D0151929

Digital Nonlinear Editing

Second Edition

Digital Nonlinear Editing

Editing Film and Video on the Desktop

Second Edition

Thomas A. Ohanian

Focal Press

Boston Oxford Johannesburg Melbourne New Delhi Singapore

Focal Press is an imprint of Butterworth–Heinemann.

Recognizing the importance of preserving what has been written, Butterworth–Heinemann prints its books on acid-free paper whenever possible.

Butterworth–Heinemann supports the efforts of American Forests and the Global ReLeaf program in its campaign for the betterment of trees, forests, and our environment.

Library of Congress Cataloging-in-Publication Data

Ohanian, Thomas A.
Digital nonlinear editing : editing film and video on the desktop / Thomas A. Ohanian. — 2nd ed.
p. cm.
Includes bibliographical references and index.
ISBN 0-240-80225-X (alk. paper)
1. Motion pictures—Editing. 2. Motion pictures—Editing—Data processing. 3. Video tapes—Editing. 4. Video tapes—Editing—Data processing. I. Title.
TR899.042 1998
778.5'235'0285—dc21 97–46778
CIP

British Library Cataloguing-in-Publication Data
A catalogue record for this book is available from the British Library.

The publisher offers special discounts on bulk orders of this book.
For information, please contact:

Manager of Special Sales
Butterworth–Heinemann
225 Wildwood Avenue
Woburn, MA 01801–2041
Tel: 781-904-2500
Fax: 781-904-2620

For information on all Focal Press publications available, contact our World Wide Web home page at: http://www.bh.com/focalpress

10 9 8 7 6 5 4 3 2 1

Printed in the United States of America

Cover art by Jeffrey Krebs

For my brother, *Michael John Ohanian,*

who in December 1969, during a blinding snowstorm, took me to the Lowe's State Theater in Providence, Rhode Island, to see my very first James Bond film, *On Her Majesty's Secret Service.* As a result, my lifetime quest (some would argue *obsession*) for James Bond memorabilia began.

Contents

Preface

In 1992, when I wrote the first edition of this book, digital nonlinear editing systems had been introduced in 1988, and their rapid rise and adoption took only four years. In 1988, I was asked to codevelop a digital nonlinear editing system, drawing on my background as a film and videotape editor. Less than a decade later, the changes that digital nonlinear editing technology have brought are astounding.

In the first few years, editors struggled with these digital systems—with their extremely compressed picture quality, inferior audio, and rudimentary features. However, the fast working speed and the ability to create multiple versions of a sequence led to rapid use and adoption. In less than a decade, tens of thousands of digital nonlinear editing systems were sold and manufactured by more than 30 companies. From 1992 to 1997, digital nonlinear systems became more capable, picture and audio quality improved substantially, and, most amazingly, images were being put on the broadcast airwaves directly from disk, completely bypassing the videotape mastering stage!

We now have video cameras that do not record images onto videotape, but instead digitize pictures and sound directly to disk. These disks are then taken directly to a digital nonlinear editing system, stories are created, and the sequences are played directly to air and into the viewer's home. In only five years, digital nonlinear technology and work methods have made substantial changes to how postproduction is being done in film, video, and broadcast. In much the same way that videotape replaced the use of 16mm film in television stations, digital disk-based acquisition, editing, and playback systems are on a course to replace videotape in the broadcast environment.

Perhaps one of the most satisfying results of digital technology in the editing environment is occurring at the educational level. Universities that offer film and video courses once struggled with videotape editing systems that were difficult to maintain. Now, many schools offer students the use of digital nonlinear editing systems, and professors require that students hand in their final video or film projects on an optical disc!

We are now entering a stage where extremely powerful digital film and video content-creation software and hardware exist on the desktop. Systems that once cost hundreds of thousands of dollars and were out of the reach of most individuals are now affordable and easy to use. The amount of programming, diversity of stories and images, and the places where we will watch these dramas unfold will also change—we'll watch on film, television, and computer screens. The way in which we communicate, learn, and tell is changing very quickly.

And, personally, although I may have a fondness for touching film while editing, I haven't missed it for years now. I can edit and try things as quickly as the ideas pop into my head. Digital nonlinear editing systems and powerful desktop software applications, some of which can be downloaded from the World Wide Web—as free demonstration versions no less!—are putting creative tools in the hands of individuals on a grand scale. Some remarkable programs will be created on a desk in a little office, in a classroom, or in someone's basement by people who aren't professional film and videotape editors. We'll watch these programs in awe.

Thomas A. Ohanian
Rome, September 1997

Acknowledgments

There are a number of individuals who have contributed their time and counsel to this effort. This book would not be complete without both acknowledging and gratefully thanking them.

A special mention to my friend and most gifted artist: Jeffrey Krebs. Special thanks to Brian Cashman for his networking expertise, Scott Glorioso for his storage engineering expertise, and Eric Peters for his expertise on digital video compression.

Basil Pappas, Tom Poederbach, Alan Miller, Joe Beirne, Peter Cohen, Scott Ogden, Lisa Surmeian, Peter Fasciano, Tony Bozanich, Michael E. Phillips, Howard A. Phillips, Joe DiMare, Jacqui Allard, Joe Torelli, Mark Flecchia, Mark Geffen, Glen Seaman, Dave Cobosco, Ed McDermid, Pam Goyette, Jim Ricotta, Rick Grogan, Greg Staten.

Adaptec: Stephanie L. Simpson; Artel Software: Jim Rickman III; Catapult Partners: Carl Furry, Virginia Henderson; Cinebase: Martin Vann, David Trescot, Chris Valle; Denim Software: John Sievers; Digimarc Corporation: Megan Livermore; Discovery Communications, Inc., for provision of footage from Discovery Channel ECO-challenge; Discrete Logic: Emma Shield; DVision: Thomas E. Allison; ElectricImage: Karen Raz; Emotion: John J. Walsh, Randy St. Jean; Fast Electronic: Tom Patrick McAuliffe; KUB Systems: Dean P. Tucker; Matrox: Janet Matey, Elisa C. Taub; Media 100: Stacey L. Hurwitz; Megadrive Systems: Carl O'Laco; MetaCreations: Teri Campbell; Minerva Systems: Paul Collins; Mountain Gate Systems: Terese Parrish; Newfire, Inc.: Harry Vitelli; Optitek: Robert McLeod; Panasonic Broadcast & Television: Jim Wickizer; Philips BTS Co.: Al Jensen; Play, Inc.: Racine Mason; Protozoa: Marilyn Novell; Qdesign: Mandy Chan; Quantel: Bob Pank; Scitex Digital Video: Elizabeth M. Von Stein; Softimage: Mike Stojda, John Poisson, Charles Migos; Sony Corporation: Laurie Compton, Robert J. Estony; Storage Concepts: Mimi Howard; Szabo Tohtz Editing and Skyview Film & Video, Chicago; Terran Interactive: Dana Giles.

1

Word Processing, Linear Editing, and Digital Nonlinear Editing

Almost anyone who has used a word processor accepts as fact that it would be very difficult to return to using a typewriter. The ability to write, rewrite, try new ideas, move and shift sentences and paragraphs—and to do so quickly—both allows and encourages experimentation. One of the early criticisms of dedicated word processing systems, and then later of word processing software on open-platform systems, was that experimentation would be endless—that the writer would spend so much time writing, rewriting, and changing things that deadlines would be missed. Just as in any craft, writing requires discipline: the discipline both to test and to know when the goal has been met.

Film and videotape editors, producers, directors, writers, indeed anyone who must put image and sound together, will always want to try things in different places and in different ways, and usually circumstances dictate that they'll want to do this up until the last possible moment!

Linear thinking means that ideas proceed in sequential order. Idea one is followed by idea two and by idea three. But nonlinear thinking is random—thoughts pop into the head and are expressed one after another, some having reference to the one before, others having no reference whatsoever. The wonderful aspect of nonlinear editing is that ideas (shots) can be tried in any order and rearranged just as easily as words are when using a word processor.

Being able to try things and to play "what if" scenarios, not with words but with moving pictures and sounds, is the best of what nonlinear editing offers. An edit that should be shortened when you had five minutes left to make a deadline used to be an edit that you had no time to change. That no longer is the case. The change can be made, and the project can stay on schedule and on budget.

Digital nonlinear editing (DNLE) has virtually made extinct analog nonlinear editing, which until 1990 was largely confined to specialized sections of postproduction in New York and Los Angeles. These analog nonlinear editing systems, represented by the first and second wave of editing systems (Chapter 3)—those that were videotape and laserdisc based—can no longer be found in use. A survey conducted in 1997 revealed that no television shows originating from Hollywood were edited on either first- or second-wave systems—the shows had all been converted to digital nonlinear editing systems. DNLE systems have brought together not only film, video, and audio, but also a variety of other media that have never had one common environment in which to coexist.

Digital nonlinear editing offers the following benefits:

1. Creative flexibility. Technology becomes more transparent, freeing up the individual to concentrate on the needs of the presentation without regard to mastering the technical details of how the system operates.
2. Ability to integrate different media easily. Whether a program consists solely of video or a combination of video, film, 35mm slides, and so on, DNLE systems allow the user to easily combine these different media into a completed program.
3. Savings in time and money. A DNLE system offers a savings in time, resulting either in the ability to explore additional ideas or in decreased costs. Based on a seven-year usage history, users of DNLE systems postulate that they decrease the amount of time spent on a project by 25%.
4. Preparation for digital integration. We are undeniably moving to all things digital, and when to introduce and retrain staff to the concepts of digital media manipulation becomes an important question. DNLE systems provide a cornerstone of that educational process. Introducing and mastering DNLE systems in the work environment sets the stage for the digital delivery mechanisms that are being required of so many of the emerging media outlets.

WORD PROCESSING: NONLINEAR EDITING'S PAST AND FUTURE

Although IBM introduced an electric typewriter in 1935, through the mid-1960s we were using manual typewriters. Made a mistake with an important presentation? Retype the document! By the early 1970s, electric typewriters were outselling manual typewriters. With the lowered cost and increased availability of microcomputers, specialized machines were created to manipulate text. By the early 1980s, word processing was big business. Companies such as Xerox, Digital, Royal, Wang, and Data General were all making dedicated word processors.

About five years later, in the mid-1980s, word processing progressed. Dedicated word processors were cast away and began their journey toward extinction, replaced by word processing software that ran on open-system computer platforms. This was a significant step because software developed for one computer was rewritten in order to run on a different computer system. Movement was afoot: Now you could buy software instead of having to buy the whole machine, which only did word processing and could not be used for other computing tasks. Early word processing software programs were WordStar, EasyWriter, and VolksWriter. Today, the most popular word processing software is created by the Microsoft Corporation and can run on a variety of open-platform systems. An Apple Computer Macintosh, a Mac OS clone, a PC, or a PC clone can all run versions of Microsoft Word.

Has this technology made a difference in what and how people write? Does the student become a better writer because she has an opportunity to rework a paragraph? Does the film screenwriter write a better film because he can examine several different endings? Overall, the answer to these questions is a resounding yes! Writers benefit from being able to hone and develop their initial ideas. Similar benefits are realized when a digital nonlinear editing system is used.

THE EVOLUTION OF DIGITAL MEDIA PROCESSORS

Word processing software has become extremely powerful and inexpensive in a very short period of time. Anyone who buys a new computer will almost always find that a word processor has already been loaded onto the system; we have also seen a tenfold decrease in the cost of such software.

DNLE systems that are used to edit film and video are repeating the same development path that saw typewriters evolve into word processors. DNLE systems that were dedicated to only editing tasks marked history from 1988 to 1995. They were used by professional film and video editors trained in the art and craft of making programs. But beginning in late 1995, we began to see the next stage: the availability of less sophisticated and less expensive systems that were affordable and within the grasp of individuals who were less classically trained in the art of creating programming. Eventually, these new machines will undergo the word processing route: software that has evolved to the point at which the computer's hardware platform is not critical.

It is vital to note that this evolution is happening very rapidly. Powerful compositing software that lets the user layer images does not require a great deal of training or knowledge, can run on a desktop computer, and is available for only a few hundred dollars, a decrease in price from the previous several thousand dollars. Usually, the only thing separating its functionality from the more expensive version is how fast or slow its operations run.

These new types of machines, and the software that dictates what these machines are, will be known as *digital media processors* directed by *digital media managers.* We've been accustomed to seeing a machine and knowing exactly what it was and what it did. That notion will change remarkably and, instead, these media processors will be machines that are artificially created through the use of software. We now use computers to fax information. The receiver can put a computer into fax receive mode to receive the information. The open-system computer platform has been directed by computer software to become, for a small period of time, a fax machine, and thus it is no longer necessary to purchase a dedicated machine for faxing. Such is the power and evolving capability of software.

The Turing Machine

Originally a mathematical concept, the term *Turing Machine* describes a general-purpose machine that can do anything if given the right software instructions. Every computer is a potential Turing Machine, and in theory, the computer can become any existing machine if given a set of instructions that emulate how the original machine operates.

Digital video, digital audio, and digital media are all mathematical problems to be solved. The Turing Machine concept of general-purpose computers that adopt the appearance and function of any given analog environment is especially important in the evolution of digital nonlinear editing. As DNLE systems progress, more functionality is possible as more sophisticated software is written.

Here is a brief and incomplete history of the software versions of a popular DNLE system:

Version 1 Capabilities: software-based lossy image compression at 160 × 120 pixel matrix; 150:1 compression; cuts only; one audio channel sampled at 22 KHz, 8 bits per sample. No edit decision list (EDL) capability. NTSC only.

Version 2 Capabilities: software-based lossy image compression at 320 × 240 pixel matrix; 150:1 and 75:1 compression; cuts and dissolves; two audio channels sampled at 22 KHz, 8 bits per sample; EDL capability for CMX and Grass Valley editing systems. NTSC only.

Version 3 Capabilities: Motion JPEG-based lossy image compression at 640 × 480 pixel matrix; 150:1, 75:1, and 40:1 compression; cuts, dissolves, and slow and fast motion; two audio channels sampled at 44.1 KHz, 16 bits per sample; EDL capability for CMX, Grass Valley, and Sony editing systems. NTSC and PAL.

Version 4 Capabilities: Motion JPEG-based lossy image compression at 640 × 480 pixel matrix; 150:1, 75:1, 40:1, and 25:1 compression; cuts, dissolves, slow and fast motion; superimpositions, freeze frame, and titles; two audio channels sampled at 44.1 KHz, 16 bits per sample; EDL capability for CMX, Grass Valley, and Sony editing systems. NTSC and PAL.

Version 5 Capabilities: Motion JPEG-based lossy image compression at 640 × 480 pixel matrix; 150:1, 75:1, 40:1, 25:1, 10:1, and 5:1 compression; support for real-time two-stream

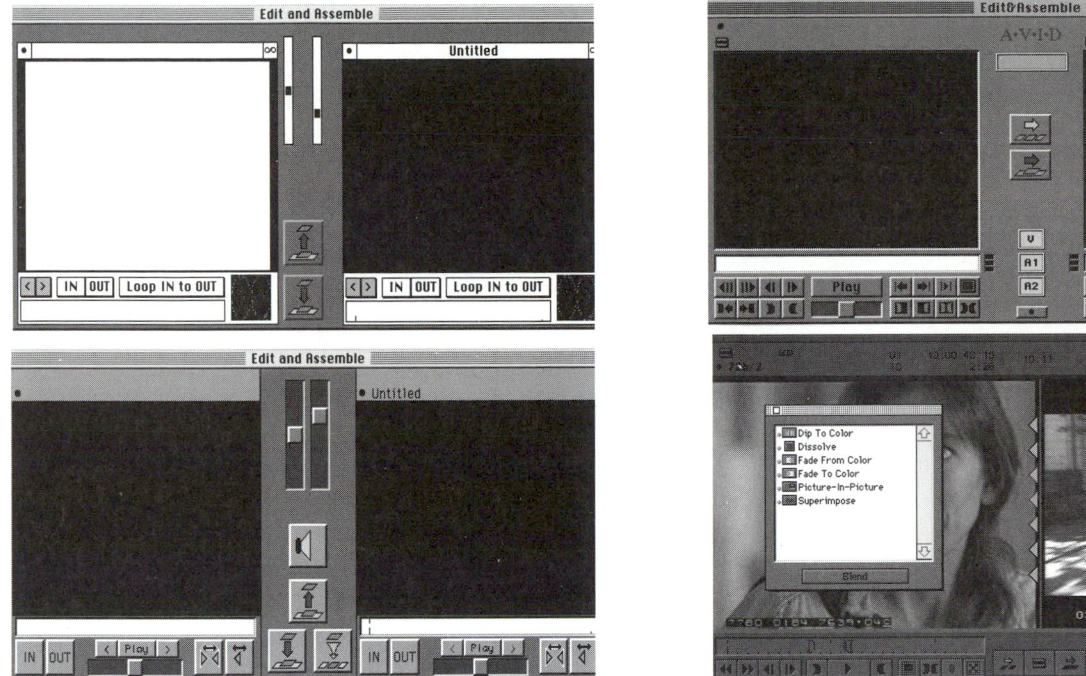

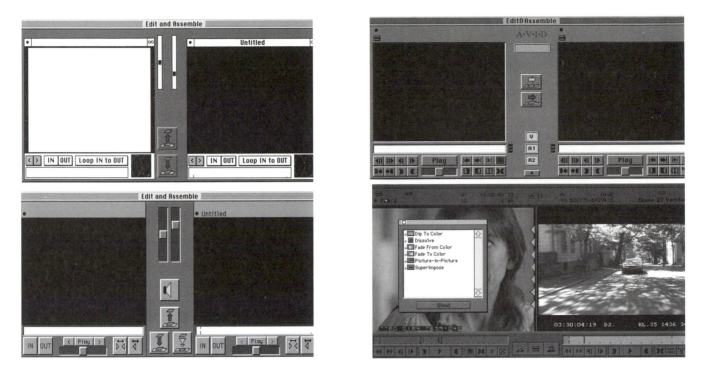

Figure 1-1 The various interface designs of the Avid Media Composer over an eight-year period. Courtesy Avid Technology.

effects, cuts, dissolves, slow and fast motion, superimpositions, freeze frame, and titles; multicamera; grouping; consolidate; abridge; user-based settings; third-party plug-in support; color correction; 24 video tracks; 24 audio tracks; four audio channels sampled at either 44.1 or 48 KHz, 16 bits per sample; EDL capability for CMX, Grass Valley, and Sony editing systems. NTSC and PAL.

Version 6 Capabilities: Motion JPEG-based lossy image compression at 720 × 486 or 720 × 576 pixel matrix; 150:1, 75:1, 40:1, 25:1, 10:1, 5:1, 3:1, and 2:1 compression; support for real-time two-stream effects, cuts, dissolves, slow and fast motion, superimpositions, freeze frame, and titles; multicamera; grouping; consolidate; abridge; user-based settings; third-party plug-in support; color correction; 24 video tracks; 24 audio tracks, four audio channels sampled at either 44.1 or 48 KHz, 16 bits per sample; EDL capability for CMX, Grass Valley, and Sony editing systems. NTSC and PAL.

It is precisely this enriching of a system's capability via software that has affected the process of editing and is changing how presentations in the professional, institutional, and consumer arenas are made. Figure 1-1 shows examples of the various user interface iterations of a popular DNLE system over an eight-year period. Figure 1-2 shows the iterations of this system's timeline, also over an eight-year period.

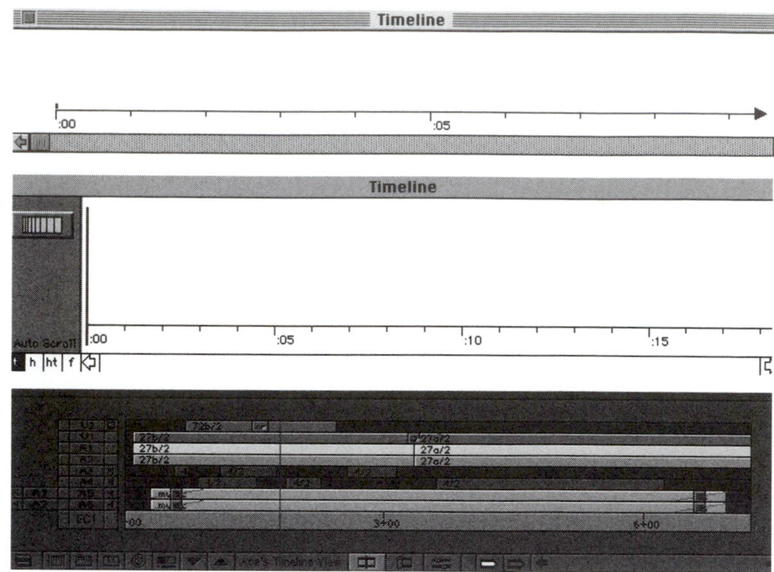

Figure 1-2 The various interface designs of the Avid Media Composer timeline over an eight-year period. Courtesy Avid Technology.

THE EDITING PROCESS HAS BECOME COMPLEX AND REQUIRES SOPHISTICATED TOOLS

Film and videotape editors manipulate images and audio to tell a story. They sift and sort through the hours of footage to ensure that the best possible performances are crafted and will be seen on the screen. They use their skill to give a scene its rhythm and an edited sequence its drive. Balancing the creative aspects of the craft with the technical details of film and videotape editing can be a formidable juggling act.

Images that we are exposed to on television, in film theaters, and on the World Wide Web (WWW) have become extremely sophisticated. The number of visual layers, painted images, fast and slow motion, live action, and animation that are frequently combined today require powerful tools that can be easily used. The work done to images even before they are edited into final program form can be quite significant. Shots may have to be blown up, repositioned, or painted, and any number of other changes may be required to make the shot believable. If done correctly, most viewers are completely unaware that these fixes have been made. All are attributed to the magic of movies.

Although it is usually video-based programs that people consider to be undergoing the most rapid visual change, consider the 35mm motion picture. Traditionally, most feature films were shot using 35mm film. The film negative was loaded into the camera, exposed, and processed. A print was then made from the processed negative, and this print was the film that the editor cut together to form the movie. For decades, films were made in exactly this fashion: Shoot the live action, edit the film, finish the sound for the film, and finish up by putting the opticals, titles, and credits on the finished film.

But even feature films have changed considerably. Yes, we can still see the feature film that consists of cuts and dissolves and few, if any, special visual effects. However, it is also very commonplace today for portions of the film to include material shot on 35mm film, 16mm, Super 8, professional videotape (such as Digital Betacam), and consumer videotape (such as DVCPRO, DVCAM, Hi-8, and VHS). Most often, these formats are enhanced or degraded electronically and then are recorded back to film negative. Integrating these different formats into the feature film can provide exciting visual results to support the director's vision.

Digital tools are constantly used to manipulate film and video. Sometimes the tools are used to enhance creativity, to save money, or to fix problems that occurred during shooting. If a period piece is being filmed but the camera must frame a house that now has telephone poles in the background, digital painting systems are used to erase the telephone poles and replace these sections with a sky background.

Audiences have become accustomed to seeing new worlds and computer-generated environments and characters. Never-before-seen synthetic characters are routinely composited with live-action actors against artificial backgrounds. These advanced images are being duplicated by television, corporate, business, educational, training, CD-ROM, and World Wide Web content. Now more than ever, there is a reliance on new digital technologies to provide these capabilities.

Film and Video Editing Tools Have Merged

The art of editing film was long considered to be resistant to technology because film editing requires a modicum of equipment. But only five years after 24 frame-per-second (fps) DNLE systems were introduced to the film editing community in 1992, more than 70% of films were edited digitally. The use of computers, software, and digital technology has reduced both film and video into a common element: the digital bit. This is critical, because more and more programming will be manipulated in the digital realm. There already is and will continue to be less actual film editing. Analog- and digital-based linear video editing rooms are being replaced with hybrid videotape/disk-based systems and will eventually be completely replaced by digital systems running on nonproprietary computer platforms.

Converging Forms of Media under Digital Manipulation

Shooting film and videotape will continue for quite some time. The resolution of video that is shot will increase under digital television (DTV) and its subset, high-definition TV (HDTV).

The method of putting together all the elements that make up a program, regardless of whether it will be seen in the theater, on television, or over the Internet, will be the exclusive realm of digital nonlinear editing environments. As different media types come together, so too will the work methodologies. Systems will be operated as standalone units, and they will also be interconnected over local and wide area networks. Files will be sent from one state to another and from one country to another. A director who wants to work with a graphics designer who lives thousands of miles away can communicate and send files back and forth until the final acceptable result is reached. All of these items will converge within the digital media processor.

2

Film and Videotape Editing, the Offline and Online Process, Digital Video Processing, and Defining the Digital Nonlinear Editor

Charting the development of different editing techniques, we find the following:

Film editing	c. 1900
Analog audio editing	c. 1945
Videotape editing	1956
Videotape editing with timecode	1970
Digital disk-based audio editing	1985
Digital disk-based picture editing	c. 1989

For approximately 90 years, the process of editing films remained essentially unchanged—it was the quintessential low-tech method of editing in the face of other sophisticated digital video editing systems. In 1992, however, with the appearance of DNLE systems, film editors began to digitally edit their films, and Hollywood, Europe, and the biggest center of film production, India, all began to make the inexorable move to digital postproduction.

FORMATS AND STANDARDS

Although there will be exceptions, in general, projects that are shot on film fall into the categories of theatrical films, made-for-television movies, film-based television shows, and high-end commercials. Video tends to be used for everything else—video-based television programs, mid- and low-end commercials, training and educational videos, entertainment programs intended for home game machines, and so forth. Of course, there are variations, specifically with programs shot on video, edited on DNLE systems, and then transferred to film for theatrical film showings.

One clear benefit of film editing over videotape editing is that experience has developed work methods that are understandable and shared throughout the world. Film is a unique standard in a world in which standards are difficult to achieve. A 35mm film can run on any 35mm projector anywhere in the world. This perhaps sounds quite inconsequential, but, in contrast, a videotape edited in the United States cannot be played on equipment in Europe because the technical standards differ. In the United States, video plays back at 29.97 frames per second (fps), while in Europe the standard is 25 fps. When a producer faces the issue of how to ensure that his program can be seen anywhere in the world, shooting it on film and having a completed film at the end of the postproduction process will realize that goal.

Audio signals are easily interchangeable. Digital audio has a fixed amount of information (resolution) and can be interpreted at various speeds. For analog recordings, the common speed is 15 inches per second (ips); for digital recordings, the common sampling rates are 44.1 KHz and 48 KHz. These recordings can be played back on capable equipment anywhere in the world.

It is critical to have interchange from country to country. While cries are often heard for standardization so that video signals could be interchangeable, there are so many different types of videotape formats that this interchange is very unlikely to be achieved. In film, the economic importance of foreign markets to a film's earning potential requires that the medium itself be easily transportable and transmittable from country to country. Film, not videotape, offers that flexibility.

Digital technologies, however, represent the potential for electronic forms of media to be interchangeable. If we examine various videotape formats, such as D1, D2, D3, D5, DVCPRO, and so forth, we find that they are, indeed, all digital. However, each of these formats is incompatible with the others. By reducing information to its most simple form, the digital bit, we can begin to create ways of interchanging these bits in the same way that digital audio files are interchangeable on compact discs from one player to another.

Even the process of film postproduction is highly standardized, for it has developed work methods that translate well throughout the world and has developed a personnel hierarchy that is similar from place to place. Apprentice editors and assistant editors each know their own responsibilities. Film labs, title design companies, and optical houses all know their roles in the postproduction process.

In videotape editing, this hierarchy never matured. There is too much diversity in equipment and formats, and there is no standard way of doing anything. From one editing facility to another, methods and approaches can vary greatly. Further, an assistant videotape editor in one facility can be doing totally different things from a counterpart in another facility.

HOW A FILM IS EDITED

Digital nonlinear editing's roots are in film editing. Today, programs for training or television commercials are rarely edited on film. Though they may be shot on film, they are almost always edited on a DNLE system or on a conventional analog or digital linear system. This is a great contrast to history, for as late as 1993, commercials were still being edited on film. We do not find this in today's marketplace: DNLE systems have come to represent normal methodology.

Instead, editing film has been almost exclusively reserved for feature film projects. There are several reasons, but typically there are three major factors: the editor's preference, the cost of the DNLE system, and the amount of footage that must be loaded into the DNLE system's disk drives. If you are so inclined, examine the end credit roll of a film and watch for a description of how it was edited. You will surely see either an "edited on a DNLE system" credit or an "edited on film" credit.

The steps below describe the traditional film editing process. If you have not been exposed to these ideas, they bear examination because each step in this process must be addressed by the capabilities of the DNLE system.

Shooting and Preparing for Editing

The most common type of film used for feature motion pictures is 35mm four-perf (perforations per frame). A film roll is loaded into a camera in what is usually a ten-minute load. Sound for the film is recorded on separate 1/4" reel-to-reel audio tape, the most common of which is the Nagra recorder. Alternatively, digital audio tape (DAT) is commonly used. Because two systems are used, one for picture and one for sound, film shooting is often called a *dual-system approach.*

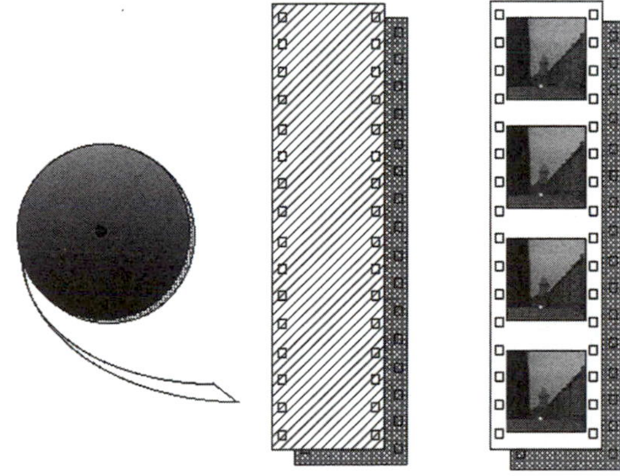

Figure 2-1 The quarter-inch sound roll is first transferred to 35mm magnetic track. This magnetic sound track is then combined with the 35mm picture track. Picture and sound now exist in the same 35mm format, and editing can begin. Illustration by Jeffrey Krebs.

At the end of each shooting day, the exposed camera rolls and sound rolls are gathered together. The exposed film negative is processed by a film lab, and the negative is used to create a positive, or print. The takes that the director wants printed are usually referred to as *circled takes.* These are noted on a log sheet and given to the lab so that the correct portions of the negative are printed. These are usually *one-lite* prints, because extensive color correction will be done later.

Thirty-five millimeter film editing requires that the picture and sound ultimately be edited together. The audio reels are transferred to 35mm magnetic track (mag track). The circled takes for audio are transferred to provide the accompanying sound for the circled picture takes (Figure 2-1). The audio takes that are transferred to mag track are noted on the sound transfer report, which is a log sheet.

Synchronizing Dailies

While the film is being processed, the mag track is marked at the sound of the clapsticks striking together at the beginning of each take. When the printed takes of film arrive, these *dailies* are marked with an X at the point where the clapsticks (also known as a *slate* or *clapper*) first join together during the slating process.

The next step involves synchronizing, or synching, the sound track to the picture. By lining up the reference point for the picture and the reference point for the audio, the 35mm film and the 35mm mag track are now in sync. If we look at an actress deliver her lines, we will see and hear perfect synchronization.

Synched dailies are reviewed by the director, editor, producer, and possibly the cast and crew. It is necessary to see how new material will affect previously shot material both from a contextual point of view as well as from a performance perspective. This continues as more film is shot.

Thirty-five millimeter film has unique identifying codes spaced at specific intervals. These are *edge numbers*, and they are essential in being able to describe, numerically, what frames are being used in the project (Figure 2-2). While we are editing with the work print, we must eventually have a way of matching the work print to the original camera negative. Edge numbers let us do this.

However, the mag track does not have any identifying edge numbers. The process of *coding* (also known as *inking*) places ink numbers along the edge of the mag track. These new numbers are coded on both the film and the mag track instead of trying to match the original edge numbers. In this way, both picture and sound share identical reference numbers. This is one of the reasons why the editor can easily put picture and sound back in synchronization if synchronization is lost through an editing operation: Simply realign the numbers and synchronization is restored.

Finally, dailies are broken down into one roll that combines the film and mag track for one take. This roll is wound and labeled with the scene and take number (for example, Sc 7, Tk 31). In addition, some editors prefer to have a short description about the scene on the label.

Figure 2-2 A film negative has edge numbers that identify the film frames. When a print is made from the negative, the same numbers are printed through from the negative to the positive. In this way, the same frames have the same numbers. Illustration by Jeffrey Krebs.

The Nonlinear Mindset

Usually, editing occurs simultaneously with shooting in order to have the film finished as quickly as possible after shooting ceases. Obviously, costs cannot be recouped until there is a film that can be shown to an audience. Often, editors excel at certain genres: Some are masters with music videos; others

Figure 2-3 The Moviola, an early mechanical film editing system. Photo by Michael E. Phillips.

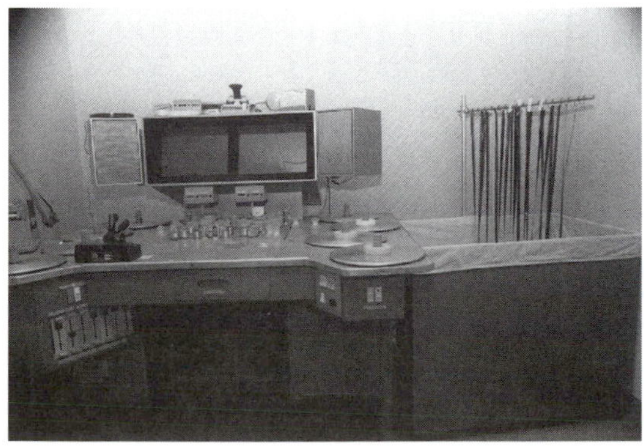

Figure 2-4 In the film editing room, strips of film representing work in progress are hung off metal hooks in the film bin shown on the right. Photo by Michael E. Phillips.

excel in films that have a great deal of action sequences. Some editors are great at cutting comedy films, while other editors are great at creating multiple layers of composite images. There are specialists in sound editing and those who are brilliant in special visual effects. Editing, clearly, is a general term that covers quite a range of work. Each of these specialists can benefit from thinking nonlinearly. The film editor may want to edit a scene that is very late in the film in order to have enough time to revisit it, while a commercial editor is thinking of flow and rearranging shots in a montage for a specific product. They could start at the middle of a scene and work outward or start at the end and work backward—whatever method they use is supported; all that is required is to make the nonlinear leap in their thinking process.

Editing the Film

Although certain technical tasks must be mastered, film editing is an artistic craft that allows the film editor to work in a nonlinear fashion. A scene can be constructed by working backward with the editor knowing how the scene must end. Or it can be edited from its logical starting point. Editing the best possible piece requires the flexibility to experiment and enough opportunity to reedit!

For film editing, there are various systems such as Moviolas, Steenbecks, and Kems (Figure 2-3). If a Steenbeck is used, the editor begins by threading a segment of film and its corresponding mag track. In general, there will be at least one picture head and two sound heads. Thus, the editor can see picture and hear two sound tracks. Usually, flatbeds can be modified to offer more picture and sound heads. If an editor is working with footage from multiple cameras, as would be the case with an intensive action sequence, several picture heads may be required (often, multiple flatbeds are synchronized together).

Once picture and sound track are aligned using the ink numbers to ensure synchronization, the film editor can run the footage at normal, slow, or fast speed. The film editor works from left (feed reel) to right (take-up reel). When the editor reaches the frame where a shot should start, the frame is marked with a Chinagraph marker. The end frame is also marked. Now it is time to cut the film. The film and mag track are placed in a sync block (synchronizer), and a film splicer (butt splicer) is used to cut the film on the line between frames and to cut the mag track. The same occurs for the end frame.

This is the first shot that will be used. The material that will not be used from this take is called the *trim*. The frames before the marked start frame are called *head trim;* the frames after the marked end frame are called the *tail trim*. Trims are important because they may be needed again. Head and tail trims are hung off a hook in the *trim bin* (Figure 2-4).

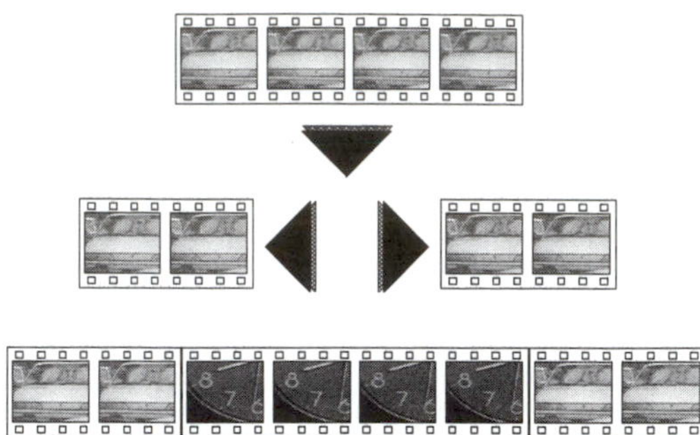

Figure 2-5 Nonlinear editing at its simplest. A single piece of film can easily be added between two pieces of film by physically cutting the film apart and splicing additional material between the sections. Illustration by Jeffrey Krebs.

This process of selection and cutting continues as the editor juggles all of the material that has been shot for a particular scene. Some scenes may have very little coverage—a dialogue scene between two people may have one angle for person A and one angle for person B. Conversely, some action sequences have been known to have 14 or more hours of material for a scene that, when edited, will be less than one minute in duration. Eventually, the editor finishes choosing all the shots that will be used in the scene. Now it is time to edit. Because film is physically cut into segments called *film clips,* the individual pieces of film can be rearranged easily. Each film splice represents a cut, and a splice can be made anywhere in the roll of film. If we have three pieces of film and want to change their order, we simply remove the segment we want to move, put it in the new position, and resplice it. Conversely, if a shot is added that simply doesn't work in its place, it can just as easily be removed (Figure 2-5).

As editing continues, there will be a number of strips hanging in the trim bin, and there will be a roll of film on the take-up reel, which is the rough assembly of the scene. The editor plays back the scene and decides where changes should be made. If shots must be rearranged, splices are removed and the shots are reordered.

Trimming shots is a different matter. If a shot needs to be shortened, the editor can move back and forth over the splice point to determine how many frames need to be removed from the shot. The film and mag track are then placed in the splicer, and those frames are cut out and placed in the trim bin. The film is spliced together again, and the cut is judged. If a few more frames need to be removed, the trimming process is repeated. Obviously, as these trims get more and more exact, the trims become smaller and smaller. This is one reason why film editors often joke about having to "find my trim in the bottom of the bin." (Actually, small trims such as these are usually placed in a box rather than in the bin.)

If the editor has trimmed a shot and then decides that the shot should be longer, the trim is located in the bin, and the desired number of frames are added back to the shot. Film editing is limited to picture cuts and sound overlaps. An *overlap* occurs when both picture and sound do not "transition," or cut, together. For example, if we see two people having a conversation, we can cut from one person talking to the other person talking. This is called a *straight cut* since both the picture and the sound cut together as we switch from person to person. However, if we want to continue to see the first person for a few frames while we hear the second person talking, this is an overlap. We overlap the picture of person A onto the audio of person B. Eventually, we cut to person B's picture.

Film editors cannot see optical effects, such as dissolves, wipes, and fades. Instead, when a transition other than a cut is desired between two shots, the editor provides directions for the optical laboratory. These directions are indicated by marking the film with a Chinagraph marker (Figure 2-6). During the

Figure 2-6 By specifying where a dissolve should occur, the film editor directs the optical laboratory to create a new piece of film for the optical effect.

editing process, the optical effects are not seen. Instead, the editor will use the markings to judge where the transitions will be. One of the major reasons why DNLE systems have been embraced by the film editing community is the ability to see many different types of optical effects during the editing process instead of waiting for the effect to be created by the lab and returned to the editor.

Eventually, the editor reaches the first assembly, called the *rough cut* or *first cut*—the first complete viewing of the entire program. Changes are noted and scenes are reworked. Reediting can be extensive or minimal. This process of review, reedit, and change continues until the *final cut* is achieved. The final cut is the point at which the picture portion of editing is complete, or "the picture is locked."

Work then begins on all of the sound elements, such as sound effects, sound design, dialogue replacement, and so forth. Much of this work could be happening simultaneously, but traditionally, audio work begins after the picture is locked because it can be ensured that the picture portion is finished. After the optical effects are delivered by the laboratory, they are spliced into their correct position, and the entire film, broken down into ten-minute reels, becomes available for final audio dubbing. Each reel is projected while the different sound elements are mixed together for that reel of film.

While dubbing is occurring, the original camera negative is being *conformed* based on the work print. That is, the original negative that was first loaded into the film camera is cut in the exact manner that the work print was cut. Negative cutting is as final as the process gets since, once the negative is cut, it cannot be replaced (though there have been countless examples where unique fixes have been used in dire emergencies, such as replacing a torn frame with a similar frame).

The first version of the film with optical effects and the mixed sound track is called the *answer print.* Here is a last-minute opportunity to check everything involved in the presentation, with particular attention to the quality of the sound track mix and the scene-by-scene color correction. Scene-by-scene correction is a process of adjusting color values to match from one scene to the next.

The last stage is the *release print*. Additional film copies will be made from a copy of the original negative to distribute to theaters or to use to make videotape copies. The film editing process is based on years of refinement and practice and is supported by the film industry infrastructure: the writers, directors, producers, film laboratories, sound houses, optical houses, and dubbing houses.

While film editing is laborious, it is very flexible. Shots can be rearranged and audio from one take can be used to replace audio from another take. The editor can construct backward, forward, or from the middle outward. Film is a nonlinear process. It simply requires time to entertain every thought with regard to manipulating the footage.

THE DEVELOPMENT OF VIDEOTAPE

Before we had videotape, a process called *electronic transcriptions* was used. These were electrical signals recorded onto glass discs, somewhat similar to the methods used to create phonograph records. These discs represented the only method to record visual signals before magnetic tape. Electronic transcriptions are not to be confused with Kinescopes, film recordings of televised signals, which appeared and became quite popular in the 1950s.

The first videotape recorder was developed by the Ampex Corporation in 1956 and used 2" recording tape. Clearly, videotape's advantage is that it does not have to be processed as does film in order to see the recorded images. Videotape is known as *single-system recording*. Image and sound are simultaneously recorded to the same piece of videotape, unlike film, where picture and sound are recorded on separate media.

While the playback speed of film is 24 fps, videotape speeds vary. In NTSC (National Television Standards Committee) countries, the frame rate is 29.97 fps; in PAL (phase alternate line) countries, it is 25 fps. NTSC tapes cannot be played on PAL machines and vice versa. Videotape frames are not visible to the eye since it is a magnetic medium. There was no way to edit videotape until 1958, when Ampex introduced a videotape splicer and special magnetized particles that were spread on the tape (Figure 2-7). Control track pulses, signals recorded onto the videotape and used to identify the frames, became visible through the use of these particles. The editor could then cut between the frames. When the desired frames were aligned, the videotape would be joined with special cement.

It is interesting to note that videotape editing began as a completely nonlinear form of editing, just like film. How ironic it is that so much time and effort would be spent building electronic nonlinear editing systems designed to emulate film editing! Editing videotape by actually cutting continued throughout the 1960s and into the early 1970s.

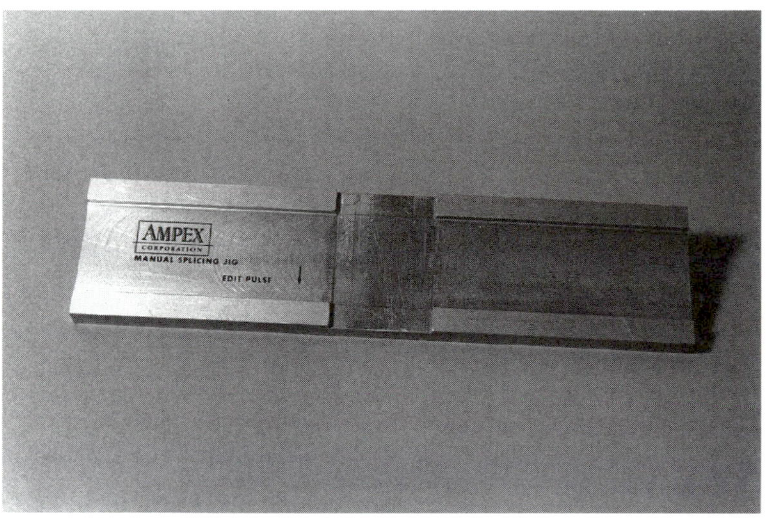

Figure 2-7 The Ampex videotape splicer was used to join the ends of two-inch videotape in the same fashion that film is spliced together. Courtesy Peter J. Fasciano. Photo by Michael E. Phillips.

As television viewership grew, the appetite for programming also grew and it became necessary to develop more reliable means of being able to view an edit before committing to it. Audio cue tones were recorded onto two-inch videotape, the tones would be sensed, and the edit made. This became a way of being able to repeat edits in a reliable fashion.

In 1967, a method of consistently identifying videotape frames was developed. Borrowing from film, with its edge numbers, *timecode* in the form of hours, minutes, seconds, and frames (such as 01:05:12:20) is a signal that is recorded onto videotape to identify each and every video frame. Timecode was developed by the EECO Company, and in 1972, the Society of Motion Picture and Television Engineers (SMPTE) and the European Broadcasting Union (EBU) standardized the code, which became known as *SMPTE timecode*.

Timecode was revolutionary. It meant that frames could be quickly identified. The precise location of timecode points and repeatable edits became a reality. Just by typing into an edit controller the number 01:04:31:20 will cause a tape machine to shuttle to precisely that frame.

HOW VIDEOTAPE IS EDITED

Videotape editing and the associated equipment vary greatly. Walk into any film editing room anywhere in the world, and the equipment will bear great similarity: There will be some type of editing table and film bins. Walk into a video editing room (called a *suite* or *bay*) anywhere in the world, and there

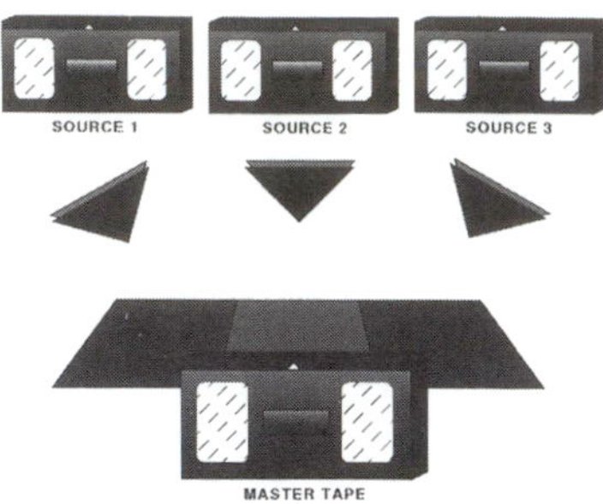

Figure 2-8 In videotape editing, selected pieces of footage are copied from a source videotape to a master videotape. Illustration by Jeffrey Krebs.

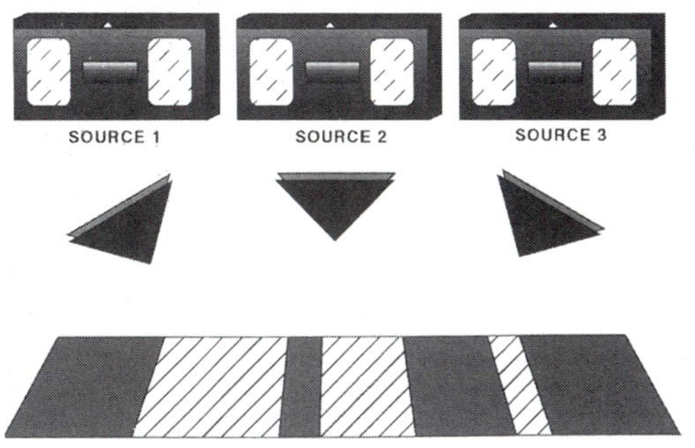

Figure 2-9 If a change needs to be made when editing with linear videotape, it is necessary to re-record all of the material after the change. Illustration by Jeffrey Krebs.

will be very little similarity. It can cost a few thousand dollars to put together a video bay, or it can well cost millions.

Video editing systems are usually composed of three machines: two source machines and one record machine. A *video switcher* is used for transitions, such as dissolves, wipes, and keys. The tape machines receive instructions from the edit controller shuttling the tapes to their specific timecode locations. An edit decision list (EDL) is a list of all the edits that were made.

Videotape editing selectively records material from a source videotape to a master tape (Figure 2-8). This is a linear copying process—the first segment is copied to the master tape, then the second segment, and so on.

However, because videotape is no longer physically cut, reordering segments is not easily accomplished. Figure 2-9 shows what happens if we have made some edits and decide to make changes. The lighter sections of the tape indicate where we have removed shots, but note that the structure of the tape cannot change because we do not physically cut videotape. If we now want to abut all the darker sections representing material we want to keep, there is no way to do this, and we must re-record the material. Note that we could just fill in the holes with new material, but we would not be able to make them shorter or longer. This is the inflexibility of linear videotape editing.

Because it is difficult to reorder shots, previews are made. The editor chooses an *in point* on both the master and source tapes, and the edit can be made, or a preview can be made. The machines will rewind to a *preroll point* (usually three to five seconds before the edit point) and then roll forward to show the edit. Since the timecode is a perfect reference for each frame, previews can be done over and over with the same result. There will be no change regardless of how many times the edit is previewed. Sophisticated switcher set-ups can also be automatically triggered via timecode. All of these operations must proceed in a linear fashion—a ten-second edit will take ten seconds plus preroll time before it can be seen.

Completing Audio for Video as a Separate Stage

Audio can be edited at the same time as video editing or can be left to an audio sweetening session. A multitrack audio recorder is used for additional sound effects, music, and so forth. The audio is then mixed: Items that are intended to be softer and louder than other elements are arrayed accordingly. In film, this process is called the *dubbing stage.* In video, this process is called *mix to pix*—mixing audio to the locked picture. The master videotape, now with its final sound track, is then copied, or dubbed, for distribution. The term *dubbing* means something quite different in the video world than in the film world!

LINEAR VERSUS NONLINEAR EDITING

If you had to create a compilation tape of three weekly meetings, you would connect two videocassette machines and make the recording based on chronological order:

1. Meeting 1 on March 14
2. Meeting 2 on March 21
3. Meeting 3 on March 28

But what if you were supposed to make the tape with the most recent meeting first? You must throw away all your work. The lengthy process must be undertaken again, until this order is reached:

1. Meeting 3 on March 28
2. Meeting 2 on March 21
3. Meeting 1 on March 14

Nonlinear editing refers to the concept that the physical nature of the medium and the technical process of manipulating that medium do not enforce or dictate a method by which the material must be physically ordered.

Random Access

Although film lets us edit nonlinearly, film does not give us random access. Random access is related to speed, an inherent part of electronic nonlinear editing. Consider a roll of film. If the roll is positioned at the beginning and we want to get to a shot that is in the middle of the roll, we must wind the film through all the intervening material to get to the desired shot. We cannot simply point to the desired shot and immediately go to it. Nor does videotape offer random access. To get from one shot to the next on a reel of videotape, we must shuttle from point to point.

Nonlinear + Random Access = Free Form

Free Form = The Way We Think?

While editing, ideas will often surface at random. Someone will suggest something, or a direction will become apparent as two shots are juxtaposed. Free-form editing, like free-form thinking, must be encouraged, and the editing system must provide easy access to these free-form thoughts. Videotape editing, with its linear thought requirements, makes the user think ahead to plan how a sequence will be edited. It's no wonder that there is no time for the cut to evolve.

Consider the following general statistics about videotape editing:

1. A well-paced video will have edits every two to six seconds. Therefore, there are about 10 to 30 edits per minute.

Some frantically paced commercials may have 10 edits a second.
2. Based on studies done in professional video editing facilities, each edit will take about five minutes, including shuttle time, video and audio setup, and preview time.
3. As a result, a range of one to three hours of editing will be required for each finished minute of program.

While we can preview as many times as required, at some point we must commit our decision to videotape. Going back and making changes is not a scenario that anyone editing linearly likes to consider. Preparing for an editing session where few changes are made was precisely the reason why videotape editing was divided into two stages: *offline* editing and *online* editing.

In offline editing, the resulting program is not finished; it is in a form of preview. In online editing, the program is finished and is ready for final distribution. Traditionally, offline systems and online systems differed greatly in their capabilities, and the distinction between the two was clear. DNLE systems have forever blurred that distinction because they have combined the capabilities of both offline and online editing.

THE OFFLINE–ONLINE LINK

By 1974, videotape had divided into two camps: offline and online systems. Because online equipment was expensive, the offline process of making all shot and preediting decisions was useful in assuring that online time would be used more efficiently. The CMX 50 editing system (the CMX Corporation was a joint venture of CBS and Memorex) was an A/B roll edit controller that could control three 3/4" tapes and permitted dissolves. One purpose of the CMX 50 was to provide a less expensive alternative to the more functional CMX 300 edit controller, which was used to edit 2" videotape.

After the offline session, the source tapes and the EDL were brought into the online room and the program was finished. The offline steps were

1. Window dubs
2. Logging footage
3. Creating a paper edit list
4. Offline editing and EDL generation

Window Dubs

Window dubs are also called *burn-in* copies. The original source material is copied to another tape format. VHS is a common choice because the tapes can be taken home and viewed. During the copying process, the timecode from the original footage is read by a timecode generator, and a visual overlay is displayed over the footage (Figure 2-10).

Logging Footage

The process of logging the footage should have begun during the shooting stage. If a log is not available, one is created by viewing the window dubs. The burn-in tapes are viewed for approximate start and end timecodes for the desired sections.

Paper Edit List

Using the log sheets, a paper edit list is created that has the source reel number, the timecode points for the shot, the tracks used, and the type of transition. This editing process is entirely conceptual. Since no tape-to-tape editing is being done, it is left to the person creating the paper edit list to imagine how everything will work together.

Offline Editing

Offline editing—copying source material to a record tape—creates two tangible work products. The first is the edit decision list, and the second is the record tape that can be referred to during the online session. Table 2-1 is an example of an EDL.

Figure 2-10 When window dubs are created, timecode information is placed as an overlay window over copies of source footage as a step in the offline process.

Table 2-1 SEQUENCE 1

FCM: NON-DROP FRAME							
FCM: DROP FRAME							
001	051	V	C	01:02:49:15	01:02:58:06	01:00:00:00	01:00:08:21
002	051	AA	C	01:02:49:15	01:02:57:06	01:00:00:00	01:00:07:21
SPLIT: VIDEO DELAY = 00:00:01:00							
003	051	AA	C	01:11:01:11	01:1:12:04	01:00:07:21	01:00:18:14
003	051	V	C	01:11:02:11	01:1:12:04	01:00:08:21	01:00:18:14
004	051	AA/V	C	01:11:42:24	01:11:51:10	01:00:18:14	01:00:27:00

THE PROCESS OF ONLINE EDITING

In 1978, standardized 1" type C videotape became the online mastering format of choice. Later outfitted with timecode, online editing on 1" videotape became the mastering standard for the 1980s. In the 1990s, digital video formats, such as D1, D2, D3, Digital Betacam, and D5 were introduced and used for online finishing. Along with the tape machines, online rooms have many peripheral devices: switcher, audio console, digital disk recorder (DDR), character generator, and monitors (Figure 2-11).

Figure 2-11 In the online edit suite, final editing takes place. Courtesy Szabo Tohtz Editing and Skyview Film & Video, Chicago.

The usual flow of online editing is as follows:

1. The offline EDL is loaded into the online edit controller.
2. If no offline editing was done, editing begins with little or no preparation.
3. Attention is paid to the final quality of video and audio.
4. The program is either mixed or sent for audio sweetening.
5. The finished picture and sound are married together to create the videotape master, which is ready for duplication.

If an offline edit was done, the majority of decisions have already been made and online editing is the step-by-step process of replicating offline decisions. The EDL is loaded into an online edit controller, the appropriate tapes are loaded, and the program is put together. There are usually reference signals for picture and sound at the beginning of each tape reel. These signals are made up of color bars and tones and are standardized so that setting a machine to play back the reference signals ensures that the recorded picture and sound are played back at their intended levels.

The color test pattern comprises several bars, beginning with white and continuing in descending order of brightness: yellow, cyan, green, magenta, red, and blue. White is measured at 77 IRE (International Radio Engineers) units, and black is measured at 7.5 IRE. All of the remaining color bars are measured at 75%. The white level is set to 75% of full level to accommodate the high levels of chrominance. Audio tone is generally at 0 dB.

Careful attention is paid to picture and sound quality. If an actor's facial tones are slightly green, or if audio is too low, they are corrected now, for this is the final stage.

Usually, online editing is not just a strict running of the offline EDL. It may be necessary to use a digital video effects device to increase the size of a picture, or there may be reasons why something that needs to be created during online editing could not be created offline. This is especially true of multilayered sequences.

Audio Editing in the Online Room

Until the late 1980s, audio editing went hand in hand with video editing, and picture and audio were finished together.

The limitation of two program audio tracks on 1" type C videotape (four tracks on other formats such as D2 and Digital Betacam) meant that any additional tracks of sound required additional steps. Many television commercials have what is known as a final mixed track, in which the final audio track is finished before the online session begins. This final track is laid down on what is to be the final master videotape, and the the picture is cut onto this final track. Usually, however, the picture is locked and then sent on to the audio sweetening stage.

The Reasons for Online Editing

As will be evident in following chapters, the distinction between the offline and online editing process has blurred, and DNLE systems and their incessant improvements are affecting the amount of work that is done in traditional online rooms. A common question, given the evolution of linear online rooms into digital nonlinear rooms, is whether linear online rooms are still necessary.

There is no doubt that over the next five years there will be a huge impact made on linear analog or digital online rooms. Traditionally, the most common areas where linear online editing had been superior over DNLE systems were uncompressed picture quality, special visual effects, and graphics creation and manipulation. The natural advancement of DNLE technology is addressing these areas.

DIGITAL MANIPULATION OF VIDEO

Computers manipulating video and audio began in the mid-1970s, when timecode-based computer-controlled editing systems appeared. Once timecode provided unique identification numbers to each video frame, computers were required to get to those numbers rapidly.

Manipulating the analog video signal through the use of digital methods has its roots in the creation of timebase correctors. The timebase corrector (TBC) is an electronic device that manipulates the analog waveform of a video signal and is used to correct and stabilize the playback of a video signal. Vertical and horizontal sync pulses ensure that a video image is displayed in a stable fashion. Making copies of a videotape without a TBC can cause signal degradation not only of the picture but also of these stabilizing signals; there may also be mechanical intolerances from machine to machine.

Narrow-window analog TBCs were developed to process and replace unstable sync signals. *Narrow window* refers to the amount of time distortion that the TBC is capable of correcting, specifically, two microseconds. By reprocessing these sync signals, there is a better chance of correctly playing back a tape that had distorted sync information.

Wide-window digital TBCs appeared in the late 1970s and provided 1 to 12 lines of error correction. This breakthrough allowed original 3/4" videotape to be broadcast by digitally correcting the error between studio playback machines and field recorders.

From Digital Timebase Correctors to Digital Framestores

Digital TBCs paved the way for digital framestores, devices that can store from one frame to several seconds of video.

Since digital TBCs were being used to correct and synchronize video signals by delaying and then reprocessing the signal, advances in technology allowed multiple frames to be digitally stored prior to playback. Framestores were originally developed to facilitate broadcast transmissions in which many different video sources must be synchronized together.

Genlocking is the process that provides this common synchronization. When sources are genlocked together, a master sync generator provides outputs for horizontal and vertical sync signals and the subcarrier, the basic stabilizing signal. Sources are matched to these signals and thus run at the same frequency and phase as the master.

When a live camera sends a signal back to a television station via microwave transmission, there is no way to genlock that camera. However, by using a digital framestore, the signal can be processed and genlocked. If the transmission suddenly becomes faulty, the framestore will usually freeze and display the last complete frame that it processed. If you have ever watched a program broadcast via satellite, you may have seen the live action freeze occasionally. You were watching the digital framestore display the last complete frame while trying to lock on to the next series of incoming frames.

From Digital Framestores to Digital Video Effects Systems

At the moment that digital framestores could delay multiple frames, it became possible for those frames to be manipulated in some way before they had to leave the digital framestore prior to the next series of frames entering the framestore. This led to new and revolutionary devices in the mid-1970s, such as digital video effects systems that could move and reposition moving video signals (Figure 2-12).

Digital video effects units could move pictures across the screen and shrink or expand their size, which led to new visual styles. Such units became deeply entrenched in the editing process. These early devices were created by manufacturers such as Vital (SqueeZoom) and NEC (E-Flex). Decreasing costs and technology advancements from 1980 to 1995 led to a huge increase in the number of systems, such as Abekas's A53D, Grass Valley Group's Kaleidoscope, Ampex's ADO, and Pinnacle's DVEator. Further, these effects could be saved to computer disk and recalled weeks later. Most important, realtime interaction and decision making became possible—you could create the effect, see it, change it, and do so rapidly.

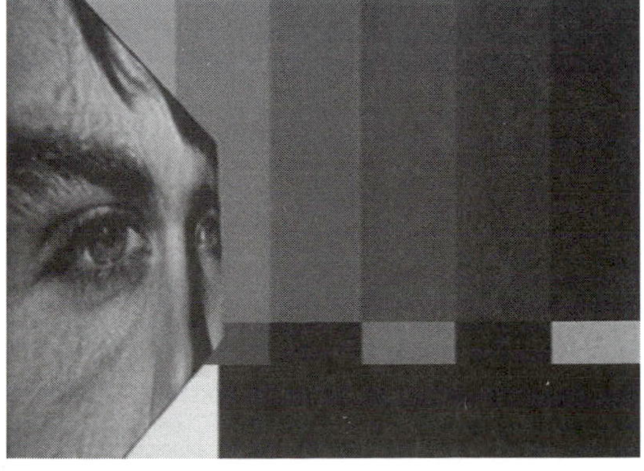

Figure 2-12 The use of digital video effects units to warp and shape analog or digital video is based on the ability to hold the video signal in framestores long enough to manipulate the video before it must leave the framestore.

From Digital Video Effects Systems to Digital Still Store Devices

The next breakthrough was the introduction of digital still store devices in 1983. The Abekas A42 was an early still store. Although the framestore unit could process frames, and digital video effects boxes could manipulate frames, they were not designed to store and recall frames. Digital still stores could store and recall frames on demand. Further, full-resolution, uncompressed video could be stored, so the exact quality of the original video was preserved by the digital still store. Before these devices appeared, 35mm slides were used to recall graphics. In the same way that videotape had replaced the use of 16mm film in broadcasting stations, digital still stores completely replaced the use of 35mm slides. Because the graphics were digitally stored, they could be recalled by typing in a number that retrieved the desired graphic from a specific address on the digital disk.

In actuality, the storage of analog video signals on computer disks had been in regular use through the 1970s. One of the earliest reasons was for slow-motion playback for television sporting events. The Ampex 100 used large-capacity disks on which analog video signals were recorded as FM signals; the disk could then be played back at speeds other than normal play. The disks could record directly and could hold approximately 30 seconds of motion video.

From Digital Still Store Devices to Digital Disk Recorders: Simultaneous Digital Playback and Recording Capabilities

Visual styles in the 1980s were characterized by the use of digital still stores and digital video effects systems. In the same way that the Ampex 100 was used to play back material, digital still stores led the way to digital disk recorders (DDRs). DDRs allowed the stored digital frames to be simultaneously played back and recorded. Before DDRs, creating multiple layered special effects was done by running many tape machines in parallel while blending the images together through the switcher. DDRs allowed frames to be played back digitally, combined, and recorded back to disk without signal loss. In 1985, the Abekas A62 DDR used magnetic computer disks and an internal digital keyer to combine hundreds of layers of images into a final visual effect.

EARLY EXPERIMENTS IN DIGITAL NONLINEAR EDITING

While DDRs are primarily used for combining images, there were early experiments in using them as digital nonlinear editors. Since it is possible to rapidly cycle from one frame to another with full random access, you could edit with these devices. The process was cumbersome, however, and it never came into widespread use, mainly because of the limited storage time—usually 50 to 100 seconds of full-resolution images.

Still, digital nonlinear editing at full resolution had never been available before, and it was especially helpful in building montages from a very limited number of shots—experimentation that could take quite a lot of time on videotape and could be very frustrating. This was digital nonlinear editing, albeit to a very limited degree, but it certainly set the stage for the introduction of dedicated DNLE systems.

DEFINING THE DIGITAL NONLINEAR EDITING SYSTEM

DDR technology and its widespread use led inevitably to the desire to store more material, play it back, and edit the material together to create programs. A digital nonlinear editing system has as its basic definition four elements:

Digital The system is driven by a computer that provides speed, data management, and graphical interfaces between the user and the system hardware. Further, media that is manipulated resides on computer storage mechanisms as digital files and not as analog material.

Nonlinear The physical nature of the medium does not impose constraints on how the material must be ordered. Shots can be tried in a different order, and a series of shots can be easily moved around as a group.

Random access The system allows the user to seek a particular section of material without having to proceed sequentially through other material to reach that location.

Editing system A combination of hardware and defining software that allows the editor to manipulate film- and video-based material. Work products can include an EDL or the direct video and audio output from the system serving as the final program. Finally, the digital files may be directly used, as would be the case if the program were being made for CD-ROM or another digital format.

DNLE systems seek to provide the nonlinearity of film editing while providing fast, random access to material by manipulating picture and sound as digital files. Figure 2-13 shows the

Figure 2-13 The Avid Media Composer is a digital nonlinear editing system that consists of CPU, computer storage, video and audio coprocessing hardware, editing software, and peripheral video and audio input/output devices, such as videotape recorders and audio mixers. Courtesy Avid Technology.

basic components of a digital nonlinear editing system. DNLE systems are discussed in depth in Chapter 4.

MAKING MULTIPLE VERSIONS EASY

An important advantage of DNLE systems is the easy creation of multiple versions. With film and video editing, it is time-consuming to have several versions of a sequence. Yes, we can reshuffle film as long as we want, but if we want to have two versions, we must send the first version to the lab, order a copy (called a *dupe*), and make our changes to that dupe. With videotape, we can make an exact copy of our first sequence and then make changes to the second copy, although we will be editing linearly. Most DNLE systems provide easy tools for the user to copy a sequence and have multiple versions that can be compared.

FILM AND VIDEO EDITING AND THE DIGITAL NONLINEAR EDITOR

Film and videotape editing each have their own advantages. Combining these advantages in a system that offers an easy-to-use graphical user interface is the goal of digital nonlinear editing systems. From its roots in the early digital TBCs and still stores, DNLE systems burst on the scene in 1988 and in seven years completely dominated the offline editing process. In 1996, they began to encroach upon the online process. But before such digital facilities and DNLE systems could be built, nonlinear editing was first brought into the electronic realm. This led to the first wave of nonlinear editing systems.

3

The First and Second Waves of Nonlinear Editing: Tape- and Laserdisc-Based Systems

There are six specific waves of nonlinear editing systems; each of these waves will be discussed during the course of this book. The first two waves—tape-based and laserdisc-based editing—are discussed in this chapter.

Through the early 1970s, 35mm film was the dominant medium for commercials, and 16mm film was used for nightly news segments. As the use of 2" videotape increased, machines decreased in cost, and more programming was shot and edited on tape. A natural question evolved: Could there be a way to combine the strengths of both film and videotape editing?

The development of electronic nonlinear editing systems began in 1970. These systems sought to

1. Achieve random and rapid access to material
2. Edit nonsequentially
3. Make changes easy to perform
4. Output work products that would reduce the time spent conforming

The first electronic nonlinear editing system, the CMX 600, was a hybrid that used videotape, computer, and analog recording techniques; it was unique, and it was quite revolutionary, paving the way for the videotape-based wave.

THE CMX 600

The CMX Company was a joint venture by CBS and Memorex. The CMX 600 was developed in 1970 and saw regular, though limited, use by 1972 (Figure 3-1). The basic operation of the CMX 600 involved using magnetic computer disks that were modified to store analog video. Film was transferred to videotape, or the original 2" videotape was transferred onto six to

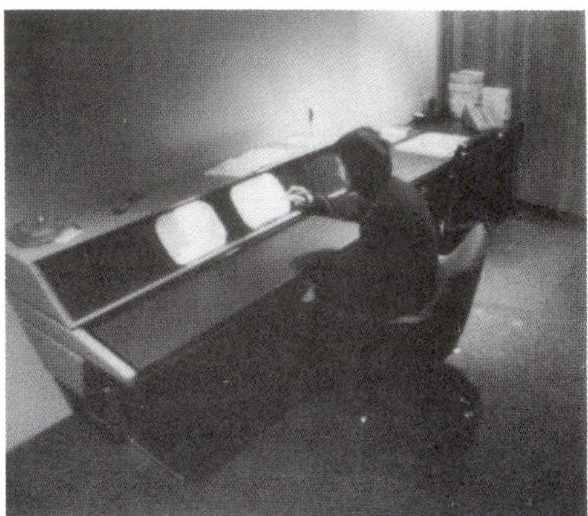

Figure 3-1 The CMX 600—the earliest electronic nonlinear editing system. Courtesy Art Schneider and CMX Corporation.

twelve 39-megabyte (MB) computer disk drives. At the time, 39 MB disk drives were considered to be gigantic!

Although the CMX 600 recorded analog signals from videotape and stored them on computer disks, it was not a digital system because the intrinsic nature of the material was not transformed from analog to digital. The CMX 600 was the first electronic nonlinear editing system, but it is classified as a hybrid system. Each disk could hold approximately five minutes of video for a total of approximately one hour on 12 disks; as a result, the system was used primarily for commercials, with their smaller amounts of original footage. And while the picture quality was quite grainy, the CMX 600 was innovative and offered instant random access to all the frames stored on the disks. Priced at over $200,000, it was expensive and not many systems were made, but it proved that film and video editing techniques could be combined in an electronic nonlinear system.

THE BASICS OF TAPE- AND LASERDISC-BASED EDITING

Tape-based editing systems (first wave) and then later, laserdisc-based systems (second wave) followed these basic steps:

1. First, the original footage is transferred to either an identical or a different medium.
2. Multiple playback devices are used to achieve nonlinearity and random access.
3. The editing process replicates the film editing model.
4. The work product stage is a video edit decision list (EDL), a film cutlist, a viewing copy of the program, a final auto-assembled version of the program, or direct output from the system.

THE FIRST WAVE: TAPE-BASED SYSTEMS

From 1972 to 1984, no new electronic nonlinear systems were introduced. Film editing was considered "safe"—it worked, it was proven, and it did not require any change. Meanwhile, electronic linear videotape editing evolved rapidly: timecode, computers, and digital video effects devices were all being used and improved for editing videotape-originated material.

The tape-based systems were nonlinear, but they were not random access since access to material was still sequential—the editor still had to wait for the videotape to cue to the desired points. Nonlinear editing borrows from film techniques the ability to splice or remove a shot anywhere in a sequence while the sequence accordingly expands or contracts, and from video techniques the ability to see optical effects, such as dissolves. Nonlinear systems also need to be *dual-finish cognizant,* that is,

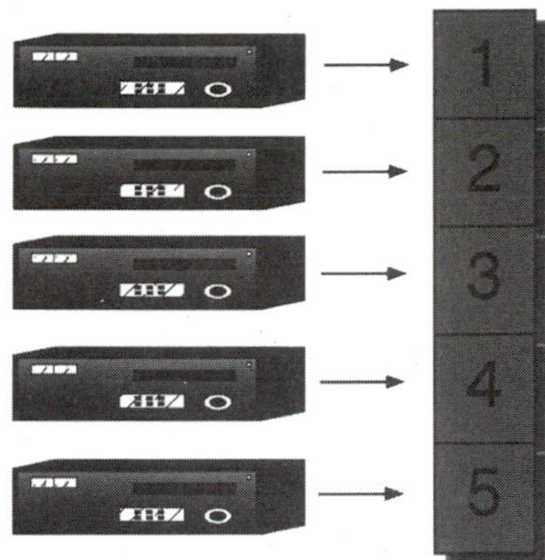

Figure 3-2 In first-wave nonlinear editing systems, multiple machines were used to seek out the desired sections on videotapes. After reaching their cue points, the machines played back the sequence in its intended order: shots 1, 2, 3, 4, 5. Illustration by Jeffrey Krebs.

to create both a negative cutlist and a video edit decision list (EDL). Finally, the system had to create an interim version of the show—a screening copy.

From 1984 to 1989, true electronic nonlinear editing systems appeared and prospered. In 1984, the first system was the Montage Picture Processor™. The name itself is an analogy to word processing, but with pictures and sounds. 1985 brought the Ediflex system, followed by TouchVision in 1986.

Tape-based systems achieved their nonlinear aspects by using multiple videotape machines. A sequence was created by cueing each machine to a different shot and then playing back the shots in their intended order (Figure 3-2). In so doing, nothing has to be committed to a final order until the editor is content with the way the shots work together (Figure 3-3).

Each of these systems used multiple VHS videotape machines. First, original material was copied to identical videocassettes; thus, each videocassette had identical footage and identical timecode. A complete load offered 4.5 hours of material. Some systems used up to 27 playback machines! Each machine would cue to a different shot, and then all the shots were played back to form the sequence.

THE PLAYLIST

It is important to realize that nonlinear editing does not involve actual recording, but, instead, the order of shots is changed to represent a different playback order. Nonlinear editing, regardless of the wave, is based on the concepts of a *playlist* and of *virtual recording*. The sequence being edited is not actually being recorded anywhere. Viewing an edit or a sequence of edits gives the impression that the entire sequence has been recorded, but what is really happening is that the order of the shots is being played back, changed, and replayed.

The playlist determines how shots are played back. If we create a sequence where we see a shot of the sky, then a falcon flying, and finally a shot of the sun, the playlist, represented by timecode numbers, looks like this:

Segment	*Play*	*From*	*To*
1	Sky	05:00:02:01	05:00:05:12
2	Falcon	05:05:08:09	05:05:18:09
3	Sun	05:02:04:01	05:02:09:01

In this example, the first tape machine is cued to shot 1, the second machine cued to shot 2, and so forth. At the conclusion of shot 1, shot 2 plays back and provides seamless viewing of the sequence. When the editor wants to change the sequence, the playlist order is changed. When the editor wants to change the length of shots, they are simply trimmed so that their duration is shorter or longer. The playlist could just as easily be

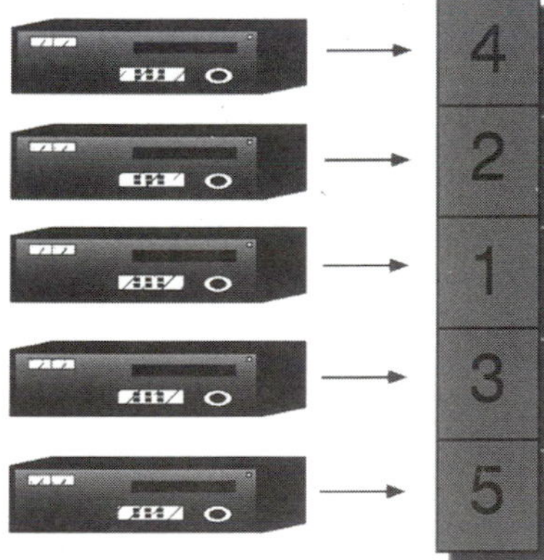

Figure 3-3 By directing the machines to cue to different sections of videotape, the sequence being edited appears to have been reordered. Here, the original sequence of shots (1, 2, 3, 4, 5) is changed by merely directing the source machines to play back material in the new order of 4, 2, 1, 3, 5. Illustration by Jeffrey Krebs.

represented by a reordering of shots and a changing of their timecodes:

Segment	*Play*	*From*	*To*
1	Falcon	05:05:03:09	05:05:16:09
2	Sky	05:00:02:01	05:00:05:12
3	Sun	05:02:02:01	05:02:08:12

WHY 27 MACHINES WEREN'T SUFFICIENT

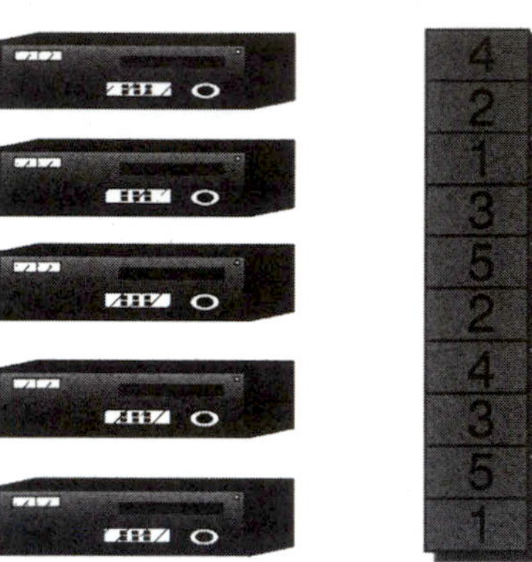

Figure 3-4 As the number of cuts increases, trafficking problems can arise if the number of tape playback machines remains constant. Will the additional cue points be reached in time? Illustration by Jeffrey Krebs.

The tape-based nonlinear editing systems were extremely popular for one-hour television shows. Conversely, they were not as successful for editing television commercials. The main reason for this was cutting density—television shows require fewer cuts per minute, whereas commercials usually have a greater number of cuts. This is also the main reason why so many playback machines were necessary: If the demands of the playlist stressed the cueing limitations of the machines, playback would fail. For example, if we only have ten playback machines and have twelve very fast cuts, and there isn't enough time for a machine to get to the material needed for the eleventh cut, we will not see pictures. These *trafficking* problems (Figure 3-4) were addressed by adding playback machines and writing software that assisted in looking ahead to determine which machines would play back material. And, of course, before playback of the sequence could even begin, there was always a waiting period while all the machines cued up to the required material.

VIRTUAL RECORDING

All nonlinear waves are based on the concept of *virtual recording*. With videotape editing, material is copied from source machine to record machine. But in nonlinear editing, nothing is ever recorded during the editing process. Instead, the virtual edit—that is, the edited sequence that we see playing back—is merely a running of the playlist. Editing, therefore, is simply manipulation of that playlist—how much of a shot is run, how it transitions to the next shot, and how many layers of material are composited upon one another.

Playlists are relatively small files—a list of numbers really—and do not take up much space in the computer's memory. The actual picture and audio files are the most storage-intensive files. Virtual recording is often referred to as using pointers to the original material by means of how the playlist is ordered. Without virtual recording, at some point the sequence would have to be recorded to tape. However, if the cutting density is high and cannot be managed by the playback machines, a portion of the sequence may need to be recorded to tape. At this point, of course, we would have severely compromised our nonlinear editing: Once we commit to tape, changes become difficult.

MULTIPLE VERSIONS

One of the benefits of the playlist is that, as a list of numbers, it can be easily duplicated. This can be thought of as the same as duplicating a computer file—once we edit a scene, the playlist is duplicated, and we have an exact copy of the scene. If it sounds simple, it should be. Changes can then be made to the new copy, not only for purposes of experimentation, but also to create multiple versions. Many programs require different language versions, for example. This is easily done: Finish the program in one language, duplicate it, and change just the language tracks.

Multiple versions can be used in many different ways. Certain shot changes can distinguish between versions, or can radically change the focus of a sequence. For example, if we create a film trailer that showcases the lead actor, the sequence can be easily duplicated, and wherever there was a shot of the lead actor, it can be replaced with the lead actress. This experimentation can be done without a great deal of effort.

USER INTERFACE

This first wave of nonlinear editing systems was instrumental in setting the stage for the creation of graphical user interfaces that blended film and videotape editing tools. Equally important was the use of manual interface knobs, wheels, and pens, all designed to provide film and videotape editors the same tactile feedback to which they had been accustomed. In 1984, personal computers were in their infancy, film and television editors' exposure to computers was limited, and computers were viewed as not being thoroughly reliable. It was therefore critical that the user interface and the screens with which the user interacted were designed to provide familiar toolsets.

THREE SYSTEMS FROM THE VIDEOTAPE-BASED WAVE

Montage

The Montage system attempted to duplicate the concept of the film editor's cutting room, and representations of footage (the pointers) were stored in electronic bins. As the material was input, shots were identified, or tagged, and a head and tail frame established for those shots. These head and tail shots were displayed as black and white digitized frames. Digitizing is the conversion of an analog signal to a digital signal. The digitized

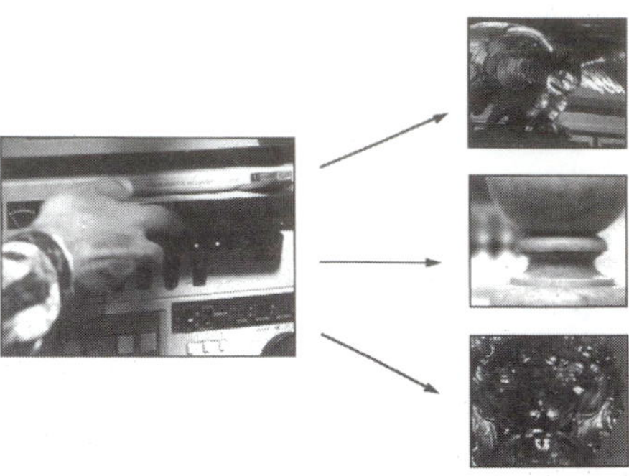

Figure 3-5 Footage contained on an original videocassette is digitized into the nonlinear editing system and displayed as representative frames.

frames were stored on the computer's magnetic disk, while the actual footage was stored on the videotape cassettes. Digitizing the first and last frame of a shot was a unique approach that employed the developing digital technology (Figure 3-5).

The user interface was largely menu driven, with tools to copy, trim, discard, splice, dissolve, and insert material. An electronic grease pencil let the editor write directly on the digitized frames to make notes and comments. The control mechanisms, two large wheels with paddle controls, were used to shuttle through footage, and they preserved some of the tactile sense of controlling the material by hand. And—a first for film editors—optical effects such as dissolves and wipes could now be seen without waiting for the effect to be created and returned from the laboratory. While film editors had not embraced linear videotape editing, the first nonlinear wave offered the ability to make trims easily, to try different versions of an edit, and to see optical effects during the editing process.

At the completion stage, the playlist was transformed into a negative cutlist and a videotape EDL. The finished sequence was recorded to 3/4" videotape for viewing; while each videocassette player cued to the appropriate material, the sequence was recorded in its edited form to the 3/4" machine. These work products were then taken into the online editing room, and the program was finished.

Ediflex

In 1985, the Ediflex system was introduced for regular use (Figure 3-6). Its inventor was Adrian Ettlinger, who had previously invented the CMX 600. Also using multiple VHS machines, the Ediflex offered a user interface that linked images to script text.

A distinct aspect of the user interface was the link between footage and the printed script. During logging, a light pen was

Figure 3-6 The Ediflex nonlinear editing system. Photo courtesy Ediflex Systems.

tapped against the computer screen to associate videotape material to sections in the script. Because of this script connection, the Ediflex enjoyed great success with one-hour television episodic programming that was entirely script driven. In addition, a particularly useful feature called *horizontal play* allowed the editor to see all the options for an actor's dialogue in a specific scene, playing take after take.

BHP TouchVision

In mid-1986, Bell & Howell's Professional Division, through a subsidiary, created TouchVision. As Montage had offered work bins, and Ediflex had offered links to the script, TouchVision furthered the interface innovation by replacing text-driven commands with graphical icons and using a touch-sensitive screen.

The *graphical user interface* (GUI) provided icons that represented visual parallels to traditional tools. For example, a film roll was represented by a drawing of a roll of film instead of a text-only menu. The GUI instantly created a visual instruction set for the user. Many editors felt that the icon-based format led to a shorter learning period and an easier transition from film and videotape to electronic nonlinear editing.

Multiple versions, film-style splicing, and trimming were available. The system created a negative cutlist, video EDL, and a screening copy. Eventually, the original IBM-compatible computer was replaced by an Apple Macintosh computer, increasing the sophistication of the graphical menus.

EVALUATING THE FIRST WAVE

The videotape-based wave introduced electronic nonlinear editing to film and videotape editors. These systems were primarily used for long-format programs—typically 60-minute television shows and some feature films. This wave did not offer random access, but each system offered unique tools and interfaces. Unlike the CMX 600, which may have been too early for its time, electronic nonlinear editing was definitely here to stay. However, random access, virtual recording, playlists, multiple versions, and graphical user interfaces could all be improved. This first wave reached its peak in 1988. Less than six years later, no first-wave systems were in use.

THE SECOND WAVE: LASERDISC-BASED SYSTEMS

The second wave began in 1984 with the introduction of the EditDroid, followed in 1986 by the CMX 6000, a descendant of the pioneering CMX 600. In 1989, the Epix system was introduced. Each of these systems used laserdiscs instead of videocassettes as the playback medium, which brought them something that the first wave did not have—random access.

Instead of having to cue sequentially through videotape, material now could be reached in as little as 900 milliseconds (ms) to a maximum access time of two seconds (Figure 3-7).

The first-wave systems suffered from long cueing times, and commercials, with their fast cutting ratios, required a medium that could be accessed quickly. Laserdiscs provided the solution. As was the case with the first wave, identical material was loaded onto multiple laserdisc machines.

LASERDISC TYPES

There are two types of laser videodiscs: constant angular velocity (CAV) and constant linear velocity (CLV). The important differences are summarized in Table 3-1. Both types of videodiscs evolved during the late 1970s. The second-wave systems used CAV laserdiscs, limiting the amount of footage to 30 minutes per disc.

Original material was first transferred to a premaster tape, and then played back into a laserdisc mastering machine. The video and audio signals excite a laser, and the resulting light beam creates a corresponding value as a frequency modulation (FM) carrier. The recording laser exposes the photochemical layer and burns reflective pits into the surface of the disc. When the disc is played back, the playback laser illuminates the pits, and then a photosensitive cell interprets the laser light that is bouncing and reflecting off the pits. These very tiny signals are carried to an amplifier and demodulated back into video and audio signals, which we can see and hear.

Figure 3-7 The CMX 6000, a second-wave nonlinear editing system that used laser videodiscs to provide improved random access to material. Photo by Michael E. Phillips.

Table 3-1 Comparison of Laserdisc Types

	12" CAV	*12" CLV*
Capacity	30 minutes per side	60 minutes per side
	54,000 frames	108,000 frames
Channels of sound	2	2
Slow motion	Yes	No
Step frame	Yes	No
Still/freeze frame	Yes	No
Use	Industry	Consumer

There are significant differences between CAV and CLV discs. A CAV disc, which stores 30 minutes of material per side, rotates once per video frame. Each track consists of two fields that make up one video frame. A CAV disc revolves at a constant speed of 1800 revolutions per minute (RPM) and does not waver, which allows a CAV disc to provide steady freeze frames. CLV discs store 60 minutes of material per side. The innermost tracks of the disc revolve at 1800 RPM, but when the outer tracks are reached, the rotational speed slows down significantly, to about 600 RPM. As a result, the CLV disc is not able to achieve a full video frame for each rotation and thus cannot offer freeze-frame capability.

LASERDISC CHARACTERISTICS

Discovision Associates (DVA) Code

DVA codes are five-digit codes encoded onto the glass master by the laser. These can be thought of as a laserdisc's version of videotape's timecode and represent how the disc is searched. When a request is made for a frame, the laser beam must leave one spot, get to the next spot, and begin displaying the requested frame. This time interval is referred to as *access time.*

Erasable or Nonerasable

Laserdiscs can be *write once, read many* (WORM). Once material is transferred to the disc, the disc can only be played back. No additional material can be recorded, and it cannot be erased. There are also *write many, read many* (WMRM) discs which can be erased and recorded to multiple times.

Disc Skipping

Disc skipping, a troubling aspect of the second-wave systems, was due to the effects of humidity, which could "fog" the disc. The laser's beam wound up being diffused in this fog.

TYPICAL SECOND-WAVE EDITING SYSTEM DESIGN

The CMX 6000, introduced in 1986, incorporated the familiar conventions of film bins, lift bins, and trim bins (Figure 3-8). One screen displayed source material, and the second screen displayed the sequence being created, similar to film's feed and take-up reels.

Previsualization Tools

The second wave continued to build on the set of previsualization tools. Dissolves and wipes were previouly available, but the use of CAV discs now allowed editors to have an array of motion effects as well, such as slow motion, fast motion, freeze frames, and reverse motion (called *reverse printing* in film). Second-wave systems also added another new capability—titling—in which text characters could be keyed over background video to previsualize titles and credit rolls. One of the continuing themes in the development of nonlinear systems is that each new wave brings with it new tools and capabilities designed to previsualize more completely or to finish the program outright.

Improvements to the Graphical User Interface

The second-wave systems furthered the use of the graphical user interface. The essential idea behind these GUIs and

Figure 3-8 The CMX 6000 laserdisc-based editing system is shown in the main editing console along with the rack-mounted laserdisc players. Photo by Howard A. Phillips.

how they sought to represent a program was borrowed from the common film synchronizer, which is used to keep film and magnetic tracks in sync (Figure 3-9). On a nonlinear system, the film synchronizer is represented as "software synchronizers," which are text representations of the film and magnetic tracks (Figure 3-10).

These graphical synchronizers soon became known as *timelines* and became a fundamental part of nonlinear editing systems. Now, for the first time, both film and videotape editors were able to see—in a graphical form—the overall structure of the programs they were creating.

Later, in 1991, manufacturers of traditional linear videotape editing systems recognized the importance of graphical interfaces and replaced rows and columns of timecode numbers with picture icons.

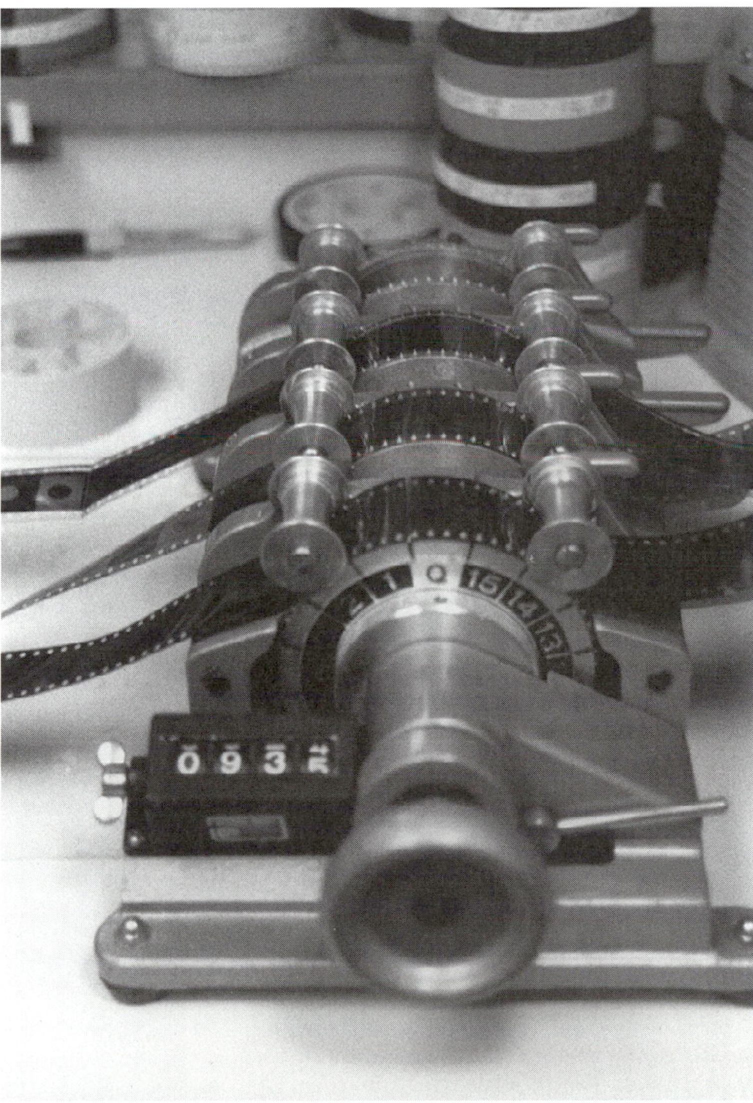

Figure 3-9 The film synchronizer is used to keep film and magnetic sound tracks in sync. Photo by Michael E. Phillips.

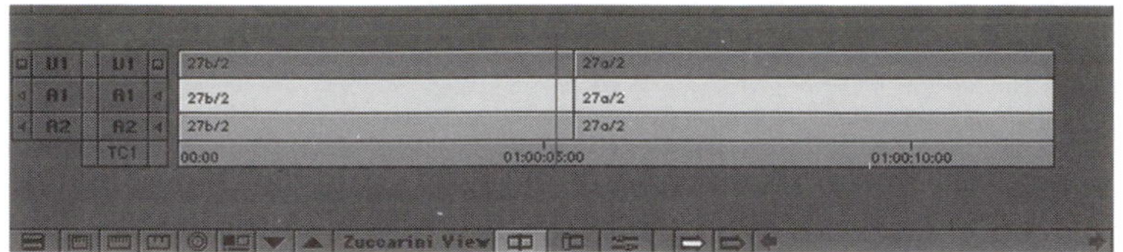

Figure 3-10 The software counterpart to a film synchronizer allows an editor to easily view the structure of a sequence.

AUDIO EDITING

Traditional Film Sound Editing

In film editing, the editor usually has two tracks of audio to work with. If we have a dialogue-driven scene between a man and a woman, the actor's dialogue will be on one mag track while the actress's dialogue will be on the second track. With two tracks of dialogue, the editor can accomplish a *straight cut*, in which one character finishes speaking before the other character begins speaking (Figure 3-11).

A *picture overlap* occurs when there is an interval of time in which one character is speaking while we are seeing a picture of another character. Structurally, it would appear as in Figure 3-12. The picture (V1) cuts from actor Russell to actor Nicholas. However, note that we continue to hear Russell's audio (A1) over Nicholas's picture. Eventually, Russell finishes, and the audio straight cuts to Nicholas.

A *sound overlap* occurs when there is an interval of time in which both actors are speaking (Figure 3-13). When Russell begins to speak, note that there is corresponding black film leader on Nicholas's sound track (A2). However, while Russell is speaking, note that Nicholas's sound track begins and that there is a period of time during which both actors are speaking over one another. Eventually, Russell stops speaking, and his sound track is shown in black leader while Nicholas continues speaking.

Next, if the film editor wants to rehearse some sound effects (sfx) against the scene, one of the magnetic tracks is removed, and the sound effects, already transferred to mag, are placed in their specific sections.

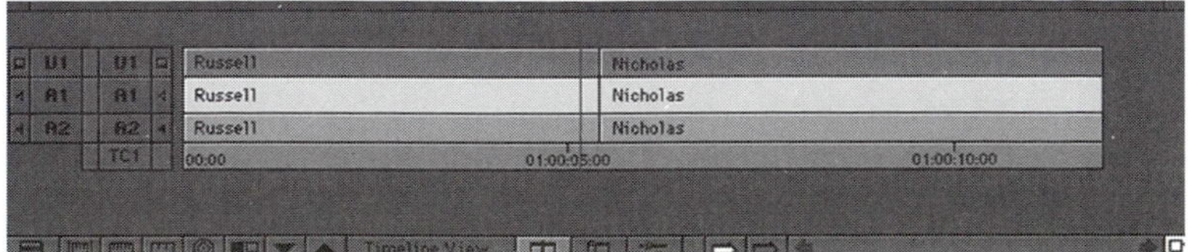

Figure 3-11 In a straight cut, all tracks cut, or transition, from one character to the next with no overlap.

Figure 3-12 A picture overlap occurs when one actor is speaking while we are seeing the second actor.

For example, let's say that when Russell begins to speak, there is a bit of off-screen applause. Later, when Nicholas is speaking, the sound of crashing dishes is heard, and the actor reacts to this sound. The editor would also like to rehearse some temporary music for the scene. Recall that, if editing in film, it would not be possible to hear all of these tracks at once; we would have to take down tracks in order to make room for new tracks. However, *if* we could put up all these tracks, they would appear as in Figure 3-14.

Second-Wave Audio Editing

Tape-based and laserdisc-based editing systems each offered two tracks of sound, making them as capable as film sound editing. Later, in the third wave—the digital wave—vast and impressive improvements were made to audio editing capabilities. Achieving multiple tracks of sound (as shown in Figure 3-14) became simple to accomplish.

Analog versus Digital Scrubbing

The second-wave systems differed from tape-based systems in how audio playback was achieved when audio was played at less than normal speed. When a film or videotape editor is trying to locate the beginning of a word, the playback speed is slowed down while the editor searches for where the word actually starts. This is called *scrubbing the track.* The film editor physically rocks the mag track back and forth along the sound head and can isolate the desired start point of a word. As the audio playback speed is decreased or increased, there is an accompanying change of pitch. If playback is faster than normal, there will be an increase in pitch; if playback is slower than normal, there will be a decrease in pitch. Therefore, pitch can be thought of as the height or depth of a tone (or of sound),

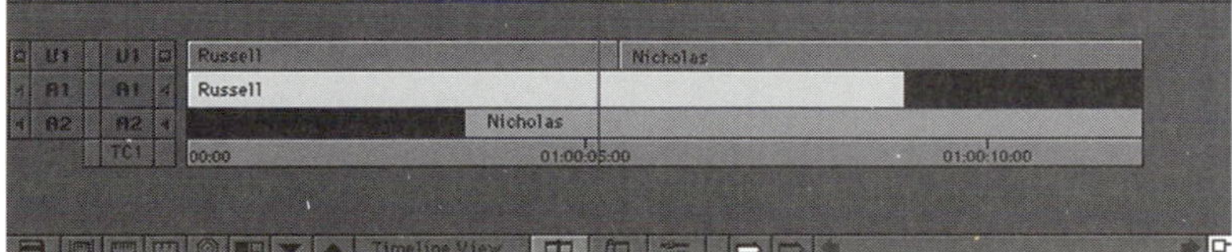

Figure 3-13 A sound overlap occurs when there is an interval of time during which both actors are talking simultaneously.

Figure 3-14 Adding more sound tracks in order to hear sound effects and a temporary music track.

depending on the relative speed of the vibrations that produce the tone or sound.

If scrubbing is performed at less than normal playing speed, the analog vibration that is created produces a pitch that is decreased from the sound's normal pitch profile. Conversely, if scrubbing is performed at faster than normal play, there is an increase in the pitch of the sound. In essence, the audio scrub is accompanied by a pitch change: a benefit film and videotape editors enjoy not as a feature, but simply as a technical characteristic of playing back an analog medium.

But second-wave systems and early third-wave systems playing back audio at slower or faster than normal speed did not recreate the analog vibrations that affect pitch. Instead, the best that these systems could provide were sample points of audio. For example, when a CAV disc is being searched, the laser beam skips from one section to the next, and there is no continuous audio vibration. Instead, what is heard is the exact sound at each point at which the laser is currently located. This "digital scrubbing" takes some time to get used to: The human ear and the craft of film and videotape editing have evolved into hearing sounds in the natural analog representation, with an accompanying change of pitch.

Several years after the introduction of both the second and third waves, manufacturers created special software designed to offer analog-style scrubbing. This is accomplished by writing a portion of audio into a memory location and using these additional samples to represent a continuous audio signal. These same audio buffering techniques had to be applied to videotape formats such as D1 and D2 to offer analog scrubbing.

Resolution: Cutting a Perf versus Cutting a Frame

Film editing can cut audio on the perforation (perf) level; that is, one can make an audio edit at less than a one-frame resolution. In both the first- and second-wave systems, and indeed on videotape itself, the smallest increment to which one can edit audio is one frame. However, with DNLE systems, subframe audio editing is possible.

Audio Mixing Tools

Another improvement over film editing was the addition of a simple audio mixer that allowed the editor to transition between the two tracks of audio. Audio dissolves are called *crossfades*. If the editor has created a scene where two people are talking and wants to run a music track underneath the scene, by controlling the audio mixer by hand, he can do a temporary mixdown *(temp mix)* of the two tracks onto the presentation tape to judge how the different sound elements work together.

THE FIRST TIME FOR 24 FPS

The second wave also brought the native film playback speed of 24 frames per second to electronic nonlinear editing. When film is transferred to video, it is played back at 29.97 fps. During the film-to-video transfer, film frames are essentially recorded to video more than once (see Chapter 14). Since the laserdisc index could trace where the true film frames were on the disc as opposed to the additional video frames, the video frames were not displayed. As a result, editors were, for the first time, able to view 24 fps material at 24 fps on the electronic system.

EVALUATING THE SECOND WAVE

The laserdisc-based wave brought with it new tools that built on the feature set of the tape-based wave. New features included slow and fast motion effects, titling, audio crossfades, and audio mixes. Laserdiscs improved access times, and it is this wave that certainly fits the definition of an electronic, nonlinear, random-access editing system. There was also a greater emphasis on graphical user interfaces, and the use of color, shapes, and visual timelines became mainstays of nonlinear systems.

SETTING THE STAGE FOR THE THIRD-WAVE SYSTEMS

The second-wave systems were in widespread operation for approximately eight year—from 1984 to 1992. By 1994, it became very difficult to find these systems in use, and in 1996, only one laserdisc-based system, that is, one physical unit, was in use in all of California. During the eight-year period, a new set of tools were created and user interfaces were redefined. From the dual-monitor CMX 6000 to the script-based Ediflex to the graphically rich Epix, second-wave systems brought color, icons, and familiar film and video conventions to users.

Whereas the first wave was used primarily for long-form programming, the second wave was adopted primarily for short-form work such as commercials. With their fast access times and random access, laserdiscs could keep up with the fast cutting ratios of commercials. Still, the second-wave systems continued to suffer from trafficking problems. If one wanted to cut between two synchronized sound sources, as is the case with two people talking, one required four discs and four machines: two discs for the "from" and "to" pictures and two discs for the "from" and "to" audio tracks. There were technical refinements made to assist in these trafficking issues; for example, the Laser Edit system introduced a dual-headed player that could read both sides of the disc, reducing the number of required discs to two.

Another inventive solution sought to address complex editing scenarios. Even with their fast access times, so many cuts in commercials began to stress even dual-headed laserdisc systems. By integrating one WMRM (write many, read many) disc player/recorder, the series of difficult-to-access shots were recorded as a *prebuild* onto the writable *slop disc*, as it was called.

The second-wave nonlinear systems were analog, but they satisfied the requirements of an electronic, nonlinear, random-access editing system. The principles, interfaces, and tools that they provided formed a significant level of functionality. Over their eight-year history, second-wave systems were used as the offline editor of choice in markets that could sustain the cost of purchasing or renting these systems—mainly Chicago, Los Angeles, New York, and Toronto, all significant centers of commercial postproduction. Over time, second-wave systems began to be used for longer-format work such as television shows, documentaries, and feature films.

Today, laserdiscs are primarily used for either presentation or archiving purposes, including displays for museum exhibits and interactive training programs. They are also, of course, used by consumers for home viewing (although this will be threatened as DVD, digital video disc, increases in use).

Even with laserdisc's occasional problems—disc skipping due to humidity, slop disc usage, and inability to reuse WORM discs—editing nonlinearly and being able to see optical effects were compelling reasons that furthered their use and acceptance. The same route of enhanced feature sets, and the trials and tribulations of both the first and second waves, was about to be repeated by the digital, third-wave systems.

4

The Third Wave: Digital Nonlinear Editing Systems

Digital-based systems represent the third wave of electronic nonlinear editing. In this wave, analog signals are converted into digital signals that are then stored on computer disks. The analog-to-digital conversion is called *digitization.* The process of reducing the amount of data that represents the original information is called *compression.* Compression is usually, but not always, applied, because the quantity of information in video usually exceeds storage capacities.

Digital nonlinear editing (DNLE) systems began to appear in 1988 and coexisted with first- and second-wave systems. Figure 4-1 shows an early DNLE system. By 1991, first-wave systems had lost market share to second-wave systems, and by 1994, second-wave systems had in turn lost their market share to the digital third-wave systems. By 1995, both first- and second-wave systems were virtually extinct. In 1997, only one laserdisc-based system was being used, and the fact that there was actually one still in use was somewhat astounding!

It also interesting to note the difference in the number of manufacturers for each wave. There were three manufacturers for the first-wave systems and three manufacturers for second-wave systems. Yet in only a four-year period, from 1988 to 1992, over 15 different DNLE systems from as many manufacturers were introduced. By 1996, there were over 38 manufacturers, and by 1997 there were over 60! Clearly, the third wave, during its critical years from 1991 to 1996, completely obviated the use of the earlier two waves. Digital-based systems were here to stay and offered remarkable capabilities, though certainly not at first.

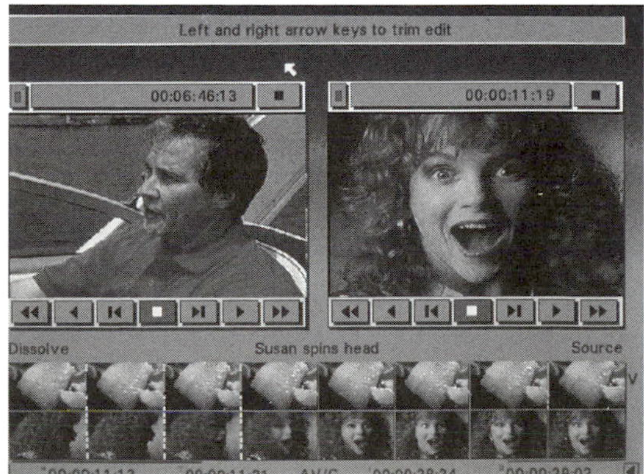

Figure 4-1 An early DNLE system, the EMC2. Courtesy Editing Machines Corporation.

Film editing, as we know, is a nonlinear process, but it is also a destructive process. We must physically cut the film, splice it to another piece of film, and judge the results. If we continue to experiment endlessly with the same frames of film, we will need to get a duplicate made because the originals will be too marred to be used effectively. Although videotape editing is a nondestructive process, it is a linear process. We must commit to a decision, and we must commit edit by edit. After committing, it becomes a time-consuming endeavor to review and make changes.

DNLE systems change the nature of the material being stored and accessed because the signals are no longer analog in nature—they are now digital. This is a critical difference in third-wave systems. The digital editing system is a unique blend of computer and advanced digital coprocessors, all built on computer interfaces designed to duplicate the film editor's traditional work place.

With any new technology, the price of entry when the technology is new is always quite high. After several years and iterations, the associated costs of building the systems decrease. This fact, combined with a competitive marketplace, usually means that systems become more powerful and cost less. Traditionally, digital equipment and digital processing techniques were expensive and unproved and, of course, staffs needed to be educated and trained. While these same concerns were voiced when DNLE systems burst on the scene, another question had to be answered: Why invest in analog when all of the active development is being spent on creating digital systems?

What do digital data and digital manipulation provide to users of DNLE systems? Essentially, digital provides greater signal processing capabilities, improvements over analog signal loss through successive generations, and, perhaps most important, an array of software that cannot easily be duplicated by any specific transitional machine. Although the compression stage reduces the original quality level of the pictures, a variety of image resolutions are often available on a system; these images are usually more than adequate for making editorial decisions. Once pictures and sounds are in digital form, they can be arranged and rearranged with the same flexibility as film, but without the manual labor.

HOW DNLE SYSTEMS WORK

General System Objectives

DNLE systems are often described as "word processors for pictures and sounds." Although it has now become a cliché, it clearly is a deserved analogy. If you have ever used a word processor, you'll recognize that they usually offer a set of tools loosely termed *cut, copy,* and *paste.* These tools are used to cut a section of text out of a document and delete it, or to easily copy a section of text from a document and paste it (place it) into a new location. Such moving, refining, and rearranging operations are at the heart of the editing of images and sounds as well as words. It seemed, therefore, a quite natural step to utilize such concepts in the creation of DNLE software.

What digital systems sought to do by virtue of their conversion of analog signals into digital data was to offer improvements in random access. With picture and sound signals in digital form, it is possible to have random accessibility to any material in, at the very best, 6 milliseconds (ms) or, at the very worst, 13 ms (1 ms = 1/1000 second). Obviously, this is a considerable time savings over shuttling videotape and is a 150% improvement over the access time of laserdiscs (about 900 ms).

Another objective of the digital wave was to facilitate the inclusion of late-arriving material. With both the videotape- and laserdisc-based systems, new material had to be duplicated before it could be incorporated into the edit session—either a new tape load or a set of laserdiscs had to be created. With digital systems, material is transferred in real time, and as a result, a new piece of footage that is 30 seconds long will take slightly longer than 30 seconds to load into the system in preparation for an editing session.

Reusability was also an issue. Videotape is certainly reusable, but the endless cueing and shuttling that took place with first-wave systems precluded reusing tapes. And with WORM laserdiscs, no additional recording was possible. Erasable WMRM discs could be re-recorded, but the high cost of media and recorders were barriers to widespread use. But DNLE systems have a great advantage: The magnetic and optical media disks are erasable and extremely reliable. In the case of magnetic disks, about 40,000 hours of use is a typical minimum rating. Even if a system based on magnetic disks were used for 80 hours a week, 52 weeks a year, it would be 9.6 years before 40,000 hours were reached. Optical discs are rated in excess of 1 million rewrites.

Figure 4-2 shows the general components found in a DNLE system. They include a computer, storage drives, monitors, and peripheral devices for video and audio signal input and output.

Figure 4-2 The components of any DNLE system include a computer, a monitor that displays the user interface, a set of disk drives for storing material, and a keyboard or similar device for input. Peripheral devices, such as a videotape machine and audio mixers, are used for assisting in the input and output of the system. DVision PostSuite courtesy DVision.

System Work Flow

Path 1: Originate on Film, Edit Digital Nonlinear, Finish in Linear Online

This method (Figure 4-3) is used when film is the original material, but the end product of the editing process will be videotape. For example, most television commercials are shot on film and are broadcast on videotape. The pathway to and from the digital system is as follows. The film is shot, and the processed film and film sound are transferred to videotape. Next, picture and sound are digitized to computer disk. Editing is done on the DNLE system, and the resulting edit decision list (EDL) and source videotapes are taken to the linear online suite to conform the finished program. This has been a very traditional course, and much work continues to follow this path. An in-depth discussion of how computers are affecting this work flow is presented in Chapter 6.

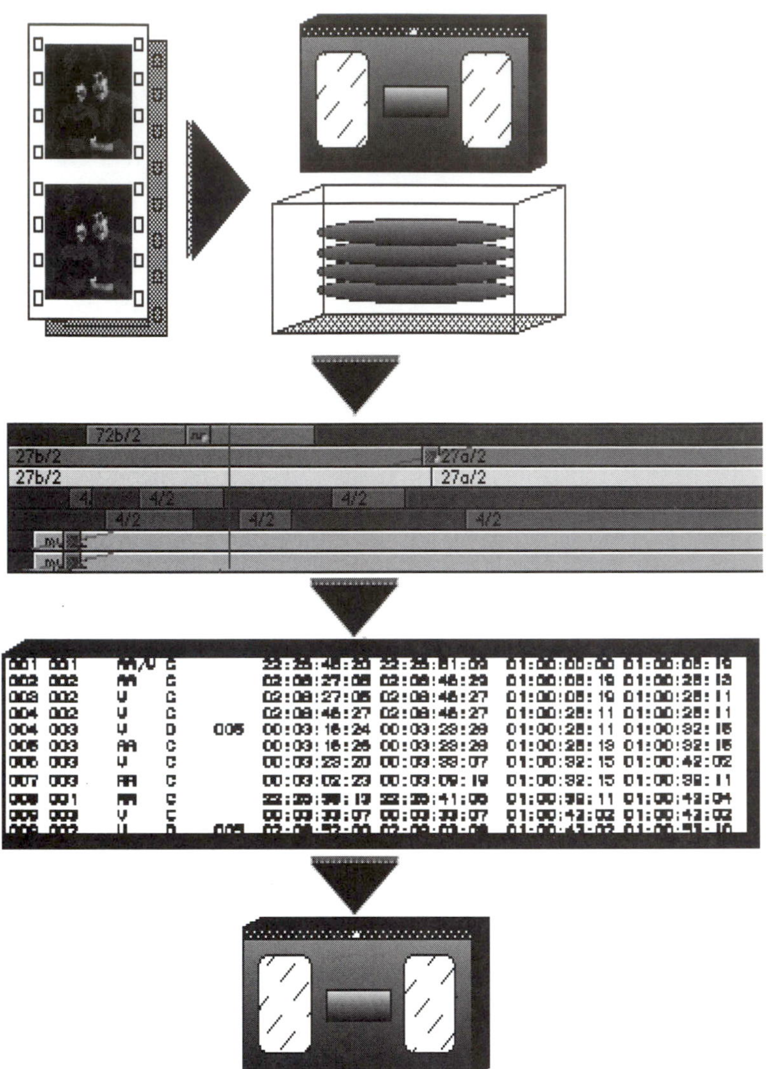

Figure 4-3 Path 1: Originating material on film, editing on a DNLE system, and finishing in the linear online room. Illustration by Jeffrey Krebs.

Path 2: Originate on Film, Edit Digital Nonlinear, Finish on Film

This method (Figure 4-4) is used when film is shot, and the end product is not a videotape but, instead, a film release. For feature films edited on a DNLE system, there must be a way to eventually return to the original film and to conform it according to the nonlinear editing session.

Here, original film is shot and transferred either directly to the DNLE system's disk drives or to videotape and then digitized into the DNLE system. Editing then takes place and a *negative cutlist* is created instead of an EDL. It contains the instructions for which frames of the film negative need to be cut and the order in which they should be spliced together. The original film negative is cut, and then a positive print is created. Later, when a videotape release is required, the conformed original negative is used to create a videotape master for duplication.

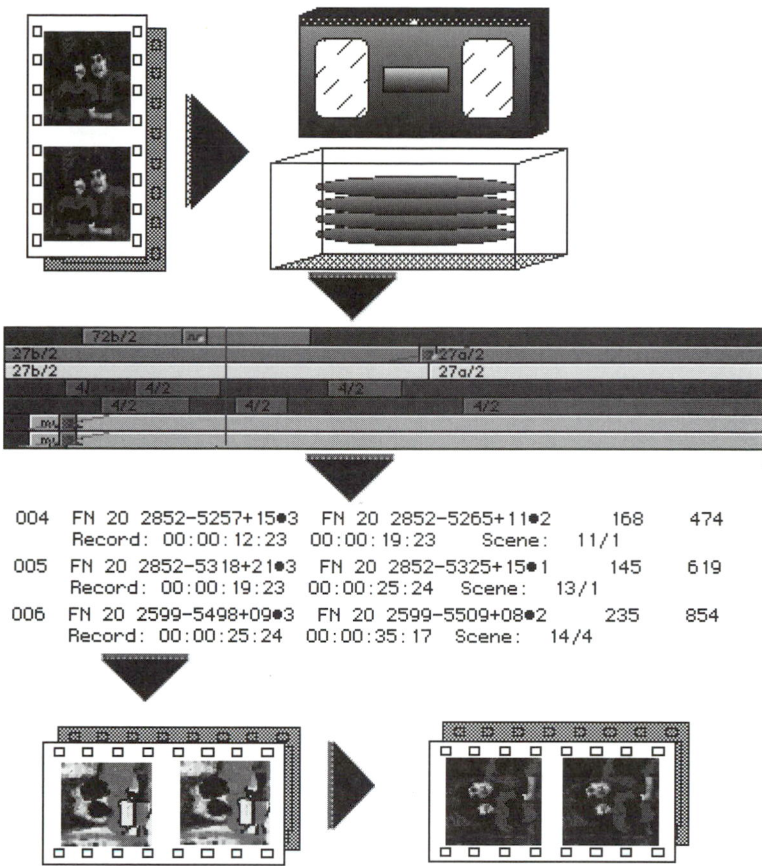

Figure 4-4 Path 2: Originating material on film, editing on a DNLE system, and finishing on film. Illustration by Jeffrey Krebs.

Path 3: Originate on Video, Edit Digital Nonlinear, Finish in Linear Online

This method (Figure 4-5) is essentially the same as the first path except that the original footage is videotape rather than film. Here, original source videotape is digitized into the DNLE system and edited, and an EDL is created. The original source tapes and EDL are used to assemble the final program. Through 1996, this method represented a majority of the work being done on DNLE systems. In late 1996 and beyond, significant advances in DNLE technology began to affect this traditional work path (see Chapter 6).

Path 4: Originate on Film or Video, Edit Digital Nonlinear, Finish in Digital Nonlinear Using Hybrid Auto-Assemble Option

Some DNLE systems are capable of performing a linear videotape auto-assembly. Here, the DNLE system controls three machines—a traditional A/B roll assembly—while a video switcher is used to make the transitions between the two source machines. This is essentially the same as Figure 4-5 except that the DNLE system serves as the hybrid edit controller.

Figure 4-5 Path 3: Originating material on video, editing on a DNLE system, and finishing in linear online. Illustration by Jeffrey Krebs.

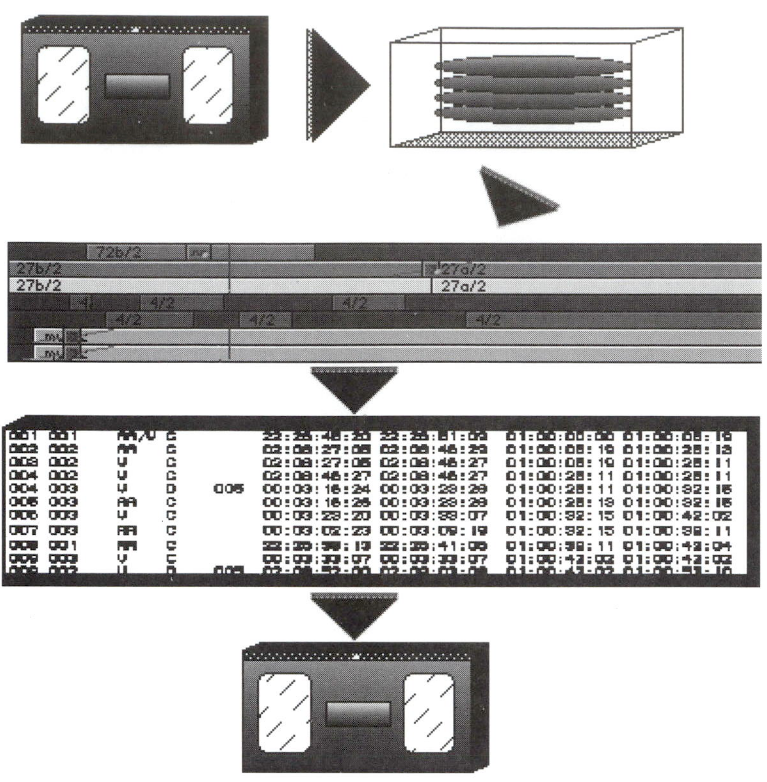

While this path still exists for those users who will not accept the picture resolution output of the DNLE system, it is most definitely on its way to extinction, and will become extinct as picture resolution from DNLE systems improves.

Path 5: Originate on Film or Video, Edit Digital Nonlinear, Finish in Digital Nonlinear Using Direct Output

When DNLE systems first began to appear in 1988 and were brought to market in 1989, they were viewed as being appropriate only for offline editing. Given the limitations in picture resolution (see Color Plate 1), this was a logical attitude—after all, it was unthinkable to broadcast an entire program done at a picture resolution at which it was impossible to see whether a person's eyes were open or closed!

However, when the picture resolution is deemed satisfactory for finished work, the direct output of the disk drives—that is, digitized picture and sound—is recorded directly to videotape (Figure 4-6), which becomes the show master for duplication.

The issue, of course, is whether picture and sound quality are acceptable enough to avoid having to return to the original source videotapes and do an online session. There are several

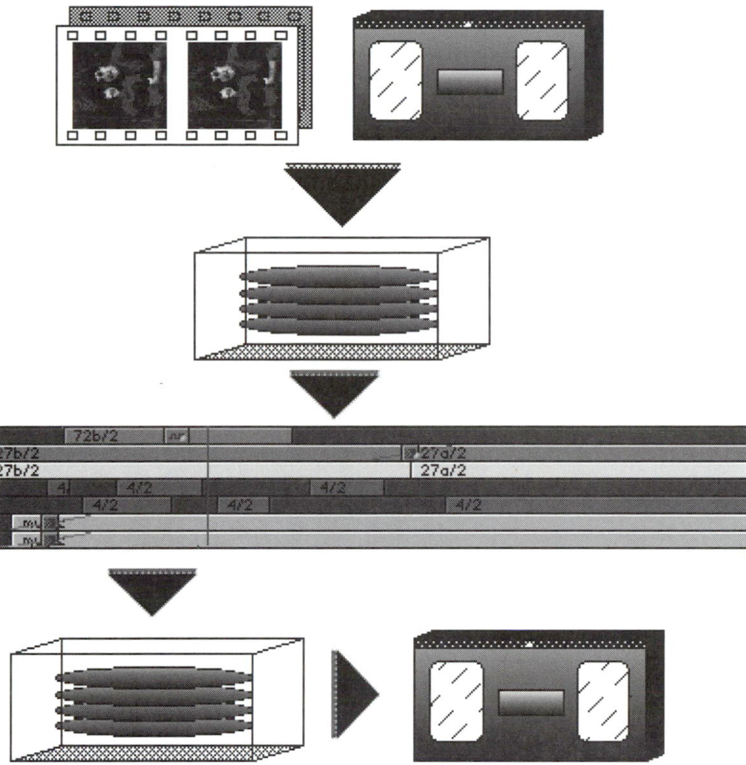

Figure 4-6 Path 5: Originating material on either film or video, editing on a DNLE system, and finishing using the direct output of the disk drives. Illustration by Jeffrey Krebs.

factors that influence this decision: What did the original material look like? What is the ratio of compression? If a low ratio was used, there will be minimal picture artifacts introduced during the compression stage.

CREATIVE AND ECONOMIC BENEFITS OF DIRECT OUTPUT

There are two main reasons why direct output is important and advantageous. The first is creativity. DNLE systems, at least in their first five years (1988–1993), offered software that basically served as offline software—everything that could be done and previsualized on the DNLE system could be recreated perfectly during online editing. When combined with the highly compressed picture resolutions, this reproducibility prevented most people from using the direct output from the disk drives. This situation began to change in 1994 as DNLE systems became more powerful. Suddenly it was possible to have acceptable picture quality for finished programs. In addition, impressive software enhancements made it possible to begin to create things on the DNLE system that could not easily be replicated during online editing (Chapter 6).

Second, economically, there is a huge benefit in being able to combine both the offline and the online stage. A considerable cost savings can be realized if online time can be completely removed from a program's completion budget. There are a range of programs that do not conform to the somewhat rigorous requirements of broadcast television. This area of programming is usually referred to as *not for broadcast* and can range from, say, two-minute new-employee introductory programs to business, educational, and training videos. When both the quality is adequate and significant money can be saved by avoiding online editing, there is no question that there will be an increase in direct-from-disk finishing.

OFFLINE OR ONLINE?

As we know, the offline and online stages were always quite separate and distinct. But the direct-from-disk method splinters the barrier between offline editing and online editing. If a program can now be finished in the offline system, what do we call that system? Is it offline, or is it online? It is inevitable that improvements to the digitizing and compression stages will ensure that results indistinguishable from original material will be achieved. From the moment that compressed video is no longer noticeable, great ramifications will arise for the post-production process. Indeed, the entire offline to online process will be affected as more users of DNLE systems use the direct output option.

PARADIGMS OF THE DNLE SYSTEM

When we look at the software that makes up DNLE systems, we can identify four basic concepts. Some of these conventions evolved from tried and proven concepts in film and videotape editing, while others are inventions introduced specifically for the digital-based systems. The four paradigms are the clip, the transition, the sequence, and the timeline. Although different manufacturers may have differing terms for these concepts, they will be clearly identifiable from system to system.

The Clip

When a film editor is making a movie, the shots that are being put together are small pieces of film that are ordered in a specific way. When the film editor has a close-up of an actress that needs to be joined to another piece of film, the close-up will be judged, handled, and spliced into the appropriate location.

As an example, if the editor has a one-second close-up of a character and is working in 16mm film, the piece of film that the editor holds is about seven inches long. To the editor, those seven inches represent the one-second shot. As the editor becomes more experienced, initial decisions as to how long a shot should be are often made by virtue of the length of the film strip the editor is holding. Often, when a film editor thinks about how long a shot should be, one image that comes to mind is how much film would be held between outstretched arms. The conversation proceeds in the following manner:

> "How long do you think this shot should be?"
>
> "About that long."

To the film editor, these little pieces of film, whether they measure seven inches or ten feet, represent all the segments of the film that must be joined to form the movie. A *clip* is simply a model based on these individual pieces of film. A clip represents the way that film editors are used to working: A clip starts and ends at a film splice. If a film splice can also be judged as a shot, then a clip represents that shot (Figure 4-7).

Film editors enjoy this simple concept of the clip because film exists in space rather than in time. This concept is absolutely essential in understanding why film editing is a nonlinear process while videotape editing is a linear process. Film images, as things that can be touched and judged by their length, allow the film editor to make judgments on how long the piece of film should be and, therefore, how long the shot should be held on the screen. These little sections of space can be easily rearranged; they will occupy the same overall space, but the order will be different.

The concept of the clip became universal in DNLE systems. When an editor sits down to any DNLE system, there will be some reference to the clip. To the film editor, of course, this reference means that the traditional working methods have been preserved.

The Transition

While the film editor can judge shots based on the space that they occupy, the videotape editor does not have this feedback loop. The film editor picks up a piece of film, estimates the appropriate length, and works much closer with, and to, the

NAME	Tracks	Start	End
34	V	18:34:27:01	18:34:31:02
34/2	V	18:34:21:26	18:34:24:09
34A/1	V	18:09:09:05	18:09:11:24
34A/2	V	18:08:49:16	18:08:57:06
35/2	V	00:15:40:23	00:15:49:27
35A/1	V	00:12:43:01	00:13:15:10
35A/2	VA1A2	00:12:38:25	00:13:16:16
38	V	00:20:23:08	00:20:30:08
38A/1	V	00:19:57:11	00:20:03:23
39	V	00:18:08:16	00:18:11:16
39	VA1A2	00:12:38:25	00:13:16:16
40/3	V	02:22:25:11	02:22:29:25
40A/1	V	02:17:35:01	02:17:41:05
40A/2	V	02:17:24:25	02:17:29:15
42	V	17:00:40:00	17:00:48:11
42/1	V	15:24:35:08	15:24:40:16

Figure 4-7 The clip. While it can be represented in many different ways, the clip is commonly shown to users as an icon, a text, or an actual picture frame representing the shot.

material. But the process of videotape editing proceeds at a greater distance, since the editor cannot manually hold the images. Videotape editing is therefore based not on the clip, but on the *transition*.

When a videotape editor makes an edit, what is really happening is that a decision is being made about a point in time. While the videotape is being played on the monitors, the editor chooses that point in time, a timecode point, and hits the mark in button on the edit controller. This in mark serves as the location where the previously laid down shot on the videotape master will be joined to this newly chosen point. When the in point has been chosen, the editor usually makes the edit as an open-ended edit with no set out point. Next, the recording is made, and when the shot is no longer useful, that is, when the action is over, the editor presses the out button. This action simply means "Stop. The useful length of this shot has been reached."

When the next edit is made, the editor replays the shot that has just been laid down and judges where the old shot should stop and the new shot should begin. This process, and the thinking that accompanies it, is very different from that used by the film editor, who picks shots based on the space that they occupy. Instead, the videotape editor is picking shots based on how they "transition" with other shots. This is because videotape exists in time and not in space. In the video editing room, then, conversation proceeds as follows:

"How long do you think this shot should be?"

"About three seconds."

Editing videotape means adding or subtracting timecode numbers that realign the transition between two shots. As these numbers are manipulated, the desired transition is achieved. The reason that film and videotape editing are different is not because one is nonlinear and the other is linear, but because of space versus time. Space will always be nonlinear, and time will always be linear.

Consider two shots joined together. The editor wants these shots to transition not as a cut, but as a dissolve (refer to Figure 2-6). The film editor draws a mark across the shots to indicate the amount of space that the dissolve will span over the length of the two shots, but the videotape editor types a duration in frames for the dissolve. While the tasks don't sound very different, it is as if the film editor says, "This dissolve should happen over this *range of space,*" while the videotape editor says, "This dissolve should take this *amount of time.*" This is a subtle, but quite real, division of thinking.

The concept of the transition is the second item that has found a place in the digital nonlinear tool set. Transition-based editing tools on the DNLE system consist of a model in which shots can be determined by their timecode length and by views that show the transition between the outgoing and incoming material. In this way, the editor's working methods have been preserved.

The Sequence

In film, clips are edited together to create a sequence of shots that forms a scene. This sequence of images becomes the film editor's *cut.* With video, transition editing is done, and the videotape editor's cut becomes the master tape. On a DNLE system, the third item in the tool set is the sequence. When either film editors or videotape editors sit down to the digital system and ask where the cut is, the *sequence* represents that cut.

The Timeline

Before building a house, a blueprint can be viewed and modified, and during construction the blueprint is consulted at critical points. This blueprint provides feedback to the builder. In traditional film and videotape editing, there is no similar way of viewing the entire program—it just is not possible or practical to take all the individual clips and the transitions between those clips and spread them out on a table like a blueprint.

Film and videotape editors can benefit by having a global view of the program being edited, a tool neither film nor video has been able to offer in the past. Instead, to judge the overall pacing of a sequence, the film editor using traditional methods has to run the film over and over, judging the individual length that each shot occupies. Similarly, the videotape editor must run the tape back and forth to judge the flow from transition to transition.

A timeline on a DNLE system can show an all-encompassing view of the program or a very specific section of the program in the same fashion that a blueprint can show the overall vision as well as microscopic details. The timeline represents pictures and audio tracks in the graphical form of boxes or can display actual images from the program. The timeline seeks to preserve and display, on-screen, the film synchronizer, where the film and magnetic sound tracks are laid out and manipulated (Figure 4-8). Now, the conversation can be more like the film editor's conversation:

"How long do you think this shot should be?"

"A little longer than those other shots next to it."

Most DNLE systems divide the computer monitor into two sections—one in which images are displayed and one for the timeline—where the editor can visually locate a clip or a transition

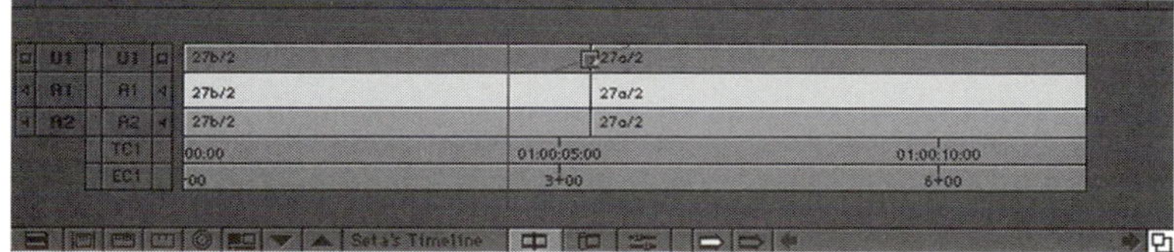

Figure 4-8 On the DNLE system, the timeline represents the sequence being edited. The sequence can be shown graphically or pictorially.

and manipulate the space that the clip occupies or affect the type of transition by changing the profile of the timeline for that section of the program. The essential difference between the editing features that are found in the timeline and editing based on the clip or the transition is that timeline editing is a direct manipulation of both the components (clips) and the joining points (transitions) in a simultaneous fashion.

The timeline is a new tool for both film and videotape editors. While the concept of the clip is deeply entrenched in film editing, and videotape editing is firmly rooted in the transition, DNLE systems augment these roots with the timeline's simultaneous clip- and transition-based editing tools. The goal is simple: The timeline attempts to combine the space and time elements of film and videotape editing.

DIGITIZING AND STORING MATERIAL

What is it like to edit on a DNLE system? The informational flow of a digital system begins with the source material. Whether the footage is on film, videotape, or directly from the camera, the first step in any DNLE system is to transfer these signals to computer disks. Of course, it may be necessary to use many different types of media in the program that is being edited. Computer graphics, sound effects from compact discs, and graphics from paint systems all may appear in even the most basic programs. All these elements must be digitized into the system. When it is necessary to derive an EDL, material must be digitized from sources that have ascending SMPTE timecode because it will be impossible to create an EDL for any material that does not have some identifying timecode.

The process of converting the analog video and audio signals into digital signals and transferring these to computer disk before one can actually edit is usually a real-time procedure (although there are systems that can transfer material faster than real time). If one has five minutes of material, it will take slightly more than five minutes to digitize the material (taking into account the tape machine's preroll time). Once the footage resides on the computer disk, it can be accessed quickly and treated like a word in a document. Think about how rapidly a very powerful computer can spell-check a document or search for a word. This speed allows the editor to very quickly scan and edit footage. A film editor cannot simply point to a roll of film and go to a specific location within that roll, but in a DNLE system, the material can be instantly cued to the point and the frame displayed. The editor can then go about deciding which portion of the footage is appropriate.

When signals are converted from analog to digital, is there information that is lost in the transformation? There are important things to understand about this conversion because just one frame of video takes up an enormous amount of disk space. For a picture displayed on a Macintosh computer at a pixel matrix of 640 horizontal × 480 vertical multiplied by 24

720x486=
~1 MB/
Frame

Figure 4-9 The demands of storing just one frame at video and film resolutions. One frame of NTSC video at 720 × 486 pixels sampled at 24 bits per sample requires approximately 1 MB of storage. The same frame in 35mm Academy format requires approximately 36 MB!

bits of color, one second of NTSC video requires about 30 MB of storage—slightly less than 1 MB per frame. How much footage (without audio) will fit on a 600 MB magnetic disk? About 20 seconds. In PAL, with its larger pixel matrix, the demands are even greater. With film images, depending on their original horizontal and vertical aspect ratio, it is possible to have a single frame of film that requires 36 MB per frame (Figure 4-9).

To provide storage amounts that are practical, the solution is to compress the video coming into the system. This means, of course, that the original image quality is compromised; these compression schemes are termed *lossy* because some amount of the original picture's data is irretrievably lost. How much compression is applied to an image often determines whether or not the direct output from the DNLE system is acceptable.

Digitizing the Footage

Loading material into a DNLE system is usually a straightforward procedure. In general, a videotape is played back, and the DNLE system is put into digitize mode. Figure 4-10 depicts the three components that are digitized in real time: picture, audio channels, and timecode. The number of audio channels that can be digitized usually varies from between two and eight. These signals are processed through processor boards resident in the computer, and the digital data is stored to computer disk. A large number of disks can be linked together to provide massive amounts of storage.

Tape machines can be controlled either via remote control or manually. The 422 serial protocol is the standard for remote deck communication and is common to most professional videotape and audio tape devices. DNLE systems will almost always be able to work with either non-drop frame (NDF) or drop frame (DF) timecode.

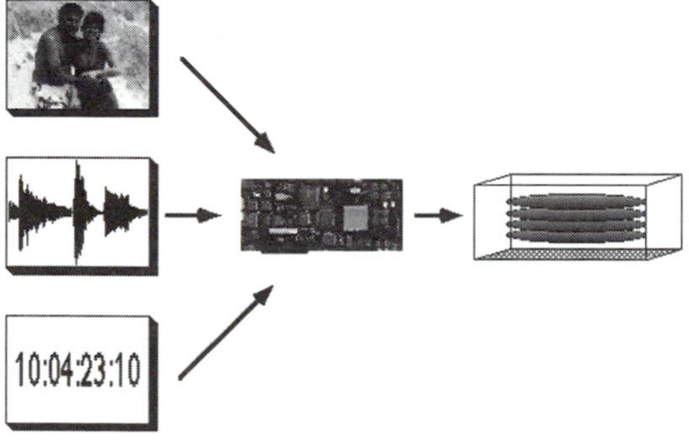

Figure 4-10 Video, stereo audio, and timecode are digitized in real time from the source videotape. The video is compressed, and all signals are stored to computer disk. Illustration by Jeffrey Krebs.

Playback Speeds for NTSC, PAL, SECAM, and Film

It's important to note that "normal playback" is different in various parts of the world. For countries that follow the NTSC (National Television Standards Committee) standards, motion video is normally played back at 29.97 fps (not the 30 fps that is commonly quoted) at a scan rate of 525 lines at 60 Hz. NTSC is used in the United States, Japan, and Canada, among other places.

PAL (phase alternate line) format is characterized by a normal playback speed of 25 fps at a scan rate of 625 lines at 50 Hz. PAL is dominant in Europe. An NTSC tape will not play on a PAL monitor and vice versa.

SECAM (*séquentiel couleur à mémoire*), like PAL, has a normal playback of 25 fps with a similar scan rate. There are actually two forms of SECAM; it is primarily used in Eastern Europe and France.

The only consistent world standard for playback is 35mm film at 24 fps. A 35mm film can be made, transported, and played anywhere in the world. Actually, the original choice for a normal playback speed of 35mm film fluctuated between 16 and 18 fps. The goal was to determine at what speed film could be exposed while preserving the semblance of natural movement. There was also an economic reason to use fewer frames per second: It would save money. Eventually, to ensure that film sound could be adequately reproduced, 24 fps was chosen. Most DNLE systems can be augmented slightly to work in both NTSC and PAL. However, not all systems are capable of playing back at 24 fps.

In film, each frame consists of one picture, and a series of these still frames, when projected in rapid succession, provides the appearance of movement. In video, each frame consists of two fields of information. To draw all the pixels of the television signal, the video signal is alternately scanned: First, the odd lines of information are drawn, and then the even lines of information are drawn. This sequence of odd, even, odd, even, scan lines are then combined, or interlaced, to present the complete picture. These odd and even lines are called *fields.* When two fields are put together, the result is one video frame. As we know, there can be different playback speeds for video: either 29.97 fps (60 fields) or 25 fps (50 fields).

Early versions of DNLE systems were not all capable of providing full frame rate playback. For example, depending on the picture quality chosen and the number of audio channels, in parallel with the architecture of the system and the disk subsystem, getting a system to play back at 30 fps may not have been possible. From 1988 to 1991, several DNLE systems could only play back at 10 or 15 fps. In these cases, at 10 fps, every third frame was repeated to equal 30 fps; alternatively, at 15 fps, every second frame was repeated to equal 30 fps.

As the data requirements increase for any frame of picture and sound, it is important to determine if the system will continue to offer playback at normal speed. There is also a cost trade-off in assembling a system that can play back the highest-quality pictures and sounds. Some of the systems covered in Chapter 6 can cost from between $500,000 and $1.5 million dollars (U.S.). Contrast this with DNLE systems, which can cost from a few hundred dollars to tens of thousands of dollars. Although there are many reasons to justify these cost differences, two major items are the quality of the images and how many of those images can be played back in a one-second period.

DNLE systems that can play back at film's native speed of 24 fps began to appear in 1992. A number of advantages are associated with true film playback, including a 20% savings in storage compared to NTSC rates.

Storing to Disk

Loading footage into the DNLE system is a continual process of digitization, compression, and storage to disk. Computer disks are extremely important to this process because not all picture

Figure 4-11 Data drives from Megadrive Systems. Note that this particular housing holds two removable storage modules. Courtesy Megadrive Systems.

and audio qualities can be supported by different disk types. As a rule, the highest-quality images and audio are always associated with magnetic disks rather than optical discs.

Digital systems can support a number of disks that can be simultaneously linked together. Usually, a minimum of seven disks is easily supported. Many more disks can be used, and some productions routinely use 49 or more disks! The number, quite honestly, is very arbitrary—some DNLE systems provide in excess of 500 gigabytes (GB) of storage. The greater the number of disks, the greater the amount of available footage given a fixed resolution. The size of each disk drive is also a variable; they usually range from 3 GB to 23 GB.

Figure 4-11 is an example of a storage module from Megadrive Systems. Note that the housing holds two disk units, which are removable.

Digitizing Parameters

During the process of digitization, the user is presented with a series of choices regarding how the material should be captured (Figure 4-12). DNLE systems will vary, but generally there will be modes for the following:

1. Image quality
2. Audio quality
3. Number of audio channels
4. Digitizing rate

Each choice affects both the quality of the picture and sound that will be stored on disk and the available storage capacity of the system.

Image Quality

There are usually a variety of image quality settings from which to choose. These settings are based on the attributes afforded by the compression scheme that the system employs. Image compression in DNLE systems is based on, but not limited to, hardware-assisted methods such as motion joint photographic experts group (M-JPEG).

In general, there are three choices that are commonly found in DNLE systems:

1. Low picture quality but maximum storage capacity
2. Middle picture quality with midrange storage capacity
3. High picture quality with lowest storage capacity

In addition, some DNLE systems offer a choice of digitizing in color or black and white. Capturing a picture in black and white will decrease storage requirements by 10 to 20% over capturing in color. While this may not seem like a significant savings, a documentary with 100 hours of material at a 15% savings equals 15 extra hours of footage that can be stored, and creatively, editors for years have worked with black and white work prints without being hampered.

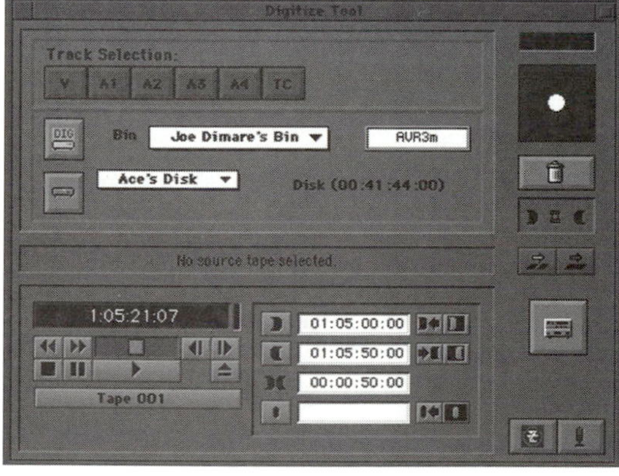

Figure 4-12 A representative digitizing interface on a DNLE system. The user is presented with a screen that allows image quality, audio quality, and number of audio channels to be assigned prior to digitization. Courtesy Avid Technology.

Audio Quality

DNLE systems have continually improved on the quality, number of channels, and number of audio tracks that are available to the user. Audio *quality* refers to the resolution of the audio measured in samples per second. Audio *channels* refers to the number of discrete and separate input/output (I/O) channels as well as the number of channels that can be simultaneously monitored (heard). For example, 4-8-4 means that four channels can be input, eight channels can be simultaneously monitored, and four channels can be output. Audio *tracks* refers to the number of virtual audio tracks that are available for editing within the DNLE software.

If we look at the evolution of audio features for one popular DNLE system, we find a steady increase in the quality and number of audio channels and tracks:

Year	*Audio Quality*	*Number of Channels (I/O)*	*Number of Tracks*
1989	22 KHz	1-2-1	2
1990	22 KHz	2-2-2	4
1991	22 KHz	2-2-2	4
1992	44.1 KHz	2-4-2	24
1993	44.1 KHz	2-4-2	24
1994	44.1 KHz, 48 KHz	2-4-2	24
1995	44.1 KHz, 48 KHz	4-4-4	24
1996	44.1 KHz, 48 KHz	4-8-4	24
1997	44.1 KHz, 48 KHz	8-8-8	24

When referring to the digital sampling of analog audio signals, it is fair to say that the sample rate should be double the highest frequency that we want to preserve. For example, if the sample is at 44.1 KHz, the highest frequency that will be preserved is 22.05 KHz. The human ear has a range of up to about 20 KHz.

To distinguish audio quality, it is fair to say that a 7.5 KHz audio sample is comparable to AM radio audio, while a 22.05 KHz realized sample (from the 44.1 KHz original sample) is the mastering standard for digital audio compact discs. The audio quality of digital videotape formats and digital audio tape (DAT) is 48 KHz.

The availability of high-quality audio on DNLE systems is extremely important because with proper procedures, duplicative work can be eliminated. Recall that very rarely was the audio from videotape offline editing ever used in the final product. However, with 44.1 and 48 KHz audio capability, the audio can be output directly from the DNLE system to the final master tape. This avoids having to duplicate the audio work during the online session.

In addition, beginning in 1995, DNLE systems began to offer direct digital audio I/O interfaces. Although we know that audio is digital once it resides in the system, how audio enters and exits the system is important. Most DNLE systems have both analog-to-digital I/O as well as direct digital I/O.

For example, if we have a digital videotape format, such as Digital Betacam, and we want to preserve the digital integrity of the audio, we can use the AES/EBU (American Engineering Society/European Broadcasting Union) inputs. Two connectors are usually found: one for input and one for output. Each connector carries both the left and right channels. If the DNLE system does not have direct digital I/O, there is only one way to bring audio into the system: in analog form.

It is also important to realize that devices that are capable of playing back digital audio may not be capable of outputting a digital audio signal. Take, for example, the audio compact disc. The signals are digital, but most compact disc players only provide analog audio outputs. However, professional CD players do provide digital outputs.

Number of Audio Channels

There has also been a steady increase in the number of audio channels that can be simultaneously digitized, monitored, and output. Although preferences will vary, many editors agree that being able to hear eight simultaneous audio channels represents an excellent baseline of functionality. Additionally, the simultaneous input of four audio channels facilitates the digitizing of audio from professional videotape recorders. On the production side, once four-channel videotape formats grew in prominence, additional microphone setups and recording began to be made on audio channels 3 and 4.

Number of Audio Tracks

While audio *channels* are the separate audio I/O conduits, audio *tracks* are the virtual number of audio tracks available from within the DNLE software. These represent the audio tracks that are part of the program being edited.

Digitizing Rate

During the first five years of DNLE systems, some systems allowed the user to specify a capture mode at other than normal play rate. In those cases, if we had 30 minutes of material to digitize and only had 10 minutes of disk space left, capturing at 10 fps would allow us to fit all the material. Conversions of files may also be an option. If we are working and find that we must digitize additional material for which we do not have storage, we may be able to convert material. If we kept every third frame, we would free up storage. The video file will exhibit a staccato motion as it holds in position for three frames, plays (updates) for one frame, holds for three, plays (updates) for one, and so on. The audio portion of the clip is left intact.

While this may seem like a compromise, there can be economic necessities for working in this fashion. There are many examples of documentaries that have a staggering amount of material—some documentaries have had in excess of 700 hours of material! Often, editors, straining for ways to fit all the material onto the computer disks, will keep only representative frames of the video and gradually work toward only the required video, which is then redigitized at full frame rates.

Storage

After digitization and compression, pictures and sounds to be edited exist as digital data on computer disks. How much footage can be stored at any one time? The answer is not straightforward. Storage capability varies from system to system and is dependent on the choices that are made regarding seven variables. Depending on the system, and in special circumstances, there will also be an eighth variable.

1. Image quality
2. Digitizing rate (e.g., 29.97, 25, 24 fps, or fractional: 15, 12, 10, 5, 1 fps)
3. Audio quality
4. Number of audio channels
5. Capacity of each disk
6. Total number of disks available
7. Media portability
8. Fixed or variable frame size

DNLE systems offer the possibility of having hundreds of hours of available material—a far cry from the 4.5 hours maximum that first-wave machines offered. Yet, with DNLE systems, many variables can have significant effects on the total amount of storage available. Evaluating DNLE systems is made easier by using the above eight variables as a guide when examining specification sheets.

Media Portability

Media portability refers to whether the computer disks are fixed or can be removed from the disk drive mechanism. Optical discs are an example of removable media in that the optical cartridges are removed from the actual disk drive. Some digital audio workstations (DAWs) use optical discs; when a second project needs to be edited, the optical discs for the first project are removed, is and the second project's discs are inserted into the drives.

Fixed magnetic disks are fixed in that the recording medium is fixed in the disk drive mechanism and cannot be removed. Faced with the same dual-project scenario, the material resident on the disks must be erased, and the new material is then recorded to disk. However, an alternative to fixed magnetic disks is removable magnetic disks. Here, the recording medium can be removed from the actual disk drive mechanism in the same fashion as optical discs.

How Storage Characterized the Acceptance of Early Digital Nonlinear Systems

DNLE systems in 1988 and 1989 were primarily used for editing television commercials. Indeed, DNLE systems would never have enjoyed the success or acceptance they did from 1989 to 1992 had it not been for their adoption by the commercial editorial community. At that time, given all the alternatives, DNLE systems were perfect for editing commercials, which tend to have a fast cutting pace, smaller amounts of selected footage, and images that tend to concentrate on single rather than multiple items in the frame. DNLE systems, with their fast access times, reduced trafficking issues, and erasable media offered an acceptable solution. Because of the high price of fixed magnetic disks, commercials, with their small amount of select footage, were natural candidates for digital editing.

By 1992, advancements in image compression technology such as the use of Motion JPEG (M-JPEG) and advances in disk technology, led to DNLE systems being used for a wide variety of programming: commercials, documentaries, television shows, and feature films.

Of course, the most critical variable affecting storage is image quality. These choices are offered by the manufacturer and are based on either fixed or variable calculations. With variable calculations—fixed or variable frame sizes (see Chapter 10)—if a disk drive indicates that we only have space for one minute of material, we may or may not actually achieve that one minute of capacity. In fact, we may find that we were able to store more or less than one minute because simple images may allow us to store more than the one-minute estimate, while a complex series of images may require more storage.

How Image Complexity Affects Storage Requirements

As listed previously, an eighth variable affecting storage is whether the system is capable of dynamically adjusting how much information is allocated to the picture frames as they are digitized and compressed. If the DNLE system is capable of dynamically adjusting its compression algorithms as complexity in the frames increases or decreases, what your original footage looks like will affect how much storage you will have. For these purposes, let's identify three categories of programming: commercials, episodics (one-hour television shows and theatrical films), and news gathering (which includes sports and documentary footage).

Tests have indicated that the type of programming greatly influences the storage numbers that can be achieved. A more in-depth discussion on how digital video compression works

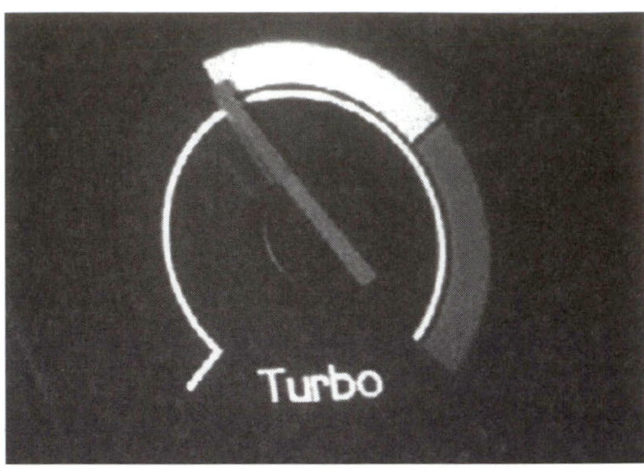

Figure 4-13 Commercial footage typically consists of one principal item of interest and a nondescript background, which serves to center attention on the item being advertised.

is found in Chapter 10. For now, consider the test results discussed below.

Commercial Footage

In general, television commercials fall into two categories. The first type has detailed foregrounds and little action occurring in the background, since the intention is often to direct the viewer's attention to one simple visual, placed in the center of the screen (Figure 4-13). And while there can be dynamic camera moves, they are usually short in duration. Art direction obviously plays an important role in commercials, and vibrant color schemes are common. The second category is commercials that are highly stylized and contain a great deal of graphics and graphic compositing.

For the storage test, a variable M-JPEG compression scheme was chosen on a 500 MB partition, with an estimated potential yield of 30 minutes, 57 seconds. In Table 4-1, the KB/frame column refers to the number of kilobytes (1000 bytes) required for each frame at 29.97 fps. The actual amount that the disk yielded was 41 minutes, 53 seconds. *Disk default* refers to the average amount of information that can be stored based on the digitizing parameters chosen and the capacity of the computer disk. As we can see, however, under a variable compression scheme, disk defaults can only be estimates.

In this case, when less complex pictures presented themselves, the system needed less space to store the frames; as a result, more material could be loaded than originally indicated. If we examine the KB/frame column, we can see how the action occurring within each segment changed the amount of kilobytes required. Lower KB/frame values indicate more storage available; higher KB/frame values indicate less storage available.

Table 4-1 Test 1: Commercial Footage

Digitize Clip	*Duration*	*KB/Frame*
Clip 1	6:06:10	4937
Clip 2	4:08:01	4308
Clip 3	9:14:13	4872
Clip 4	7:14:13	4880
Clip 5	5:00:00	5030
Clip 6	3:00:00	4783
Clip 7	2:59:17	5120
Clip 8	3:14:13	4847
Clip 9	56:10	N/A
Total	41:53:17	

Episodic Footage

Medium and wide shots tend to be used more often in episodics than in commercials (Figure 4-14). There tends to be less camera movement, and when movement is present, it is usually slow. Of course, there are exceptions—we've all seen television shows that are completely shot with hand-held cameras. But, in general, frames are usually static: People enter the frame, action progresses, and there is a transition to the next scene. These longer sections are usually balanced with shorter, more action-driven scenes.

Under the same guidelines as the commercial footage test above, the disk default was again 30 minutes, 57 seconds. However, the actual amount that could be stored on the disk was 32 minutes, 34 seconds (Table 4-2). Although we stored more material than the estimate indicated, note that we stored considerably less footage than the commercial material. The episodic footage, being more complex in terms of the action occurring within the frame, required a greater amount of data to be stored per frame. The KB/frame column shows that the average KB/frame is higher in this footage category; thus, less material could be stored.

Figure 4-14 Scenes that are longer in duration and that involve dialogue passages are representative of episodic footage.

Table 4-2 Test 2: Episodic Footage

Digitize Clip	*Duration*	*KB/Frame*
Clip 1	20:00:00	6993
Clip 2	5:00:00	5899
Clip 3	4:59:24	6259
Clip 4	2:30:00	7136
Clip 5	5:00	7876
Total	32:34:24	

News-Gathering Footage

In news-gathering, sports, and documentary footage, the action occurring in the frame is often quite unpredictable, with dynamic camera movement and ceaseless foreground and background action (Figure 4-15). Just think of a soccer match in which the camera follows action on the field and then pans to follow the ball in flight while a panorama of cheering fans swishes by in the background—those will certainly be complex frames to digitize.

Following the same test guidelines, the disk default again indicated 30 minutes, 57 seconds. The actual amount captured was 29 minutes, 47 seconds (Table 4-3). When we examine the KB/frame column, we see the largest amount of data required per frame compared with the other two types of footage. This results in a decreased capacity of about 12 minutes compared with the commercial footage. As a result, the last segment could not be stored in its entirety.

Figure 4-15 News footage is often associated with dynamic action in both the foreground and the background with unplanned and unpredictable camera movement.

Table 4-3 Test 3: News-Gathering Footage

Digitize Clip	*Duration*	*KB/Frame*
Clip 1	8:27:06	7428
Clip 2	4:21:05	7616
Clip 3	4:18:05	7620
Clip 4	8:19:06	7426
Clip 5	4:00:00	7502
Clip 6	22:00	6696
Total	29:47:22	

It is important to note that not all DNLE systems offer variable frame size compression. If the system cannot adjust instantly to a picture's simplicity or complexity, storage will be used unnecessarily, or portions of an image will not be drawn intact. Although the digitization process should appear to the user as an uncomplicated procedure, successfully digitizing video, multiple audio channels, and timecode necessitates that all subsystems work together, from the digitizing interfaces (which convert picture and sound to digital data) to the timecode reader (either internal to the system or in the videotape machine) to the ability of the computer disks to sustain the storage of video and audio second after second.

THE USER INTERFACE

How footage is organized, presented, and manipulated falls into the domain of the user interface (UI). While one machine can be more powerful than another, a computer can be faster than another, and a computer software program can offer better features than another, if the door into that power, speed, and depth of features requires too much user effort, the benefits of the system will be unrealized, leaving both user and manufacturer highly frustrated.

Whether the user is a professionally trained film or videotape editor, a producer, a director, or a writer makes little difference. If the interface and design are truly intuitive, it should not matter if the user has actual training in editing. At the same time, there is much to be gained if the system retains familiar paradigms from classic film and videotape editing (Figure 4-16).

The explosion in desktop publishing systems created a vast industry as a result of having easy-to-use tools that did not require intensive training or capital investment. Of course, we also saw many examples of difficult-to-read publications as a result of people using these technologies without being aware of certain layout design rules. Nonetheless, people embraced these technological changes, and more people were able to create publications than was possible before. This same explosion is happening with desktop video production.

As DNLE systems become more sophisticated, technological impediments will disappear, allowing people more time to be creative rather than worrying about the technical aspects of a system's operation. For the first ten years of DNLE systems, roughly from 1989 to 1999, there will have been a competition between picture quality and system cost. But when that conflict has been equalized, as began to happen in 1997, we will be left with the power of the software tools and the user interface at a reasonable price. Many manufacturers who do not realize this will find that they will eventually be out of business.

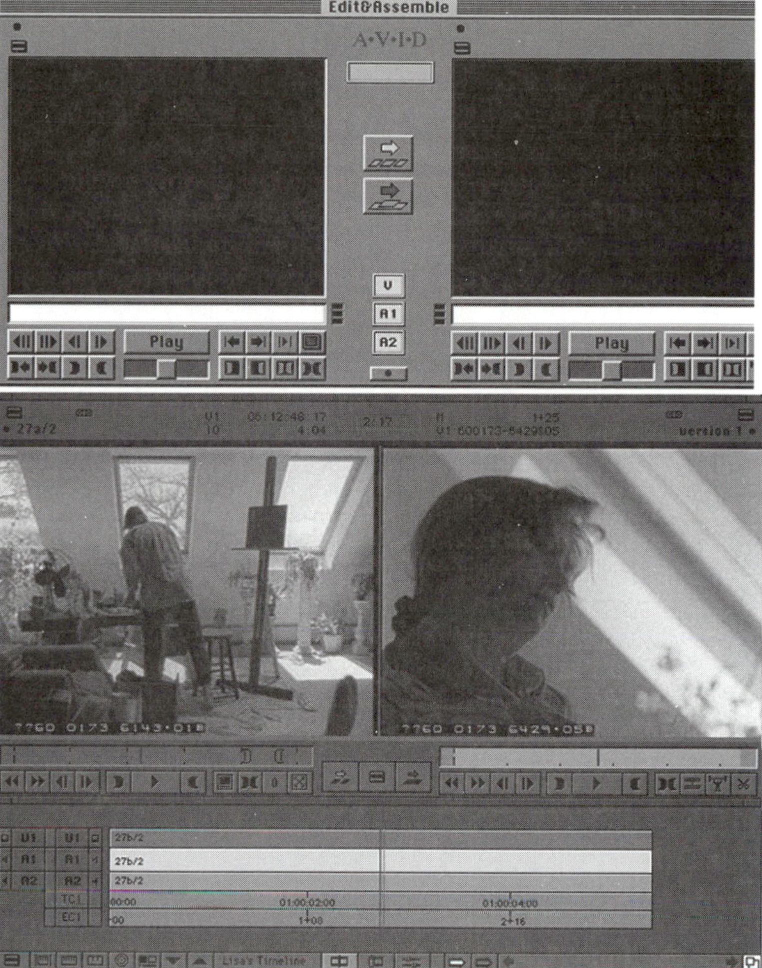

Figure 4-16 The software evolution of a user interface for the same DNLE system. Above is the original interface (1989), while below is the interface from version 6. While the layout has not considerably changed, button positioning, depth, alignment, and font styles—all important choices to be made when creating any successful interface—have evolved. Courtesy Avid Technology.

The buzzwords for characterizing user interfaces are *graphical* and *intuitive.* Many system designers are very pleased when a new user sits down and figures out how to use a software application by just trying things on the user interface. This points to a well-designed, simple-to-follow interface. But a system's interface must be viewed as much more than the manner in which buttons are displayed on a computer screen. When a user says, "I like that system; it's got a great interface," often what the person means is that not only does the system present information in an easy-to-comprehend manner, but that it also operates in a sensible fashion.

It is important to consider and evaluate any system's interface from a complete perspective. When this author is designing a DNLE system or functionalities, hours and hours are spent on where to put button functions based on how often they are to be used—for example, often-used buttons are put under fingers that are stronger, such as the index or middle finger, whereas little-used buttons are put under the small finger.

GENERAL DESIGN OF DNLE SYSTEMS

Although all DNLE systems are unique, three areas are usually represented in some fashion on the computer monitor of almost every system:

1. An area where footage is displayed
2. An area where the main editing tasks are accomplished
3. An area where a graphical representation of the edited sequence is shown

On a DNLE system, there is often an analog to the film editor's canvas bin, namely, an electronic "bin" where footage is usually displayed. These pictorial representations can be thought of as pointers to the digitized video and audio files that now exist as digital data on the disk. Figure 4-17 shows these clips in their bin display form. When the user wants to play back a shot, the system associates that shot with one or more digital files on the disk (representing a combination of video and audio tracks), and the user sees and hears the shot playing back from the disk.

There are usually two designs for the actual area where editing takes place. The first approach is to create one main editing screen, which holds both original footage and the destination window where the program being edited is displayed (Figure 4-18).

The second approach is to display two screens: one that serves as the source display and one that serves as the edited program display (see Figure 4-16). This convention recalls the feed and take-up reels of film editing or the source and record machines in videotape editing.

Which approach is better? It is impossible to answer this question fairly—whichever is favored by the user is the best approach. One important thing to remember is that these displays are created by software. Some systems allow the user to access portions of the software to, in effect, customize the editing environment. For example, Figure 4-19A is an example of a DNLE interface that shows many buttons and on-screen tools, whereas Figure 4-19B shows a very streamlined interface on the same system, with few buttons and tools visible. Making such changes allows the user to easily customize the environment.

This is the real power of software-intensive systems: Design layout and tool palettes can be left up to the discretion of the user. A key point of the evolution of DNLE systems is that as more online tools are offered from within the software environment, the user will not be obligated to follow the mode of operation imposed by the system.

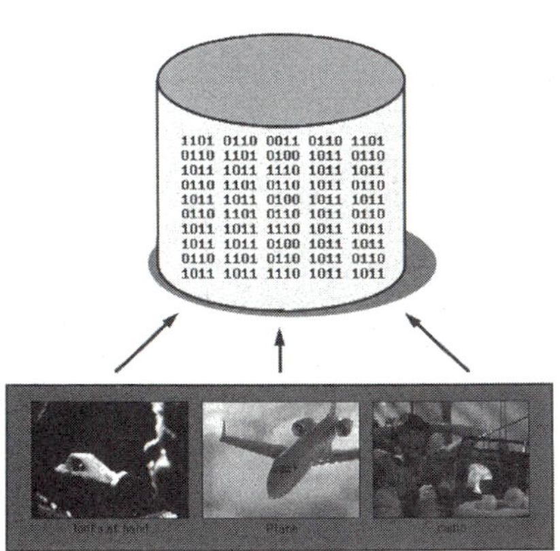

Figure 4-17 Digitized representations of the original images point to data files on the computer disk. Illustration by Rob Gonsalves.

Representing the Footage

After the selected footage, or *selects,* have been loaded into the computer disks, editing can proceed. Often, the type of

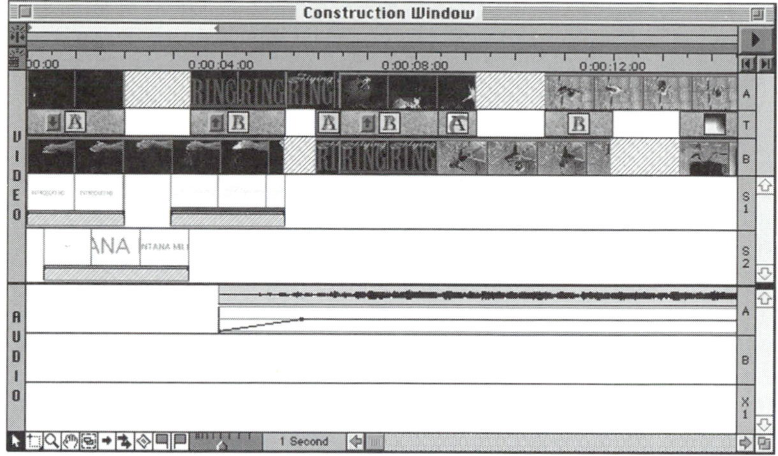

Figure 4-18 A single-display editing interface for the Adobe Premiere editing application. Courtesy Adobe Systems.

program being edited influences whether all the footage or only a portion of it will be stored. If we are creating a training film and have videotaped seven takes that illustrate how a process is done, and only one take is correct, there really is no need to waste valuable disk storage with the other six takes. However, in the case of feature films, all of the footage is almost always loaded as there is no way of knowing just exactly what pieces from different takes will be used to create the film.

Often the display of footage is via a computer window that serves to emulate the film editor's canvas bin (Figure 4-20).

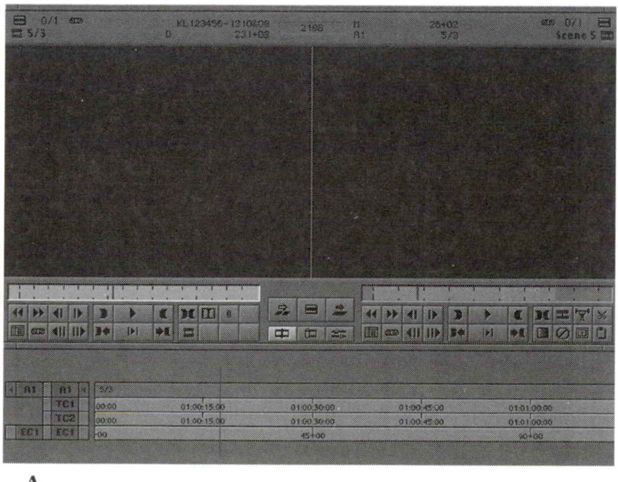

A

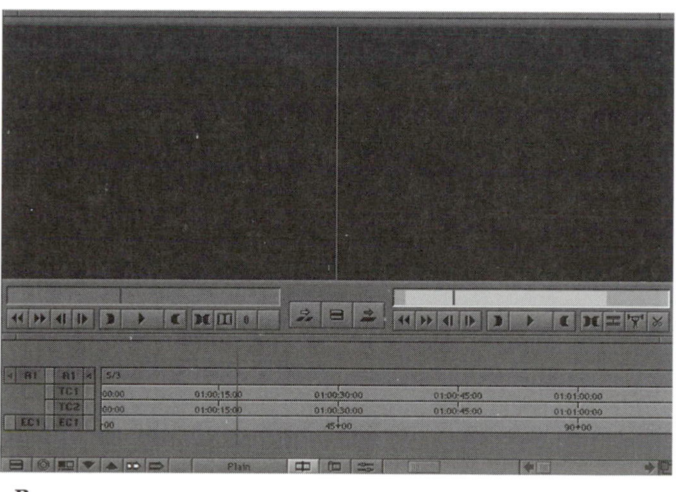

B

Figure 4-19 **(A)** A DNLE interface that shows many icons and on-screen tools. **(B)** The same DNLE interface customized by the user to show fewer on-screen graphic icons. Courtesy Avid Technology.

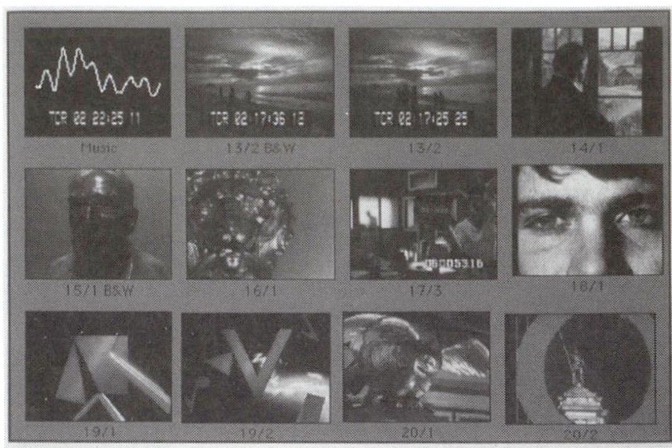

Figure 4-20 The electronic version of the film editor's canvas bin, where representations of the digitized footage can be viewed.

This *electronic bin* serves to store material and allows for a number of powerful organizational routines; just as traditional film editors have random access to any strip in any bin, digital systems offer the same flexibility.

Because the bin is really the editor's view into the footage, a bin's organization and presentation tools are extremely important. More than one editor will say that editing is a craft dependent not on what footage to include, but on what footage to exclude! If footage is easy to identify and locate, less time will be spent looking for the right shot. Also, because DNLE systems can search and retrieve footage so rapidly, they all tend to have extensive logging and database features. If we only want to work on a specific scene, and do not want to see all the clips that we have digitized, sifting and searching engines are critical (Figure 4-21).

Storyboarding has become a basic method of preediting in which individual shots are arranged and rearranged. The purpose of storyboarding is to obtain a visual impression of how shots will work together in sequence before actual editing is begun.

NAME	Description	Director Comments	Script Lines
34	Good	*	Get out of here...
34/2	-	-	"
34A/1	Boom in Shot	-	"The money was here all the time...
34A/2	Nice	*	"
35/2	Good Take	-	
35A/1	Statue	-	Voice Over...
35A/2	Best Take	*	"
38	Logo Draw	-	
38A/1		-	
39	Eyes / Keeper	**	Voice Over...
39	Eagle	-	"
40/3	Stereo	-	
40A/1	Beach	-	Music Under
40A/2	Beach	*	"
42	Logo Expands	-	"Tough driving through fog...
42/1	-	*	"Kim couldn't have predicted...

NAME	Description	Director Comments	Script Lines
34	Good	*	Get out of here...
34/2	-	-	"
34A/1	Boom in Shot	-	"The money was here all the time...
34A/2	Nice	*	"

Figure 4-21 Extensive databasing and media management tools allow sifting and organizing bin footage. The original bin has been sifted to show only those clips that relate to Scene 34.

The Editing Interface

What is the best way to recreate a film editing table or a computerized videotape editing system in software? There are a limitless number of alternatives, and manufacturers must constantly struggle with knowing and understanding their user population. Should the editor look at one screen, or do two screens make more sense? Does the system take more of a film approach or a videotape approach to editing? How do editors work? What tools does the editor use constantly? Many DNLE systems borrow strongly from the operation of film flatbeds (Figure 4-22).

It is very easy to judge DNLE systems based solely on their capabilities—what picture quality they offer, how many channels of audio they provide, and so forth. But it is truly in the interface of DNLE systems where it is possible to see how the use of pictures, layout, and graphical icons

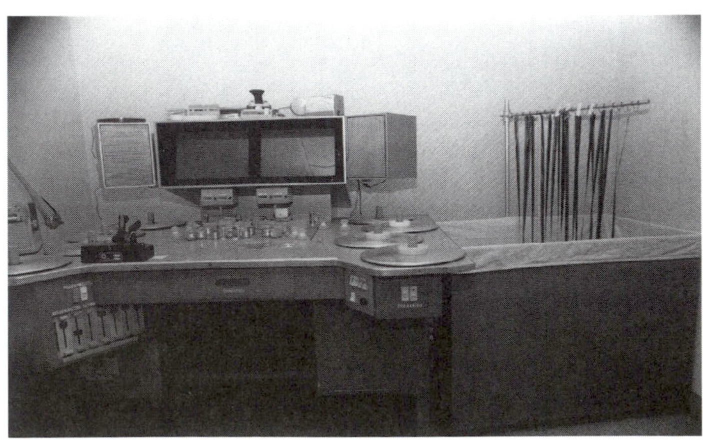

Figure 4-22 A standard flatbed for the film editor—a Steenbeck editing table. Photo by Michael E. Phillips.

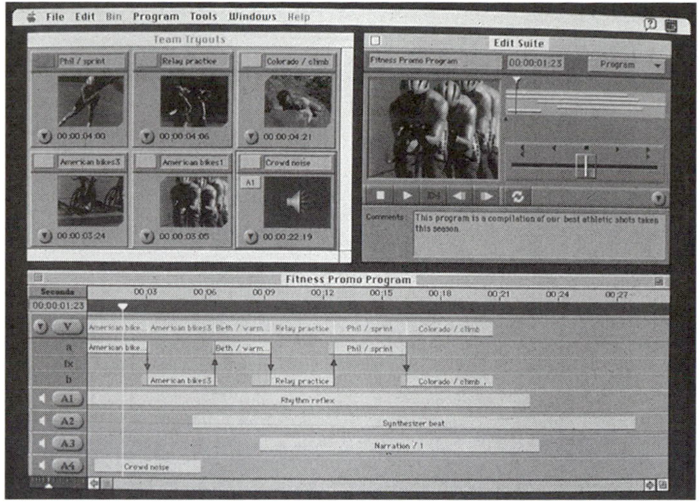

Figure 4-23 An editing interface display of Media 100, a DNLE system. Courtesy Media 100 Corporation.

form the basis of operation and of user acceptance or rejection (Figure 4-23).

DIGITAL NONLINEAR EDITING'S DOMINANCE AND PROMISE FOR THE FUTURE

DNLE systems rapidly became the dominant system of choice for offline editing within a five-year period (1989–1994), and by the mid-1990s, they began to encroach on online editing's tool sets. There are certain stages to editing on a DNLE system and decisions to be made concerning input and output, editing tools, and file compatibility with other computer-based applications. In the next chapter, we shall examine what it is like to edit on a DNLE system.

TALKING WITH EDITORS

What do you feel have been the most significant reasons why DNLE systems have experienced such explosive growth in the postproduction industry?

Joe Beirne

Postproduction facility owner, Stable Edit, New York

Nonlinear Editing History: I have supervised postproduction on nonlinear systems since 1986 (Quantel Harry) and on desktop DNLE systems since 1990 (Avid/EMC/Epix/Lightworks, etc.). I have owned Avid editing systems since 1992.

Credits: Among Stable Edit's clients are Colossal Pictures (Rock & Roll Hall of Fame), Ralph Lauren, Giraldi-Suarez-Klein, ABC, CBS, USA Networks, Calvin Klein, Frontline, Miramax Pictures,

Florentine Films, Mortal Films, MTV Networks, Good Machine, Dennis Earl Moore Productions, and many others; for projects ranging from feature films and documentaries to interactive and multichannel destination entertainment.

> I think that as much as the technology, digital nonlinear editing has been advanced by a profound change in editorial culture. Motion picture and commercial editorial flowed from a kind of mechanical technology (for example, the upright Moviola), and professional video postproduction was basically an outgrowth of the broadcast television industry, both of which had fundamentally been unchanged since the 1940s and 1960s, respectively. The culture of editing reflected these origins.
>
> I think more than an enabling technology, DNLE provided access to the editorial process in an attractive and inspiring setting. Rather than the nuclear submarine ambiance of an online facility, desktop DNLE systems brought sophisticated editing capability anywhere that a director and editor wanted to work. (Of course, this is a simplification. One could argue that Calloway had just the same effect. But Calloway didn't explode in the same way that nonlinear did, because they only had part of the equation: cost and portability but not flexibility and ease of use.)
>
> DNLE software was also more graphical and less forbidding than say, a CMX edit screen. That accessibility brought new vitality to the post "problem," just as desktop publishing revitalized the graphic design world in the 1980s. (The fact that Avid was on a Macintosh aided the adoption of that product in environments in which the Mac had made inroads: advertising agencies, print design firms, and animation shops.) New talent and new clients came to a more collaborative process. Also, random access did for editing what vector-based graphics did for print design: It sped up the time necessary to visualize an idea. Consequently, more editing is done.

Peter Cohen

Executive in Charge of Postproduction

Nonlinear Editing History: Avid Pioneer

Credits: FILM: *The Big Gig, The Cottonwood, Peep Hole, Pushed to the Limit;* TELEVISION: *Tarzan: The Epic Adventures,* "Andrew Dice Clay: Assume the Position," "Robbie Robertson: Coming Home," "AJ's Time Travelers," "Harley-Davidson: The American Motorcycle."

> The growth of DNL Editing in the postproduction industry is simple; it is the way editing should be. Film editing was always nonlinear. Video editing became linear because of the limitations of the technology. The analogy I like to make is to the space program. After World War II, Chuck Yaegar tried to fly a plane into space, but the technology wasn't there. We got into a space race with the Russians, put guys on the top of huge explosives and blasted them into space. Now we have the space shuttle, which is back to what Chuck was trying to do in the first place.

> There was electronic nonlinear editing almost three decades ago, but the technology wasn't quite there. The biggest drawback was that it was black and white, and clients in the video world were used to working in color. The concept returned a couple of decades later with tape-based systems and evolved into the digital systems we use today. We now have the true marriage of the versatility of film editing with the speed of electronic editing. This gives the client more control over his product.

Alan Miller

VP Postproduction, Moving Pictures, New York

Nonlinear Editing History: Bought Avid Media Composer Serial #001 in 1989.

Credits: "Fool's Fire," *American Playhouse;* "Road Scholar," feature documentary; Bill Moyer's "The Home Front"; "Power to the People"; VH1, *The 70s;* "Roger Daltry at Carnegie Hall," The Disney Channel.

> Number one is ease of use. Anyone who still remembers editing "the old way" knows they never want to do it again. Remember the agony of going multiple generations just to make a small change? Or remember the art of talking the producer or director out of a change because it would take an extra day? How about searching a 60-minute tape from one end to the other and waiting nine minutes? Just a few of the many reasons why DNLE has exploded. Now it's happening with online. Most producers say, "If I never have to go to another traditional online room again, I can die happy." Add to these reasons all the truly innovative ways to manipulate media, and editing becomes easier while creativity soars to new heights.

Scott Ogden

Senior Editor, Creative Domain (Film Advertising/Trailer Production) Los Angeles, CA

Nonlinear Editing History: I edited my first nonlinear trailer on an EMC2 in 1989. It was a disaster. The EMC2 was very difficult to work with, and after calling the company for help and getting none, I ended up finishing the project on a linear system. I was convinced that the nonlinear revolution was a ways away. About six months later, I was on staff at Mad River Post in Santa Monica, and they bought one of the first Avid Media Composers. I walked in at 9 A.M. and looked over the machine. I asked if I could cut on it . . . three hours later I was sitting with a couple of producers cutting a commercial promo for *Hard Copy.* We all had a grand time.

Credits: Trailers for *Air Force One, Absolute Power, Devil's Own, Michael, Stargate, Patriot Games, Jacob's Ladder.*

> DNL editing systems contain the best of all worlds. They bring to postproduction the freedom of nonlinear film techniques and

marry them with the immediacy of video. Once an editor learns nonlinear editing, he/she will never go back. Producers love nonlinear because it gives them the freedom to experiment with different cuts, and they can do so much more in a short amount of time.

Basil Pappas

Film/Avid Editor

Nonlinear Editing History: 1977: film; 1986: Ediflex; 1987: Touchvision; 1988: CMX 6000; 1989: Avid Media Composer.

Credits: Currently editing for CBS's *48 Hours.*

> The explosive growth is due to relatively low cost, ease of use (user interface is logical and easily learned), integration with common graphics formats, erasable media, ability to shave significant time off postproduction schedules, more flexibility for editor/director/producer, and high image quality.

Tom Poederbach

Director/Editor

Nonlinear Editing History: Seven years with Avid.

> I believe there are two reasons that I see here in Europe. First, some of today's users are more computer literate and not afraid of operating these systems. Previously, some film and tape editors were more or less afraid of computer-operated systems. The demand for programs to be turned out quickly is very high. When real editors finally discovered the creative freedom these systems could give them, they almost turned to DNLE en masse.

5

Editing on a Digital Nonlinear Editing System

Editing on a DNLE system can be described as a combination of the nonlinear aspects of film editing, the repeatability of computer-controlled videotape editing, and the flexibility of a word processor. In this example, we'll begin with film footage, edit on a DNLE system, and finish on videotape and film. This method is used when we require two end results: a finished videotape program and a finished film program.

Here is the pathway that we'll follow:

1. Film is shot, and processed film and film sound are transferred to videotape.

1. Picture and sound are digitized to computer disk.
2. Editing takes place.
3. Direct video and audio output from the DNLE system form the finished video program.
4. The database of the DNLE system is used to generate a negative cutlist that is used to cut the original film negative to create the film release.

STEP 1: TRANSFERRING FILM TO VIDEOTAPE

After original film is shot, the picture and sound elements are synched together during the telecine stage—the process of transferring from film to tape. This transfer to tape is from the original film negative and not from a film work print created from the negative, which is an unnecessary step. Depending on pricing, perhaps as much as 25¢ per foot of film can be saved by eliminating this step. Multiplied by 100,000 feet, a savings of $25,000 can be realized.

In telecine, original audio recordings, either from 1/4" audio tape or digital audio tape (DAT), are synchronized to the appropriate picture. Next, automatic film logging hardware and software are used to establish relationships among film edge numbers, the videotape timecode, and audio timecode. These relationships are important and form the database for the eventual creation of an edit decision list (EDL) and a film cutlist. Figure 14-5 (Chapter 14) shows an example of a telecine transfer log, which can be imported into a DNLE system.

It is important to note that it is also possible to bypass the videotape recording stage and transfer directly from telecine to disk. The most important benefit of this method is that the process of digitizing from tape is no longer necessary.

STEP 2: DIGITIZING THE MATERIAL

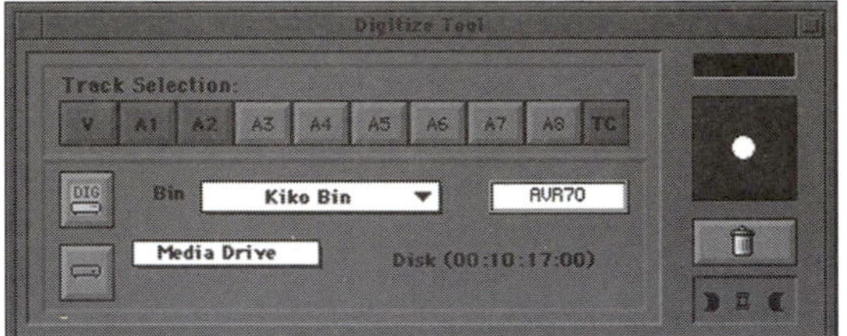

Figure 5-1 Choosing the digitizing parameters. This window shows various choices that can be made for picture and audio resolution and number of audio channels prior to digitization. Courtesy Avid Technology.

The digitization stage is a real-time process—transferring five minutes of footage from tape to disk takes roughly five minutes. First, the floppy disk created in telecine is loaded into the DNLE system and imported into a bin. This footage database provides the DNLE system with all the information required to automatically digitize the material from the videotapes. Failing this automatic file transfer, the material must be logged manually from either the telecine report or by entering timecode start and end points. Clearly, the time savings can be significant under an automatic procedure.

Next, digitizing parameters are chosen. Image quality, audio resolution, and number of audio channels all affect the amount of storage required. The videotapes will have been SMPTE timecoded, and this code will also be digitized (Figure 5-1).

STEP 3: THE EDITING STAGE

Figure 5-2 A representative DNLE system editing interface. Courtesy Avid Technology.

After the digitizing process, editing begins. Now is the time to take advantage of both the computer's databasing and storyboarding tools to organize and array footage prior to actual editing.

The interfaces of DNLE systems vary considerably but usually there will be one or two computer screens. One screen is used for the organization of material while the second is where the actual editing is done. There may be an optional NTSC or PAL monitor, which will show the sequence being edited as a full-screen display.

Figure 5-2 shows a representative DNLE interface. The upper portion is where the majority of editing takes place and is composed of a source window (left) and a record window (right). The lower window is the timeline, which will graphically show the structure of our sequence as we begin editing. Also shown is a clip, which has been loaded into the source window. The record window is blank because we have not yet begun to edit.

Editing is done by moving material from the source window to the record window in much the same way that the film editor moves material from feed reel to take-up reel. As we edit, the structure of our sequence is drawn in the timeline.

Figure 5-3 After making the first splice, video is shown drawn on the timeline.

What quickly becomes apparent is the reliance on the clip, the splice, the transition, and the timeline.

Two Basic Tools: Splicing and Extracting

We begin by choosing the desired in and out points of the Sailboat clip, and we make a splice of video (V). Figure 5-3 is the view after we make the splice. In the timeline, picture is shown as the V band. Note that the timeline preserves the name given to the Sailboat clip.

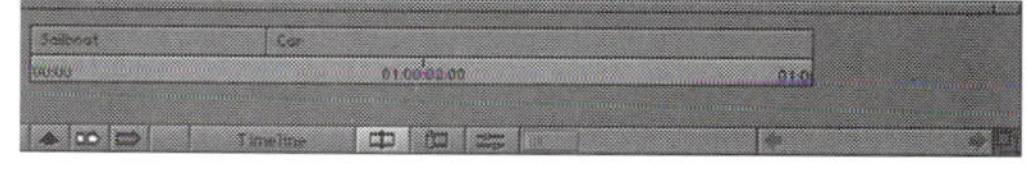

Figure 5-4 After making another splice, the sequence now consists of two shots, with the Car clip longer than the Sailboat clip.

Next, we choose in and out points for another clip labeled Car, and we splice this clip directly after the Sailboat clip. Figure 5-4 shows the two splices that we have made. Note that without referring to either film footage or timecode indicators, we can see that the Car clip is longer than the Sailboat clip: Such is the advantage of such a visual interface.

Next, it is time to make our first nonlinear edit. By marking an in point between the Sailboat and Car clips, we can splice in the Nightscape clip between the two other clips (Figure 5-5). This is the essence of nonlinear editing—being able to splice or extract material anywhere in the sequence while the sequence expands or contracts accordingly.

Trimming Shots

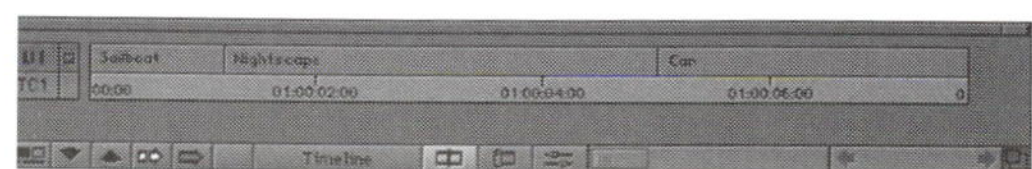

Figure 5-5 Nonlinear editing! The new clip is spliced between the two existing clips, and the sequence is now longer as a result.

On a DNLE system, it is very easy to trim shots wherever they may be in the sequence. In trimming, we use the transition to easily add or delete frames from any clip in our sequence (Figure 5-6a). Several tools are used as part of the transition editing device. There may be numeric trim keys to type in the number of frames that should be added or deleted, and there likely will be graphical icons such as scissors, used to "cut out" the unwanted frames of picture or sound.

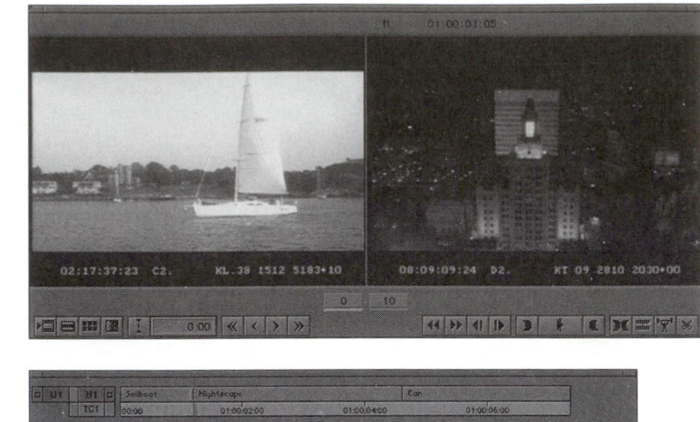

Figure 5-6 Trimming on a DNLE system. **(a)** The editing interface displays the transition frames between the tail of the outgoing shot (left) and the head of the incoming shot (right). **(b)** Adjusting the highlighted transition on the timeline will add or remove frames from either or both sides of the transition. Courtesy Avid Technology.

As shown in Figure 5-6a, we have chosen the splice between the Sailboat and the Nightscape clips. The interface above the timeline no longer shows source and record monitors but instead now shows the outgoing and incoming material—the transition between the two clips. In the timeline (Figure 5-6b), note the indicator on the transition. By adjusting this indicator, we can make the Nightscape clip shorter or longer. In this case, we have deleted ten frames from the Nightscape clip and made it shorter without affecting the other two clips. This task took mere seconds to accomplish as opposed to the many minutes it would have taken to rerecord the material in proper placement on a linear system.

Rearranging the Order of Clips

Just as it is easy to trim shots on a DNLE system, so too can shots be easily rearranged. If we decide that we do not like the order of the clips, we do not have to laboriously reedit the sequence. While editing, we may want to retain the original sequence; we do so through the use of a powerful DNLE feature: *multiple versions.* We label our original sequence Version 1 and then duplicate the sequence to create an exact copy of Version 1. Duplicating a sequence is almost instantaneous because we are not duplicating the actual digital video and audio files but instead are just making a copy of the original playlist, which we can then manipulate. We label this playlist Version 2 (Figure 5-7).

Figure 5-7 Making use of the multiple versions, the original sequence is duplicated and is labeled Version 2.

Now, to quickly rearrange shots, we change the timeline view to another useful mode, one which shows the clips in terms of their head frames, that is, the first frame in each clip. Rearranging shots may involve moving a representative frame of one clip from one location to another (Figure 5-8). In this case we have moved the Car clip from the last position (top) to the middle position (bottom). The result is that the playlist and the sequence are reordered. The power of such rearrangement cannot be overstated: Imagine the ability to experiment so quickly without the drudgery of reassembling!

Figure 5-8 Displaying the clips in head frame (H) format. Rearranging the shots is easily accomplished by choosing a clip and dragging it to a new location. Courtesy Avid Technology.

We have thus used two methods of digital nonlinear editing: the transition-based trim tools and the clip-based rearrangement tools.

Optical Effects

In film, dissolves can't be seen during editing. Instead, the optical effect is created by the lab, returned to the editor, and then cut into the program. In video, dissolves are easy to see through the use of a video switcher. In fact, in video, a wide variety of optical effects, such as fades, dissolves, wipes, and keys, can all be seen.

Depending on the DNLE system, it may be possible to see optical effects in real time in the same way that a video switcher operates, or the opticals may have to be *rendered* (precomputed), a process in which the A and B material or the layered material is combined to create the optical effect. Whether an effect can be played in real time or requires rendering will depend on the DNLE system being used, the computer processing power, the number of pixels that must be combined, and the length of the optical effect.

When a film editor specifies how long a dissolve should be, the interface is the film itself and a Chinagraph marker. The film editor makes a dissolve mark over the frames that should be dissolved together, whereas the videotape editor chooses a number of frames for the dissolve's duration. Figure 5-9 is an example in which the cut between the Sailboat and the Car clips has been changed to a dissolve. In Figure 5-10 we can see the result of this blending of frames.

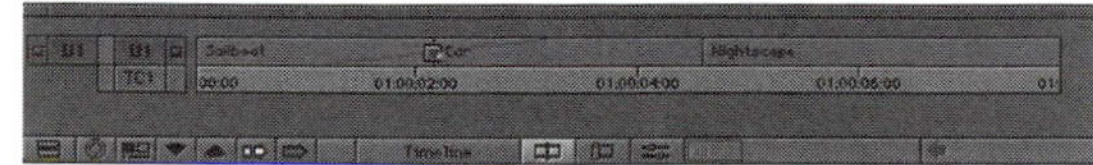

Figure 5-9 Optical effects such as dissolves can be created directly on the DNLE system without the use of an external video switcher. Here, the cut between the Sailboat and the Car clips has been changed to a dissolve.

Figure 5-10 The blending of the Sailboat and the Car frames.

Complex Layering, Digital Video Effects, and Multiple Video Tracks

DNLE systems can create complex layered and digitally manipulated imagery. Recall that many DNLE systems offer multiple video tracks, which can be used to build layers of clips on top of one another. In Figure 5-11A, we have layered the Sailboat clip onto the Nightscape clip by creating a second video track (V2). The resulting superimposition is shown in Figure 5-11B.

Next, we decide that the Sailboat clip needs to be made a little larger. By applying a digital video effect to the clip, we

B

A

Figure 5-11 **(A)** By creating a second video track, multiple-layer sequences can be created. **(B)** By using a superimposition effect, the Sailboat clip is layered onto the Nightscape clip.

Figure 5-12 The resized and repositioned Sailboat clip superimposed over the Nightscape clip.

are able to increase its size and also reposition it to the left. Figure 5-12 shows the resized and repositioned clip and the resulting superimposition (compare with Figure 5-11b).

Virtual Audio Tracks

The term audio *channels* is used to indicate the number of separate audio I/O connections as well as the number of audio voices that can be simultaneously monitored. *Tracks* refers to the number of audio tracks onto which we can edit. The term *virtual tracks* is used because on DNLE systems there are almost always more tracks than there are channels.

If we are using two tracks of audio to edit overlapping sync dialogue and we want to place stereo music and stereo sound effects within the scene, we require four additional audio tracks. Figure 5-13 shows a sequence to which we have added four virtual audio tracks (A1 to A4). By adding four new virtual audio tracks, we are able to add our stereo music and sound effects. DNLE systems vary in their number of virtual audio tracks, usually having between 8 and 24 tracks. Simultaneous channels of sound range from combinations of two, four, or eight.

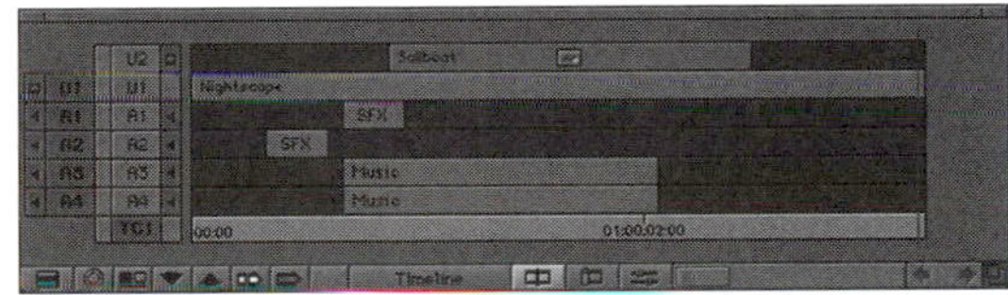

Figure 5-13 Virtual audio tracks can be added to a sequence in order to accommodate split dialogue, stereo music, and sound effects. It is common for DNLE systems to offer 24 virtual audio tracks. Courtesy Avid Technology.

Audio Editing and Waveforms

Audio editing can be made easier by giving the ear an additional tool: the eye. Displaying audio waveforms for a piece of dialogue can assist in finding exactly where a word starts or where an audio cut should be made. This is especially true if we are cutting between syllables when doing a particularly precise audio edit. By displaying the digital audio signal as a visual waveform, it becomes easier to hone in on a particular sound that we want to extract (Figure 5-14).

It should be noted that in film, audio edits can be made down to perforation level, that is, one-quarter of a frame resolution. On videotape, audio editing is limited to one-frame resolution. But with certain DNLE systems, audio editing can be done at the sample level. For example, with 44.1 KHz audio, we would be able to edit any of those 44,100 samples!

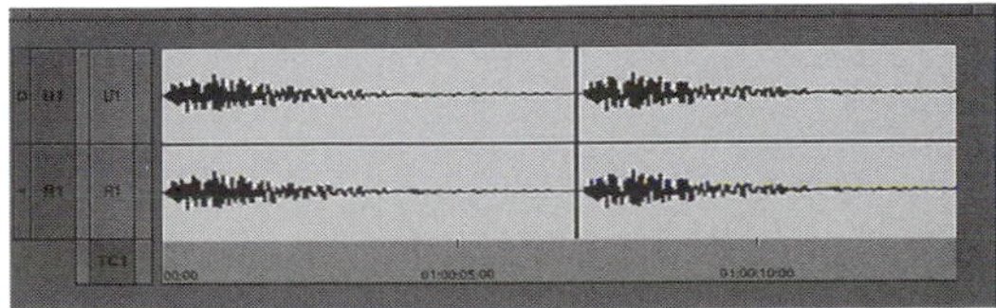

Figure 5-14 Audio waveforms are displayed as yet another component of the timeline and assist in making precise audio edits.

Customizing the Timeline

It is critical to note that the timeline is not simply a passive user interface invention that only shows the structure of a sequence. Indeed, well-designed timelines offer both the possibility of manipulating the edit points as well as customization for specific editorial tasks. Figure 5-15 is a combined view that shows the sequence in both graphical and pictorial form. This view is helpful because the editor is accustomed to seeing pictures, along with the additional graphical feedback that shows the structure of the sequence. The question "What did I do

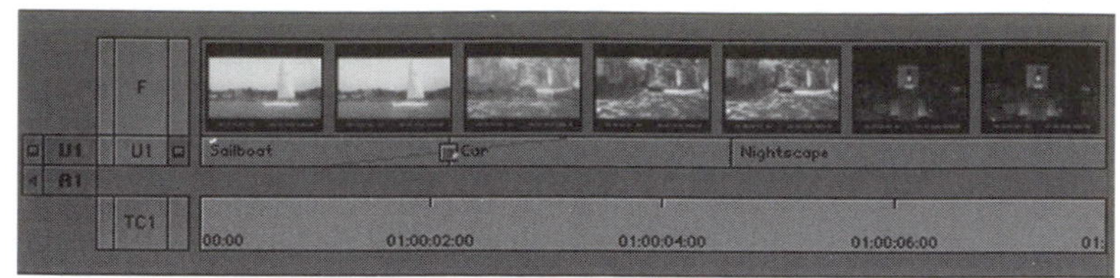

Figure 5-15 A combination layout that shows a graphical depiction of picture and sound tracks and pictorial representations of the actual footage.

there?" becomes easier to answer when the layout is in front of the editor.

Timeline views of the sequence being edited do not really have counterparts in the film or videotape worlds. Many film editors actually listen for the film splices as the film moves through the projector, since the cadence of the splices can be useful in determining the cutting rhythm.

STEP 4: DIRECT OUTPUT FROM THE DNLE SYSTEM

Traditionally, after using a DNLE system, the next phase would be to output an EDL and take it and the original source videotapes into the online room to finish the program. Prior to early 1993 (when M-JPEG-based video compression began to show marked improvements), DNLE systems were never considered as being able to finish a program due to their limitations in providing acceptable picture quality. However, as compression ratios decreased, bringing marked improvement in picture quality, more programming came to be finished direct from disk. In this instance, direct finished output means that the DNLE system is both the offline and the online system. Once the original footage has been transferred into the system, editing, optical effects, titling, and audio mixing are all performed in the system, and the completed program is recorded to videotape.

EDLs

The most common formats for EDLs are for CMX, GVG (Grass Valley Group), and Sony editing systems. Both CMX and GVG controllers use RT-11-formatted disks; Sony controllers use DOS-formatted disks. The disks are usually double-sided, double density.

Screening Copy

During the editing process, it is often necessary to send versions of the program to various individuals for review. The direct output of the DNLE system is recorded to tape and can then be viewed and judged.

Hybrid Editing and Assembly

From 1989 to 1993, DNLE systems offered auto-assembly capabilities in which the DNLE system acted as the edit controller, directing multiple videotape machines and a video switcher. During those years, the picture resolution offered by DNLE systems was not acceptable as finished picture quality.

While the machine-to-machine auto-assembly function was made extinct by DNLE systems in late 1993, the auto-assembly process migrated toward another important function—hybrid editing and assembly. Some DNLE systems act as the edit controller that controls source videotape machines to bring both disk-based media and tape-based media together to create the finished program. Why, we may ask, is it necessary to have hybrid systems? A common reason has to do with news programs. For example, it is often not possible to take the time to digitize material and then edit it together for news production. Instead, the DNLE system plays material from both disk and videotape recorder (VTR) to create the finished program.

STEP 5: CREATING THE NEGATIVE CUTLIST FOR THE FILM RELEASE

Recall that there are two objectives of our editing session: to create both a video and a film release. Using the DNLE's database of the relationship between film frames and videotape frames and how the frames were used (the edited sequence), a film cutlist is created that provides the necessary instructions for conforming the film negative to agree with the edited program. This cutlist is used by a negative cutter to conform the original film negative.

DOES USING A DNLE SYSTEM SAVE TIME?

There certainly can be no argument that a DNLE system saves time over conventional linear editing systems when it comes to making changes. But is there an overall savings in time? Some users of DNLE systems estimate a savings on the order of 30 to 40%. For other users, it is not the time factor that is important but that in the same span of time more versions and experiments can be attempted and a better finished piece created.

SYSTEMIC ISSUES

The Operating System versus the Software Program

Computers use two important, and different, routines. The first routine is the computer's operating system, often referred to as the *OS.* The OS is the set of instructions that forms the basic communications link among the various components of the computer. The second routine is described under the generic banner of *software programs.* Software operates within the restrictions of the OS.

What's important to keep in mind is that the methodology of the OS is usually different from the methodology of any of the software programs that operate within the OS. There are certain aspects of operating systems that can be called on by DNLE software (see Chapter 7).

File Organization

As you evaluate DNLE systems, it is important to know how the system organizes the files that make up your edited program. It should be easy to find the digitized files and understand their organization.

Documentation

Computers are machines, and they require maintenance. The hardware, the OS, and the DNLE software program can experience difficulties. Almost all software programs come with release and bug notes. Release notes outline the program's specific features, while the bug notes outline any known problems in the release.

Thinking Nonlinearly

Often, first-time editors, writers, producers, and directors bring a linear mindset to the DNLE session. They start with an orthodoxy of presumptions that are based in the linear mode of the editorial process and, consequently, the storytelling process. This can be a problem because it is important to play "what if" scenarios with footage, especially if you are very close to the footage. Often, the first-time user of a DNLE system begins in a linear fashion. Only after significant minutes or hours have passed do the first-timers magically discover that editing nonlinearly is easy; it's thinking nonlinearly that can be difficult at first.

It is important that once you feel you are done with a sequence, you entertain the notion of trying something else. In going for the single solution or direction, you can fall into an orthodoxy. Therefore, it is extremely important to constantly remind yourself to remain as flexible as the DNLE system. If you do this, you'll get the best possible results from your footage.

This discussion of a representative DNLE session has been brief and could not possibly delve into every feature available. However, some of the operations that we performed and the tools that we used are very common to any session. As important, the philosophical concerns of the nonlinear mindset must not be overlooked. In the next chapter, we will discuss the evolution of DNLE systems into the fourth wave: digital nonlinear online systems.

6

The Fourth Wave: Digital Nonlinear Online Editing

It has been a relatively short period since audio tape was edited with a razor blade and videotape was edited by using tracing powder to locate track pulses. In only five years, DNLE systems completely made obsolete the first two waves of nonlinear editing systems. Moreover, the various technologies that form the basis for DNLE systems are progressing very rapidly. Two questions are obvious: How long will the third wave last? What will characterize the fourth wave?

Before we answer those questions, it's important to state that the ultimate goal of DNLE systems is to finish directly from the computer disk drives regardless of the program type or where and how it will be viewed. You may be wondering if this is even possible. In 1989, when DNLE systems first appeared, it was unthinkable that anyone would broadcast digital video that had been compressed at a ratio of over 250:1. However, as compression methodologies improved, and as lower compression ratios were introduced, compressed digital video began to be aired. A full comparison of various compression ratios can be found in Chapter 10. In general, compression ratios from 2:1 to 25:1 are put on the air regularly, every night, in many parts of the world!

THE DEATH OF LINEAR OFFLINE AND THE DOMINANCE OF DNLE SYSTEMS

The main reason that the linear offline process was eclipsed by DNLE systems was that traditional linear offline editing posed too many creative limitations. If directors or clients cannot get a good indication of how the project will appear as it exits the offline stage, how can they be expected to agree to the online session without reserving the right to make changes? DNLE systems, with their enhanced feature set, allowed users to see and try more; their creative capabilities simply surpassed those of linear editing systems.

There has been unprecedented use and development of DNLE systems. It is worth noting that first-wave systems numbered no more than several hundred, while second-wave systems numbered less than 500. By 1992, there were over 2000 DNLE systems in use; by 1997, there were over 25,000 systems in use. From the manufacturer's perspective, there clearly is a thriving series of markets here—offline, online, and broadcast alone potentially account for hundreds of millions of dollars that could be spent on such equipment.

The migration of analog video and audio signals toward digital processing simply makes sense. More digital transmission is taking place in the broadcast industry, and the ultimate origination of video and audio as digital data will increase as the all-digital production system and the "digital media processor" stages begin to appear.

THE TRANSFORMATION TO DIGITAL NONLINEAR ONLINE

As we now know, the third wave, the digital wave, will have its ten-year cycle from 1989 to 1999. It is a fairly common idea that new technologies and inventions run their course over a period of ten years. About eight years into the history of the invention, it is usually enhanced and redefined—almost always as a result of improvements in the core technologies that made up the invention in the first place.

This is the crossroads that allows the third wave to give way to the fourth wave—digital nonlinear online editing—where jobs are begun and finished on the DNLE system. There are several variations within the DNLE online wave: those systems that utilize compressed digital video and those that utilize uncompressed digital video.

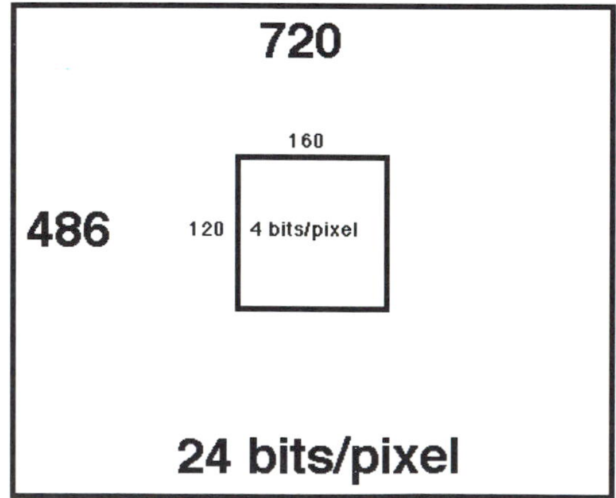

Figure 6-1 Improvement in picture quality is the single most important characteristic defining DNLE online systems. Shown within the larger 720×486, 24 bits/pixel box are the original capture and compression statistics (circa 1989) of 160×120, 4 bits/pixel.

Picture Quality Improvements

DNLE systems were born offering single-field compressed resolutions. A video frame is made up of two video fields; early DNLE systems only digitized the first field of every frame, thus immediately discarding one-half of the information in the frame. For NTSC video, this meant that 30 fields per second were digitized. By reducing the amount of image compression, greater picture quality is available to the user. Figure 6-1 depicts how improvements in picture quality were achieved. Original picture quality was limited to a pixel matrix of 160×120, single-field (30 fields per second, NTSC) capture of 4 bits per pixel, and a compression ratio of 250:1. In late 1996, the picture resolution offered was based on a full NTSC pixel matrix of 720×486, two-field (60 fields per second, NTSC) capture of 24 bits per pixel, and a compression ratio of 2:1. As a result, program makers looked very carefully at these improvements in picture quality and began to finish programs directly on DNLE systems.

Input/Output Connections

One of the important variables that directly affects the quality of the picture that is stored to computer disk is the manner in which video enters the digitizing subsystem of the DNLE system. The most common input/output (I/O) routes for picture are listed below.

Composite A composite video signal is one in which the luminance and chrominance signals are combined. Composite video is an analog signal, coded in either NTSC, PAL, or SECAM. The biggest criticism of composite video connections is that the signal is created by adding chroma signals to the luminance channel. As a result, there may be difficulties in separating the two, and chroma interfering (bleeding) into the luminance channel may result.

Component analog (Y, R-Y, B-Y) A component analog signal is one in which the original red, green, and blue signals (RGB) are separated into their luminance and chrominance components. Specifically, luminance is known as Y, while chrominance is separated into R-Y (red) and B-Y (blue). Luminance can be defined as the levels of brightness that a picture contains, while chrominance consists of the color values of the picture.

S-Video An S-Video signal is one in which the luminance channel is separated from the chrominance signals, but, unlike component analog, the chrominance signals are not separate.

Serial digital A serial digital interface (SDI) provides connections for both ITU-R 601 and composite digital video and four channels of digital audio. SDI obviously differs from the other coding schemes in that it is a digital medium. SDI has a transfer rate of 270 Mbits/sec.

With first-generation videotapes, component analog and serial digital I/O will provide superior results over composite and S-Video. Most DNLE systems offer composite and S-Video I/O, while more capable systems also offer component analog and serial digital I/O.

VIDEOTAPE FORMATS AND DIGITAL SAMPLING FOR DNLE SYSTEMS

There are many different types of videotape formats, and new types are introduced every year. The important aspects of these various videotape formats for digital nonlinear editing are the type of signal that can be recorded, the sampling rate, and the actual physical dimensions of the tape and the tape cassette. One very clear trend is high-quality picture and audio capabilities in extremely small cassettes.

As DNLE systems continue to improve, they must take into account certain aspects of sampling, color space, and pixel depth issues.

Tape Formats

D1 This component digital tape format (19mm) conforms to the ITU-R 601 standard 4:2:2, 8-bits-per-pixel sampling. D1 is especially useful in situations where multiple compositing layers are necessary with little to no generational loss.

D2 This composite digital tape format (19mm), like D1, employs 8-bits-per-pixel 4:2:2 sampling, but unlike D1, is not a component system. As a result, D2 is much more susceptible to generational loss when multilayered composites are required.

D3 This composite digital tape format (1/2"), like D2, employs 8-bits-per-pixel sampling. Much of the same performance characteristics of D2 are found with D3, the chief advantage of the latter being the smaller size as well as a 1/2" digital composite camcorder.

D5 This component digital tape format (1/2") employs 10-bits-per-pixel sampling. As a result, D5 provides superior performance to D1, especially with regard to keying operations for multilayering.

Digital Betacam This component digital tape format uses the ITU-R 601 standard and then employs discrete cosine transform (DCT) compression at a very low ratio (1.77:1).

High-definition television (HDTV) In 1985, the equipment necessary for recording HDTV (format nonstandardized) was akin to the size of a small refrigerator. Yet by the late 1990s, a portable HDTV recorder was introduced.

Sampling Rates

Digital tape formats, and the digital video compression algorithms that enable DNLE systems, all process original signals and assign numerical values to those signals. These sampling rates are directly responsible for determining how much of the original signal can be recreated. Some of the sampling rates found in videotape formats are described below.

4:2:2 The Y, R-Y, and B-Y components are sampled in a ratio of 4:2:2 (four samples of Y at 13.5 MHz, while R-Y and B-Y both equate to 6.75 MHz). Common tape format: D1. Note that it is technically correct to refer to the digitized luminance value (Y) as Y, while the color component R-Y is referred to as Cr, and B-Y is referred to as Cb.

4:2:0 The Y, R-Y, and B-Y components are sampled in a ratio of 4:2:0. While this ratio may give the appearance that the B-Y signals are never sampled, this is, in fact, not true. Instead, every other line is sampled, so that we sample the first scan line at 4:2:2 and then sample the second line at 4:0:0 (four samples of Y at 13.5 MHz while R-Y and B-Y both equate to 6.75 MHz sampled every other line). Common tape format: DVC (digital video cassette).

4:1:1 The Y, R-Y, and B-Y components are sampled in a ratio of 4:1:1 (four samples of Y at 13.5 MHz; 3.75 MHz for R-Y and B-Y). Common tape format: DVC. Compression format: MPEG 1.

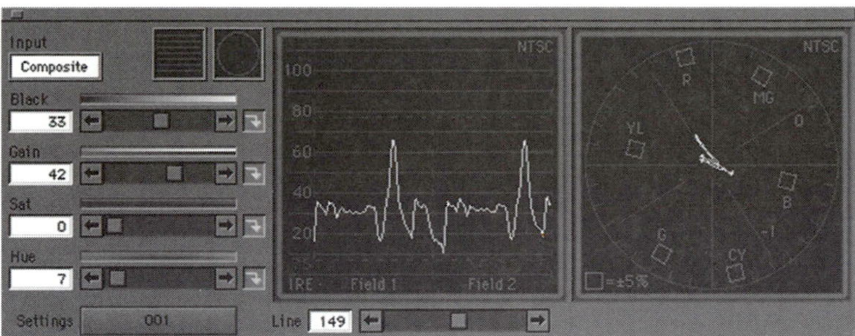

Figure 6-2 Representing waveform and vectorscope in software. Adjusting the sliders affects the luminance and chrominance levels of material entering and exiting the DNLE system. Courtesy Avid Technology.

4:4:4 The Y, R-Y, and B-Y components are sampled in a ratio of 4:4:4 (equal samples for each component). A greater amount of samples for each of the signals will generally result in greater quality (as long as information is not lost in "rounding off" routines, which are often encountered when 4:4:4 material must be processed by 4:2:2 devices). Also, 4:4:4 sampling can be applied to RGB signals.

4:2:2:4 Whenever a fourth sampling figure is encountered, it equates to the alpha channel required for keying applications.

Waveform and Vectorscope Monitoring

DNLE systems also offer software-based models for setting the I/O levels for video that enters and exits the system. Figure 6-2 is an example of a software waveform/vectorscope; a waveform monitor is used to set luminance levels, whereas a vectorscope is used to set saturation and hue adjustments for chroma.

TWO ONLINE WORK SCENARIOS: BATCH REDIGITIZE VERSUS DIGITIZE ONCE

Two of the most popular scenarios whereby programs can be finished directly from the DNLE system are shown in Color Figures 2 and 3. In a *batch redigitizing* scenario, the DNLE system is first used as an offline device. As shown in Color Figure 2, picture and sound are digitized from videotape, but picture is digitized at a lower-than-final-resolution quality. The program is then edited, and the low-resolution picture files are erased while the sound files are kept. Then, using the instructions contained in the edited sequence, only the picture files are redigitized at a higher resolution—one deemed by the user as being sufficient for finishing directly from disk. The step-by-step process of batch redigitizing proceeds as follows:

1. Picture and sound are digitized; picture is digitized at low resolution.
2. The program is edited.
3. Picture files are erased; audio files remain.

4. A new picture resolution is chosen: one that will be the final picture quality for the program.
5. The sequence is batch digitized.

The data display shown here is used to prompt the user to reload the original source tapes for digitization:

Tape 010 1:05:00:10 1:05:13:18V

This example means that videotape number 10 is put back into the tape deck, and the DNLE system automatically cues the tape to the first timecode number, 1:05:00:10, and digitizes video only (V) to the out point, 1:05:13:18.

The digitize-once scenario means that footage is digitized at the picture resolution required to finish directly from disk. This requires having enough disk space to accommodate the footage storage needs, but it avoids having to redigitize the material. This process is shown in Color Figure 3, where original footage is digitized from videotape at a high picture quality, editing takes place, and then a recording is made directly from disk to tape. Here, the offline and online processes have merged and as soon as the editing is done, the program is finished. It may not always be possible to do this, of course, due to the storage requirements of low-compression-rate video. For example, a 2:1 compression rate, depending on the complexity or simplicity of the images, may only yield three minutes per gigabyte. As the price of disk storage continues to decline, this will be less and less of an issue.

REAL-TIME PROCESSING

Real-time processing of both transitions and effects is assumed when one enters an online room. Multiple videotape recorders and digital disk recorders are used to provide the playback sources and the recording mechanisms, while a switcher is used to blend these various sources together. *Real time* refers to the ability to see certain operations happen without having to wait for the DNLE system to *render,* or create, a new piece of media before the effect can be seen.

Let's take the case of a four-machine online room: We use three of the machines to play back our source material while the fourth machine acts as the record machine. If we want three images to be superimposed together, with each image at a different level (in order to be more or less prevalent), each of the sources is routed through the switcher, and the fader bars on the switcher are adjusted in order to set the level of each source as it is superimposed over the others. As long as there are enough mix busses on the switcher (the bus and the fader bar for that bus are used in this case to set the blend level between sources), this is an effect that can be seen in real time. While all four machines play, the video from the three source machines is blended together, creating an effect that can be seen immediately, adjusted, and recorded on the fourth machine.

On a DNLE system, this type of effect may be done in real time, or it may require rendering before the effect can be seen. Early DNLE systems offered no real-time capabilities. If the user wanted to see a dissolve, the effect would first have to be rendered before it could be viewed. However, DNLE systems in the third wave began to add real-time capabilities for some transitions and effects. The most common real-time capabilities of DNLE systems are

Dissolves
Luminance (luma) keys
Chrominance (chroma) keys
Wipes
Slow-motion effects
Superimpositions

Real-time DNLE capabilities are divided into two categories:

1. *Convolving* effects, in which pixels of different clips are blended together in some fashion, such as dissolves, superimpositions, and keys.
2. *Pixel manipulation* effects, in which pixels of different clips are moved over time, such as wipes and digital video effects.

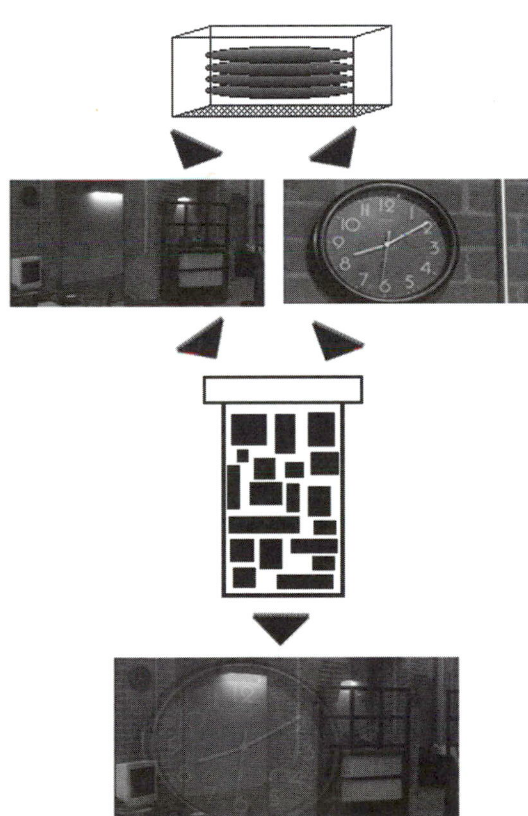

Figure 6-3 How a dissolve is accomplished in real time. Files exit the disk drive, and pixels from Stream A and from Stream B enter a blender chip that mixes the pixels, thereby creating a dissolve. The effect can be seen as soon as the user hits Play, and no rendering is required.

How Real-Time Processing Works

For convolving effects, two *streams* of video must be blended together in real time. Figure 6-3 diagrams how this can be accomplished. The files representing the two images to be dissolved together exit the disk drive, and each file, now referred to as a stream, enters a coprocessor board populated with various computer chips.

Within the coprocessor board, each stream is decompressed from its specific coding state (how the files were stored on the computer disk) and enters a blender chip, where the pixels of each stream are combined. What is meant by "specific coding state" is that systems may differ with regard to how the video is sampled and stored on disk. Let's say that video is sampled and stored on disk in YUV color space. If the effects subsystem (in this case, the routines that blend the streams together) operates in RGB color space, a conversion from YUV to RGB is necessary.

In the case of a dissolve, pixels from Stream A are turned off after a time while pixels from Stream B are turned on; there is, of course, an interval of time during which pixels from both streams are on; that is the dissolve duration.

Is the Number of Real-Time Streams of Video Finite or Infinite?

In the above example of real-time dissolves, two video streams are involved—the *from* source and the *to* source. However, DNLE systems, unlike an online videotape editing suite, do not

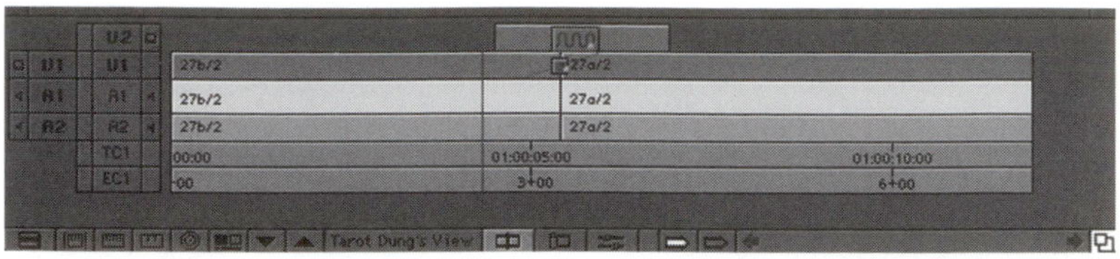

Figure 6-4 Unlike a dissolve, which involves the real-time playback of two streams, this is an example of an effect that cannot be accomplished in real time on a two-stream system: Three tracks need to be playable in real time.

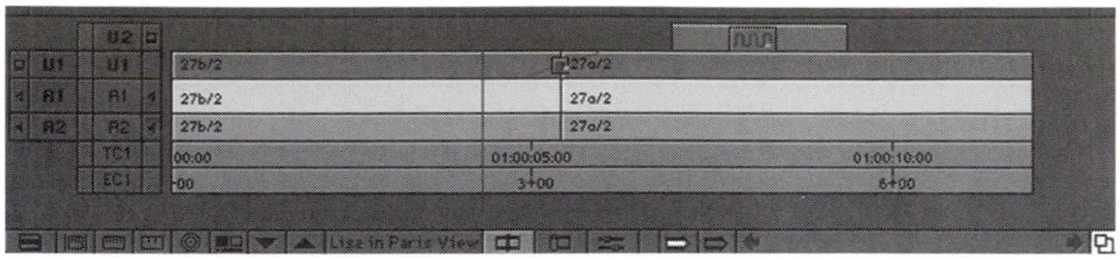

Figure 6-5 By moving the position of the superimposition, only two streams need to be played at any one time.

offer a limitless number of real-time streams. In the online room, if we want to have seven different images all mixed together as a superimposition, we are only limited by the number of playback devices available in the room: If we have seven different tape machines, we can achieve our goal.

Figure 6-4 shows an effect that cannot be accomplished in real time on a two-stream DNLE system. The dissolve, shown on video track 1(V1), can be shown in real time, but the clip on video track 2 (V2) cannot be shown in context with the dissolve in real time. To accomplish this, three-stream functionality is required—two streams for the clips dissolving together and one stream for the superimposed material.

Note, however, that in Figure 6-5 the position of the superimposition has been adjusted so that it does not overlap the dissolve. As a result, *at any one time* only two streams need to be played together.

REAL-TIME DIGITAL VIDEO EFFECTS: 2D AND 3D

Real-time three-dimensional (3D) digital video effects are, of course, common in the online room. But until 1993, digital video effects were not available on DNLE systems. That year, real-time two-dimensional (2D) digital effects became available. 2D and 3D digital video effects differ in that 2D effects cannot transform the image with perspective. Figure 6-6 shows three examples of 2D transforms. The original image is at left. Next, the image is "flopped" (middle). That is, it has been transformed on the *x*-axis so that the sailboat is on screen left. Finally, the image is transformed on the *z*-axis to create a *blow-up,* in which the image is larger in frame than its original size (right).

Figure 6-7 shows how both 2D and 3D integration are accomplished. From disk, Stream A enters the blender card, while Stream B enters either a 2D or 3D transform card. Note that it is often possible to fit all the logic necessary for 2D and 3D transforms onto the

Figure 6-6 Examples of 2D transforms. The original image (left) is transformed on the *x*-axis to flop the image's screen direction (middle) and affected on the *z*-axis to create a blow-up (right). Footage courtesy Fox Point Films.

actual blender card, but this will vary among different manufacturers. Stream B is then transformed in either 2D or 3D and enters the blender card, where it is combined with Stream A. The final effect is shown at the bottom of Figure 6-7.

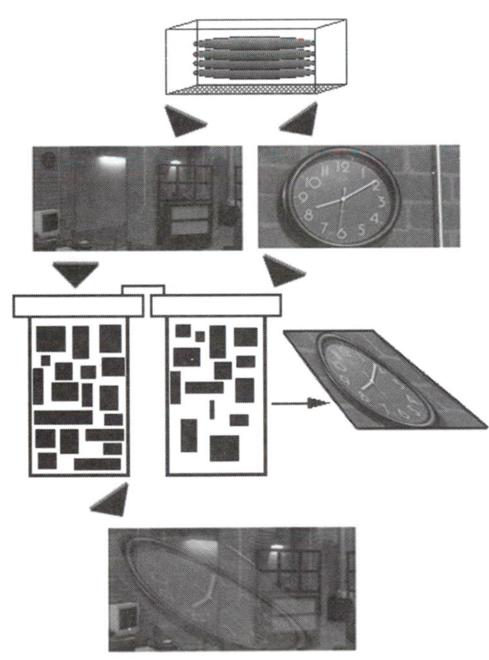

Figure 6-7 How 2D and 3D effects were introduced into DNLE systems. By inserting a 2D or 3D transform chip or card in parallel with the blender card, either stream can be affected in 2D or 3D and then combined to create the final result (bottom).

Integration of 3D: Third-Party Suppliers or Programmable Chip Sets

3D integration was a natural progression for DNLE systems, and in 1995, such functionality became available. A key difference between 2D and 3D implementation is the manner in which the integration occurs. With 2D systems, DNLE manufacturers found that it was relatively easy to take 2D transform chips and integrate them on a coprocessor board that could be used in the DNLE system.

Yet with 3D systems, quite a lot of work had already been done by several manufacturers—popular systems included the Grass Valley Kaleidoscope, Abekas DVEous, and Pinnacle Mercedes. While a 3D coprocessor can certainly be built, DNLE system manufacturers must choose whether to build such complicated systems themselves or to use the products of third-party suppliers. This latter approach has been the most popular. Referring to Figure 6-7, we would replace the 2D transform chip with a 3D chip or a connection to an outboard 3D digital effects device. After the 3D transforms are made, the streams then exit and return to the CPU-resident coprocessor board, where they enter the blender chip. Figure 6-8 shows an example of software-based 3D effects. The original figure (left) is transformed via software controls (middle) to achieve the final effect (right).

Judging the Level of Hardware Integration—Can I Always See the Effect?

It is important to note that not all 3D implementations are equal. While it's true that they all require the video streams to exit the disk drives to be transformed, the level of integration can differ wildly from system to system. For example, some implementations do not allow the user to step through the effect frame by frame. This means that after hitting the Play

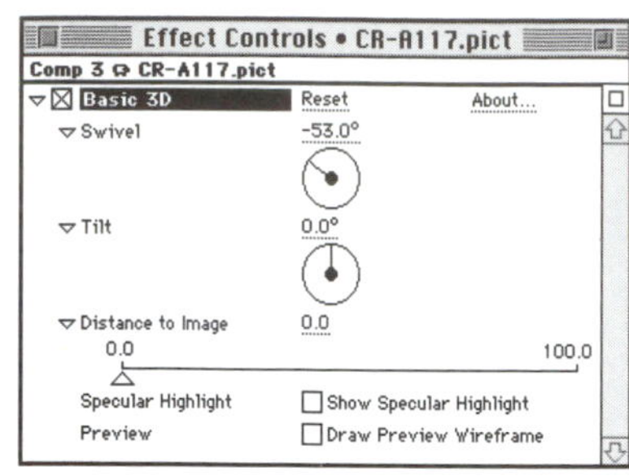

Figure 6-8 A software-based application that can be used to create 3D transforms. Adobe AfterEffects courtesy Adobe Systems.

button, the user must see the effect in its entirety. If the user stops at a specific point in the timeline—somewhere within the effect—the digital video device is not cued to the appropriate location because it can only be triggered at the start of the effect! This, obviously, is not the most desirable situation. Systems that allow the user to stop at any point and see the digital video effect at that specific point in relation to the other clips and how they are aligned are most useful.

Combining Effects: 3D and Plug-Ins

Plug-ins refer to software tools that are created by third-party manufacturers and which can be used directly by the DNLE system. Figure 6-9 shows a representative interface and transform effect from within Adobe Photoshop. Plug-ins extend the capabilities of DNLE systems by offering a wide range of effects. Most DNLE manufacturers realize that if the system is open to working with third-party applications, then a greater degree of functionality can be provided to the user.

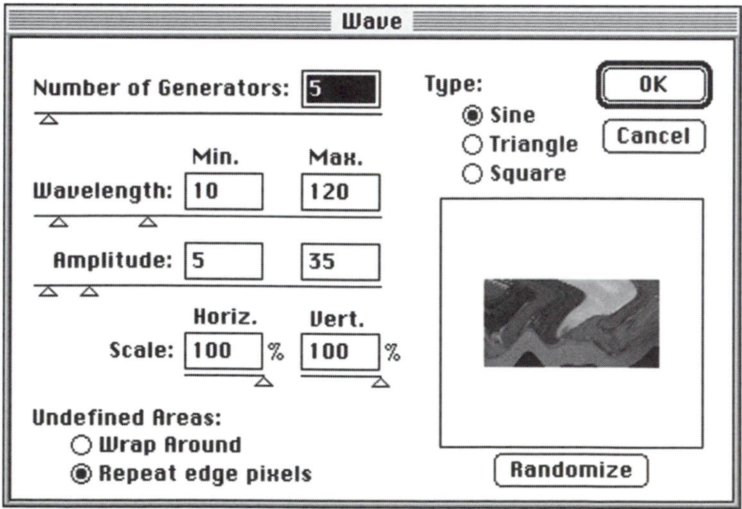

Figure 6-9 A representative interface and transform effect from a third-party plug-in application (Adobe Photoshop), which is used to enhance the capabilities of the DNLE system. Courtesy Adobe Corporation.

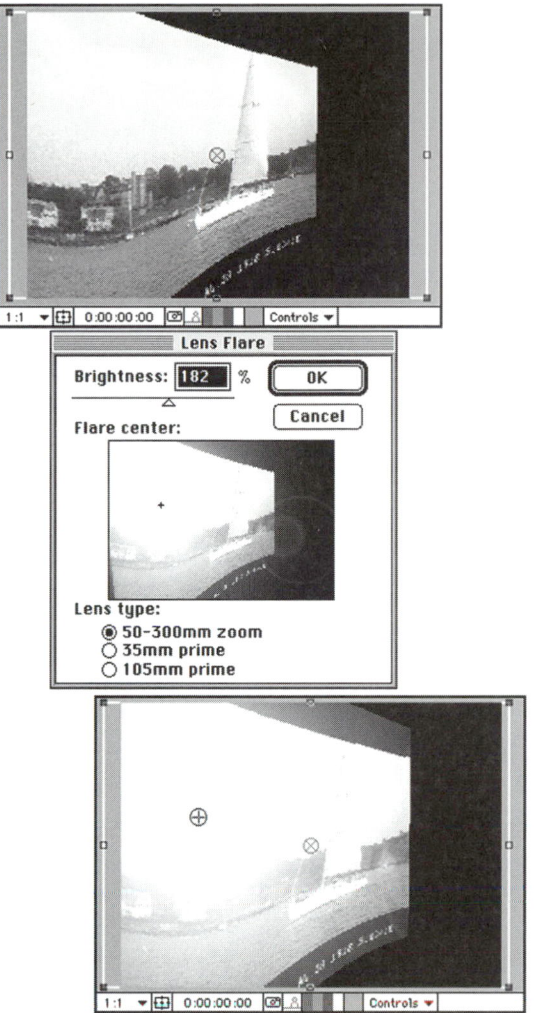

Figure 6-10 An example that combines a 3D transform and a plug-in. The 3D transform (top) is augmented by manipulating the settings of a lens flare plug-in (middle) to create the final effect (bottom). Adobe AfterEffects and Adobe Photoshop courtesy Adobe Systems.

Figure 6-10 is an example in which 3D transforms have been combined with a plug-in to create the effect of a lens flare. Note that the 3D transform has been manipulated to create a "flag-waving" effect (Figure 6-10, top). To this, a plug-in is added that will result in the creation of a lens flare, and the settings are adjusted (Figure 6-10, middle) to create the final effect (Figure 6-10, bottom).

RENDERING

When an effect is desired that cannot be accomplished in real time, the entire effect, or a portion of it, must be rendered in order to see the effect play in real time. Note that some DNLE systems do not require effects to be rendered if all we want to do is to see, but not play, the effect. It may very well be possible to build a very complicated, multilayered effect and to see the effect by stepping through it on a frame-by-frame basis. This, of course, can be very helpful in the design phase of creating the effect—especially so if the effect is very complicated and will require many hours of rendering.

Figure 6-11 shows the before and after versions of a clip to which an image processing effect has been applied. However, this effect cannot be seen in real time; we cannot just apply the effect, hit Play, and see all the frames of this particular clip affected in the desired fashion. Instead, in order to change the original pixels that make up an image, the effect is accomplished either with the assistance of hardware or must be created solely in software. The general rule is that if an effect has hardware assistance, that is, if there is a computer coprocessor board that works in conjunction with the software, then the effect can either be seen in real time or will be rendered faster.

The Factors That Affect Rendering Times

After the user applies an effect to a clip and then wants to see the affected clip play in real time, the system will render the effect. The original pixels that make up each frame will be transformed according to the properties of the specific effect. And, of course, certain properties take longer to apply to the pixels than other properties. There are three factors that affect rendering times:

1. The type of transforming effect. How the pixels of an image must be affected has an impact on the amount of time it will take to render the effect. In general, convolving functions, in which pixels are blended together and changed in some way, will be faster to render than those functions that require a movement of pixels from one location to another.
2. The size of the image. The smaller the image, the fewer the pixels contained in that image and therefore there are fewer

Figure 6-11 An example of the before and after results of a software-based effect that requires rendering.

pixels to be transformed in some fashion. An effect applied to an ITU-R 601 frame sampled at 720×486 pixels will be rendered faster than that same effect applied to an HDTV frame sampled at 1920×1080.

3. The render speed as accomplished by the host CPU. There are a number of factors that affect how the actual process of rendering is done. If there is no hardware-accelerated rendering board present, the host CPU carries out the rendering tasks. The operating speeds of CPUs are rated in terms of megahertz (MHz). Given all other conditions equal, a CPU operating at 350 MHz will render an effect faster than another CPU operating at 132 MHz.

How Rendering Is Accomplished

Rendering is accomplished by reading one or a series of frames from disk, bringing them into a temporary location, applying the desired effect to those frame(s), and then writing the new frames back to disk. When the rendering process is CPU dependent and not hardware assisted, the frame(s) will be read into RAM (random access memory), where the transform is made. With hardware-assisted rendering, the frame(s) will be read into memory (some type of RAM) on the hardware board and the transform applied. Also, some effects may be *hard coded* into the hardware board. This means that a particular transform and the instruction set that makes up that transform will be coded directly into chip(s) present on the board; think of this as being similar to a third-party 3D digital video effects unit in which the functionalities are specified in hardware.

The Different Types of Rendering

Destructive versus Nondestructive

Rendering can be a destructive or a nondestructive process. A destructive process is one in which the transforming algorithm is performed on the original frame. Thus, the original frame is no longer available and only the affected frame is stored back to disk after the effect has been applied. A nondestructive process reads the original frame into memory and applies the transforming effect on a copy of the original frame, thereby preserving the original frame. The disadvantage of nondestructive rendering is that additional disk space is required because we now have two versions of the original frame and we have not freed up any space, as is the case with destructive rendering. However, this is perhaps a small price to pay, given the ability to return to the original image.

Background Rendering

How a render is accomplished also merits examination. Some DNLE systems do not allow any other operation, such as viewing clips or editing, to take place while rendering is being done. However, in the case of background rendering, renders occur as a secondary operation, thus allowing the user to continue working. When there is a pause in user action, or when the type of work the DNLE system is accomplishing leaves enough free CPU cycles, some of the rendering tasks are done, thus maximizing the efficiency of the overall process.

Distributed Rendering

Distributed rendering is a process whereby software can distribute the rendering load either to various coprocessors resident in the same CPU or to other CPUs. For example, some CPUs contain multiple processors. Instead of just one CPU processor—the main chip (set) that powers the CPU—there may be multiple processors—multiple chips—that can all be used in tandem. A single-processor CPU that normally is rated at 175 MHz could be rated at 700 MHz if we put four processors into the system. The system is then capable of much faster operating speeds, which will definitely affect rendering times.

It is also possible to distribute rendering over multiple CPUs. Imagine that we have an effect that has been distributed among four processors in a single CPU and that the effect is also distributed to four CPUs. We now have 16 processors that can all be used to process our effect. If, in addition, we can background render, the users of all four computers can proceed working as normal while the distributed background rendering occurs. Note, however, that the DNLE software must support background and distributed rendering.

Multiprocessing and Multithreading

Multiprocessing refers to the use of more than one CPU processor to accomplish a task, as described in the previous section. Another important computer processing term is *multithreading,* which refers to the ability to run several different processes from either the same or different software packages simultaneously on a file. For example, let's say we want to apply three different transforms to the same file. If we are using a software package that does not support multithreading, we are likely to get an error message informing us that the file is busy. We must then wait until the first transform is finished before the second transform can begin. However, with multithreading capability, all three transforms can proceed in parallel without waiting for a file to be released by a preceding transform.

ADVANCED AUDIO

DNLE online systems, while offering very advanced audio capabilities, do not usually offer as many functions as dedi-

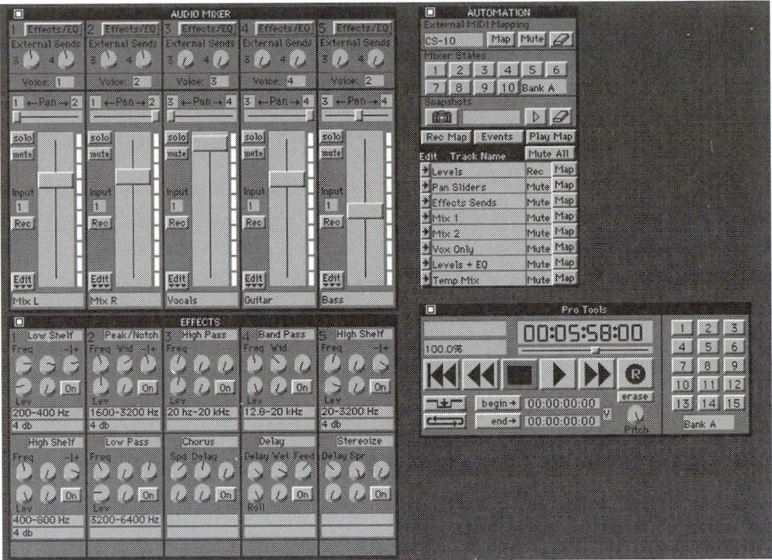

Figure 6-12 A software-based mixing interface used for setting volume, pan, and overall mix. Courtesy Digidesign Corporation.

cated digital audio workstations. However, many of the audio processing tools from the online room have been incorporated into online DNLE systems. Figure 6-12 shows a software-based audio mixing interface that is used to set volume and pan for individual clips as well as set the overall mix for a sequence. Each time the sequence is played, the faders will dynamically adjust for the mix.

Equalization

Equalization (EQ) tools are used to smooth out the sound between shots as well as to create specific audio effects. Figure 6-13 is an example of a software equalization interface. By adjusting the controls, audio effects and environments can be created, such as equalizing the low and middle range while boosting the high end to achieve the effect of a person speaking on a telephone.

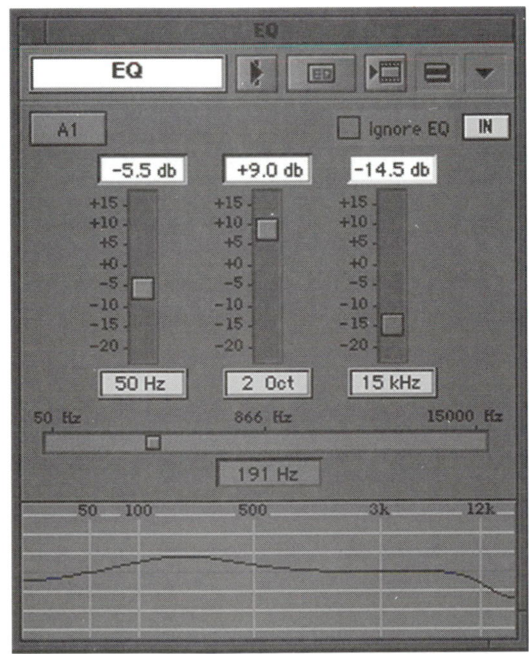

Figure 6-13 Equalization tools recreated in software. Courtesy Avid Technology.

Rubber Banding

Rubber banding is a term used to describe the setting of audio volume parameters. Figure 6-14 shows the basic operation of rubber banding. The top figure shows our two audio tracks. Below, the second figure shows two faint lines that form the audio data for the two audio tracks. By clicking (pointing) at a specific point in the clip's audio, a keyframe is added, shown here as a triangle in the third figure. Finally, by dragging up or down on each triangle, an audio profile is created, which represents the audio's volume.

Figure 6-14 Rubber banding interface used to create a profile for how audio will dip and fade. Courtesy Avid Technology.

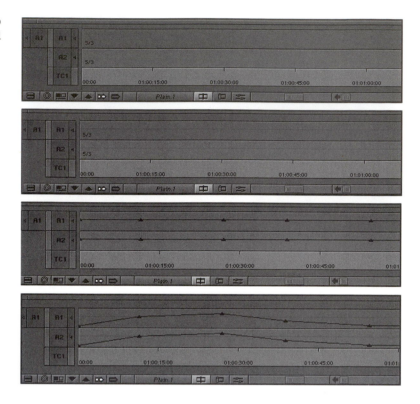

CUSTOMIZING AND SAVING EFFECTS AND USING THEM ELSEWHERE

DNLE systems should provide the ability to save any of the user-defined picture or audio effects that are created. For example, if we have a series of clips of people talking on telephones, we don't have to create EQ effects for each clip: We only need to create the effect once and then drop it onto the appropriate segments.

Another important aspect of being able to save customized effects is that they can then be transmitted from place to place. Imagine that you have a friend 3000 miles away who has created an interesting effect. Your friend can send you the effect over an electronic mailing system (e-mail), and you can use the effect in your own program—provided that both of the DNLE systems are compatible.

DIGITAL AUDIO WORKSTATIONS (DAWS)

Digital audio workstations (DAWs) first appeared in 1985 and used optical and magnetic disks to store the digital audio files, which could then be accessed nonlinearly. However, the video portion of the program was not digitized. Instead, the DAW offered extremely fast access times to the digital audio files,

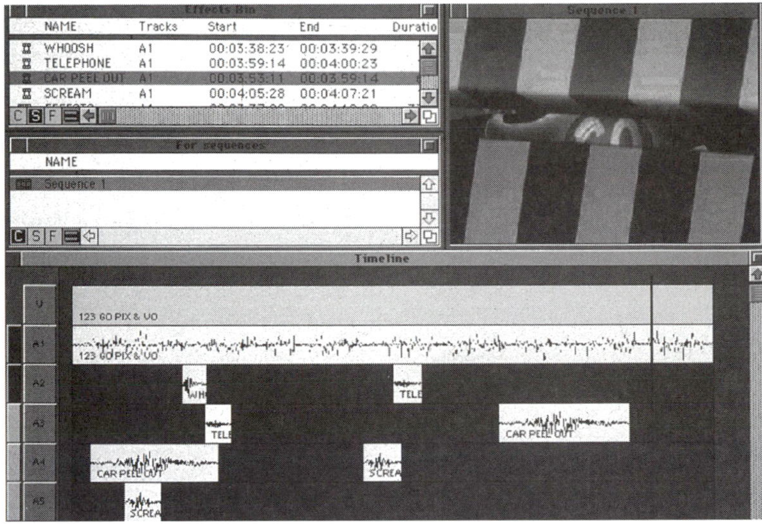

Figure 6-15 Incorporating compressed digital video playback of picture along with multi-track digital audio editing capabilities creates a unique way of accessing picture for the audio editor.

but had to function with a comparably slow piece of machinery and the shuttling of a linear tape machine.

In 1991, however, DAWs with digital video files appeared. The earliest systems employed M-JPEG-based compression (Figure 6-15) and were subsequently followed by systems using QuickTime-based video. The incorporation of digital video was so successful that only five years after its introduction, all major manufacturers of DAWs offered digital nonlinear picture access.

DIGITAL SIGNAL PROCESSING

From our exposure to film and television programming, we have experienced the manner in which audio is treated. We are all familiar with the stereotypical image of someone running in slow motion while we hear the person's heart beating in a slowed-down manner. With analog equipment, the tape speed is altered and played slower than the original recording in order to create the desired effect. However, a greater degree of experimentation and repeatability is possible by digitally manipulating sound. Digital signal processing (DSP) techniques are used to sample the original sound and modify it in some fashion.

A dizzying range of possibilities is available. Now instead of a single heart beating in slow motion, we can digitally manipulate the sound to achieve a layered effect. There can be a heart beating at one tempo layered against a different tempo, and they can be in different pitches. The degree of ease with which sound can be manipulated by digitally processing signal is, indeed, enabling (Figure 6-16).

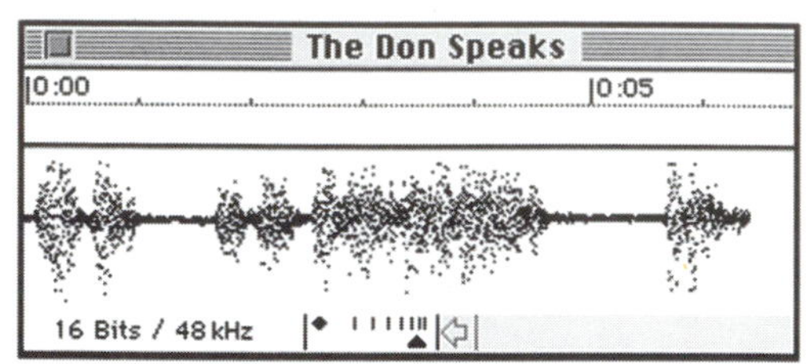

Figure 6-16 Some of the digital signal processing techniques found in SoundEdit Pro—software that can easily be applied to an audio file. Courtesy Macromedia.

MUSICAL INSTRUMENT DIGITAL INTERFACE (MIDI)

MIDI is used to translate musical information into digital terms. Linking musical instruments digitally to computers relies on a simple given: that musical information, notes, and how the notes are created can be expressed by numbers.

The MIDI keyboard is at the center of the link. When notes are played on a MIDI keyboard, signals are sent to a computer serially via a MIDI cable. These signals describe each note by a variety of characteristics: note on, note off, key pressure, attack velocity, duration, and so on. With a set of such data and an understanding of how the information should be deciphered, sounds can be interpreted and exactly played back as digital data. Sixteen separate channels of MIDI data can travel down one MIDI cable.

The software that captures these incoming signals is the MIDI sequencer portion of the computer program. As notes are played on the MIDI keyboard, the signals are sent to the sequencing program and are assigned to one track in the sequencer. Different instruments can be incorporated, such as MIDI drum machines and MIDI samplers; there are even special acoustic-to-MIDI convertors available if acoustic instruments, such as guitars or wind instruments, are required. When each instrument is played, a separate track for that instrument is created and displayed by the MIDI sequencer.

The sequencer, in effect, is similar to the concept of the playlist for the DNLE system. In many ways, the MIDI sequencer represents a log for playing music. Once the digital information that makes up a track of MIDI is resident in the computer, it can be changed through a variety of means, such as audio waveform editing and equalization. MIDI is an integral component in digital audio workstations.

When the tracks have been prepared, this "sequencing log" can be manipulated and reordered. In the same way that the DNLE system achieves multiple versions, multiple MIDI automation files can be created to play back the tracks in the sequencer in different ways. When a playback file is run from the computer, the digital data is sent back to the musical instruments. If multiple instruments have been used, these instruments will then play back simultaneously, emulating a multitrack recording. At any point, changes can be made to any of the parameters that make up the sounds being played back, and timing adjustments can be made. The output of the sequenced instruments is recorded and then laid back to the master videotape.

MIDI has had a significant impact on how finished audio for pictures is created. The concept of nonlinearly accessing audio files, sequencing them, and creating multitrack playback of instruments paved the way for refinements to the analog nonlinear editing systems and for the appearance of digital nonlinear editing systems.

DIGITAL NONLINEAR ONLINE: REDUCING THE COMPRESSION RATIO

Desktop-based DNLE systems usually offer compression ratios from as high as 150:1 to 2:1 to uncompressed ITU-R 601. The smaller ratio equates to better picture quality. A 2:1 ratio equates to a popular resolution that many users find sufficient for a majority of final program delivery applications. Of course, some users of DNLE systems find that a 5:1 ratio is acceptable—clearly, the quality of the picture that a user finds acceptable is very subjective. However, in general, a 2:1 ratio seems to be sufficient for almost all needs. The Digital Betacam format has been extremely popular in the postproduction and broadcasting markets and employs a mild 1.77:1 compression ratio.

Run-Length Encoding: Lossless Compression

Run-length encoding (covered in depth in Chapter 10) can be used to bring lossless compression to the DNLE system. Lossless compression may seem to be an oxymoron: After all, if we are compressing a file, aren't we losing information? The answer is no because there are techniques that can compress a file without losing any information. If a picture file consists of 100 MB (megabytes), it can be compressed using lossless techniques that reduce the size of the file; upon decompression, all 100 MB are returned, producing no loss of information and, thus, the original file.

It should be noted that under run-length encoding (RLE), the degree of compression is very slight and, in fact, the compressed file size on a frame-by-frame basis may actually be larger than the original file size for any specific frame. This is due to how information is compressed and the attendant overhead involved in specifying that the file has been compressed. In any case, RLE compression incorporated into DNLE systems represents an exciting evolutionary step: absolutely mathematical equality between the original picture and the digitized version. Literally, every bit of the original file is contained in the compressed file.

DIGITAL NONLINEAR ONLINE: THE UNCOMPRESSED SYSTEMS

There is also a category of DNLE systems that are completely uncompressed. These systems require very large bandwidth at the computer bus level and very high throughput from the disk subsystem in order to store the data-intensive picture files. The calculations are dependent on exactly what type of picture we are trying to store. The first DNLE uncompressed systems appeared in the early 1980s and offered ITU-R 601 picture quality. To calculate the storage requirements of ITU-R 601, we have the following specifications:

Pixel matrix	720×486
Bits per component	8 (1 byte)
Sampling	4:2:2

Thus we calculate:

$$720 \times 486 = 349{,}920 \times 2 \text{ bytes} = 699{,}840 \text{ bytes}$$
$$(\sim 700 \text{ KB})/\text{frame} \times 30 \text{ fps} \cong 21 \text{ MB/sec}$$

The amount of storage required for one minute of video at this sampling rate is approximately 1.26 GB!

As a result of this staggering requirement, early uncompressed systems offered from 7 to 15 minutes of storage. As a result, most of the programming done on these systems paralleled that of the compressed DNLE systems: commercials and short program opens and closes, each of which did not require massive amounts of footage in order to complete the final program.

Architecturally, these systems must be capable of passing specific amounts of data over the computer bus and to and from the disk mechanisms. The computer bus must be fast enough to consistently pass this data. Early DNLE uncompressed systems include the Quantel Harry, which used a proprietary computer bus system to ensure consistent and required throughput from bus to disk. Figures 6-17 and 6-18 show uncompressed ITU-R 601 DNLE systems.

Figure 6-17 Discreet Logic's Fire is an uncompressed DNLE system that runs on the Silicon Graphics Workstation platform. Courtesy Discreet Logic.

A Word on Closed versus Open Systems

As DNLE uncompressed systems evolved, manufacturers found themselves facing an important issue: whether to create a system based on proprietary hardware or develop software for open and generic computer platforms. Software that is developed to run on a nonproprietary hardware base allows the user to run other software programs on the same hardware. Both proprietary and open systems have their advantages. An in-depth discussion of open versus closed systems is presented in Chapter 13.

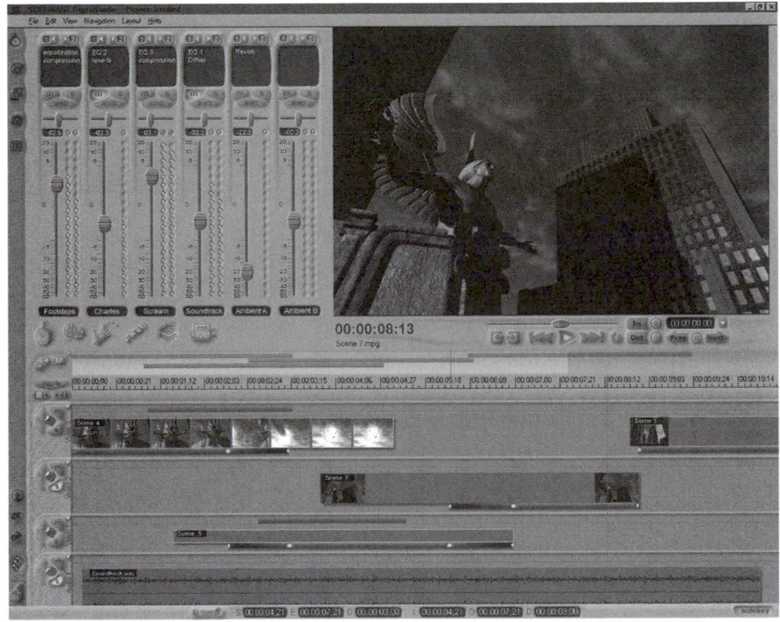

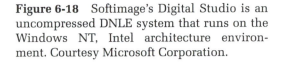

Figure 6-18 Softimage's Digital Studio is an uncompressed DNLE system that runs on the Windows NT, Intel architecture environment. Courtesy Microsoft Corporation.

RESOLUTION DEPENDENCY AND RESOLUTION INDEPENDENCE

Thus far, we have been introduced to DNLE systems that are resolution dependent. This means that the highest resolution they can provide is fixed. But with *resolution independent* systems, the resolution is not fixed. Also, whether a system is resolution dependent or independent is an issue that must take into account the system's ability to achieve a play rate of 24, 25, or 29.97 fps in real time. Thus, in determining what resolution a system provides, these are the important questions:

1. Is the resolution fixed at a specific capture size in order to ensure real-time play of 24, 25, and 29.97 fps? For example, is the system capable of capturing ITU-R 601 video at its highest resolution and ensuring that a play rate of 29.97 fps can be achieved? If so, then the system is resolution dependent at ITU-R 601 picture quality.
2. Is the resolution *scaleable*? That is, can the system scale its resolution and still provide real-time play rates? In this scenario, let's say that we have a resolution-dependent system whose maximum real-time play capability is at ITU-R 601 resolution and that we have enough disk storage to hold 15 minutes of footage. Next, let's say that we have a project that requires 30 minutes of storage. With a system that offers scaleable resolution, we can choose a resolution that will facilitate storing the 30 minutes.
3. In a resolution-independent system, we can work at any resolution we desire. For example, let's say that we are creating a special visual effect that contains extensive compositing for a commercial for television broadcast. We also want to

Figure 6-19 Domino is an integrated effects and compositing system that operates at 2K×2K resolution. Courtesy Quantel Corporation.

take this special effect and put it into a film. Finally, we want to include a still from this special effect for a magazine cover. Each of these requirements is best served by a system that offers resolution independency. The television commercial can be finished at uncompressed, ITU-R 601 resolution. But the film elements need to be at a greater resolution, approximately five times greater resolution. With resolution independency, we can scale up the resolution by directing the system to change its resolution from ITU-R 601 to 35mm Academy film resolution. Print advertising is even more demanding: For the creation of fine details on plates used for printing currency, 25,000 lines of resolution may be required!

Increasing Resolution May Affect Real-Time Playback

As we increase resolution, we may lose the ability to play back the images in real time. For example, DNLE uncompressed systems that provide resolution independency may not be able to play back the images past a certain resolution. When the image size, and consequently the data rate, increases on a resolution-independent system that normally can guarantee real-time playback of D1 images, the playback speed can well be a fraction of real time; perhaps the best that the system can provide is 10 to 15 fps.

For many years, professionals working in the digital postproduction industry processing film images waited for the appearance of DNLE and compositing systems that could play back film-resolution material sampled at 2K×2K, that is, 2000 lines horizontal×2000 lines vertical (Figure 6-19). By mid-1997, such systems appeared. Of course, they consume disk storage at a staggering rate (approximately 1.2 GB/sec), but the ability to play film-resolution images in real time was an important breakthrough in providing professionals with the ability to interact better during the creation process. Resolution-independent systems include Avid's Illusion, Kodak's Cineon, and Discreet Logic's Inferno.

Many desktop applications, such as those covered in Chapter 7, also offer resolution independency. It is only the playback capability of the underlying hardware that determines how fast we can see frame after frame as the images are played back.

DIGITAL NONLINEAR ONLINE ARRIVES IN THE BROADCASTING ENVIRONMENT

An all-digital broadcasting facility incorporates digital acquisition, digital nonlinear editing, and digital playback of images directly from the DNLE system's disk drives. In much the same way that the arrival of videotape halted the use of 16mm film,

Figure 6-20 Ikegami's Editcam, with Transport Technology created by Avid Technology, records its signals not onto videotape but directly onto a removable hard disk that is then removed and accessed by the DNLE system. Courtesy Avid Technology.

digital disk technology will gradually and inexorably supplant the use of videotape in the broadcasting industry.

Even signal acquisition, in the form of cameras and the recording technology they employ, is migrating to digital technology. In broadcasting, news events were originally recorded on 16mm film, then on 3/4" Umatic videotape, and then on Betacam and Betacam SP. In 1995, a digital disk-based camera was introduced (Figure 6-20). Instead of recording images and sound onto videotape, the signals were recorded onto a 2.5" magnetic disk with a capacity of 2.4 GB. The decrease in size and increase in capacity of disk technology is chiefly responsible for being able to create such a system having the necessary size and weight dimensions that field videographers were accustomed to using.

Further, this digital M-JPEG-based image capture negates the requirement to digitize prior to editing. Instead, the digital disk pack is simply removed from the camera in the same way that a Betacam videotape is removed and put into a playback deck. The digitized images and sounds are then instantly available to the DNLE system.

The Rise of Temporary Field Digital Networks for Broadcasting

An in-depth discussion of computer and video networking technologies is found in Chapter 12. It is clear that as streets and cities across the world become wired with more advanced technologies, the amount of data that can be transmitted from the field to the broadcasting station will be increased.

Digital camera acquisition, editing on a compact DNLE system in the field, and sending the digital material to the news station through a plug-in ATM (asynchronous transfer mode) network found in the street could represent a new age of television news gathering and broadcasting. Imagine if we were trying to get footage of a fire but could not easily drive a broadcasting van (equipped with transmitter) into the area. Instead, we carry a digital disk-based camera into the area, digitally record the material, and plug the camera's output into an ATM network. Because the camera has an Internet Protocol (IP) address, it can be addressed by computers at the television station (each computer that has access to the Internet also has an IP address, regardless of whether it is a Web server or not), and material directly from the camera can be sent over the ATM line. If the line provides the required throughput, the images can be sent in real time.

Browsing, Editing, and Airing: From Journalist to Transmitter

Digital nonlinear technology is also assisting in the transformation of the broadcasting environment at a very basic level—the journalist's desk. Figure 6-21 shows the workflow that becomes

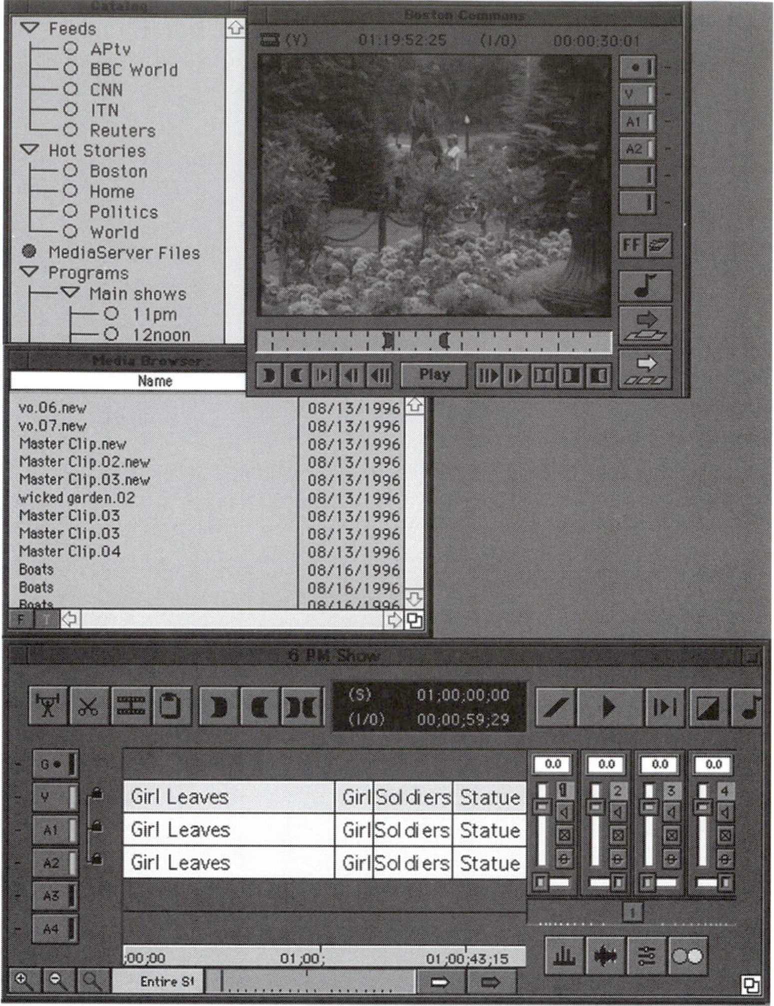

Figure 6-21 A media-serving scenario in a broadcast facility where journalists and editors are able to enter search criteria and then browse and edit the resulting footage. Courtesy Avid Technology.

possible in a digital nonlinear broadcast station. Here, the journalist is able to browse a central server that contains all the footage for a specific story on which the journalist is working. The server contains two versions of the files, at low and at high resolution. The journalist defines a search via the asset management software and is able to see thumbnail picture representations of all the footage that matches the search conditions. The images that the journalist browses have been stored to the server in MPEG (either MPEG 1 or MPEG 2) format to facilitate keeping large amounts of material available.

The journalist station consists of a more simplified DNLE interface, designed to let the journalist mix the text of the story being written with the pictures and sounds that are stored on the server. It's important to note that the journalist does not have to copy, or pull, the MPEG files from the server to a local disk. Instead, they can be played in real time over network lines that connect the journalist's station to the central server.

Once the journalist puts the story together, the sequence and the pointers it contains are electronically sent to either the DNLE station, where a professional editor then hones and finalizes the program, or directly to the playback station and the air. When either of these two options is chosen, the edited sequence's links to the lower-resolution MPEG files are broken, and new links are established to the high-resolution files that are already stored on the server.

THE TRANSFORMATION: WILL LINEAR ONLINE EDITING DISAPPEAR?

In the third wave, DNLE systems established themselves as the rightful heirs to the offline editing process. In the fourth wave, DNLE offline systems provide the tools and the digital video compression ratios that are necessary to finish programs that third-wave systems could not address. Naturally enough, fourth-wave systems will come to be known as DNLE Finishing Systems, in which material is loaded into the system, is edited, and exits in finished form.

An intriguing question is whether linear online suites will disappear and be replaced by digital nonlinear technology. In comparing DNLE systems and capabilities versus linear online suites, it is clear that the software capabilities of DNLE systems far outweigh those that can be found in the traditional online room.

Hybrid Systems: Linear and Nonlinear Editing Combined

Hybrid systems combine linear videotape machines, digital disk recorders, and DNLE systems. The main reason that hybrid systems were developed was to utilize the equipment already found in a conventional online suite and combine it with the capabilities of digital nonlinear editing. Hybrid systems usually have advantages in two areas: due to the presence of multiple videotape playback machines, more real-time streams are available; in addition, the video switcher allows for the complex compositing of images. Both of these advantages are also available on DNLE systems, but there may be a limit as to how many streams and how many effects can be handled in real time. Figure 6-22 is an example of a hybrid system that uses both A/B roll linear videotape capability as well as nonlinear disk-based capability.

Figure 6-22 Video Machine, a hybrid system that offers a combination of linear and nonlinear support. Courtesy Fast Electronic.

New Need for the Online Room

There will still be, however, a work scenario based on beginning in a DNLE system and finishing in a traditional online room. In the 1970s, 2" Quadruplex videotape was the standard for postproduction; in the 1980s, it was 1" videotape, and by the 1990s, half a dozen different tape formats vied for dominance. Yet, through the mid 1990s, the highest picture quality was based, for all intents and purposes, on the requirements of the broadcasting world—namely, ITU-R 601 picture quality with uncompressed images at a pixel matrix of 720×486 (NTSC).

But broadcasting picture quality is no longer limited to an ITU-R 601 sampling matrix. By 1997, with the standardization of high-definition television (HDTV), resolution in excess of ITU-R 601 became a reality. There is a wide variety of different sampling matrices, each patterned for specific use. Some of the different aspect ratios and matrices are defined below.

ITU-R 601

With an aspect ratio of 4:3 (horizontal to vertical units) and a pixel matrix of 720×486 (NTSC) and 8 bits per component, 22 MB/sec are required to sustain this picture quality.

Digital Television

In 1997, the Federal Communications Commission (FCC) created 1600 licenses for digital television (DTV) channels for each television station in the United States. The Advanced Television Standards Committee (ATSC) was originally concerned with preparing and developing a standard for advanced television (ATV), which was planned to be analog in nature. Over the course of deliberations, this requirement was changed to a proposal for the development of a digital television standard. This standard uses MPEG-2 video compression and Dolby AC-3 audio compression.

It is important to note that there are several possible combinations that fall under the realm of the term *digital television*. For example, high-definition television (HDTV) is simply the most intensive form of DTV. Table 6-1 lists some, but not all, of the pixel matrices that are within the domain of

Table 6-1 Digital Television Signals

Horizontal Pixels	*Vertical Lines*	*Aspect Ratio*	*Frame Rate**
1920	1080	16:9	30I, 30P, 24P
1280	720	16:9	60P, 30P, 24P
720 (704)	480	16:9	30I, 60P, 30P, 24P
720 (704)	480	4:3	30I, 60P, 30P, 24P
640	480	4:3	30I, 60P, 30P, 24P

**I* refers to interlaced scanning; *P* refers to progressive scanning.
Source: ATSC Digital Television Standard, September, 1995.

DTV signals. Note that not all DTV signals are high definition in nature. For example, a 704×480 pixel matrix with an aspect ratio of 16:9 at 30 fps (interlaced) would fall into the category of standard-definition television (SDTV).

The rise of digital television will place new requirements on the online room, which, heretofore relegated to ITU-R 601 editing, will grow in capability to allow for the editing of DTV and HDTV images. When one considers that an HDTV frame sampled at 1920×1080 pixels requires approximately 4 MB/frame (7 GB/min), it is clear that a great deal of computer storage is necessary to store only several minutes of HDTV-resolution video.

THE NEW STATUS QUO

DNLE systems, naturally, will continue to improve in terms of the picture quality that they offer. Although uncompressed ITU-R 601 picture quality requires approximately 22 MB/sec, DNLE computer subsystems that can support multiple streams of ITU-R 601 can be offered—by the mid 1990s, computers that supported a data transfer rate of 600 MB/sec were available. With the correct complement of disk drives, multiple streams of uncompressed ITU-R 601 video can be made available in a completely digital nonlinear environment.

Editing in HDTV or in an Intermediate Level?

Moving up in picture quality, let's assume that we want to be able to play, in real time, HDTV signals sampled at 1920×1080, interlaced. This equates to approximately 120 MB/sec that must be supported. And although these signals require massive amounts of storage, the computer bus and disk drive transfer rates necessary to sustain these signals are available without sacrificing real-time 30 fps playback.

In addition, it is likely that there will be instances of editing HDTV images in an intermediate level, that is, a subsampled pixel matrix of the 1920×1080 I format.

Television and Other Data

With NTSC television, an analog signal is passed down a 6 MHz channel. However, an SDTV signal would occupy only a fraction of this same channel. Therefore, additional digital data can be sent down the remaining bandwidth. This is perhaps the most interesting development in the migration from analog to digital television. Interactive content, of course, is a natural candidate to be provided on this additional bandwidth. For example, we could find ourselves watching a television program, and if there were a story that we were particularly interested in, we would be able to find out a great deal more about the "backstory"—related material with text, graphics, and so forth. Clearly, what we have heretofore perceived as "the television experience" will be radically changed forever.

METAMORPHOSIS

DNLE systems have the capability of metamorphosing, which is perhaps their greatest strength. Because of this, they have the unique ability of offering increased capabilities through software-intensive methods. Integrating features such as electronic paint capability, character generator, animation files, digital video effects, and so on, results in an editing system that has grown into something much more than just an editing system.

The fourth wave of digital nonlinear editing is characterized by the realization of DNLE online, where programming is begun and finished directly on the DNLE system. Significant changes in the manner in which projects enter the production stage and exit the postproduction stage will result. This fourth wave will lead to the fifth wave, characterized by intraframe editing and resolution independency (Chapter 8).

TALKING WITH EDITORS

What tools were developed in DNLE systems that promoted their rapid growth? Can it be attributed to the improvement in picture quality?

Joe Beirne

Picture quality is the most generally over-rated index of quality in DNLE systems: The ability to manipulate the media with ease is by far a more important reason that this technology changed the post world. I think very important capabilities introduced by DNLEs were (a) working in digital space, which increased the ability to deal directly with other computer-based media (that is, digital audio and graphics), (b) Undo and, obviously, version control was a huge factor, (c) preview of optical effects, and (d) although still primitive, the ability to deal with media as a database was important.

Peter Cohen

Picture quality was certainly a factor in the growth of DNLE systems, but for me as an editor, the functionality is more crucial. The ability to massage a cut has never been this easy and clean before. The synching abilities for Multicam and the use of alternate codes has greatly increased the speed of certain types of editing. The informational database that is created gives me faster and easier access to all of my source material. These tools are what make DNL editing a better way to edit.

Alan Miller

Picture quality was obviously important, but DNLE was great when the pictures weren't. It was being able to try ideas with no penalty. The advent of more than two or four audio tracks led to many more possibilities for intricate mixing that used to take a separate sound session. Basically, it wasn't necessary to imagine what you would do online. It was all possible offline. Plus, the price was affordable.

Scott Ogden

Truly, picture quality was the most important first step to widespread acceptance of nonlinear systems in the post industry. But several other factors were very helpful:

1. The timeline approach to cutting. Being able to see a cut in its entirety as a visual representation of a sequence and to be able to manipulate the cuts in a sequence by use of the timeline.
2. Real-time effects. Editors and producers have no creative patience these days (nonlinear editing helped promote this). So as more and more effects can be done in real time, the more critical nonlinear systems became.
3. Four or more channels of audio and CD sound quality. This has allowed the sound of spots to be very dynamic. My mixes are so much more complicated these days. I often cut my music in stereo. I'm sure that this factor alone helps sell spots.

Basil Pappas

Picture quality is a big factor, but the development of the user interface to emulate all common editing situations, along with ease of use of the Macintosh platform, made growth inevitable. The first years of DNLE were unusually successful due to clean edit decision lists and film cutlists, in a variety of formats. The ability for tape-based shows to suddenly eliminate generation loss, and filmlike editing features such as trimming and extracting, made it the obvious choice for highly creative editorial.

Tom Poederbach

The picture quality did help a lot. I do not think that most of the early buyers realized or had the vision of what the potential power of such systems would be, once migrated to computers.

7

The Desktop Applications Explosion

By the early 1990s, affordable personal computers were becoming readily available, were decreasing in price, and were increasing in computing power. Table 7-1 shows the increase in clock speed on the Apple Macintosh computer platform.

In late 1997, 500 MHz to 1 GHz (gigahertz) processing power on Apple and Windows NT desktop platforms at a cost of only a few thousand dollars greatly enabled the growth of desktop applications.

Table 7-1 Increase in Macintosh Computing Power

Model	*Date*	*Clock Speed*
Mac IIFX	1990	40 MHz
Quadra 900	1993	33 MHz
Quadra 950	1994	66 MHz
PowerMac 8100	1995	120 MHz
PowerPCI 9500	1996	200 MHz
PowerPCI 9600	1997	233 MHz
PowerPCI 9600	1998	350 MHz

DESKTOP APPLICATIONS: IS HARDWARE ALWAYS NECESSARY?

As we know from previous chapters, software is the key component defining the capabilities of the DNLE system. True, the hardware component is important, but it is not always necessary. For example, if we want to digitize audio signals, we will find that some DNLE systems employ add-in audio cards to accomplish this task. However, increasingly, computers are shipping directly from the manufacturer with built-in audio digitizing and playback capability, thus eliminating the need for add-in boards.

Figure 7-1 shows an example of this trend: the interface of a real-time MPEG audio compression software program that operates entirely in software within the Pentium Processor environment. Previously, this encoding process would have required a hardware interface card, or would have taken longer than real time if accomplished with software-only methods. However, as a result of faster CPU operating speeds and optimized software, the encoding can be done in real time.

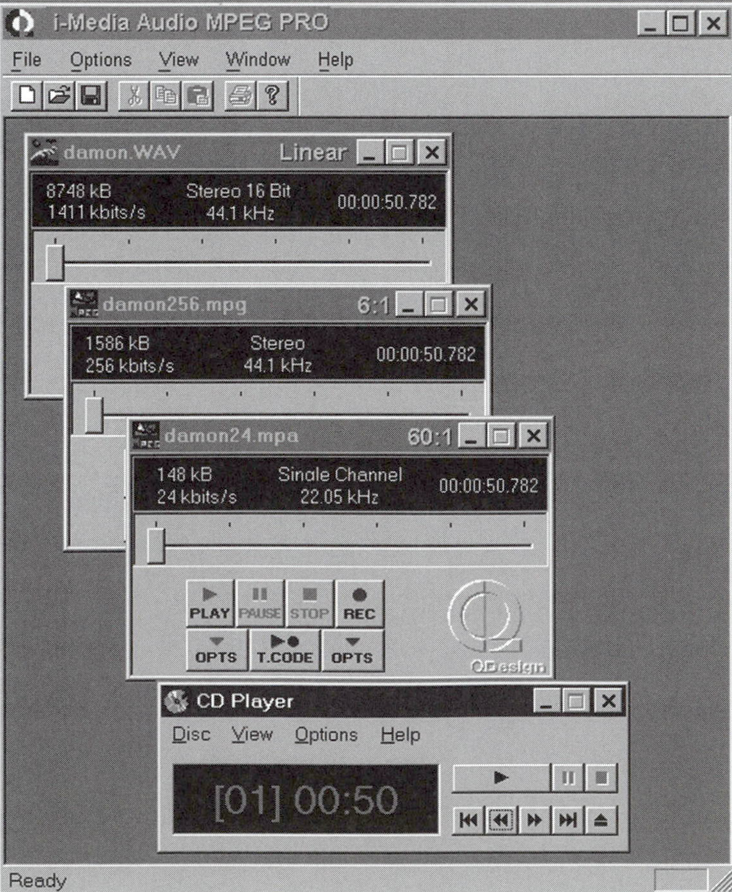

Figure 7-1 A real-time MPEG audio compression program based on the MPEG audio coding algorithm, i-Media Audio provides studio-quality encoding using the processing power of a standard Pentium PC. Courtesy QDesign Corporation.

When the Processing Power Increases, More Things Can Happen in Real Time

Consider what happens when we have two audio channels that we want to crossfade together. Normally, DNLE systems will handle this task in two ways: some systems can actually perform the task in real time through the use of the add-in audio card that is able to quickly compute the result of the two channels combined together. Other systems cannot play this effect in real time and must first render the effect before we can hear the result.

However, as the operating speed of CPUs becomes faster and faster, we will find that many tasks that required add-in accelerator boards to create the effect in real time will no longer need them, nor will it be necessary to first render the effect. Instead, the CPU, operating at a fast enough speed, will just play the effect and render it on the fly.

THE DESKTOP SYSTEM LOOKS SIMPLE BUT IS VERY POWERFUL

A desktop applications system can be defined as consisting of a personal computer, perhaps some add-in cards, software, local or shared storage, and a network. The type of work that can be accomplished on these desktop systems rivals that of supercomputers used only a few years earlier. The cost difference, as one would suspect, is equally astounding—it's possible to accomplish on a $15,000 system what previously would have cost at least ten times that amount!

Linking Multiple, Low-Cost CPUs Together and Using Multiprocessing and Multithreading

In Chapter 6, the concepts of multiprocessing and multithreading were introduced. To recap, multiprocessing is the ability to use multiple processors contained either in one CPU or over many different CPUs to simultaneously run the processes that a file requires. Multithreading allows us to run different processes on the same file simultaneously without waiting for one process to finish before the next process can begin.

Imagine that you have a digitized video file where you see a skyline, a boat, and an ocean. You first want to blur some of the sky and colorize it a deeper blue. Next, you want to add some reflections of the boat in the water. Last, you want to add some sun rays to one of the ship's sails. Using different computer applications, you would normally begin with the blurring effect, moving on to the other effects when the first effect was completed. Remember, depending on how complex the effects are, they may require very long rendering times.

However, now imagine that you have created a work environment in which you have linked together four low-cost computers, each with four very fast 500 MHz processors. You have at your disposal approximately 8 GHz of processing power (some will be required by the various operating systems). This, coupled with software that can take advantage of multiprocessing and multi-threading, will result in a radical speed-up of the transforms that you require. The result: less time waiting to both previsualize and finalize the effect you want.

Resolution Independent, not Resolution Dependent

A DNLE system whose highest resolution is at ITU-R 601 is a *resolution-dependent* system. If we wanted to work with pictures that are in excess of that resolution, the system would not provide for our needs.

Resolution-independent systems, however, allow us to work at whatever resolution we desire. For example, let's take our previous example of the beach scene. We could desire to scan this material not from video at ITU-R 601 resolution, but instead, from 35mm film at a resolution at least 40 times greater.

Software that is resolution independent allows us to determine the size and resolution of images with which we want to work. We could use a desktop painting program to create a graphic for television at ITU-R 601 resolution, or we could use the same program to create a design that will be used to make the metal plates for printing currency—at 25,000 lines of vertical resolution.

Technological Improvements Fostered the Desktop Applications Boom

When we begin to think about multiple, low-cost parallel processing computers; multiprocessing, multithreading applications; and resolution independency, it becomes clear that there is something important afoot in the adoption and creation of desktop editing, effects, and graphics. These technological trends are the reason why the desktop applications boom began in the mid-1990s. There are many different types of applications that one finds operating at this high level on the desktop. Among them are applications for the following purposes:

Painting
Compositing
Titling
3D animation

Each of these categories previously fell under the realm of dedicated computers that were designed specifically to do titling, painting, or 3D effects. Consider the videotape online room, in which there is most likely a dedicated system for manipulating ITU-R 601 video in 3D in real time. However, as should be evident now, the processing power of CPUs and sophisticated software is developing so rapidly that what was once the key benefit of dedicated systems—that they could function in real time without requiring rendering—is an advantage that is disappearing.

In no way should we equate low-cost desktop systems with quality or performance inferior to dedicated systems. Indeed, there is virtually nothing that cannot be accomplished in software. Contrast this with a dedicated system's capability, which is highly dependent on the underlying hardware. Desktop systems, on the other hand, have limitless growth due to the ever-changing nature of the software that powers them.

LOW-COST, HIGH-PERFORMANCE DIGITAL VIDEO FORMATS

We are probably all familiar with the significant growth that hand-held camcorders have enjoyed in the consumer marketplace. These small video cameras capture surprisingly good-quality video and audio, using Hi8 videotape. Professionals in the broadcast industry used Hi8 cameras to capture video, especially in locations where it was either too difficult or too obvious to use larger and higher-quality cameras. At the same time, however, professionals did not use Hi8 in the postproduction sector due to its inferior images in relation to Betacam SP and, later, Digital Betacam.

While the use of desktop applications increased, by mid-1997, CPUs began to ship directly from manufacturer to consumer with built-in audio and video digitizing capability along with powerful video and audio editing software. Having a consumer video camera that could feed directly into the CPU to transfer video was highly desirable.

In parallel, the broadcast and postproduction industries could benefit from a low-cost, highly portable, high-quality video format. Format changes in these industries is, of course, nothing new, as formats tend to change quite rapidly. However, with the development and introduction of various digital video (DV) formats, a flood of activity ensued.

WHAT IS DV?

A DV camera captures information by taking light into a three-chip lens, one chip each for red, green, and blue component. These signals, in turn, are converted into electrical signals by a charged-coupled device (CCD). Normally, the RGB color space signals are converted to YUV but differ from the ITU-R 601 format in that the sampling resolution is lower.

One of the characteristics of DV is that its signals are stored to digital video cassette (DVC), with a width of 6.35 millimeters. As opposed to the portable component analog or digital tape formats used by professional videographers in the broadcasting industry, who must change a tape after every 20 to 40 minutes, DV cassettes can provide at least one to two hours of recording time (Figure 7-2).

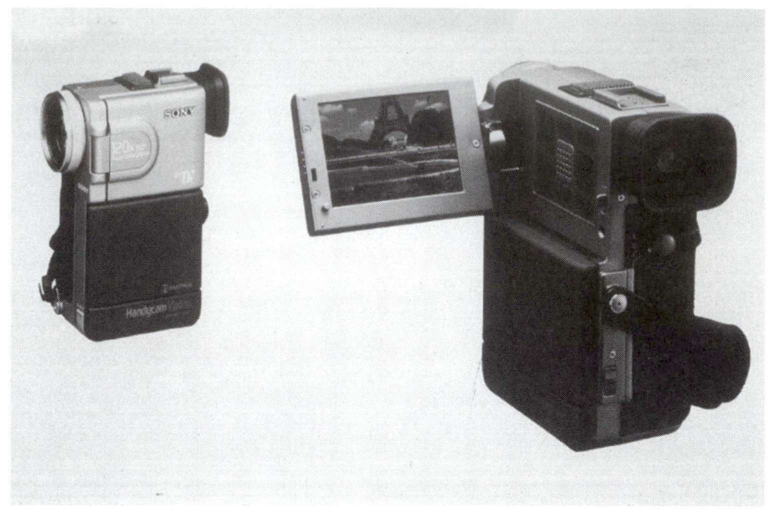

Figure 7-2 The Sony DCR-PC7 DVC camera. Courtesy Sony Electronics, Inc.

In order to reduce the data rate of digital video, YUV is sampled at 4:1:1 (NTSC) and 4:2:0 (PAL). 4:1:1 sampling decreases the required data rate by approximately one-half, to 15 MB/sec.

At this stage, hardware-based intraframe compression (the same methodology employed by M-JPEG) is used. A 5:1 compression ratio reduces the data rate to about 3 MB/sec. *Adaptive motion* compression techniques are also employed when there is a great deal of movement from frame to frame. In such a case, each field is individually compressed, and multiple quantization tables (see Chapter 10) may be used. One of the major benefits of this standardized way of compressing the DV signal is that we always know the data rate that will be required of the playback mechanism.

DV Audio: High Quality, Multichannel

DV, despite its small tape size, provides for high-quality, multichannel audio. Two channels of 44.1 KHz or 48 KHz audio can be recorded. If the user desires more audio channels, DV allows the sampling rate to be lowered to 32 KHz, and four audio channels can then be recorded.

Total Data Rates

When the data rates of DV's video and audio are combined, the total figure is approximately 5.1 MB/sec or 25 Mbits/sec. This makes DV extremely easy to incorporate into industry and consumer uses of digital video. At 5.1 MB/sec, storing a half-hour of DV video requires one 9 GB disk. If we employ a desktop DNLE system that further introduces compression, we may find that a 1 GB disk, which is usually the minimum found on mass-market computers, can hold up to one hour of video and audio.

DV and Its Variants: The Professional Formats

There are several variations of DV, introduced by two large manufacturers of digital video equipment: Panasonic and Sony Corporations. Among them are the following formats:

DVCPRO Introduced by Panasonic, this format adds both analog cue and control tracks. The cue track can be used to hear audio when the tape is being shuttled. It has been formally submitted to be recognized as D7 by the Society of Motion Picture and Television Engineers (SMPTE).

DVCAM Introduced by Sony, this format uses a slightly larger tape width, and inside each tape cartridge is a memory chip that is used to store small thumbnails each time the camera is started. Figure 7-3 shows the DSR-85, a DVCAM recording unit from Sony Corporation.

Sampling Rates of DV Formats

For news and field acquisition, the 4:1:1 sampling rate of DV is perfectly adequate, but, as mentioned earlier, for postproduction and especially in cases in which multilayered compositing is necessary, this sampling rate has been deemed to be inadequate.

Approximately one year after DV began to make a substantial appearance in the broadcasting industry, 4:2:2 versions became available from major manufacturers. These versions, which increase the data rate from 25 Mbits/sec to 50 Mbits/sec, have relatively quickly removed many of the objections professionals had to digital video.

Any chart of videotape formats is most likely to be out of date in a short time period. However, from a historical perspective, it is interesting to note the various sampling rates of the different DV formats, especially in relation to more traditional digital videotape formats (Table 7-2).

It should be noted that DV formats will certainly be used for more postproduction applications in the future, especially as variations with mild and lossless compression are introduced. In addition to 25 and 50 Mbits/sec versions of DV, there will most likely be a 100 Mbits/sec version, and perhaps data rates beyond that as well.

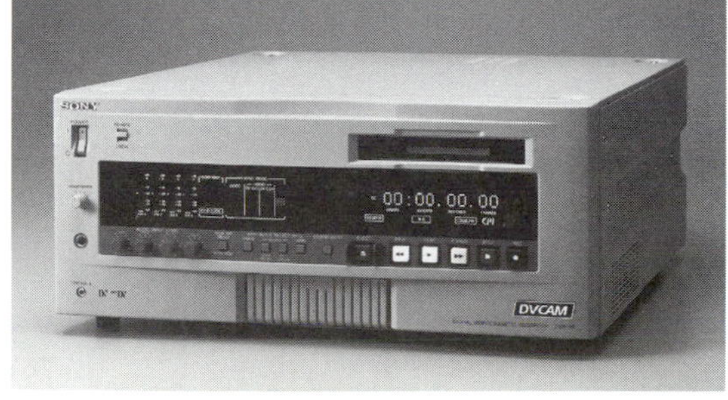

Figure 7-3 The DSR-85, a DVCAM recording unit from Sony Corporation. Courtesy Sony Corporation.

Faster than Real-Time Transfers to the DNLE System: No Digitization Stage

One of the characteristics of editing with DV-native video and audio files is that the digitization stage is completely bypassed. Since we are capturing our video and audio content with a DV camera, the material is already, in essence, being digitized. As long as we use a DV-native DNLE system, the digital files that exist on the digital video cassette can be brought into the DNLE system and editing can begin immediately.

Table 7-2 DV Sampling Rates

Format	*Bits/ Component*	*Sampling*	*Compression*
Betacam SX	8 bits	4:2:2	0:1 interframe
D1	10 bits	4:2:2:4	Uncompressed
D5	10 bits	4:2:2:4	Uncompressed
DV	8 bits	4:1:1	5:1 intraframe
DVCAM	8 bits	4:1:1	5:1 intraframe
DVCPRO	8 bits	4:1:1	5:1 intraframe
DVCPRO 50	8 bits	4:2:2	3.3:1 intraframe
Digital-S	8 bits	4:2:2	3.3:1 intraframe
Digital Betacam	10 bits	4:2:2	1.77:1 intraframe

Most important, the process of transferring the DV files from cassette to the DNLE's disk storage system does not have to be a real-time process. Under certain circumstances, a transfer four times faster than real time can occur (that is, transferring four minutes of footage would take only one minute) because what is being done is akin to a computer file transfer as opposed to a real-time digitization of picture and sound files. Obviously, being able to immediately start editing without first having to undergo the digitization process, while also transferring material from tape to disk in faster than real time, is a great advantage that DV affords to the user.

THE IMPACT OF FIREWIRE

FireWire, also known as IEEE (Institute of Electrical and Electronics Engineers) 1394, was developed by Apple Computer and is a standardized method for high-speed connections among a wide variety of professional and "pro-sumer" equipment.

Figure 7-4 An example of a FireWire-capable chip developed by Adaptec, Inc. Courtesy Adaptec, Inc.

In its initial incarnation, FireWire provided data transfer rates of between 100 to 400 Mbits/sec, but its standard provides for transfer rates in excess of 2 Gbits/sec. In addition, multiple FireWire controller cards can be used simultaneously to increase the data transfer rate. Figure 7-4 shows the AIC-5800, a FireWire-capable chip developed by Adaptec, Inc. Figure 7-5 shows a FireWire adapter card, ready for computer installation.

There are additional characteristics of FireWire that make it most interesting. For example, unlike SCSI (small computer system interface) with its very thick cabling and limited overall distance, FireWire consists of a single wire that is highly flexible, offering a connection that resembles a simple telephone jack.

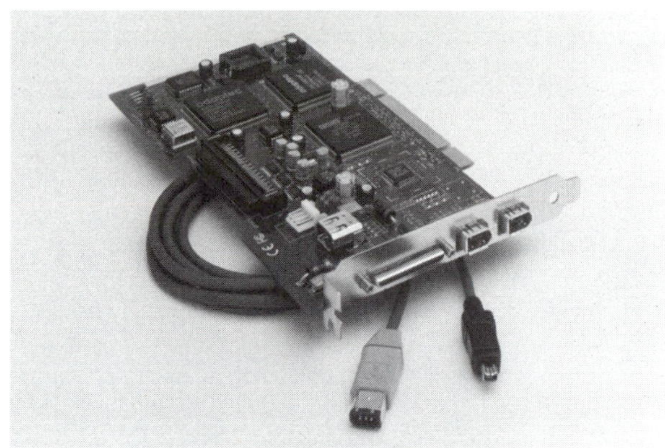

Figure 7-5 A FireWire adapter card, ready for computer installation. Courtesy Adaptec, Inc.

The FireWire standard supports 63 devices on a single FireWire port, and multiple FireWire ports can operate in parallel. In addition, whereas SCSI requires each device (for example, scanner, hard disk, or optical disc) to have a unique address that cannot conflict with another device, FireWire operates based on self-initialization when the device is connected.

FireWire and the Home DNLE System

For consumer electronics, FireWire is very exciting because different consumer machines can be interconnected and controlled by a FireWire-capable computer. This is especially important as DNLE systems enter the consumer marketplace. For example, as the use of small DV camcorders increases, DNLE systems will be more widely used in the home. These extremely portable cameras offer excellent picture quality, and some units offer 500 lines of resolution with a very high signal-to-noise ratio. As a result, consumer camcorder quality rivals that of professional broadcasting Betacam units.

Figure 7-6 shows the basic components of a FireWire-based editing system: computer, FireWire adapter card and cabling, and hand-held digital video camera.

Figure 7-6 The basic components of a FireWire-based editing system: computer, FireWire adapter card and cabling, and hand-held digital video camera. Courtesy Adaptec, Inc.

DIGITAL NONLINEAR EDITING AND THE HOME AND BUSINESS USER

Most home computers in the early 1990s came equipped with built-in analog and video I/O ports for the digitization of video and audio signals. With the advent of FireWire (as well as lesser adopted alternatives), however, transferring a consumer camera's digital video and audio signals directly into the home computer via an all-digital path becomes very easy to accomplish.

Further, it is only natural to assume that computer manufacturers will create partnerships with DNLE manufacturers so that DNLE software is included within the home computer. As a result, hundreds of thousands of consumers will have the ability to make an easy connection of camcorder to computer while using extremely easy-to-use, intuitive DNLE software.

One such example of consumer-oriented DNLE software is Avid Cinema, whose various user interfaces are shown in Figures 7-7 and 7-8. Notice the streamlined interface and the user-oriented index card motifs, which are designed to provide only the necessary tools to the user.

QUICKTIME

QuickTime was developed by Apple Computer and is a standard for the creation and playback of video, audio, graphics, and textual information, the form of which is generally known as a QuickTime "movie." QuickTime is unique in that it is capable of delivering motion video without the use of video and audio add-in cards. QuickTime was developed not only for Apple computers (QuickTime for Mac) but also for PC-based systems (QuickTime for Windows).

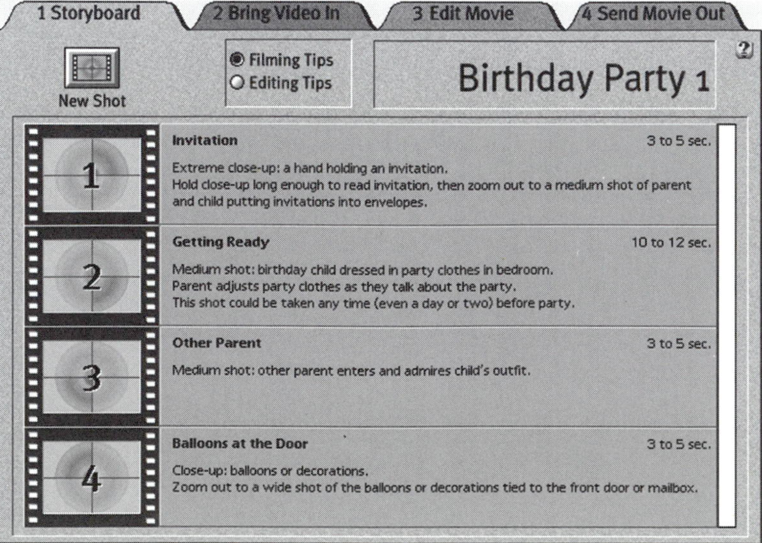

Figure 7-7 The consumer-oriented DNLE software, Avid Cinema. Courtesy Avid Technology.

Figure 7-8 Avid Cinema's user interface.

For example, let's say that we receive an e-mail message from a relative who has taken some footage with a DV-based camcorder and then edited a few minutes within a DV-native DNLE software package. This program can be exported into a QuickTime movie and, using only a software QuickTime codec (compressor/decompressor) loaded into the home computer's operating system, the movie can be played back with all its video, audio, graphics, and text. Depending upon the CPU's processing speed, the movie may be limited in its playback capabilities. For example, it may not be possible to view the movie at a pixel matrix of 640×480 or 720×486 and at 30 fps. Instead, we may have to view the movie at 320×240 and at 15 fps. After placing a QuickTime accelerator board in the CPU, we would be able to achieve full-screen, full-motion playback. As CPU processing power increases, however, full-screen, full-motion QuickTime movies without any additional hardware support will become the norm.

Along with consumer-friendly DNLE software, editing on the desktop—at home, and with professional-quality video and audio—will result in millions of individuals editing and crafting their camcorder-originated footage into finished programs. Some of these programs will be seen on traditional over-the-air television, while the Internet will play host to much of this programming.

QUICKTIME VR

QuickTime VR (virtual reality) is a variation of QuickTime that allows the user to view a movie that is not limited to 2D space. With QuickTime VR (QTVR), a series of still images is seamlessly woven together, allowing the user to pan and tilt around the scene in 360 degrees. Figure 7-9 shows a series of frames from a QTVR movie. Note how it is possible to pan around the image in order to obtain the same perspective that we would get if we were looking at the location with our own eyes.

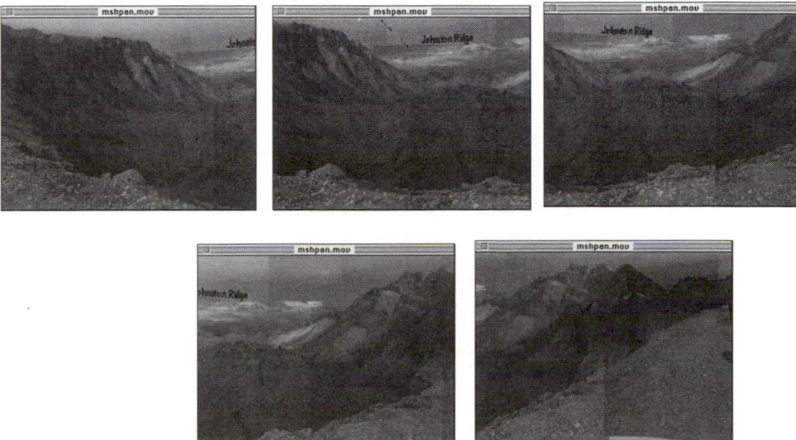

Figure 7-9 This series of frames shows the result of a QTVR movie, where the user can determine the motion and view. This QTVR movie was created by Brad Klein, who carried a Macintosh Powerbook and an Apple QuickTake camera during a climb up Mount Saint Helens. Mr. Klein shot 75 images to document the climb and created the panorama by patching 20 digital photos together using Adobe Photoshop. The 20×5-inch digital image was then converted into a QTVR movie using the Make QTVR Panorama application. Note how the images show how the user has panned around Mount Saint Helens. Courtesy Brad Klein and VolcanoWorld.

Figure 7-10 Creating a QTVR movie. A series of photos is taken at 30-degree angles. While edge-to-edge placement results in overlap, QTVR warps the images and matches the seams. This results in a warping of the combined image. Finally, when the QTVR movie is opened, the distortion is corrected. Courtesy Apple Computer.

Creating a QTVR movie can be done by using images taken from stills or from motion video. Generally, a scene will be photographed with a relatively wide-angle lens. After each exposure, the camera is panned slightly, and another photograph is taken. These photos are then digitized and are overlapped into what appears to be a continuously panning shot. QTVR must slightly warp these individual images in order to seamlessly blend the edges of each individual frame (Figure 7-10).

The result is that the user can now control the panning and tilting of the QTVR movie in order to observe the scene in a highly interactive fashion. As CPU power develops, real-time QTVR full-screen playback, at varying resolutions, becomes possible.

ACTIVEMOVIE

For PC users (PCs are categorized as those which utilize Microsoft Corporation's operating system, or OS, as opposed to

Color Figure 1 Originating material on either film or video, editing on a DNLE system, and finishing using the direct output of the disk drives. Illustration by Jeffrey Krebs.

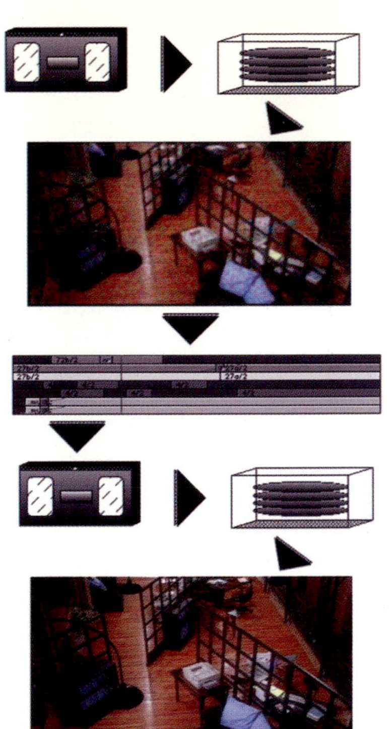

Color Figure 2 The batch redigitization process begins with using the DNLE system as an offline system, and then redigitizing picture at a higher picture quality in order to finish the program directly from disk.

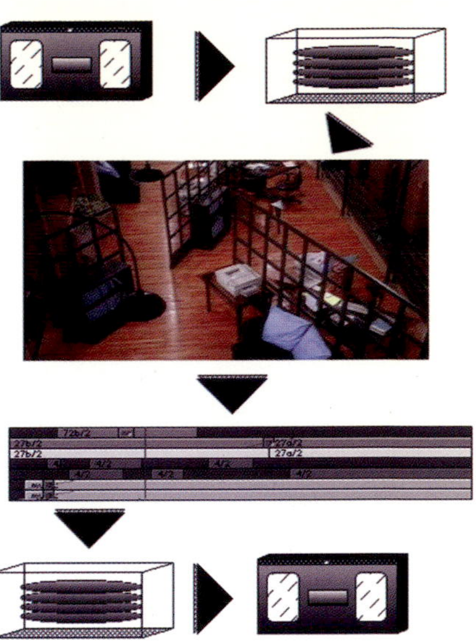

Color Figure 3 In a digitize-once scenario, original footage is digitized at a high picture resolution, editing is done, and the finished program is recorded directly from disk to tape.

Color Figure 4 Frame-based effects are those that are applied to a single frame of a shot and then must be applied to all successive frames that make up the shot. Shown here is the original frame (top) and the tinted frame (bottom). Footage courtesy Fox Point Films.

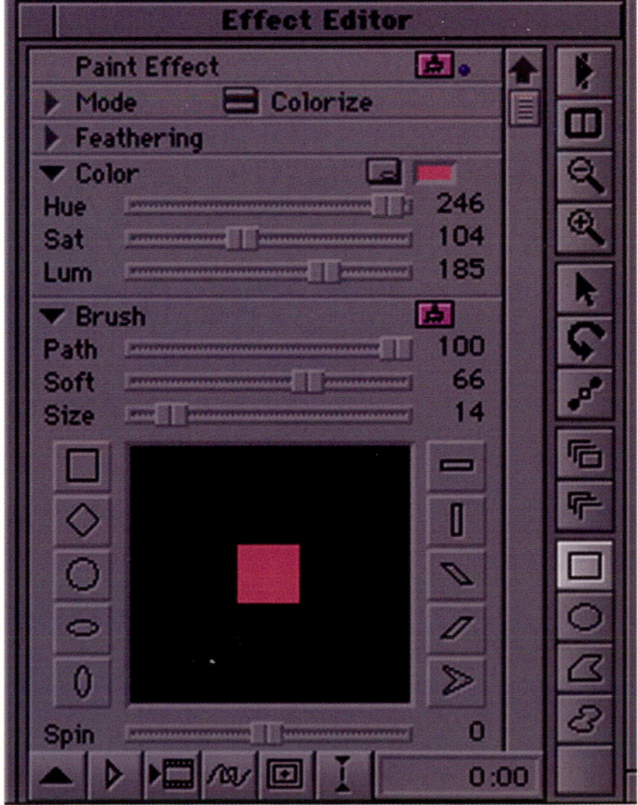

Color Figure 5 Using the DNLE tool set to create a color effect. Courtesy Avid Technology.

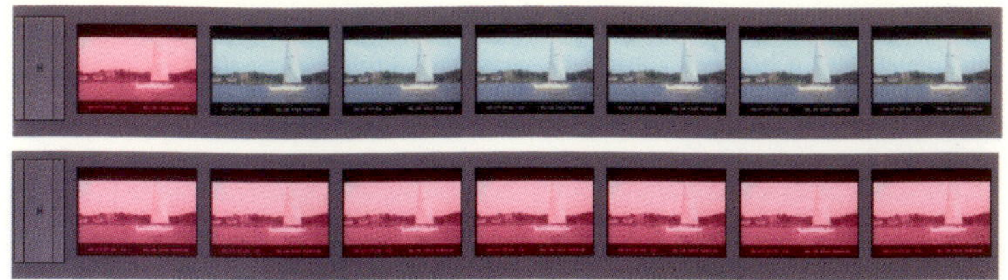

Color Figure 6 With frame-based tools, the effect is applied to a single frame (top), while with clip-based tools, the effect is applied to every frame in the shot (bottom). Footage courtesy Fox Point Films.

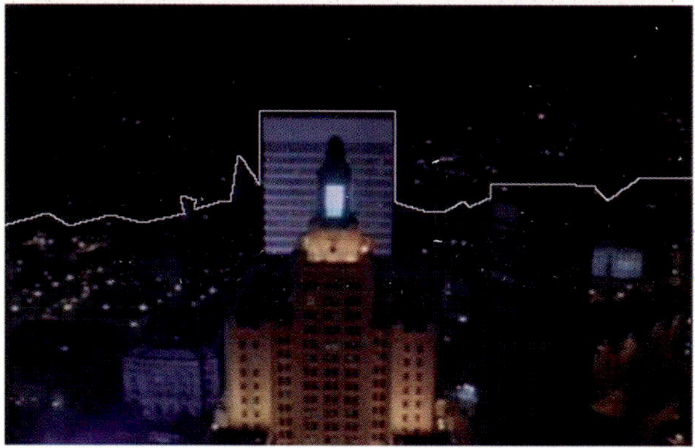

Color Figure 7 The original city scape image (top). A hand-drawn matte is drawn to isolate the cityscape from the background city lights (bottom). Footage courtesy Fox Point Films.

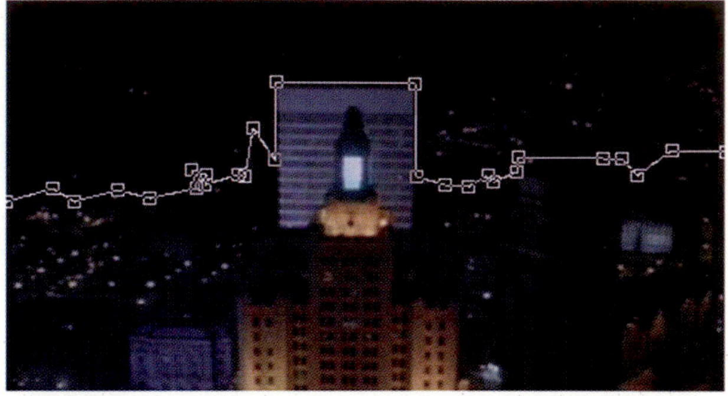

Color Figure 8 The matte is adjusted via control points (top). A blur process is applied to the frame areas not protected by the matte (bottom). Footage courtesy Fox Point Films.

Color Figure 9 Manipulating the control vertices of graphics and text to create different styles with Fractal Expression. Courtesy MetaCreations Corporation.

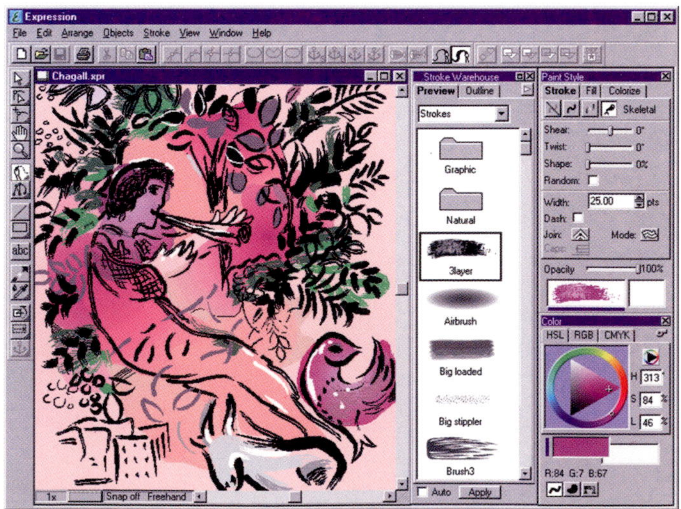

Color Figure 10 Using Fractal Expression for electronic painting. Courtesy MetaCreations Corporation.

Apple Corporation's OS), the software-based playback system equivalent to QuickTime was originally called Video for Windows (VFW), which gave files an .AVI extension name. However, several limitations, such as the need for precise audio-to-video synchronization and a screen size of 320×240, prevented VFW from being widely adopted.

The Microsoft Corporation followed VFW with ActiveMovie, a component of Microsoft's ActiveX, later reestablished as Direct Show. ActiveMovie is an API (application programming interface) that can be used to create synchronized full-screen video and audio. ActiveMovie is specified to be able to play QuickTime video, MPEG video and audio, and AVI video, both locally as well as for streaming video for World Wide Web programming. DirectX, another component of ActiveX, is an API for integrating 2D and 3D graphics.

PLUG-INS AND FILTERS EXTEND THE CAPABILITIES OF DESKTOP SYSTEMS

As stated in Chapter 6, plug-ins are a category of software tools that conform to the API of a specific application. Plug-ins drop in to, and are called by, an application through the use of API support. APIs allow one software package to use the instruction sets of other software applications by integrating a general-purpose library with a specific application, which uses the library via function calls (the actual programming interface).

For example, let's say that we are using a DNLE system and want to create a greatly exaggerated echo for an actor's line of dialogue. However, the DNLE system that we are using does not have any tools that allow us to create this audio effect. We could solve the problem by using a plug-in that conforms to the DNLE system's API for third-party plug-in effects. In this way, we can order a package of software audio effects from another manufacturer, and our DNLE system will now be capable of creating all types of audio effects.

Figure 7-11 contains several examples of different effects created by using third-party filter effects from Gallery Effects.

DESKTOP APPLICATIONS AND THEIR INTERFACES

3D Animation

Figure 7-12 shows part of the user interface of ElectricImage Animation System, a powerful desktop 3D animation tool. Figure 7-13 is an example of a 3D world rendered in ElectricImage.

Figure 7-11 An example of various transforming effects from a popular third-party plug-in application. The original file is on the upper left. Courtesy Aldus Gallery Effects.

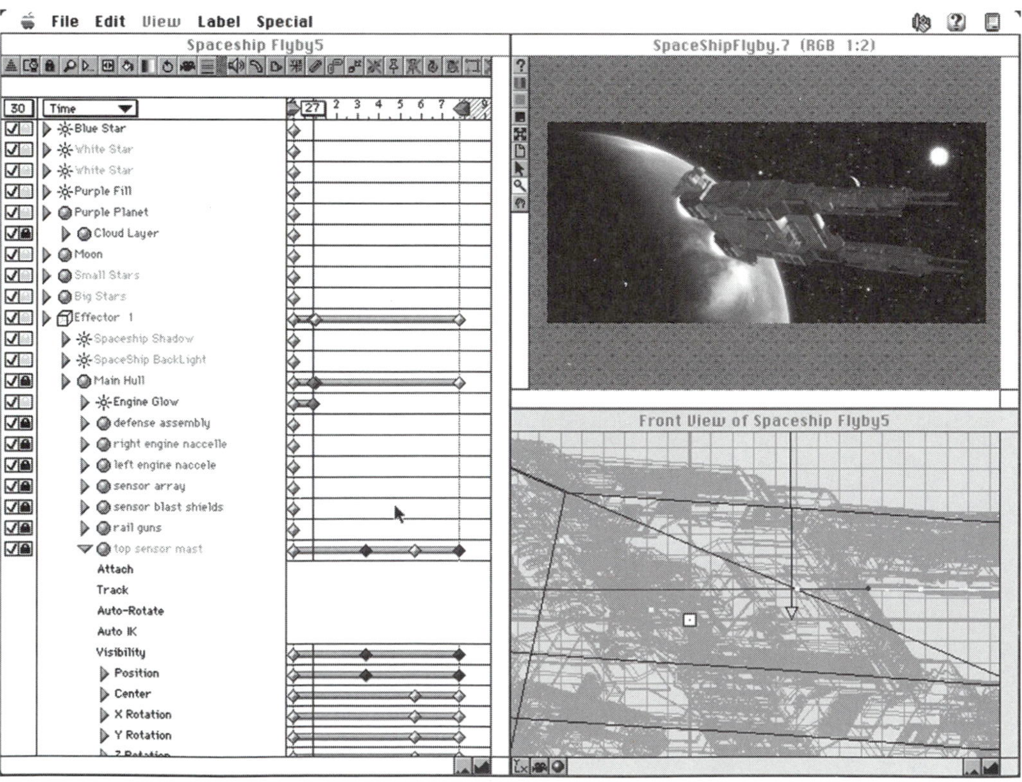

Figure 7-12 A user interface screen from ElectricImage Animation System, a desktop 3D animation tool. Courtesy ElectricImage, Inc.

Figure 7-13 An example of a 3D world rendered in ElectricImage Animation software. "Castle" created and copyrighted by Chuck Carter. Courtesy ElectricImage, Inc.

Audio

Figure 7-14 is an example of ProTools, desktop digital audio software used for film, music, and video production and post-production.

Compositing

Figure 7-15 is an example of a desktop compositing application, Illuminaire Composition, for Apple Macintosh and Windows NT computers.

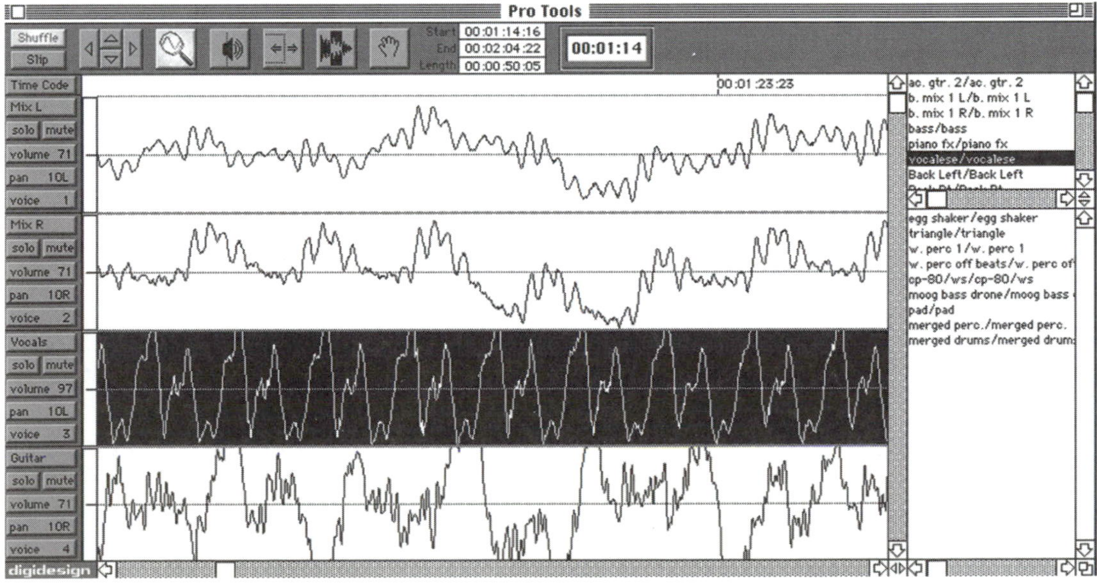

Figure 7-14 ProTools, desktop digital audio software. Courtesy Digidesign Corporation.

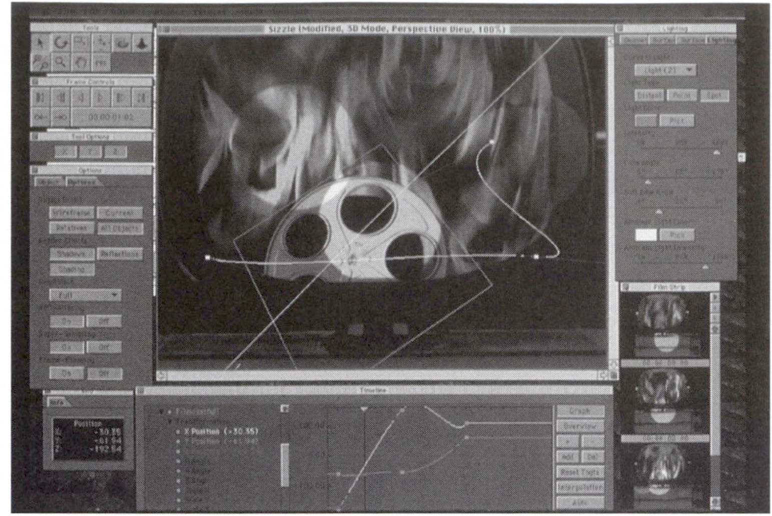

Figure 7-15 Illuminaire Composition, a powerful desktop compositing application for Apple Macintosh and Windows NT computers. Courtesy Denim Software.

Figure 7-16 Avid Matador, a powerful desktop painting. Courtesy Avid Technology.

Painting

Figure 7-16 is an example of Matador, a desktop painting application.

TALKING WITH EDITORS

What are your views on the wide range of low-cost desktop applications?

Joe Beirne

> Essentially every creative media tool is available in an inexpensive analog for the desktop. There is nothing that you can do on a

Domino or Cineon system that you can't do in one Adobe desktop product or other.

We use AfterEffects and PhotoShop on the Mac OS even for 70mm film projects. The trade-off, of course, is throughput. Ignoring speed, there is more you can do with inexpensive applications than you can do with expensive ones.

Our clients don't care exactly how we do anything, but they often need to interact with and/or approve our process. This means we will probably always have some call for purpose-built, expensive systems for some projects. But we don't always need to own these systems to retain control over the process and the creative culture employed in doing this work. Sometimes we can model a project on one system and render it on another, once key creative decisions are made. We prefer the tools to scale with the demands of the project.

We look forward to greater scaleability, extensibility, and programmability in our DNLE and desktop media manipulation tools.

Peter Cohen

The proliferation of desktop applications for editing and compositing has given me greater flexibility and control over my projects. On a recent project I was able to use these tools to offline complex effects shots. This greatly decreased the amount of time and money required to finish an episode. We used desktop tools for offline, visual effects, dialogue, and sound effects editing. The more functionality that becomes available on the desktop, the more control I have.

Scott Ogden

I hardly ever use these. Occasionally I will use Photoshop or Illustrator for title and matte creation, but that is about all. Luckily, I am able to call upon the talent of others in creating titles, but if I worked in a small shop, I would definitely need to know these tools intimately.

Alan Miller

This is a great breakthrough that is still under-appreciated by the majority of edit clients. Basically, it's the power of a Paint Box or Harry for under a thousand dollars. It's a little slower but getting faster. We just installed a four-processor Genesis doing Photoshop and AfterEffects at 700 MHz. It's blazingly fast and does everything we need. Add a few more key pieces of software, and you can do most anything.

Basil Pappas

I edit primarily in the documentary world, and even there I make use of image editing tools such as Photoshop and AfterEffects. These relatively inexpensive tools displace traditional high-ticket items such as Paintbox and Harry, allowing the editor to quickly accomplish various types of effects. These desktop graphics applications have also had the wonderful effect of changing the look of what the viewers enjoy, adding variety at low cost. Integration of DNLE tools with the desktop graphics applications is expected, and clients quickly learn how to rely on them.

Tom Poederbach

Everybody likes to have access to manipulation tools when they are affordable!

8

The Fifth Wave: Intraframe Editing

The fifth wave of nonlinear editing is a combination of the fourth wave, digital nonlinear online, and a new set of tools that allow intraframe editing. Intraframe tools operate within the actual film frame or video field.

Now, we can think of digital nonlinear editing as comprising the following:

1. Horizontal editing: Shots are chosen and transitioned together to create the basic flow of the story being told.
2. Vertical editing: Shots are layered together to form a collage of images.
3. Intraframe editing: The actual pixels that make up the frame (or fields) can be manipulated.

Intraframe tool sets are not a new introduction for DNLE systems. Indeed, there have been several systems that allowed users to work on an intraframe basis. However, the cost of systems that combined horizontal, vertical, and intraframe editing had traditionally been over six figures in U.S. dollars. Fifth-wave systems are a fraction of that cost. As years pass, we should find that fifth-wave systems cost somewhere in the vicinity of 25% of traditional systems.

INTRAFRAME FEATURE SETS

There are several pertinent features typically found within the intraframe tool set. Among them are matte cutting, paint, spot (secondary) color correction, image stabilization, image tracking, and user-definable transitions.

CLIP-BASED VERSUS FRAME-BASED EFFECTS

Traditionally, intraframe tools have been frame based. For example, let's say that we have a picture of a nightscape and the shot is 100 frames long. We want to paint a light into the shot, and so we apply a paint element to the shot. With frame-based effects, we must paint the same effect onto each individual frame.

Let's examine frame-based versus clip-based effects further. Color Figure 4 (top) is a frame of video of a sailboat. In order to create a tinted effect, we have applied a color-correction effect to the sailboat (bottom). Color Figure 5 shows the settings we used to create the desired color effect.

The difference between frame-based tools and clip-based tools is shown in Color Figure 6. With frame-based tools, the effect we create is for a single frame (top of Color Figure 6), and therefore the other frames are unaffected. However, clip-based tools work by applying the effect to the entire shot. This means that we can apply the effect to the shot and the effect is instantly applied to all of the frames that make up the shot (bottom of Color Figure 6). The amount of work that is therefore required by the user is greatly diminished.

FIXING PROBLEMS

Various intraframe tools can be used to fix problems that may exist in images. For example, if we have a boom microphone that is visible in the frame, we can use intraframe tools to isolate a section of the image. This section can then be copied, or cloned, and used to cover over the section of the image that contains the boom, thus "removing it" from the shot.

Mattes and Matte Cutting

Let's say that we have an image in which we want to blur the background in order to draw more attention to the objects in the foreground. In order to create this effect, we must isolate the object that is to be kept in sharp focus. This is done by creating a *matte*, or *mask*, around the object. Color Figure 7 (top) is the original shot; below, we have used intraframe tools to hand-draw a matte around the cityscape, which we want to keep in focus.

Next, in order to better align the matte to the various city objects, we are able to adjust the various control points that make up the matte (Color Figure 8, top). Finally, the matte protects the foreground cityscape, and a blur process is then applied to the areas of the frame that are not protected by matte (Color Figure 8, bottom).

Spot (Secondary) Color Correction and Enhancement

Color correcting an image is necessary for any number of reasons. An image may be too light and may require darkening. For creative reasons, we may decide that we would like to

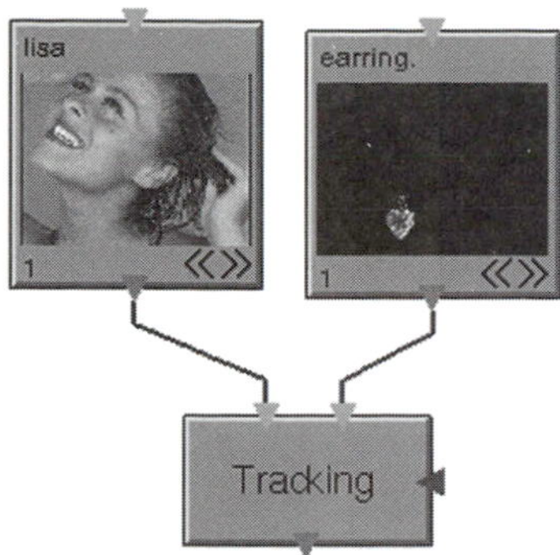

Figure 8-1 Image tracking can be used to add an earring to the model's ear. Control points are matched, and the computer-generated earring tracks perfectly as the model turns her head. Courtesy Parallax Software. Graphic artist: Jacqui Allard.

change an image from color to black and white. Further, it may be desirable to create certain effects by color enhancing only a specific color or section of an image. For example, let's say that we have an image of basketball players and we want to take the image and make the players and the basketball court gray and blue in color. At the same time, we want to enhance the color of the basketball, in effect, making it the only item in the image that has a bright orange color.

Image Tracking

Image tracking refers to the ability to place, or attach, an object to another object in the frame. For example, let's say that we have a series of frames in which a female model is turning her head. However, when the footage was shot, we forgot that she was not wearing the earrings she wore in the previous scene. It may be cost prohibitive to attempt reshooting the scene. In a situation such as this, image tracking can be used to fix the problem.

Figure 8-1 is an example of how an object is tracked to an image. Control points are chosen and tracked from among the frames of the shot. Next, a computer-generated earring is created, and points are associated between the model's ear and the earring. Appropriate size and perspective add to the necessary effect. The result is that the earring can be made to track perfectly as the model turns her head.

Image Stabilization

Image stabilization is yet another aspect of intraframe editing that can prove invaluable. For example, let's say that we are shooting from a helicopter and have our camera trained on a car speeding along the highway. However, despite using special shock-absorbing camera-mounting equipment, significant air turbulence introduces a noticeable amount of shaking in the resulting footage. It is possible to use image stabilization to steady the footage.

Image stabilization is a means whereby we can designate certain areas of the image that should be mapped to each other, regardless of the motion that occurs from one or more frames to the next. The image stabilization algorithm, in effect, directs these specific control points to match to one another; the difference that is thereby canceled out represents the shakiness from frame to frame.

USER-DEFINABLE TRANSITIONS

Most transitions and effects that are provided to the user by the DNLE system are fixed in nature. That is, they are defined by the DNLE manufacturer. The most common transitions are dissolves,

Figure 8-2 Two images that transition together with a user-defined transition. Both images are combined using a hand-drawn matte, and control points are aligned to the contour of the sailboat (top). The result is an animated transition that wipes the sailboat over the car in a sailboat pattern. Footage courtesy Fox Point Films; software interface courtesy Avid Technology.

fades, and shape wipes: circles, squares, rectangles, diamonds, and so forth.

However, in fifth-wave DNLE systems, considerable power is available anytime a "dedicated" effect can be changed and augmented. These user-definable effects and transitions can be thought of as being organic in nature. Since they can be changed and defined to fit the individual user's desires, incredibly diverse visuals can result.

For example, Figure 8-2 (top) shows two images, a car and a sailboat. Referring to the timeline for this graphic (bottom), we see that the sailboat has been layered on the car. Notice that instead of a standard wipe, which would place both images on screen at the same time, we have hand-drawn a matte around the sailboat's contour. This hand-drawn shape becomes the transition element between the car and the sailboat (middle). The transition can then be animated, resulting in a hand-drawn transition that wipes across the screen from car to sailboat in the shape of a sailboat. Normally, without being able to hand-craft transitions, we would have been limited to the transitions provided by the DNLE system.

User-definable transitions combined with intraframe tool sets provide powerful functionality. Figure 8-3 (top) is the original sailboat image. Using a 2D transform tool, the image is then enlarged; in effect, we have zoomed into the homes on the shoreline. Next, by applying a hand-drawn matte, we isolate the water area from the land area (Figure 8-3, bottom). Last, we add color-correction to these two isolated images.

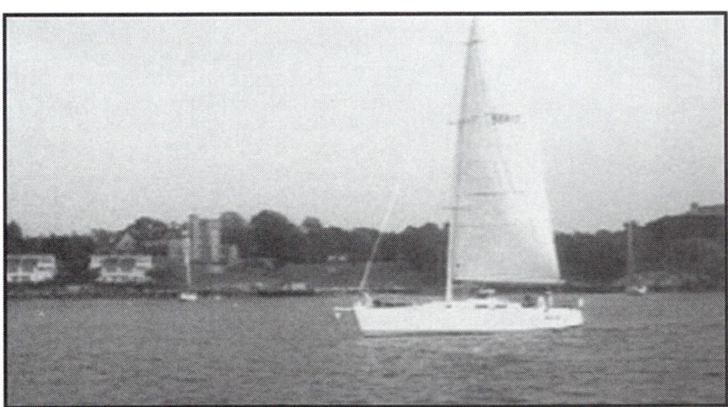

Figure 8-3 Using a 2D transform, the image is enlarged. A hand-drawn matte isolates the land and water areas, and different color-correction transforms are applied (bottom) to create quite a different look from the original image.

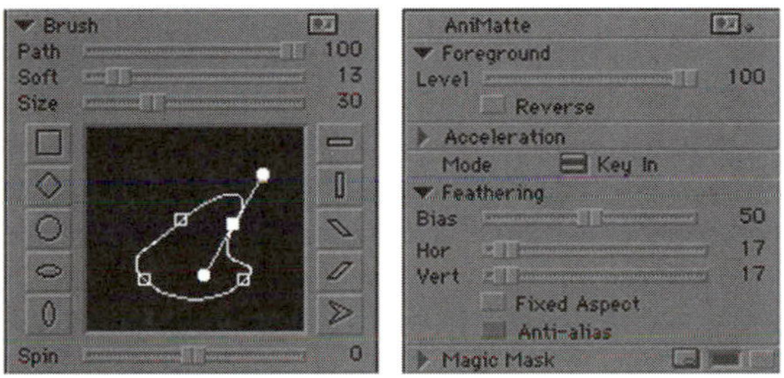

Figure 8-4 Using the color-corrected water from Figure 8-3, we hand-draw a matte and composite the water into the street scene (top). We then soften the matte's edges (middle) using software tools (bottom).

In Figure 8-4, we use the color-corrected water from Figure 8-3 and hand-draw a matte that combines the water with the car image (top). We then adjust the softness and feathering of the matte's edges to blur the edges of this matte (middle) using the software interface tools (bottom).

APIS AND THIRD-PARTY APPLICATIONS

APIs (application program interfaces) allow one software package to use the instruction sets of other software applications by integrating a general-purpose library with a specific application, which uses the library via function calls (the actual programming interface). In this way, it becomes possible to extend the native functionalities of the DNLE system.

For example, let's say that we are creating a program open and that we want to place a small lens flare near one of the letters of our title. There are actually several programs that provide such specific effects as different types of lens flares. If the program (often called a third-party application) conforms to

Figure 8-5 A third-party application for a variety of 3D transform effects. Courtesy Artel Software.

the DNLE's API, the DNLE user is able to access the tools of that third-party application. Further, if the DNLE application provides additional API information in the form of how the third-party application should map to the DNLE interface, the DNLE user will not be accessing these new tools from within the interface of the third-party application but, instead, will be using the new tools from within the DNLE interface.

Figure 8-5 shows the interface and the feature set of a third-party application that provides 3D transform functionality.

CONTROL POINTS AND CREATIVITY

It is very interesting to note that the presence of intraframe tools can assist in creating an atmosphere whereby the look of a particular visual is enhanced differently than originally intended. Color Figure 9 (top to bottom) contains examples in which being able to manipulate the control points that form the vectors of a drawn line and a line of type allows us more flexibility and creativity. In this example, we have drawn a line and have then highlighted the various control points that make up that line. By manipulating those points, we can create completely different line shapes.

The same is true for a line of type. Here, we have typed the word *style*, highlighted its control points, and manipulated them to create a new font style that previously did not exist. When intraframe tools are presented to the user in such a way as to create an inviting atmosphere for experimentation, such quick changes to something as simple as this title treatment become very important to increasing creativity. Color Figure 10 is an example of creative painting using Fractal Expression's tools.

GRAPHIC ARTIST OR EDITOR? WHO USES THESE DNLE SYSTEMS?

One of the more controversial subjects that is raised regarding intraframe tool sets centers on the issue of just who will use such systems. Will the user be an editor or a graphic artist? The thinking behind this issue has to do with opinions as to whether an editor has the necessary skill set to use the graphics capabilities that are available from within the intraframe tool set. Conversely, another question that arises is whether a graphic artist will be comfortable using the editorial tool sets of the DNLE system. DNLE systems are designed with the goal of making the tools accessible enough to accommodate both types of users.

The fifth wave of DNLE systems combines horizontal, vertical, and intraframe tools. Having these tools available at the beginning of the editorial process, when footage first arrives, and being able to shape the material throughout the editing process—in essence, to do the offline editing as well as the online with one system—are exciting developments of this wave, as well as all the finishing qualities that are associated with intraframe capabilities.

During the rise of the third wave of DNLE Systems, real-time video manipulation became vital to the further use and growth of DNLE systems. The incorporation of intraframe editing capabilities and the creative possibilities that they will unleash will define all future versions and waves of DNLE systems. Having all the tools—horizontal, vertical, and intraframe—available will contribute to the manner in which programs are approached from the very first moment that the raw footage arrives in the cutting room to their final look.

TALKING WITH EDITORS

Where is DNLE going?

Joe Beirne

I think the future of DNLE is multipronged. It basically boils down to four areas of development:

1. Media database issues. There is much to be done here.
2. Resolution versus throughput. [Having] multiple streams of ITU-R 601 and beyond on the desktop is one goal; [having] lightweight deliverable media for networks and massive (multiple terabyte) searchable media libraries is another goal. These require simultaneous solutions and tend to pull one's efforts in opposite directions.
3. Intraframe (coined by Tom Ohanian) manipulation, and particularly "reality" effects. (Einstein was wrong: Reality is

more important than imagination.) These consist of such things as compositing, rotoscope/retouching, grain and noise reduction/enhancement, color correction, etc.).

4. Extraframe (coined by Joe Beirne) manipulation, particularly incorporating 3D and multistream "environments" in interactive and/or immersive projects. I would also include programmable and "intelligent" media types in this category.

Theatrical film and television are only a small portion of the media spectrum. Architecture, engineering, urban planning, industry, finance, science, and medicine all have their own visualization spaces. Moving media has a role in all of them. The huge market for computer-based training hints at the vast potential that this inclusivity holds for the future of time-based media.

Peter Cohen

As the picture quality continues to improve, DNLE systems move into the realm of finishing machines. Many of the systems now have compression ratios better than 2:1. Most of my recent projects have required delivery on Digital Betacam. If I am delivering compressed video, why do I have to conform uncompressed video? Moving DNL editing into the area of online creates a whole new set of problems. This is an industry of specialists. The sensibilities of a good online editor and a good offline editor are not necessarily the same.

Alan Miller

DNLE is in its infancy. It's inevitable that you will be able to do everything in a DNLE system that you would traditionally do in an online room. The boundaries between online and offline are blurring and will soon no longer exist. 2:1 compression is probably good enough for most programming, and uncompressed is just a matter of computer power and storage space, two things that seem to double every year. Picture quality is a non-issue. If it's not good enough today (and it is), it will be good enough tomorrow. Flexibility and ease of use are more important in the long run. Digital means total control. The ability to manipulate every pixel like you can do in Photoshop is around the corner. Shoot tape, apply a filter, make it look like film. Bend it, twist it, shape it, cut it—it's all possible in a DNLE world.

Scott Ogden

Since all my work is in an offline environment, the use of intraframe editing tools has little effect on my work. But I see that the move to seamlessly bridge the gap between all levels of post-production, maintaining a digital environment throughout the entire process, from telecine all the way to transmission, will have a profound effect on the way editors work. It is only a matter of when this will happen.

Personally, the ability to take my offline cut and to seamlessly move it to a DNLE online environment would be very useful, and I see this happening in the not-too-distant future. The best reason for this would be that I would see less chance of creative error, since duplicating online what I do in offline is not always easy. Once in the online environment, the use of intraframe editing tools becomes very important. All these tools are currently available in online bays, so in order for wide acceptance of DNLE in the uncompressed online world, these tools would need to be there.

Basil Pappas

Clearly there are no areas of film and video postproduction that will *not* benefit from DNLE tools. Almost any effect can be emulated or accomplished in extremely high resolutions, with less and less rendering time. The systems are in danger of becoming too complex, in that they give most traditional editors tools beyond their abilities or scope. The flipside is that editors can now try the ideas that they once relied on others to accomplish. That allows for more challenging types of decisions that can now be in the realm of the editor rather than [that of] other postproduction artists. Pixel manipulation will become a necessity as DNLE becomes the dominant postproduction tool.

Tom Poederbach

The possibilities are actually unlimited if you think of it, but I see still two separate ways: Horizontal and vertical editing both require different skills. While both could live in one system, I see different functional workstations on a network, which will eventually be worldwide. As a result, pieces of the project will make a journey from one specialist to another, each adding his own portion to the job and then sending it to the next artist.

9

Video and Computer Fundamentals

A wide range of material finds its way into the DNLE system. Film- and video-originated footage must be combined with still graphics, audio, animation files, and so forth. Yet these different media types, of course, do not originate from one common file type. In integrating each of these different media types within a DNLE system, it is important to have a basic understanding of some of the fundamental aspects that characterize video and computer signals and how they function.

Some of the most fundamental problems that users of DNLE systems encounter are due to the inherent differences between computer and video signals. This chapter is concerned with the basics of video and computer operations and includes some of the specific issues that are commonly encountered when video and computer signals converge.

COMMON DEFINITIONS, TERMS, AND ISSUES

Pixel

A pixel (picture element) refers to an individual element or sample of a picture.

Bit

The bit, or binary digit, is a fundamental basic of computer operation. A bit can have only one of two possible values: 0 or 1. Eight bits equal one byte. Computer graphics and digital video systems classify their media forms in terms of the number of bits assigned to each image.

For example, a computer graphic that consists of 1 bit is monochrome: It can only be either black or white. An 8-bit image may display up to 256 colors, and a 24-bit graphic can support 16.7 million colors. Note that a 32-bit graphic is similar to a 24-bit graphic but that the extra 8 bits are used to represent the graphic's alpha channel.

The number of bits assigned per pixel (bits per pixel) can also vary. For many feature-film special effects, between 12 to 16 (and sometimes as many as 64) bits per pixel may be required to perform the intricate special effects compositing required.

Color Space

As we now know, there can be a variable number of bits per pixel as well as a variable number of pixels per component (luminance, color, alpha components). To further complicate matters, the manner in which color is assigned and remapped from a component in one medium to another component in a different medium is critical to ensuring acceptable results.

For example, if we are working with computer-generated objects, we could be working in RGB (red, green, blue) color space, or perhaps in HSL (hue, saturation, luminance) color space. On a DNLE system, we most likely will be working in in Y, R-Y, B-Y (analog luminance and color difference); in Y, Cr, Cb (digital luminance and color difference); or in RGB. Finally, in the print medium we would be working with images in CMYK (cyan, magenta, yellow, black) color space.

It becomes very obvious that if we are working in our DNLE system in Y, R-Y, B-Y color space and need to integrate graphics created on an RGB-based system, then a color mapping routine must be utilized. Further, not all colors can be represented from one medium to the other, and therefore, some averaging must occur.

Many developers of DNLE systems choose to work strictly in RGB to avoid a conversion between Y, R-Y, B-Y to RGB and back. The only negative aspect of this method is that more storage is required when video is stored in RGB.

COMPUTER BASICS

All computers include the following basic items: CPU, memory, and operating system (OS). The CPU is the central processing unit, the OS is the software that dictates the operation of the CPU's hardware, and memory is where CPU-OS operations are run.

Computer Bus Architectures

In the PC environment, both 16-bit ISA (industry standard architecture) and 32-bit EISA (extended industry standard architecture) busses are used. Until the late 1990s, the Apple Macintosh utilized a 32-bit bus, the NuBus. Other computer

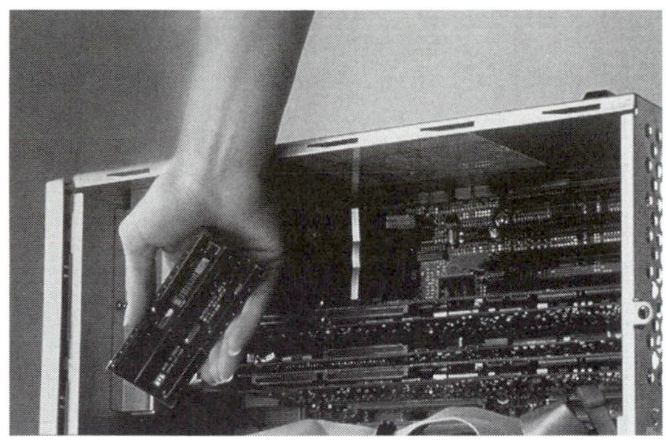

Figure 9-1 The Movie-2 expansion bus, which can be utilized by ISA, EISA, and PCI busses. Courtesy Matrox Video Products Group.

manufacturers may use proprietary bus structures. These busses communicate with peripheral devices in different ways and can communicate with a variety of different devices, such as disk drives and printers.

By the late 1990s, the standardized PCI (peripheral computer interconnect) bus became widely adopted and integrated in computers using the Mac OS, Windows NT, and UNIX.

The Movie-2 expansion bus (Figure 9-1) was introduced in the late 1990s and is a computer bus structure that is designed to sustain an aggregate data bandwidth of 240 MB/sec.

Computer Clock Speed

All computers are rated in terms of *megahertz* (MHz), which refers to the number of cycles (in millions) that the computer has available to carry out its instructions. Personal computers and workstations are rapidly increasing in their MHz rating. Moore's Law, attributed to Gordon Moore of Intel Corporation, states that a computer's speed will double approximately every 18 months.

Computer Operating Systems

The major computer operating systems that are readily available to the DNLE user include Macintosh OS, MS-DOS, Windows 95, Windows NT, and UNIX. Each is different, although there can be a level of interoperability in that certain interchange programs will allow files created from within one OS to be recognized by a different OS.

Mac OS: Developed by the Apple Corporation, the Mac OS is a 32-bit OS that is used in all Apple CPUs as well as third-party Mac CPU clones.

MS-DOS: Developed by the Microsoft Corporation, MS-DOS (Microsoft disk operating system) is perhaps the most famous OS simply due to the large numbers of computers that utilize it. This OS originated as a 16-bit OS.

Windows 3.1 and Windows 95: Developed by the Microsoft Corporation, Windows 95 is a hybrid OS of 16-bit and 32-bit elements.

Windows NT: Developed by the Microsoft Corporation, Windows NT is a true 32-bit OS, and not a hybrid as is Windows 95.

UNIX: Developed by Bell Labs, UNIX is the standard choice for powerful workstation computers, such as those developed by Silicon Graphics. UNIX, originally developed as a 16-bit OS, now functions in both 32-bit and 64-bit mode.

Open GL: Open GL, or Open Graphics Library, is a standard that makes it far easier to develop graphics and 3D applications for multiple operating systems.

Types of Computer Memory

RAM: Random access memory. RAM chips have many different applications. RAM forms the additional computer memory into which a software application's instruction set will load, or RAM chips can be found in digital video effects units and timebase correctors. In general, the more RAM that is applied to an application, the faster the application will run (although there are entropy limitations that can be encountered).

DRAM: Dynamic random access memory. DRAM chip sets are extremely fast, high-density integrated circuits (see Chapter 10). More than any other commercially available chip set, DRAM chips are perfect for incorporation into DNLE MPEG-based systems in order to perform the I, B, P frame searches that are necessary.

Network Computers versus Workstation Computers

When we think about most computers—those that sit on our desks and which we use as DNLE systems or to run word processing and e-mail software—we are thinking of workstations. These computers have onboard ROM or RAM into which an OS and then software applications are loaded. However, there is a different kind of computer known as a network computer (NC). An NC has no internal hard disk or resident OS; instead, it connects to a network and downloads both the OS as well as the application software that the user requires. This is accomplished as a result of the NC using Java virtual machine (VM) software. The NC can then run connected to the server or can disconnect and run in standalone mode.

Codecs

Codecs (coder/decoders) are useful tools because they assist in the coding and decoding of data. Any system that employs a particular codec becomes capable of reading the information contained in that type of file. Among the better-known codecs are the widely adopted Cinepak, M-JPEG, MPEG 1, and MPEG 2.

Codecs can be software-only or dependent on hardware. A software codec will usually be asymmetrical and will require more time for coding than decoding. Let's say that we are using a DNLE system and we want to save our files in a format that can be put onto a cross-platform (PC and Macintosh) CD-ROM and played on both PCs and Apple Macintosh computers. We first convert our files from M-JPEG to Cinepak, which allows us to compact and optimize the files so that they can be played by any system that supports the Cinepak codec.

The Intel Corporation originally developed Indeo, based on digital video interactive (DVI), but achieved little success with that codec. However, Indeo video interactive (IVI) is a codec based on wavelet compression that has been more successful.

VIDEO BASICS

Figure 9-2 A video frame is composed of two fields that are interlaced together to form the complete frame.

Fields and Frames

As shown in Figure 9-2, video is composed of two *fields* that combine to make up a single *frame*. In the NTSC system, a total of 525 horizontal lines are used to make up the picture that we see. When a picture is scanned from left to right, top to bottom for all the odd lines, Field 1 is created. Next, the even lines are scanned to create Field 2. Fields 1 and 2 are then combined in a method referred to as *interlaced scanning*. In total, NTSC signals utilize 29.97 frames per second (fps) or 59.94 fields/sec. In PAL, 625 horizontal lines make up a single frame at 25 fps.

Active Lines and Blanking

Note that the total number of lines that make up a frame are not all assigned to displaying a visible picture. A certain number of lines are reserved for special signals, where picture is not available. This area is referred to as *blanking*: Picture is blanked out to make room for other information. There are several types of data that can be inserted into the blanking area, such as close-captioning information.

The number of active lines in an NTSC signal of 525 lines (720×486 pixels, ITU-R 601) is 486 lines and 711 samples to form the picture that we see.

Even a cursory glance shows the obvious differences between computer and television monitors:

Computer Screen	*Television Screen*
Progressive display	Interlaced: 2 fields
Variable scan: 50–72 Hz	59.94 Hz

COMPUTER VERSUS VIDEO

Square and Nonsquare Pixels

It is important to note that computer and video signals fundamentally differ in the aspect ratio that they assign to the individual pixel. Video signals are composed of pixels that are not square, while computer-based pixels are square.

To calculate the aspect ratio of an individual pixel in video, we first take the scanning method and the actual active lines that are used to draw the picture. For an NTSC picture, the actual active lines are 486 lines with 711 samples. To determine the aspect ratio of each pixel, we calculate as follows:

NTSC video: 486 (active vertical lines) ÷ 711 (active pixels) × 4/3 (aspect ratio) = 0.91

PAL video: 576 (active vertical lines)÷702 (active pixels) ×4/3 (aspect ratio) = 1.094

Thus, we can see that video consists of nonsquare pixel spacing. The spacing between pixels is not a square. and in fact there can either be more height than width (NTSC) or width than height (PAL).

However, computer-generated signals are composed of square pixels, and the space between pixels is a perfect square, unlike video. As a result of this mismatch, signals must be scaled from their original aspect ratio to the target aspect ratio. For example, if we have a computer-generated graphic that we want to edit into our video program, during the import process of the graphic to the DNLE system, a scaling procedure will be applied to convert the aspect ratio accordingly. An alternative to this would be to originally create the graphic in the aspect ratio that video requires.

Interlaced and Progressive Scanning

As we know, television signals are created by interlacing odd and even scan lines to form the viewable, interlaced image. However, with computers, interlaced scanning is not used. Instead, progressive scanning, where each line is drawn progressively, or sequentially, results in the final, viewable image.

Digital Television Scanning Methodologies

In Chapter 6, an outline of digital television (DTV) and high-definition television (HDTV) scan rates was provided. Under the ATSC (Advanced Television Standards Committee) standard, the issue of square versus nonsquare pixels and interlaced versus progressive scanning is addressed as shown below:

DTV Form	*Scanning Method*	*Pixel Aspect Ratio*
HDTV	Interlaced	Square
SDTV	Interlaced and progressive	Square and nonsquare

Note that with some standard-definition television (SDTV) resolutions, both square and nonsquare pixels are supported.

10

The Digitization and Compression Processes

DNLE systems operate using both compressed and uncompressed picture quality. DNLE systems are based on a fundamental principle: Pictures and sounds are first converted to digital data and are then manipulated in the same way that a writer manipulates words with a word processor. The process by which moving pictures and sounds are transferred from their originating form into digital data is known as *digitization*.

BASIC TERMS

It is helpful to define some basic terms relevant to the digitization process:

Analog In analog recordings, the changes to the recording medium are continuous and analogous to the changes in the waveform of the originating sound or to the reflectance of the original scene.
Compression To reduce in volume and thereby force into less space.
Digital In digital recordings, numbers are used to represent quantities. Numbers in rapid sequence represent varying quantities.
Digitize To convert continuous analog information to digital form for computer processing.
Sample points The amount of data used to represent an original form.

AN EARLY SAMPLING EXPERIMENT

In the early 1970s, Bell Laboratories in Murray Hill, New Jersey, performed several studies as part of their research for the picture phone. The goal was to transmit a caller's likeness over standard phone lines. These studies sought to ascertain how much information would have to be sent over the phone line for the person to be recognized. Additionally, what methods would have to be developed whereby light information could be turned into energy that could then be transmitted?

The examples shown in Figures 10-1 to 10-5 recreate these experiments. One can see varying degrees of recognizability based on how much information is present in each of the photos.

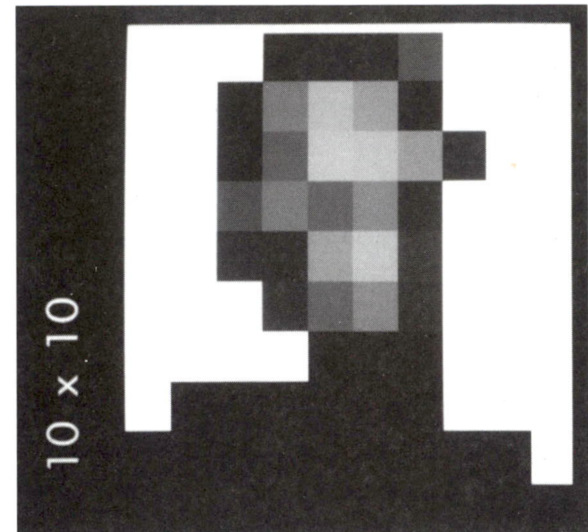

Figure 10-1 A 10×10 sampling of a portrait. How much information must be present to recognize a picture? This basic question is at the heart of this chapter.

Figure 10-2 By increasing the number of samples to 20×20 (400 sample points), more of the image becomes apparent. By holding the image a distance from your eyes and squinting, the subject of the photo may become clear.

Figure 10-3 By increasing the sampling to 40×40 (1600 sample points), the picture becomes clearer.

Figure 10-4 In this 80×80 sampling, the subject of the photo should be recognizable.

Figure 10-5 The normal view shows President Abraham Lincoln.

Bell researchers, seeking to preserve the intent of the image (the recognizability of the face) with as little information as possible (thereby limiting the amount of data that would have to be transmitted), came to the conclusion that the samples of a picture could be limited and that recognition would be aided by the tendency of the eye to blend contiguous areas. They concluded that, while it is difficult to identify minimally sampled pictures, blurring and blending the steps of such samples will improve recognizability.

Years later, in the mid-1990s, video compression became a standard component in the creation of picture phones and videoconferencing systems.

PIXELS AND SAMPLE POINTS

A *pixel* is the smallest element that makes up a picture. In essence, pixels are the patterns of dots that make up an image on a viewing screen. *Pixel matrices* are calculated by multiplying the number of pixels that are contained both vertically and horizontally over the span of the viewing screen.

The Bell Labs experiment, one of the first to involve the digitization of a picture, first reduced a photo to a series of 100 blocks (10 vertical×10 horizontal = 100) in a process of selective sampling. Each block had its own shade of gray. When viewed normally, the photo looked like 100 blocks of information with varying shades of gray. But when the interconnecting blocks where blurred, a portrait became more obvious.

This early Bell Labs experiment forms the basis for representing visuals in a digital form. The number of samples that are assigned to a signal and the storage of this data are two fundamental issues that the DNLE system must address. A great number of samples for a signal have to be stored; too few samples may not adequately represent the original signal so that it can be recognized.

How are units of information defined within a digital video medium? Each pixel that makes up a portion of the image that will be converted from its original form to digital data is categorized based on its brightness value. Once these digital data have been stored to computer disk, pictures and sounds exist as numbers to the computer operating system. These digital data are a result of the sampling process. A sampling includes the following characteristics: how often a signal is measured, the quantity of its amplitude, and the definition of its frequency over the span of the signal.

The number of samples assigned to represent a signal can vary. One very simple form of a digital sampling system is the facsimile machine used to transmit documents. Fax machines that operate in black and white mode have only two samples that can be assigned to a pixel: 0 = black, and 1 = white. The goal of incorporating such a scale is simple: to transfer high-contrast information reliably.

The more information preserved with regard to samples of a pixel, the better the perceived result. In general, here are some sampling guidelines for pictures and sounds. For pictures, if the sampling frequency is very high, the perceived picture will have a lot of spatial definition. If the sampling frequency is very low, there will be fewer stages of brightness to recreate the original picture; therefore, it will be compromised. For sounds, if the amplitude definition is very high, the perceived fidelity of sound will be high. If the amplitude definition is very low, the fidelity of sound will be decreased; therefore, it will be compromised.

THE FLASH CONVERTOR

How do you get pictures and sounds into a computer, and how can we instruct the computer to figure out what to preserve in the picture and what to discard if we want to compress the pictures? The photo of Lincoln can be sampled into the computer with all the information necessary to reproduce the photo without a noticeable change. Conversely, the original photo can be sampled into the computer with fewer references to the original. In that case, the integrity of the photo is compromised.

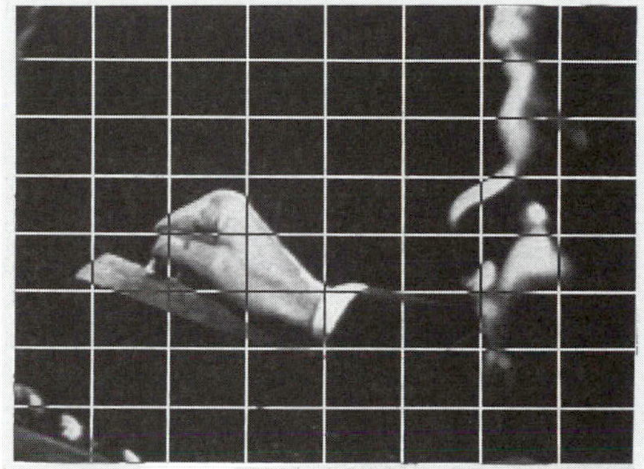

Figure 10-6 The flash convertor divides the computer screen into a grid pattern to define each pixel in the grid's array.

A method of converting video signals into data that computers could process arrived in the late 1970s. *Flash convertors* were expensive and able to process only black and white pictures, but they represented a very fast way of converting analog signals to digital signals. With a flash convertor, it was possible to convert one frame of video at a time into data that could then be interpreted by computers. Although they could quickly convert analog signals to digital signals, these flash convertors were not able to keep up with the stream of 30 NTSC video frames each second. They were only able to handle about one frame each second.

How Does a Flash Convertor Work?

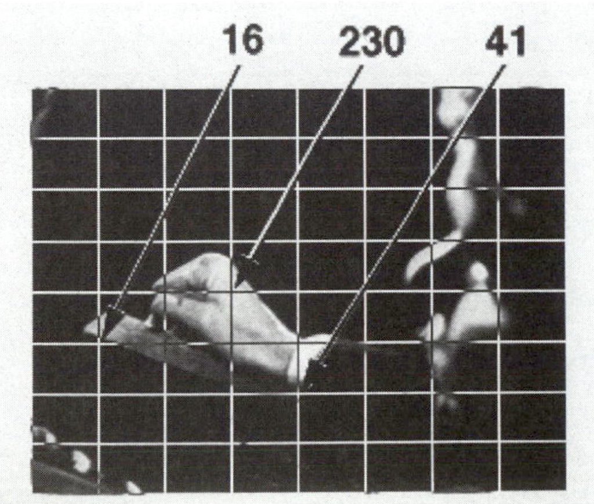

Figure 10-7 The flash convertor next evaluates the brightness of each pixel and assigns to it a number.

The flash convertor first divides the computer screen into a grid pattern so that each pixel making up the grid array can be located (Figure 10-6). As a picture is processed by the flash convertor, what becomes apparent is that a picture is composed of a number of precise elements, pixels. At its simplest level, the flash convertor takes each pixel and converts its brightness value into a number (Figure 10-7). The establishment of these numbers for brightness values is based on a grayscale chart consisting of 256 steps, in which 0 equals full black, and 255 equals full white.

Finally, the flash convertor processes the image and assigns values for each pixel of the image. These numbers are put into memory, and at that point, the image is regarded as a set of values (numbers) that the computer then can manipulate. Early flash convertors did not preserve full detail of the picture. With only 256 steps to represent an image, which may originally have had thousands or millions of shades of gray, the reduced sampling level compromised the full detail of the original image.

When any signal is flash converted, or digitized, the signal is converted into binary data via an analog-to-digital (A/D) convertor. Like all A/D convertors, the flash convertor's function is simply to take the instantaneous value (pixel duration sample) of an analog signal voltage and convert it into binary data form. One byte can express a range of values between 0 and 255, but the video scale is expressed between 0 and 100 IRE units. If one section of a picture is measured at 47 IRE units, how are that portion of the picture and the pixels that make up that portion converted to digital data?

Let's mathematically convert one video pixel with an IRE value of 47 units into a byte.

Pixel (P) = 47

Byte range (B) = 100 units

We begin by dividing B (100) by 2 to find the midscale (50). Is P now larger than this new value of B? The first bit will be set to a "1" if the answer is yes. Since a byte consists of eight bits, we will repeat this test eight times at eight decreasing test values for each bit. Before each successive test, we will again divide B in half. Whenever P is larger than B, we will set the corresponding bit's binary value to a "1," and we will subtract B from P. Otherwise, the bit remains unchanged at "0," and P also remains unchanged (Table 10-1). Thus, 47 IRE units of video are expressed as the byte 01111000.

The conversion task, as expressed in Table 10-2, is quite close to the way in which even a simple computer language such as BASIC would handle it as a software routine. Instead of using software, the flash convertor is a dedicated piece of

Table 10-1 Pixel-to-Byte Conversion

B = 100	*P = 47*			
B = B÷2 = 50	Is P larger than B?	No	Bit 1 = 0	No changes
B = B÷2 = 25	Is P larger than B?	Yes	Bit 2 = 1	P = P – B = 22
B = B÷2 = 12.5	Is P larger than B?	Yes	Bit 3 = 1	P = P – B = 9.5
B = B÷2 = 6.25	Is P larger than B?	Yes	Bit 4 = 1	P = P – B = 3.25
B = B÷2 = 3.12	Is P larger than B?	Yes	Bit 5 = 1	P = P – B = .13
B = B÷2 = 1.56	Is P larger than B?	No	Bit 6 = 0	No changes
B = B÷2 = .78	Is P larger than B?	No	Bit 7 = 0	No changes
B = B÷2 = .39	Is P larger than B?	No	Bit 8 = 0	No changes

Table 10-2 Bit-to-Bit Value Relationship

Bit Number	*Bit Values*
1 = 0	50.00
2 = 1	25.00
3 = 1	12.50
4 = 1	6.25
5 = 1	3.12
6 = 0	1.56
7 = 0	0.78
8 = 0	0.39

high-speed hardware that rapidly samples the video signal as pixels and outputs binary values as bytes that are stored in a section of memory reserved for use as a frame buffer.

When we take the combined bit number for bits 1 through 8, we have the following string: 01111000. However, since there are no changes to be made for bits 1, 6, 7, and 8 (see Table 10-1), we only combine the bit values for bits 2, 3, 4, and 5. We therefore add 25.0 + 12.5 + 6.25 + 3.12 for a total of 46.87 IRE units.

Color video consists of three distinct analog signals of red, green, and blue (RGB). Thus, digital conversion is often conducted by three flash convertors operating in parallel.

To get our original analog signal back, the computer performs the tasks in reverse via a digital-to-analog (D/A) convertor.

Evolution of the Flash Convertor

By the mid-1980s, we were no longer looking at black and white computer terminals: We were experiencing the explosive entry of color into computer displays. Manufacturers of flash convertors began to add color capabilities in the same fashion as color was added to the computer. Prior to this, digitized images were limited to black and white. Although they cost thousands of dollars, flash convertors that handled color began to appear in the mid-1980s.

The pathway for moving from video to the convertor is as follows. A composite video signal is made up of four elements: red, green, blue, and a sync (stabilizing) signal. It is necessary to break this four-item signal into separate components. We began to see flash convertors that had, instead of just one frame-grabbing unit, three units, one each for the red, green, and blue signals. However, with the complexity of color images, decoding and encoding units became necessary. Through the use of a decoder, the composite signal is separated into its components, and the signals are prepared for the flash convertors.

Cost was a factor. These early three-color flash convertors ranged in price from $5000 to $8000. In the late 1980s, the combined functions of a digitizer, an encoder, and a decoder appeared in an affordable unit. Examples included the VID I/O™ from Truevision, Inc., which decoded composite video into red, green, blue, and sync signals and then encoded these signals so that it was possible to record material from the computer to videotape. Digitizing was accomplished through the use of a separate computer card. More remarkable was the price: under $1000.

In 1991, computer boards began to replace the external encoder and decoder units. These computer boards house chip sets that perform the digitizing, encoding, and decoding functions (Figure 10-8).

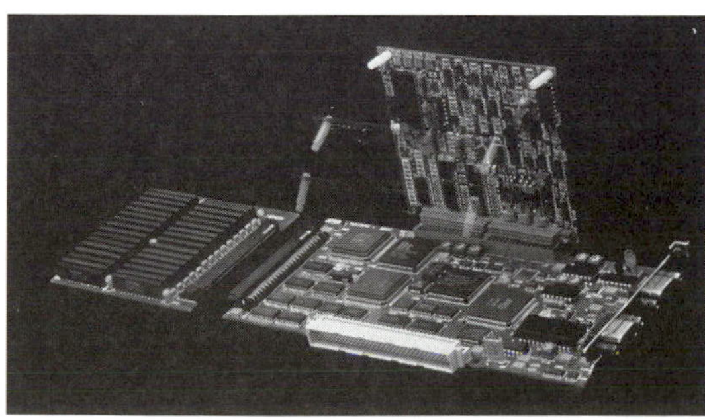

Figure 10-8 The functions of digitizer, encoder, and decoder combined into a single unit. Courtesy Truevision, Inc.

With the flash convertor, we achieved the ability to transfer the pixel array of an image into data that represented analog-based information as digital data. However, the governing process, the ability of the computer to process this data, had yet to be addressed.

APPROACHING REAL-TIME DIGITIZATION

By 1985, digital timebase correctors (TBCs) were in wide use. In addition, digital video effects devices (DVEs) had become very popular. Both digital TBCs and DVEs helped set the stage for the real-time digitizing of analog video and audio signals. In the late 1980s, improvements in several areas allowed the digitization process to proceed much more rapidly. Central processing units (CPUs), computer busses (which transfer information from one portion of the computer to a different, internal, part of the computer as well as between internal and external devices), and computer disks all began to get much faster.

With these developments, it became possible to display pixels on the computer screen much more rapidly. For the first time, it was possible to do picture subsampling from videotape rather than from computer-generated images. This subsampling was still being done in greater than real time, but much more rapidly than ever before. For example, although digitization may not have been at a full 30 frames per second, it was possible to digitize at about 9 to 10 frames per second. This was a significant breakthrough; one frame per second had been the norm. The important aspect is that real motion now could be seen and detected, even if it was somewhat staccato in nature. It was a revolutionary development: live action, moving pictures stored on computer disks!

These early attempts at digitizing video were accompanied by a great deal of quantizing artifacts, including spatial aliasing, temporal aliasing, and color aliasing (inaccurate representation of color, absence of color, or blending of colors). In addition, no form of compression was being applied to the frames as they were digitized, and therefore, the files were extremely large. In 1989, a 380 MB magnetic disk drive was considered large and was quite expensive; it was filled very quickly with these uncompressed digitized video frames. Reducing the amount of information (samples) became a necessary objective.

DIGITIZING, COMPRESSING, AND CODING

Representing Information as Bits

ASCII (American Standard Code for Information Interchange) represents the manner in which binary definitions are assigned to numbers and letters. It provides a standard for exchanging different types of files: ASCII code. Two main benefits arise from representing information in ASCII form.

First, as a common labeling scheme, it ensures that the letter F in ASCII will be given the same ASCII symbol, 70, regardless of who is doing the labeling. Second, ASCII ensures that files saved and transported in their ASCII form can be accessed by software programs that may not be compatible in and of themselves.

ASCII assigns binary definitions to numbers and letters. *Binary* means numbers that use the power of 2. Computers can only use two numbers, either 0 or 1. The smallest piece of information in the digital world is called a *bit*, which is short for "binary digit." Creating words from bits involves first creating letters; you need a series of bits to represent a letter and, obviously, a series of letters to represent a word.

For the word *FILM*, for example, the ASCII codes that make up the letters (*F, I, L, M*) are as follows:

Letter	*ASCII*	*Binary Code (Bits)*
F	70	01000110
I	73	01001001
L	76	01001100
M	77	01001101

It takes eight bits to represent any letter. If we were to save our ASCII file of the word *FILM* and bring that file to another computer, anywhere in the world, the word *FILM* would be displayed when the ASCII file was read.

Any message can be reduced to and represented by a series of bits. It makes no difference if the message is the word *FILM*, a paragraph, a Saroyan novel, a graphic from a printed page, a color photograph, or a full-resolution video frame. All information, at its heart, is a series of data in the form of bits.

Once information is represented in bit form, many things can be done with the data. One common example is transmitting the information via a modem (modulator/demodulator), which can be used to communicate from computer to computer over telephone lines. When a modem is used, letters are represented by codes, and these codes are sent over transmission lines.

There are two major concerns. First, will we be able to represent a message accurately by reducing it to a series of bits? In the case of our word *FILM*, it is straightforward: We have four letters, and each letter is represented by eight bits. Second, if we store this data or send this data, will the integrity and order of that data be preserved? If we are successful, we send a colleague 32 bits of information, and he or she receives 32 bits of information in the correct order and sees the word *FILM*.

So far so good, but what happens when we are faced with situations in which we may not be able to represent a message accurately by reducing it to a series of bits? How will a color photograph be represented by a series of bits? We now know that the flash convertor is used to represent a picture as digital data, and that one byte's worth of information relates to each pixel in the picture, for example, to provide numeric values for shades of gray. However, what considerations are made, and what compromises occur? Is there a standard such as ASCII code for representing a frame of video that needs to be digitized and sent somewhere?

Compressing a File

Being able to reduce a message into a series of numbers is a critical step in converting an analog signal into a digital signal. The quantity of numbers assigned to the message can be a fixed standard. In the case of the word *FILM*, representing the word in ASCII code leaves no arbitrary decisions to be made. If we want to represent that word and we want to adhere to the standards of ASCII, we must use the correct binary information. As mentioned, when we make this transformation, we send a series of bits, and the same series of bits is received, and the word *FILM* is decoded: We sent 32 bits, and 32 bits were received.

However, there are times when we want to reduce the size of a message being sent, but at the same time, we do not want to change the meaning of that message. The first goal is size reduction, and the second goal is content preservation.

Let's say that we have a 50-page, single-spaced document that we want to send to someone over a modem. We finish typing the document on our word processor and save the file in ASCII format. We do this because the person who will be receiving our document is not using the same word processing software we are using. However, the word processing program he is using will open up ASCII files.

After saving the file, we determine its size, and it turns out to be approximately 100 KB (100 kilobytes or 100,000 bytes), a relatively small file. We then run a communications software package that, before engaging the external modem, gives an estimate of how long it will take to transmit the file based on the size of the file and the speed of transmission. The estimate is ten minutes to send the file.

While ten minutes isn't an extraordinary amount of time, if we have many documents to send or if we simply want to work in the most economical fashion and save telephone costs in so doing, it would be advantageous if we could reduce the transmission time. What if we could reduce the time to five minutes? Two methods quickly come to mind: either find a way to transmit the file twice as fast or find a way to reduce the file from 100 KB to 50 KB.

Let's say that due to the capabilities of the modem that we are using, we cannot transmit the message twice as fast. Our alternative is to figure out a way to reduce the size of the file from 100 KB to 50 KB, or, if a 50% savings isn't achievable, to something between 100 KB and 50 KB.

Coding Techniques

Coding, in the context of reducing the size of a file, refers to how information is represented. If we had to repeat a very long

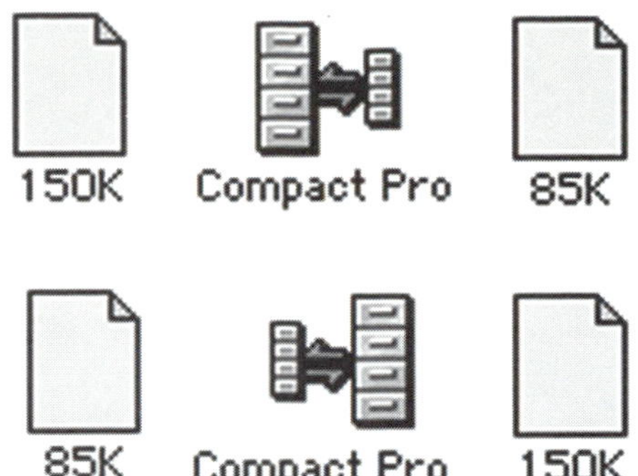

Figure 10-9 With lossless software compacting programs, such as Compact Pro, the file size can be temporarily reduced and then decompacted after the transmission of the file is complete without losing any information.

word, such as *brontosaurus*, many times, we could choose to code a shorter version: We could say *bronto* instead. We have just created a method of labeling an original name (file) while reducing the number of syllables that we must vocalize.

There are software and hardware routines that we can use to reduce the file size. For now, we will concern ourselves with software methods, which are typically marketed under the general category of file compacting programs. They use certain algorithms (an *algorithm* is a procedure or rule for solving problems, such as for finding the lowest common denominator) to determine the degree of frequency with which items appear (Figure 10-9).

Huffman coding is one such coding technique used by these compacting programs. In the case of our 100 KB document, we have to be very careful in how we reduce its size. We cannot arbitrarily chop out letters and characters because by doing so we will change the message that is received. We must have a way to reduce the 100 KB file temporarily, and then the receiver must be able to expand it back to its original size, losing no information.

If we use a computer program that employs Huffman coding techniques, we will confirm the following presumption, and we will realize a benefit from it:

> Letters and words in our document are not equally likely; there will tend to be much repetition of a certain class of letters (such as vowels) as well as words.

The previous sentence contains the following letters (for now, upper- and lowercase letters are not differentiated):

a	appears 8 times	n	appears 7 times
b	appears 1 time	o	appears 10 times
c	appears 3 times	p	appears 1 time
d	appears 5 times	q	appears 1 time
e	appears 16 times	r	appears 10 times
f	appears 1 time	s	appears 12 times
g	appears 0 times	t	appears 12 times
h	appears 1 time	u	appears 5 times
i	appears 7 times	v	appears 1 time
j	appears 0 times	w	appears 5 times
k	appears 0 times	x	appears 0 times
l	appears 11 times	y	appears 2 times
m	appears 2 times	z	appears 0 times

When we apply Huffman coding techniques to our 100 KB document, we have only one goal: make the overall message shorter. The fact that certain letters are more likely to appear than others allows us to reduce the overall document size temporarily. Huffman coding assigns codes to the letters such that (1) the most probable letters (those that appear most frequently) will be assigned short codes, and (2) the least probable letters (those that appear least frequently) will be assigned long codes.

In this way, when we need to transmit the information that the letter *s* appears 12 times, we transmit this information through a short code for that letter. Why transmit a long code when you have to transmit it 12 separate times? Conversely, when we have to report that the letter *z* appears zero times, we use a long code because, although it will take more time to transmit this information, we only have to transmit the long code one time.

For example, if we wanted to assign some codes to the message we want to transmit, we could proceed as follows: The letter *t* appears 12 times, so we assign it a transmission value of 1. We are therefore sending the smallest code for a letter that appears frequently. The letter *p* appears once, so we assign it a larger transmission value of, say, 7. Continuing in this fashion, we will ensure that the most frequently required characters have lower transmission values than the least frequently required characters.

Software programs that work in this manner and make use of Huffman coding techniques analyze the statistics of the message and determine the frequency of a message's components. Then, after ascertaining how many different codes there are, the greater number of components receives short codes and the less frequent number of components receives long codes.

It is not at all unusual for a document to be reduced by 40 to 50% after the redundancies have been analyzed and short and long codes have been assigned. Instead of using the word *reduced*, we need to begin to use the word *compressed*. Huffman coding techniques typically save about 50%, while a similar technique, LZW (Lempel-Ziv-Welch) encoding, typically saves about 75%.

We have achieved our aim, and the 100 KB file has been temporarily reduced in size by 50%; instead of having to send 100 KB over a modem, we are now sending 50 KB. The transfer takes place twice as fast. The person who receives the 50 KB file, now in its compressed form, cannot read it. To read the complete and unaltered file, it must be restored to its original form, which consists of 100,000 bytes, not 50,000 bytes.

After the compressed file is decompressed, the original frequency of components is restored, and the file again becomes 100 KB in size. The person who has received the file can proceed to read a document that has all the letters, sentences, and paragraphs in the correct order with no loss of information.

SAMPLING

Sampling is one of the first steps that needs to be taken when an analog signal is converted to a digital signal. The process of sampling involves measuring an analog signal at regular intervals and then coding the measurements for storage and transmission purposes. A *sample* is merely defined as a smaller part of a whole that represents the nature or quality of that whole.

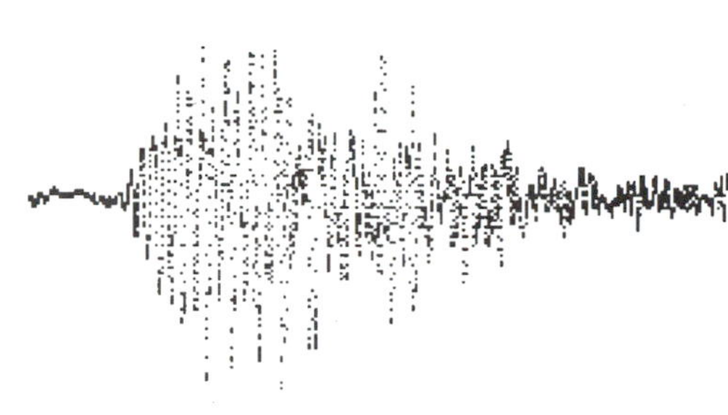

Figure 10-10 The process of sampling begins with an original signal. Here, the waveform of an audio signal is displayed.

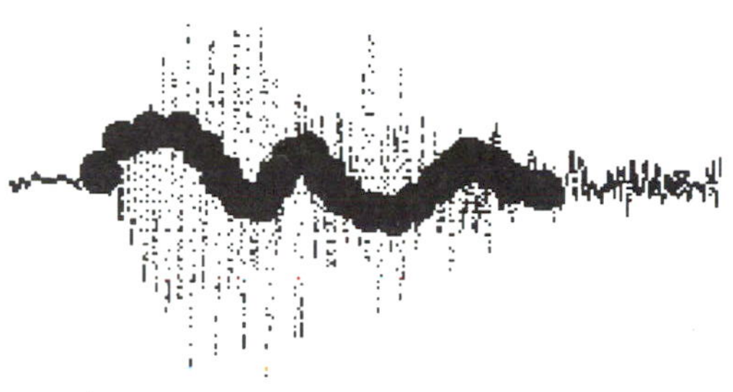

Figure 10-11 Sample points are now taken along the waveform of the signal. These numbers facilitate the conversion of analog data to binary information.

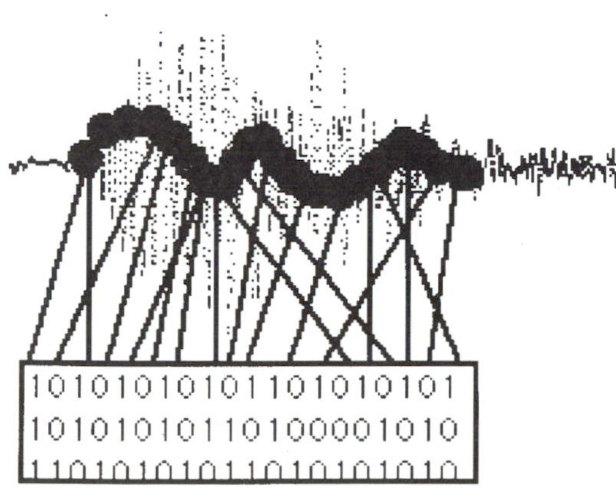

Figure 10-12 Once sample points have been taken, the binary information is then stored to computer disk.

There are a variety of sampling techniques, each yielding benefits, detriments, and artifacts; some are specific to visual signals, others to audio signals.

When we are presented with video and audio signals that must be converted from analog to digital, we must represent the analog waveforms of these signals by numbers. Where to assign the numbers and how many numbers to assign are very similar to the assigning of codes to the document that we compressed (Figures 10-10 to 10-12). Numbers represent the essential characteristics of the audio signal, but the number of sample points—the number of digits assigned to represent the signal—can vary. Sampling not only refers to how frequently a signal is measured, but also to the degree of measurement that is provided for the amplitude.

Consider, however, a representation where far fewer sample points have been assigned to the same waveform (Figure 10-13). More interpretation time must be given to this second example since there are fewer sample points to indicate the original path of the audio waveform. The process of sampling—indeed, any time an analog signal is turned into a number—yields a loss, and sampling creates a phenomenon known as *quantization*. This term refers to the limit to which the analog signal can be sampled by the analog-to-digital convertor in a samples/time relationship. Quantization can also be viewed as an acceptable loss in the original quality of the signal.

It stands to reason that if one analog-to-digital convertor can only plot three points whereas another can plot 300 points for the same analog signal, there will be more numeric samples in the latter sampling. Accurately representing and recreating an original signal with just a few samples as opposed to many samples is an impossible task. We always attempt to have as many samples as possible to represent original information. As we now know, to reduce the overall size of a digital file, fewer samples are often taken than would be optimal.

Quantization can yield several noticeable *artifacts*, which are discrepancies between the original signal and the representation of that signal. Perhaps one of the most recognizable artifacts is called *aliasing*, in which images can be distorted or appear disjointed.

The Sampling Theorem and Subsampling

The sampling theorem is a rule for obtaining acceptable representation of a signal by determining the regularity with which sampling should be done. The sampling theorem states that a signal must be sampled at least twice as fast as it can change (2 times the cycle of change) in order to process that signal adequately. Sampling the signal less frequently will lead to aliasing artifacts. For example, if we want to preserve an audio signal to the range of human hearing (approximately 20 KHz), we would sample the signal at least two times the desired result. For audio compact discs, the sampling rate is 44.1 KHz,

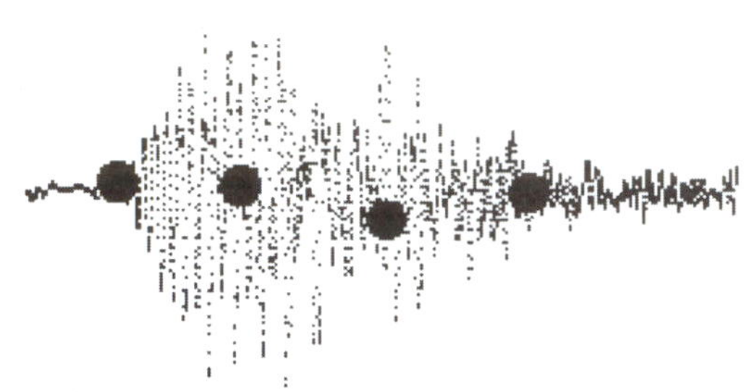

Figure 10-13 Here, the audio signal is represented by only four sample points versus the original sampling of more than twenty points.

which quite adequately preserves signals that the human ear can process.

Subsampling refers to a technique in which the overall amount of data that will represent the digitized signal has been reduced. More generally stated, when more samples are thrown away than meet the sampling theorem, we are subsampling. When the sampling theorem is violated, many types of aliasing may be noticeable.

The .sif format is a sampling algorithm that reduces the pixel matrix by one-half on the vertical and horizontal axes, in effect, sampling every other pixel and every other field.

Spatial Aliasing

In spatial aliasing, the perception of where items are positioned in two- and three-dimensional space becomes distorted (Figure 10-14). When enough samples are provided for the signal shown, it will be represented as a long and solid object. However, when too few samples are provided for the signal, that is, when the sampling theorem has been violated, the solid object is perceived as a series of objects.

This spatial aliasing phenomenon is also very noticeable when looking at computer type after it has been recorded to videotape. On the computer display, the letters look fine, with smooth edges even on fonts with fine serifs. After being recorded on videotape, these edges take on a stair-stepped appearance, often called *jaggies.*

Figure 10-14 Spatial aliasing affects the perception of the three-dimensional space that an object occupies. When we remove sample points, a solid object appears as a series of individual objects. Illustration by Jeffrey Krebs.

Temporal Aliasing

In temporal aliasing, the perception of movement over time is distorted. When enough samples are provided for the signal, the perceived direction of a wheel is not ambiguous: It appears to be moving forward. However, when the sampling theorem is violated and there are not enough samples, the direction in which the wheel is traveling becomes ambiguous (Figure 10-15). It is not clear if the wheel is moving forward or backward. If the sampling theorem were not violated, we would have enough information to be able to judge the correct movement of the wheel; but if the wheel has traveled more than halfway (180 degrees), and we do not have at least two times the cycle of change represented as information to us, we will not be able to judge the proper direction. Alternatively, as long as we can view the wheel before it reaches the halfway mark, we will be able to perceive the wheel as going forward.

Nyquist Limit

When sampling techniques are used, the sampling theorem asserts that we must sample a signal at least twice as fast as the signal can change. When we are subsampling, we are in violation of this theorem. Note, though, that the theorem states *at least* twice as fast. There are reasons why we would want to sample a signal more frequently than exactly twice the rate at which the signal can change.

The Nyquist limit refers to one-half of the highest frequency at which the input material can be sampled. For example, if the

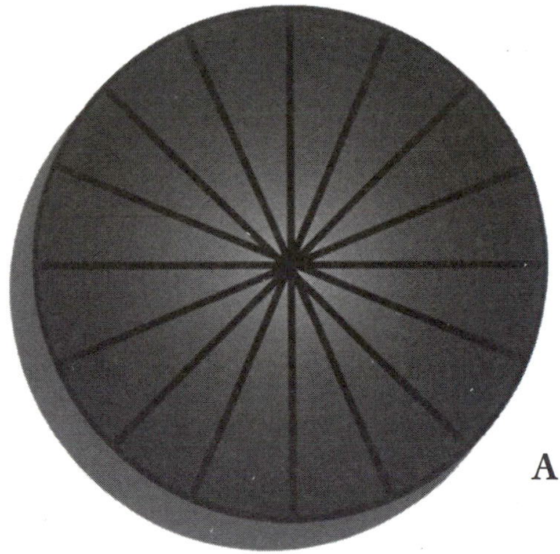

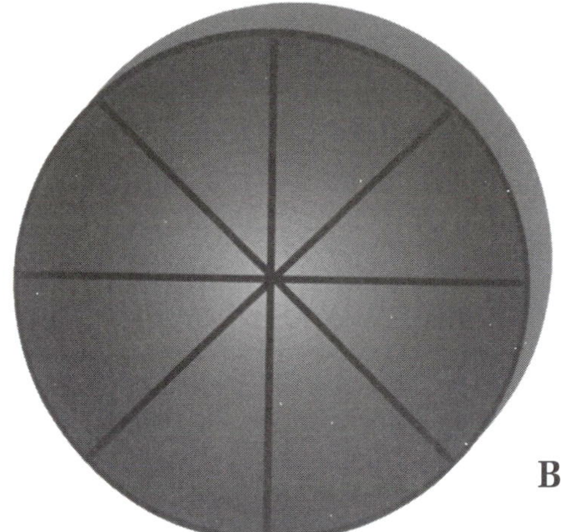

Figure 10-15 Temporal aliasing alters the perception of movement over time. When the number of samples (wheel spokes) is sufficient **(A)**, the wheel appears to be moving in a forward direction. As the number of samples decreases **(B)**, there is ambiguity regarding the direction of the movement of the wheel. Illustration by Jeffrey Krebs.

optimal number of samples for a signal is 44, the Nyquist limit would be 22 (44 samples ÷ 2 = 22 samples).

The problem with only sampling at two times the rate of change is that conditions can occur in which the resulting information is of an ambiguous nature. When that happens, it is often difficult to interpret and understand the message. Returning to our example of the wheel moving forward, we can sample points between 12 o'clock and 3 o'clock. In Figure 10-15a, we have sampled the wheel two times, at less than and greater than two times the frequency of its cycle (at 12 o'clock and 3 o'clock). Because these sample points exist, there is no ambiguity in judging the direction of the wheel. It is moving clockwise. If we draw a dotted line halfway between our two sample points (within 12 o'clock and 3 o'clock), we reach the midpoint of one of the four cycles that the wheel requires to rotate completely (Figure 10-16). This line represents one-half of the highest frequency that can be sampled: It is the Nyquist limit. Sampling a signal at less than and greater than the Nyquist limit leaves no ambiguity as to how the signal should be interpreted.

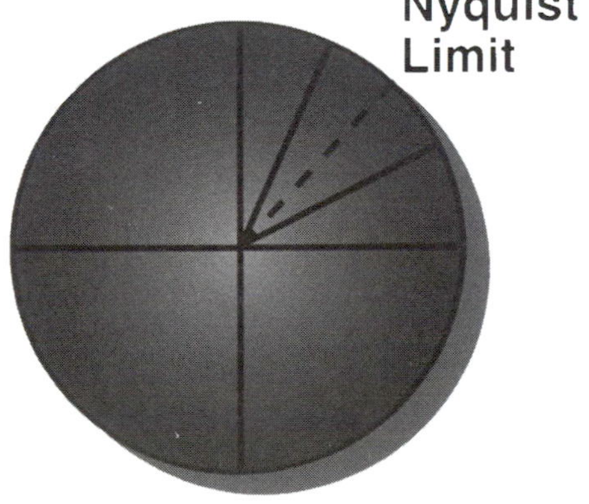

Figure 10-16 The Nyquist limit is shown as the midpoint between one of the four cycles of change. Illustration by Jeffrey Krebs.

However, if we only sample at two times the rate of change, it is not at all clear as to how the wheel is moving (Figure 10-17). We only have a sample point midway through the cycle. Is the wheel moving forward or backward? We do not have enough information to make a judgment. The message presented to us is ambiguous, and as a result, we cannot begin to make an interpretation. One of the possible ramifications of

Figure 10-17 Sampling at exactly two times the rate of change yields ambiguity. It is impossible to judge the direction of the movement of the wheel. Illustration by Jeffrey Krebs.

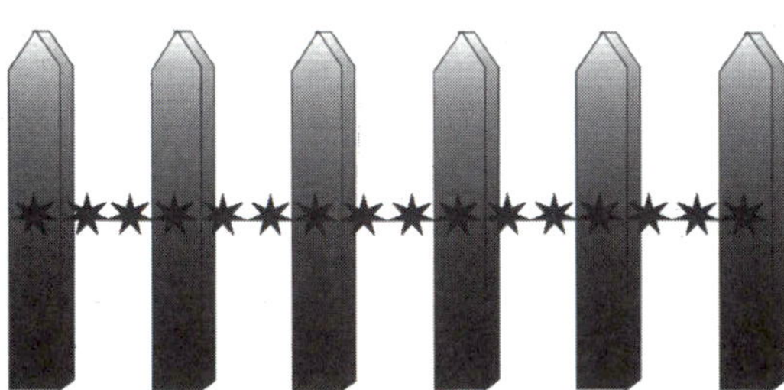

Figure 10-18 Six pickets in a fence and sample points between pickets. Illustration by Jeffrey Krebs.

sampling at *exactly* two times the rate of change is that ambiguities could occur.

Effect of Sampling and Selective Removal of Samples on the Message

The act of sampling analog signals to convert them into digital files is a process that brings with it benefits as well as possible detrimental side effects. The degree to which the integrity and intent of the information is preserved and can be adequately deciphered by the viewer/listener is dependent on the number of samples (represented by bits) in the digitally converted file.

Once an analog video or audio signal has been adequately sampled such that aliasing has been kept to a minimum, the overall number of samples can then be further reduced, and certain samples can be discarded. This process is called *subsampling*. This reduction is not arrived at by randomly removing samples. Rather, such reduction techniques are based on how images are perceived and how the human eye is attracted to certain areas of an image.

For example, if we remove pixels in violation of the sampling theorem when we sample a solid color background that has been generated on an electronic paint system, instead of a solid background, we would see a quantized background that would show aliasing. Instead of our solid background, we would see stripes of colors, most likely evidenced in a stair-stepped pattern.

Consider what would happen if samples assigned to an image were removed without ascertaining whether the samples were expendable or not. For the example shown in Figures 10-18 to 10-20, consider the drastic effects of an instruction that states, "Remove every other sample." Figure 10-18 shows a row of six pickets in a fence. We attempt to represent the fence by choosing sample points between the pickets. We assign three samples per picket, well below the Nyquist limit, for a total of 16 sample points. However, we decide that the resulting sampling is too large, and we attempt to reduce the size by 50%: eight fewer samples. We issue a command to remove every other sample point.

The arrows in Figure 10-19 indicate the sample points that will be removed. However, note that three sample points that will be removed fall on pickets. Our original instruction was to remove every other sample point. As a result, the original image of the picket fence will be altered.

In the resulting image (Figure 10-20), we have the eight sample points that we wanted, but we have only three of the original six pickets! We have lost three pickets during the sample reduction stage. Deciphering the resulting message becomes difficult; it is not at all clear where actual pickets should be placed since we are now in violation of the sampling theorem. This phenomenon of subsampling is actually known as *picket fence effect* and is often seen when computer images are taken from their original environment and

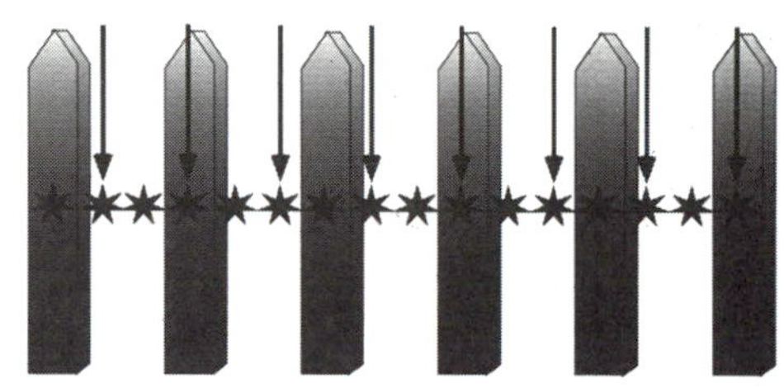

Figure 10-19 Arrows show which points will be removed. Illustration by Jeffrey Krebs.

recorded onto a medium that may compromise the sampling theorem.

Sampling pictures and sounds is an integral step in transforming analog signals into data that computers can process. The act of quantizing such signals yields artifacts, some of which can be ingeniously masked and filtered. When an analog signal is digitized, samples must be assigned to recreate the original signal accurately and adequately. Lossy compression techniques can further affect the integrity of the signal. Finally, when subsampling or discarding samples to reduce the size of a file further, as evidenced by the picket fence example, entire portions of an image can be lost forever. For these reasons, it is vitally important to understand why we cannot indiscriminately throw away portions of a picture and expect to have it always look acceptable or decipherable.

We can begin to see how pictures are affected by the number of samples used to represent the picture. There are a number of image plane schemes. With RGB signals, a typical color picture is composed of 24 bits. Each chrominance component has eight bits. With eight bits times three colors, we arrive at our 24-bit picture. Next, to calculate the number of potential colors that the 24-bit picture could represent, we have the following: 8 bits equals 256 colors. Each color can represent 256 shades of gray. Therefore, 256 for red×256 for green×256 for blue = 16.7 million potential color combinations.

Many products store varying numbers of bits per sample. Examples of videotape formats and postproduction hardware that are based on a specific number of bits per sample and total color array follow:

D2 videotape = 8 bits/sample = 256 colors at 4 FSC

4 FSC refers to 4×subcarrier frequency; 14.3 MHz NTSC and 17.7 MHz PAL. This is the sampling frequency that is most often used for digitizing composite video signals. Note that D2 is not limited to 256 colors because color information is represented by modulation of the subcarrier.

Quantel Paintbox = 24 bits/sample = 16.7 million colors

The Quantel Paintbox stores three channels for picture information: one for luminance and two separate channels for the color-difference channels. These two separate color memory planes are in full resolution.

Avid Matador Paint = 32 bits/sample = 16.7 million colors + 8-bit alpha channel

In a 32-bit system, eight bits per sample are allocated for luminance, the color-difference signals, and a new, fourth, component: the key channel (alpha) information.

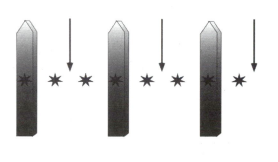

Figure 10-20 Three pickets are lost in the reduction process. Illustration by Jeffrey Krebs.

Decimation

Decimation means removing a great proportion of the elements that make up a whole. This form of subsampling occurs at the pixel level. If we have a 24-bit picture (8-bit samples for RGB), and we subsample the picture to 15 bits (5-bit samples for RGB), then to 12 bits (4-bit samples for RGB), and so on, the original picture will be drastically altered simply because much of the information necessary to represent the picture accurately will have been removed (Figure 10-21). In this example, reducing of the number of bits per pixel results in

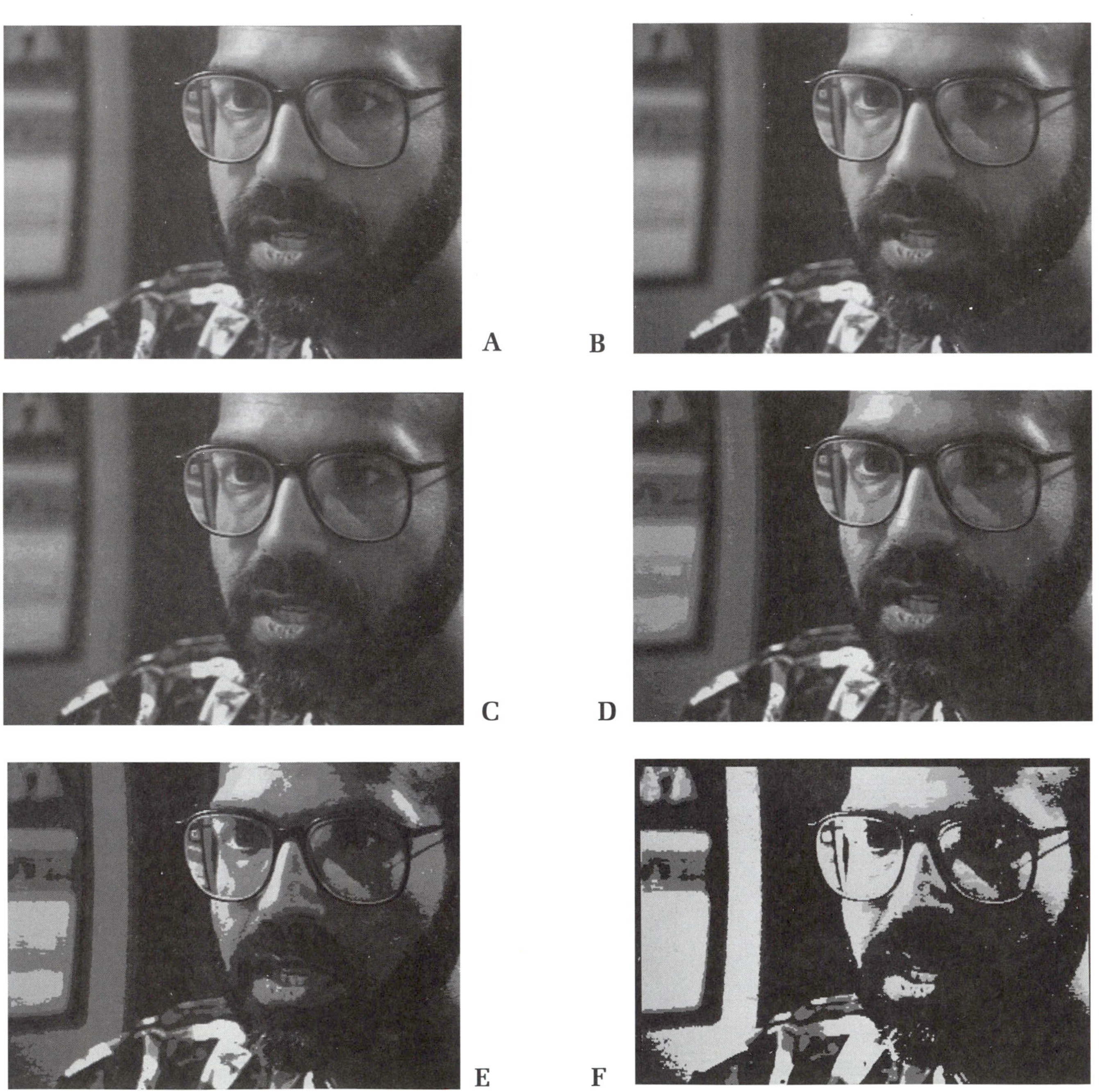

Figure 10-21 Decimation is a form of subsampling at the pixel level. Shown are the original 24-bit, 8-bits-per-pixel image **(A)** and subsampled images at **(B)** 15, **(C)** 12, **(D)** 9, **(E)** 6, and **(F)** 3 bits per pixel.

significant quantizing artifacts. Although the original quality of the 24-bit picture is affected, these pixel subsampling techniques create visual effects that can be used for artistic purposes. Many of these techniques are employed by digital video effects systems to achieve creative visual effects.

Error Masking Techniques

When a number of samples are missing from a signal, there may be ways to mask, or "repair," the affected areas. Digital recordings, unlike analog recordings, do not recreate video and audio signals by decoding waveforms for those signals. Digital recordings assign numbers to represent picture and sound. There is a specific benefit to this process: Numbers don't degrade. Digital videotape systems and compact audio disc systems still rely to some degree on *data error masking techniques* to compensate for media microfailures (dropouts), which are any brief failures of the medium to provide the data that the system is requesting.

Although video and audio signals are infinitely more complex to store as digital data than text, they enjoy an interesting advantage over characters, words, sentences, and paragraphs. Video and audio signals are much more tolerant than text (ASCII files or word processor documents) because there is a degree of predictability in video and audio. If errors occur, such as videotape dropouts, and information cannot be retrieved, it may be possible for the problem areas to be repaired. These areas can be filled in (masked) by using information from surrounding areas.

In Figure 10-22, the first image of the bridge shows the original picture, which has a defective area as a result of microfailures in the videotape medium called *dropouts*. This defective area measures two pixels wide. By taking a one-pixel wide line from above as well as from below the dropout area, we are able to repair the defective portion. This technique is a form of error masking.

Errors in playing back samples of audio can readily be heard if they fall within the normal range of human hearing, about 20 KHz. Error masking techniques are prevalent in digital audio systems, such as audio compact disc players. Compact audio discs are manufactured at a standard sampling rate of 44.1 KHz. Rather than count the exact number of samples—44,100—compact disc players often *oversample* the amount. It is normal to enter a retail store and see machines that offer "2×oversampling" or "8×oversampling."

In the case of a compact disc player that offers "2×oversampling," more samples are taken in (counted) than will be offered as signals in the output data. The disc player reads the CD and processes 88.2 KHz, but it only plays back at a rate of 44.1 KHz. If an error occurs while the machine is playing back a section of the CD, there will be redundant samples to fall back on. The benefit to the listener is that the error is internal; there is no apparent break in the sound. The "extra"

Figure 10-22 Error masking techniques can be used when an original image experiences failures in the medium to preserve recorded information. The black area in the image is "repaired" by filling in the defective portion with surrounding lines of video.

samples don't actually exist on the disc; rather, they are created in the player.

The concept of generation loss or no loss in a digital system also provides insight into lossy and lossless digital compression techniques. The same repetitive and predictive nature of video that makes it fault-tolerant and the beneficiary of error masking algorithms also makes video, as well as audio, a highly compressible signal requiring minimal data to represent the level of information perceived.

When a video signal is processed by the flash convertor, and the analog signal is converted to digital data, all the pixels take the same amount of space. Absolutely nothing is done to take into account any redundancy in the makeup of the video frame. This is because the digitizing process has no way of recognizing that there can be areas of a video frame that are similar and, therefore, that methods may exist by which this redundancy could lead to ways of reducing the data to be stored.

PRODUCTS AND CAPABILITIES BASED ON DIGITAL MANIPULATION

While the basic digitizing properties of the flash convertor permitted single-frame grabs, sophisticated machines began to appear that could digitize video in real time. This brought forth a series of products that allowed for the management and modification of the resulting digital signal. These devices began to appear in the early 1970s.

Products such as digital video effects units (which rapidly decode, digitally manipulate frames, and then encode), digital still stores (which store full-resolution video frames), digital paint systems (which are sophisticated electronic painting systems), and digital compositing devices (which allow digital images to be layered on top of one another without generation loss) are all examples of products based on digitally manipulating video frames.

Digital video tools are so ingrained in current methods of production and postproduction that the effects that they create may be familiar. These tools are used to create many of the special effects we regularly see, for example, in television commercials.

Being able to control components of a picture based on digitally manipulating the numbers that make up the picture provides the user with much more choice and control. Contrast this to the manner in which manipulating analog signals occurs: mostly by brute force approaches that do not permit for easy repetition of the task.

However, with digital techniques, modifications to a frame or a series of frames can be handled more intelligently, precisely, conditionally, and repetitively. When we have the ability to manipulate a frame of video digitally, the signal sifting becomes much easier to accomplish than trying to accomplish the same sifting in an analog world.

Figure 10-23 shows several examples in which manipulating the digital data that represent a picture can lead to interesting visual effects. The first picture (A) is the original 24-bit image. The second picture (B) shows the results of manipulating the degree of chrominance, contrast, and luminance in the image to create a visual effect. In fact, the subsampling technique of decimation is utilized. The third picture (C) is a mosaic effect, created by decreasing the number of horizontal and vertical samples used to display the picture. The fourth picture (D) is an example of adding perspective to the original image by changing its normal aspect ratio of four units horizontal by three units vertical.

Making changes to a frame of video by rearranging the digits that make up the frame has led to the creation of digital effects units, which have become standard in the postproduction world. In the ever-changing world of new machines that allow the user to paint, bend, enlarge, move, reposition, and combine frames, there are undeniable advantages of being in a digital nonlinear environment to manipulate frames of video.

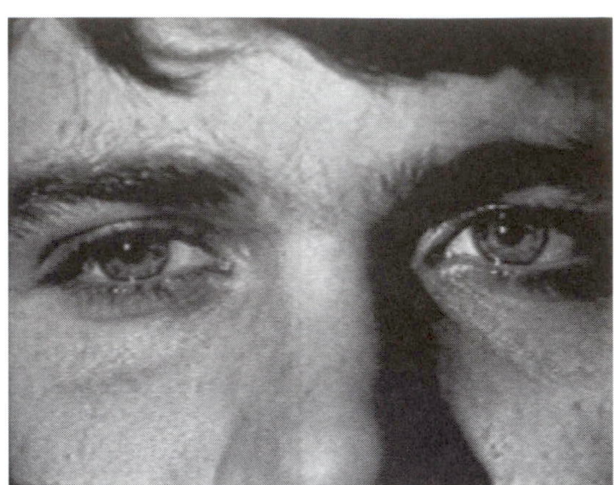

A

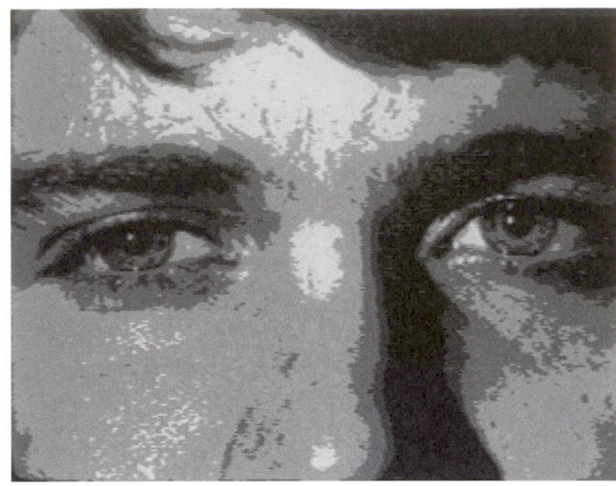

B

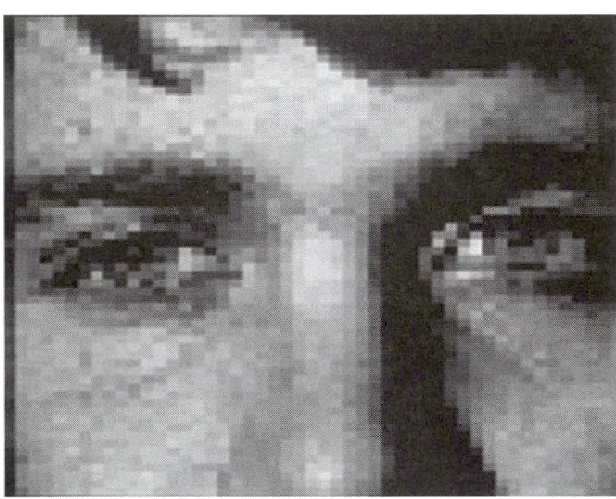

C

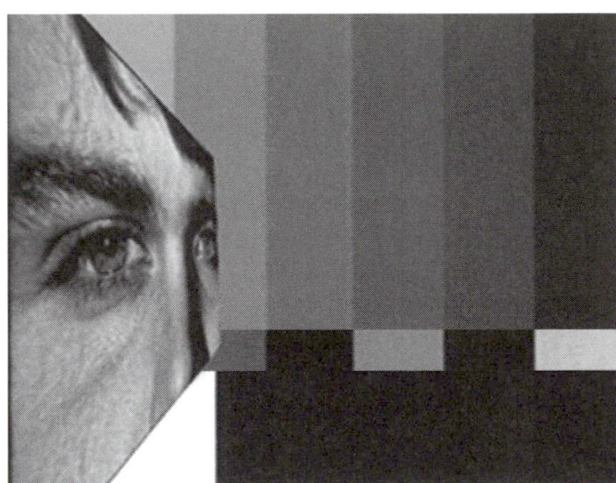

D

Figure 10-23 By manipulating the digital data that represents a picture, several creative visual effects can be achieved.

BANDWIDTH AND STORAGE

Bandwidth, in the context of the digitization process, refers to the number of bits per second of material that can be processed or transmitted within or between computers. The CPU is tasked with processing a number of bits per second when digitizing. The computer can process only a certain number of frames and a certain amount of information for each frame every second. These factors, in turn, affect how close to the original the pictures will look once stored on disk.

Basic Storage Terms

Bit	The smallest amount of information for a computer
Byte	8 bits
Kilobyte (KB)	~ 1000 bytes
Megabyte (MB)	1,000,000 bytes
Gigabyte (GB)	1,000,000,000 bytes
Terabyte (TB)	1,000,000,000,000 bytes

Note that these figures are approximate! The exact numbers are as follows:

1 KB = 1024 bytes

1 MB = 1024×1024 bytes

1 GB = 1024×1024×1024 bytes

Video Storage Requirements

Video signals, on a frame-by-frame basis, represent a large number of pixels. Large amounts of computer memory are required to store several seconds of video. Storage for one frame of video can range from 1 MB to over 125 MB, depending on the pixel matrix and depth!

ITU-R 601 NTSC

We can determine the storage requirement for one frame of ITU-R 601 (NTSC) video by performing the following calculation:

720×486 = 349,920 pixels×2 bytes = 699,840 bytes (~ 700 KB)

We multiply the number of bytes by 2 since samples of R-Y and B-Y are alternated in 4:2:2 sampling. Thus, it takes approximately 700 KB to store one video frame at this pixel matrix.

ITU-R 601 PAL

We determine the storage requirement for one frame of ITU-R 601 (PAL) video by performing the following calculation:

720×576 = 414,720 pixels×2 bytes = 1,244,160 bytes (~1.2 MB)

Thus, it takes approximately 1.2 MB to store one video frame at this pixel matrix.

High-Definition Television

In HDTV, the number of total sampling points with regard to horizontal and vertical lines includes pixel matrices that are 1180×720 and 1920×1080 at 24, 30, and 60 Hz, progressive scan. We begin with 1920 horizontal sample points and multiply by 1080 vertical sample points to get 2,073,600 pixels. We multiply this by 2 because it takes one word (2 bytes) to store each pixel in 4:2:2 sampling:

2,073,600×2 = 4,147,200 bytes

Therefore, to define one entire HDTV frame, we require 4.147 MB. For one second, we require more than 120 MB!

The constrictive factors of bandwidth limitations, economies of processing power, and disk storage capacities must be addressed to solve the essential problem: how to digitize full-motion video with sound and offer enough stored material so that an editor CAN work with a viable amount of footage. We may choose to work with completely uncompressed pictures or we may choose to reduce the amount of data stored for each video frame.

Editing Full-Resolution, Full-Bandwidth Digital Video

Of course, there are many jobs that require editing full-resolution digital video. When editing short pieces that rely heavily on graphic compositing in which layers of video and graphics are intertwined, it is very important to choose a postproduction methodology that will ensure that generational loss is nil or kept to a minimum. It is therefore very desirable to begin with the best possible picture quality and to maintain as lossless a signal path as possible.

A variety of DNLE systems digitize analog or digital signals and do not subsample or compress these signals. Avid Illusion, Discreet Logic Flame, and Quantel Henry all operate in full-resolution ITU-R 601 mode.

Resolution and Storage

At this stage, we have done nothing to reduce the amount of data it takes to represent a frame of video at its original and full resolution. We have only taken one critical step, the digitization of analog signals and the storage of those resulting data points as digital information. However, if we have a great deal of information to be stored, we may choose to employ compression.

How much resolution should be maintained for each frame of video, and how much digitized footage will be available at any one time? These two key questions determine what compression ratio we will employ. The tug of war between full-resolution pictures and large amounts of footage forms the basis for the discussion of digital video compression.

DIGITIZING THE AUDIO SIGNAL

While frames are being digitized and stored to disk, the accompanying audio signals are also being digitized. A simple pathway that four audio channels from a videotape recorder (VTR) would take is as follows: The four audio outputs from the VTR enter an A/D convertor for audio. In much the same way that our analog RGB video signals are flash converted and turned into digital data, the audio signals are sampled and converted. The resulting digital signals are then passed from the A/D convertor to a complementary card in the computer that processes the data by storing it to computer disk.

Sampling an audio signal is very similar to sampling a video signal. We can assign more or fewer samples, depending on the audio fidelity that we wish to preserve. Fortunately, the bandwidth requirements of even the most professional quality of audio pales in comparison with the requirements of full-resolution images. Whereas one frame of our 720×486 video requires approximately 700 KB, one second of two channels of compact-disc-quality audio (44.1 KHz) at 16 bits per sample (2 bytes/sample) requires

44.1 KB/sec×2 bytes/sample×2 (audio channels) = 88.2 KB/sec×2 = 176.4 KB/sec

Clearly, maintaining high-quality audio does not require nearly the amount of data that full-resolution video requires. The ability to store sufficient amounts of audio and to offer random-access audio editing is the leading reason why the development of digital audio workstations (DAWs) progressed so rapidly since their appearance in the mid-1980s. While most DAWs utilize hard disks, the relatively low bandwidth of 176.4 KB/sec (or about 10.5 MB for each minute of stereo audio) allows a variety of disk drives and optical discs to be used.

The limit of human hearing is approximately 20 KHz. Recall that the sampling theory holds that we must sample a signal at least twice as much as the highest frequency that we want to preserve. Professional audio recording systems sample slightly above two times, to over 40 KHz. Tables 10-3 and 10-4 show the audio frequencies and sampling rates of various for-

Table 10-3 Audio Frequency Rates

Format	*Audio Frequency Rate*
Film sound optical, 16mm	7 KHz
Film sound optical, 35mm	12–15 KHz
VHS linear tracks	10 KHz
3/4" video	10–15 KHz
Betacam	12–15 KHz
Betacam SP	15 KHz
Laserdisc	15 KHz
1" type C	15 KHz
1/4" audio tape (at 15 ips)	20 KHz
Hi8	20 KHz

Table 10-4 Audio Sampling Rates

Format	*Audio Sampling Rate*
Audio compact disc	44.1 KHz
D1	48.0 KHz
D2	48.0 KHz
D3	48.0 KHz
Digital audio tape	32, 44.1, 48.0 KHz
DVC	44.1 KHz

mats. The digital samples of 44.1 KHz to 48.0 KHz are designed to provide a realized resolution in excess of 20 KHz.

Hardware interfaces permit the simultaneous digitization of multiple tracks of sound. Some DNLE systems will usually digitize 2, 4, or 8 tracks of sound simultaneously. DAWs usually offer 8, 16, or 24 tracks that can be simultaneously digitized.

Most often, the A/D convertor operates in concert with an additional sound card that performs operations on the incoming audio data. The capabilities of the sound board vary from card to card; some are only capable of passing the digital data on to the disk drive, while others are capable of further filtering and compressing the data.

It is important to note that the audio signals have, thus far, only been digitized. Digital audio data are not normally compressed since digital audio data files are much smaller than digital video data files. If we elect not to compress the audio data, the information is passed from the sound card to the disk drive, and the digitization process is completed. However, compressing the audio signal can be accomplished with negligible quantization. Digital compression of audio is a common procedure when it is necessary to transmit the audio over various wide area networks.

INTRODUCTION TO COMPRESSION TECHNIQUES

Lossless Compression

Returning to the example of the document that was reduced in file size and then expanded back to its original file size, we can classify the file compacting program as a *lossless compression technique*. An original message was shortened, compressed, transmitted, and decompressed, and the original message was not changed. We ended up with the exact message with which we started. We did not receive a document with letters in the wrong order or with missing sentences.

Lossless compression techniques are clearly favored over losing information in a message, but lossless compression has boundaries. First, to be lossless, a lot of analyzing must be done. The message must be looked at, the statistics must be gathered, and the codes must be assigned. Depending on the information to be analyzed, this will require a certain amount of computer power and time. In certain circumstances, such as when video is traveling at full frame rate, there won't exist the luxury of being able to analyze each video frame at less than normal play speed; there will only be a very small amount of time in which to analyze the message and determine how it should be compressed.

Second, a stage called the *entropy* of the message will eventually be reached. Entropy is the measure of the frequency with which an event occurs in a system. Originally, we had a

100 KB file, and we compressed it to 50 KB. Now we try to compress the 50 KB file again. We may find that we are able to further compress it slightly, perhaps by several kilobytes, but we will not receive dramatic results and achieve, for example, a 25 KB file. What has happened is that we have reached the entropy point of the message that we are trying to compress. The resulting message is at its optimal point of compression.

It is important to note that the entropy of a message is different from the compression limits of the system performing the compression task. If a software compacting program has, as its limitation, a maximum file size reduction routine of 50%, this is the inherent capability of the system performing the compression and is a factor independent of the entropy point of the message being compacted.

Lossy Compression

When we make the decision to compress a file, whether that file is a document, a photograph, or a frame of video, we may have to make decisions that take us out of the realm of lossless compression and into the domain of lossy compression. *Lossy Compression* simply means that we lose information: The amount of information with which we end is not equal to the amount of information with which we started.

Why would we want to lose information? Why not always work with lossless compression techniques? Let's return to the 100 KB document. What options are available to us when we still require a file that is less than 50 KB in size? We try to compress it further, but we reach the entropy point of the message. We still want to reduce its size. The remaining option is to choose to lose some information but to leave enough clues so that the message can be deciphered adequately and accurately.

For example, consider our original sentence:

> Letters and words in our document are not equally likely; there will tend to be much repetition of a certain class of letters (such as vowels) as well as words.

What if we were to compress the sentence and make just a few changes that are lossy? We would lose information, but not so much information that we would change the readability and the decipherability of the message. For example, we could try the following:

> Lettrs and wrds in our docment are not equaly likely; there will tend to be much reptition of a crtain class of lettrs (such as vowels) as wel as wrds.

Clearly, we have lost information, but the message can probably be read and understood, even with the missing letters. This compressed file will never be the same as the original: We cannot replace information that has been deleted. Regardless, we have achieved our aim: The file is now represented by a smaller amount of data.

The readability and decipherability of this sentence depended on some very careful choices during the deletion stage. If too many letters were removed, or if letters were removed that would leave the meaning of the word ambiguous, we would have rendered sections of the message illegible. Assumptions regarding which letters to remove from which words were based on how we process language.

Assumptions regarding how much information is enough to receive the message successfully have to be made regardless of the item being compressed. Information is going to be lost, and we must attempt to ensure that it will be information that is expendable!

These assumptions about how information is processed by the human eye and intellect, theories concerning how much information is enough, and compromises therein, are decisions that will have to be made when the material to be compressed in size is no longer textual, but visual: film and video frames.

Analog Compression

Before continuing our discussion of digital video compression, it is necessary to understand those concepts that carry over from analog-based compression (Figure 10-24). Digital video compression methods have much in common with the manner in which analog compression of video signals occurs in everyday image origination and distribution. Analog video signals are routinely compressed from the time that they are originated to the time that they are viewed. When we watch a television show, we are watching the effects of analog compression. The original signal that was captured is superior to the image we get to view because of the stages that the signal has undergone. These stages may be long or short, depending on the signal path that the program must take from origination to distribution. Of course, this argument does not hold true for digital television, which is not intruded upon by analog compression.

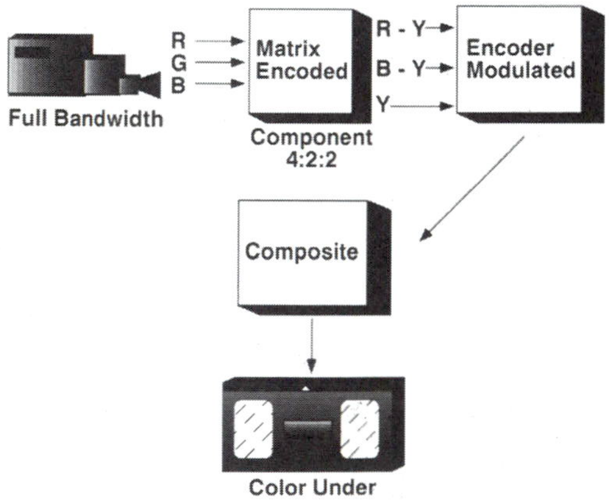

Consider the compression path that an analog video signal will take when we capture images on a video camera for distribution to our audience on a composite videotape recording. Figure 10-24 shows the original camera signal, whose red, green, and blue signals carry 10 MHz of information per channel. These signals represent the full-bandwidth, uncompressed signal that originates from the camera.

Since the distribution form in this example is a composite VHS videocassette, it is necessary to matrix-encode these individual signals. *Matrix* simply means that the individual signals must be combined, in effect, composited together. This condition is also referred to as *color under*, where luminance and chrominance first are separated while the information per channel is reduced from the original signal, then these signals are combined through a heterodyne process. Matrix encoding results in the original RGB signal being broken down into the following components: Y, R-Y, and B-Y, where Y = luminance, R = red, and B = blue.

Figure 10-24 The analog compression process for an RGB-originated camera signal shows the degradation inherent during the various compression stages as the signals approach their final distribution form on videocassette. Illustration by Jeffrey Krebs.

These Y, R-Y, and B-Y signals exist in a 4:2:2 ratio, in which there are four samples of luminance for every two color-difference signals. This process also reduces the amount of information for the individual channels, as luminance is filtered to 4 MHz per channel, and each of the color signals is filtered to 2 MHz per channel. We have encountered our first stage of analog compression.

The next stage is to encoder-modulate these component signals into a composite signal. Here, the color information is further wave-shaped down to 1 MHz or less per channel. By the time that the composite signal is introduced to the VHS machine and recorded, the color information has been limited to approximately 1/2 MHz in bandwidth. The luminance channel has been further reduced to 2 MHz.

This analog compression process is a normal affair for images that originate in RGB and that must be recorded onto composite, color-under videotape machines. From the original 10 MHz of information per channel, there is quite a decrease in the luminance and chrominance information by the time the signal is recorded to tape. This is a form of compression, and many of these same principles carry over to the digital video compression techniques outlined below.

Digital Video Compression

The digitizing experiments that scientists at Bell Labs conducted regarding visual recognition yielded certain characteristics and traits for the minimal amount of sampling information necessary to recreate an image. In the early 1980s, Sarnoff Labs, a division of RCA, conducted experiments aimed at providing a new form of entertainment. These experiments eventually led to methods of digital image compression.

The appearance of compact audio discs in 1983 heralded the ability to search and play audio in whatever order the listener wanted. RCA felt that "nonlinear home video" was a promising area for product investigation. The goal was to provide home presentation programming through the use of hardware and software systems that would put the viewer in charge of how the presentation proceeded.

To test whether these interactive programs could be successful, four pilot projects were conducted. One involved the subject of archaeology. A production crew shot every conceivable path around a historic temple, allowing the viewer to see every possible point of view to and from the temple. An archaeological dig was in progress, and the production included footage of the excavation of artifacts, the preservation of these items, and their eventual display in museums. The program combined all this motion material with still pictures, audio, and graphics.

A computer program was written that allowed the user to, in effect, explore the archaeological site at will. The user could choose to learn about the history of the site, view the site, watch the unearthing of an artifact, and then see the artifact displayed in a museum. Or if the user did not want to progress in such a linear fashion, he or she could start out by seeing the object in its museum setting and then jump to an exploration of the site.

The manner in which the material was laid down to disc didn't matter at all; the power to move through the material was in the hands of the user, so in whatever fashion the user wanted to explore, the computer program allowed him or her to do so. All this was possible because the medium on which the project was stored allowed such freedom.

How was it done, and how did the user have random access to the material? Since the material was digitized and the pathway to the material was a computer program, on what storage medium was the project recorded? The method involved compressing the huge bandwidth of video that made up the program and storing the results on a digital medium. A video compression method known as *digital video interactive* (DVI) was used. It searched for and discarded redundancies of visual information. In so doing, the resulting pictures were no longer at full resolution. However, the quality was sufficient to enable users to view the program successfully. The information for the program, now digitized and compressed, was recorded to a compact disc that included video as well as audio and played back in a compact disc interactive (CDI) system. This happened in 1987.

Combining all these different media into one medium that could then be easily accessed by the user via the computer required the use of digital video compression. Digital video compression can be achieved by software alone or by software and hardware. There are several types of digital image compression methods:

Digital video interactive (DVI)
Motion joint photographic experts group (M-JPEG)
Moving picture experts group (MPEG)

Hardware and Software Compression Methods

Compression, reducing a volume of data, can be accomplished using software-only methods or through a combination of hardware and software methods. The advantage of being able to compress in a software-only system is that dedicated hardware that aids the compression process does not have to be designed and implemented.

The most powerful compression methods are achieved through a combination of hardware and software because the addition of hardware facilitates processing more instructions per second.

Software-Only Compression

As we know, it takes time to analyze analog signals and determine how the signal should be sampled and coded. Software-only compression methods can be made to work in the real-time world of video, which moves at 30 frames per second, but the amount of information that they can process and pass—in effect, take in and move out—is limited. Software-only compression schemes can only process frames of video that have a certain number of bits representing that frame of video. When the compression scheme reaches the threshold of data that it can process and pass, more information must be thrown away, the number of frames per second must be reduced, or the process must become slower than real time.

All of these consequences are objectionable, and, as a result, software-only compression methods had a limited use in DNLE systems.

THE DIGITIZING AND COMPRESSION PROCESS: SOFTWARE- AND HARDWARE-ASSISTED

Software-only compression methods were used during the years 1987 to 1989, after which time hardware-assisted compression became the standard for DNLE system operation. Digitizing video frames requires the following components: (1) CPU, (2) flash convertor (A/D, the digitizer), (3) framestore (computer memory), (4) D/A convertor, and (5) software algorithms that orchestrate the components and the compression process by determining the amount of data that will be stored for a video frame.

Figure 10-25A illustrates the role of the digitizing engine. The process begins when composite analog video is played into the system. The video signal is decoded and broken down into Y, Cr, and Cb components. These components are then matrix decoded into red, green, blue, and sync components. Sync is composed of stabilizing signals that are present to ensure that the signals being sent to a television screen are in concert with the normal scanning operation of the screen. Note that there can be a variety of input formats supported: composite, component analog, serial digital, and so forth.

The three color components are then processed by three A/D flash convertors. Note that the decoding stage is analog, while the process after the A/D conversion is entirely digital. The digitized data (codes now assigned to represent the analog signals) are passed to a framestore in the computer (the computer's memory) and stored in a new form, as bits. The framestore is capable of handling 24-bit-wide samples.

Figure 10-25B depicts essentially the same process as that shown in Figure 10-25A, except that the process is now completely digital. Whereas Figure 10-25A shows analog decoding and matrixing stages, in Figure 10-25B these stages are digital.

The RGB framestores are connected to the CPU via a 32-bit-wide bus (Figure 10-26). This bus is usually referred to as the *computer back plane bus*. The actual speed of this bus is rated in megahertz (MHz). High bus ratings are associated with allowing more data to pass from the framestores to the CPU back plane. For example, a 60 MHz bus operates at 60 million cycles per second. Via this bus, each cycle carries up to 32 bits

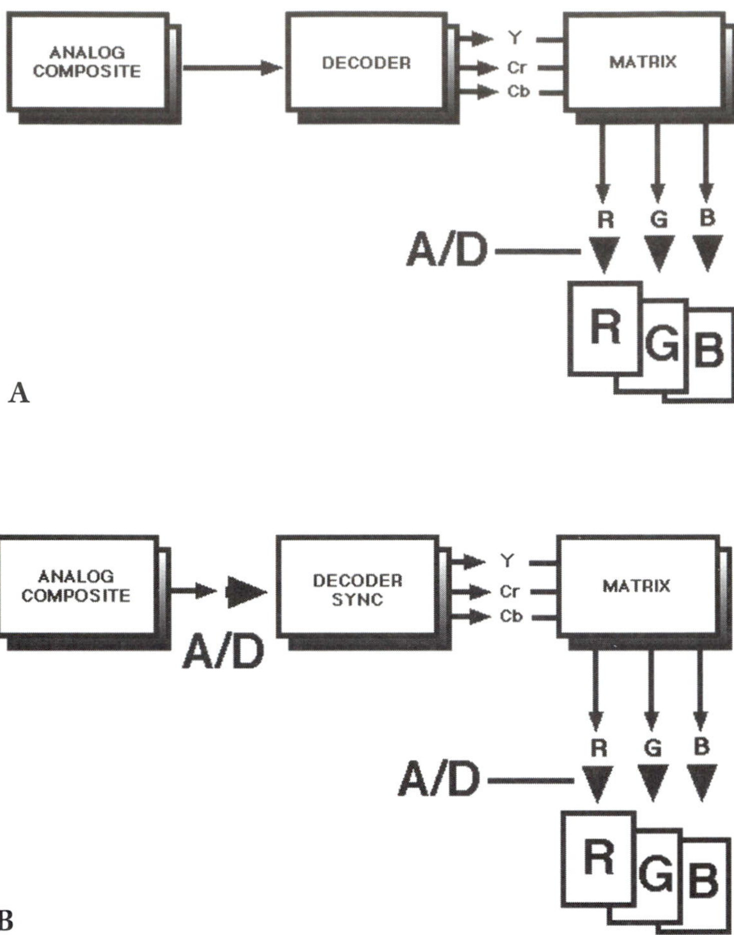

Figure 10-25 **(A)** The digitizing process begins as composite analog video is decoded into its analog components and flash converted. In this scenario, the decoding stage is an analog process while the process after the A/D stage is a digital process. **(B)** A similar process, but with the decoding and matrixing stages digital rather than analog.

of data, and the bus can operate at 60 million cycles per second. Since eight bits is one byte, four bytes can be processed:

32 bits = 4 bytes×60 million cycles/sec = 240 MB/sec

If we have a 60 MHz CPU bus, it has the capacity to transfer approximately 240 MB of data each second. Without some type of accelerator, no additional data can pass. In actuality, however, even though the bus can sustain 240 MB/sec, it would really only be used for passing 180 MB/sec. Recall that

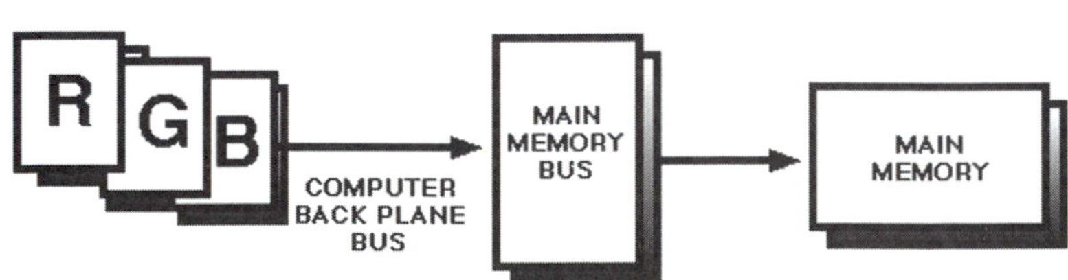

Figure 10-26 The RGB framestores connect to the CPU via the computer back plane bus. Data passing from the framestores through this bus are eventually passed to the CPU's main memory via the main memory bus. Illustration by Jeffrey Krebs.

our video frame is providing us with 24 bits of information. Therefore,

24 bits = 3 bytes×60 million cycles/sec = 180 MB/sec

The CPU is connected to its main memory by another bus called, appropriately enough, the *memory bus*. The width of these busses varies from computer to computer and can range from 8 to 128 bits or more.

What we have achieved thus far is the process of digitization: getting analog signals converted to digital signals and stored into a computer's memory. The signals can be reprocessed through a D/A convertor and encoded back to composite, component, or digital video and viewed on a monitor.

It is easy to see where potential bottlenecks can occur. If we have a bus that can support 100 MB/sec, we can easily handle two streams of uncompressed ITU-R 601 video, which requires approximately 42 MB/sec. However, the disk subsystem that we are using may not be able to support real-time digitizing at the rate of 42 MB/sec. Listed below are the capabilities of common disk subsystems (see Chapter 11):

Fast, narrow SCSI controllers support bus transfers of up to 10 MB/sec.
Fast/Wide SCSI controllers support bus transfers of up to 20 MB/sec.
Ultra Wide SCSI controllers support bus transfers of up to 40 MB/sec.

Of course, higher data rates can be supported if we employ disk striping (see Chapter 11). In addition, other technologies may be employed, such as fibre channel, with its planned rate of 125 MB/sec. At this point, we have successfully digitized video and audio signals. Prior to storing these signals to disk, we must decide whether or not to use digital video compression techniques to reduce the amount of data to be stored.

Software Compression

Compression is usually applied as frames exit the A/D convertor. Software-only methods usually involve two common themes: reducing the size of the matrix for the image by removing pixels (a technique called *scaling*) and reducing the amount of color information (*chroma subsampling*).

For example, with scaling, instead of sending the pixels based on a 720×486 matrix from the framestore to the bus and to the CPU, the first method of reducing information is to reduce the size of the pixel matrix. Thus, fewer pixels are represented in each frame of video that we have to process. For example, if we use a matrix of 360×243, we reduce the horizontal and vertical information by one-half.

We can also choose to reduce the overall amount of color that passes over the bus. Usually, we process three colors: red, green, and blue. However, to further reduce our data, we can drastically reduce the amount of color. Whereas we normally

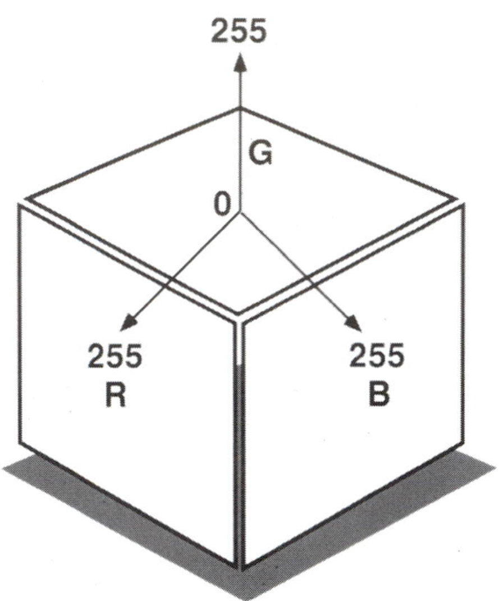

Figure 10-27 The color space occupied by a 24-bit sample. Each color is capable of representing 256 levels on a grayscale. Illustration by Jeffrey Krebs.

process 3 bytes of color (8 bits each for RGB), we could reduce 24 bits of color (3 bytes) into 8 bits of color (1 byte). There are various combinations, of course, but by representing the colors red and green by 3 bits each, and the color blue by 2 bits, we can process all our colors in 1 byte of information:

R (3 bits) + G (3 bits) + B (2 bits) = 1 byte

In Figure 10-27, we look at the color space normally occupied by our 24-bit sample of red, green, and blue. Each color is capable of representing 256 levels on a grayscale. If we multiply 256×256×256, the total number of colors that this 24-bit sample can represent is about 16.7 million.

In our subsampling example, by reducing the overall number of bits for each color and ending up with just 1 byte for each frame of video, we have lost the ability to see 16.7 million possible colors. Regardless of how complex the color scheme may be in the images being processed, we have only 1 byte to represent that color scheme. Because of this, the most colors we can possibly hope to see represented is limited to 256.

Results of Subsampling

Reducing the combined number of horizontal and vertical pixels and the amount of color information yields significant results. In the above example, not only did we reduce the overall data requirement immediately by 50% as a result of scaling, but we further reduced the data by more than 60% as a result of color subsampling. This reduced amount of data places less stress on the disk subsystem, and we are able to store more footage as a result.

However, software-only compression techniques have many limitations. Since there is so little time to make an analysis of the redundant information from frame to frame, software-only methods operate by discarding wholesale pieces of information without making genuine judgments on the relative importance of the components in the frame.

If we recall our example of the sentence from which we removed letters, certain decisions were made regarding which letters to remove. We based our decisions on knowledge we possess with regard to how language works and how it is interpreted. But making these judgments takes time. They are based on known information and require additional software programming. Yet with software-only compression methods, there is little time left over that can be allotted to analyze, judge, and recommend plans of action for each video frame being processed. As a result, hardware-assisted compression methods became the standard for DNLE system operation by 1991.

Hardware-Assisted Compression

When hardware and software are used together to compress video, several advantages are realized over software-only methods. First, hardware-based compression allows more instructions to be run per second. This provides more time to analyze and judge a frame of video before the next frame of video must be processed. Second, the wholesale discarding of information can be relegated to more of a last resort rather than a given. Instead, more time will be available to examine the video frame, identify redundancies, and assign numeric values. Intelligent decisions and plans of action can be made based on knowledge regarding how our eyes process information.

M-JPEG COMPRESSION

JPEG compression, which was proposed by the Joint Photographic Experts Group, a subset of the International Telephone and Telegraph Consultative Committee (CCITT) and the International Organization for Standardization (ISO), is a form of hardware-assisted compression (Figure 10-28). M-JPEG, or Motion-JPEG, is a derivative of JPEG for moving pictures. JPEG is based on still images, also called *continuous-tone images*, whereas MPEG, which is discussed later, is based on motion video.

Significant and powerful compression methods employ mathematical procedures to accomplish the analysis of the video frame. These mathematical procedures are referred to as *discrete cosine transforms* (DCTs). The DCT is a lossy algorithm, which simply means that when a file is compressed

Figure 10-28 Hardware-assisted digital video compression is accomplished through the use of a computer chip. A variety of M-JPEG-based computer chips is available from different manufacturers. Courtesy C-Cube Microsystems, Inc.

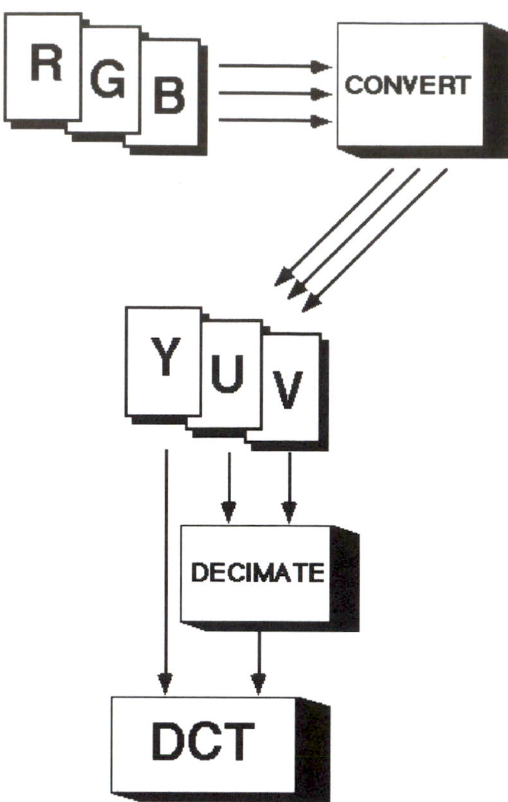

Figure 10-29 The RGB signals are converted to YUV, and the color portion undergoes decimation. Next, the signals enter the discrete cosine transform stage. Illustration by Jeffrey Krebs.

using an M-JPEG-based processor, information about the original signal is discarded and lost. Which information to discard, which information to keep, and how much information will remain versus the original signal are the key issues addressed by the DNLE system's compression algorithms.

In Figure 10-29, the RGB signals are processed by the hardware-based compression "engine," which connects to the RGB framestore. As before, the composite analog video signal is decoded into component RGB, flash converted, and processed by the secondary CPU. This hardware engine differs from the supplemental CPU added to the framestore because it performs operations based on compression rather than digitization.

Now, however, we introduce compression. Instead of the data leaving the framestore and passing directly over the bus to the CPU, which would be the case if we were capturing and storing uncompressed video, data exit the framestore and enter the compression section of our model. There, the data undergo the M-JPEG-based compression schemes, travel over the bus, and move on to the CPU.

Adding this compression engine to our model offers additional time to better analyze the video frame. The goals of hardware compression are the same as the goals of any lossy compression scheme: to preserve as much detail as possible in the picture while simultaneously discarding as much information as possible. There are a variety of concerns: how to analyze the frame, what information should be kept and what information discarded, as well as the overall amount of footage that we require to be stored.

Inside the Compression Engine

M-JPEG compression centers around the ability to decode and encode grayscale and color images at full video frame rates. Chip sets from different manufacturers will have varying capabilities: Some chip sets are limited to processing video that does not exceed ITU-R 601 resolution, while other chip sets can function with video in excess of 601 resolution. Both the chip set and the software from the DNLE system determine what compression ratio is employed.

In 1991, when M-JPEG compression was introduced in DNLE systems, the compression ratio was quite high—varying between 100:1 to 75:1. The higher the compression ratio, the lower the resulting picture quality. As years passed, the compression ratio of DNLE systems has decreased while picture quality dramatically improved. Compression ratios of 2:1 and uncompressed picture quality are choices to be made based on the project's requirements.

Chroma Subsampling

The component RGB signals from the framestore enter the compression engine. These signals are then converted into YUV: luminance and color-difference components. With 8 bits each, we have a 24-bit sample to be processed. While luminance is left untouched, the next step is to decimate color, for it is at this stage that chroma subsampling is applied. It is important to note that, although the digitization process may have introduced quantization artifacts, it is at this stage that we begin a lossy compression process of discarding information that will be irretrievable.

This stage is similar to what happens with analog component signals, such as Betacam's color time division multiplexing (CTDM) storage methods. CTDM is a basic technique used in the record and playback processes of Betacam videotape. In CTDM recording techniques, the bandwidth of the color signal is divided by 2. When a composite signal is recorded to Betacam, the signal is broken down into luminance (Y) and the color-difference signals, R-Y and B-Y. These color-difference signals are then processed through a timebase corrector.

This TBC is a special-purpose device used to provide horizontal management of the color channels. Here, the R-Y signal is shrunk to one-half of its size and placed on the left side of a horizontal matrix. The B-Y signal is also reduced to one-half of its size and then placed on the right side of the same horizontal matrix. This matrix is, in fact, one horizontal line. Both R-Y and B-Y now have only one-half of a line available to them and are, therefore, one-half of their original resolution.

When a CTDM recording is played back, the special-purpose TBC takes R-Y and B-Y and performs a 2× expansion. The luminance signal is delayed to compensate for the delay caused by processing R-Y and B-Y through the TBC. The TBC thus is used to resynchronize Y, R-Y, and B-Y so that they are back in parallel. CTDM signal processing is essentially the reason why it is impossible to purchase a Betacam machine without a timebase corrector. CTDM is an example of the lossy analog signal processing environment.

Continuing with the subsampling model, we process a sample of U while discarding a sample of V. Then we process a sample of V while discarding a sample of U. Alternately discarding samples in this fashion reduces the overall amount of data to be processed. As a result, our 24-bit sample is now reduced to 16 bits: 8 bits for Y and 8 bits for either U or V. In sequence, it would look like this: Y and U, then Y and V, and so on, with each cycle being 16 bits long. Within the 16 bits per pixel, we can represent 256 levels of color (quantization levels). This is akin to what happens with component 4:2:2 color handling.

After decimation, Y and alternating color-difference signals are sent to the discrete cosine transform. The main purpose of the DCT is to use frequencies to represent a picture, whereas, prior to this, pixels were used to represent the picture.

It is important to note that compression algorithms vary from manufacturer to manufacturer. Instead of the decimation described above, increased or decreased ratios may be employed. Alternatively, no decimation may occur, and all 24 bits will be preserved. Which algorithm to use and to what

Figure 10-30 Using an 8×8 array, a picture is analyzed as a series of shades of gray. The purpose is to ascertain levels from one section to another and to use this information to represent the entire picture as frequencies and not as pixels. Illustration by Jeffrey Krebs.

degree decimation will occur are choices that will affect the type of picture quality and amount of storage required.

The DCT

When the YUV components of a frame enter the DCT, the frame is divided into 8×8 squares. The entire picture is processed at one time, and the DCT analyzes this whole array. This is the first step in representing the picture as frequencies and not as pixels (Figure 10-30).

Representing a picture's elements via frequencies can be thought of as if we were asking the question, "How much brighter are these elements of the picture than those elements of the picture?" The baseline from which to make these comparisons is zero direct current (0 DC), which, for our purposes, equals the average gray level for the picture being analyzed. These frequency determinations continue until the entire 8×8 array has been analyzed. The data that are formed represent information concerning how the pixels were arrayed. We are able to reconstruct a picture based on interpreting the assigned frequencies that make up the picture.

In general, the overall shape and outline of a picture will be represented by low frequencies, while fine edges will be represented by higher frequencies. Another way of thinking about this is that items that are big and take up a lot of screen space are represented by low frequencies. Details for those items, such as fine serifs on a typeface, will be represented by high frequencies. In addition, most of the extraneous and unwanted noise in a video signal is associated with high frequencies.

After analyzing an 8×8 array, the process is repeated for the next 8×8 array. We started with a picture that had a matrix of 720×486 pixels, which gives us a total of 349,920 pixels. We analyze these as 8×8 blocks (64 pixels) and must do this analysis 5,467.5 times to completely analyze the picture. The process repeats itself when the next frame presents itself to the DCT.

The analysis of the pixel makeup of a picture by the DCT is a lossless step. We begin with 64 pixels in each 8×8 array, and we achieve 64 frequencies as a result of the analysis. No information has been lost. Rather, the data have been interpreted in a different and lossless fashion.

In Figure 10-31, luminance (Y) and chrominance (C) exit the DCT and are now represented by frequencies (f). The next stage, quantization, is a lossy step.

Quantization

It is during the quantization stage that a significant amount of M-JPEG compression is accomplished. Here, file sizes can be marginally or drastically reduced: Either lossless encoding can occur or lossy compression can be applied. With lossless encoding, no information will be lost. With lossy encoding, information will be lost that can never be retrieved. How the resulting pictures will be perceived affects the decisions that must be made regarding how much information should be discarded. In

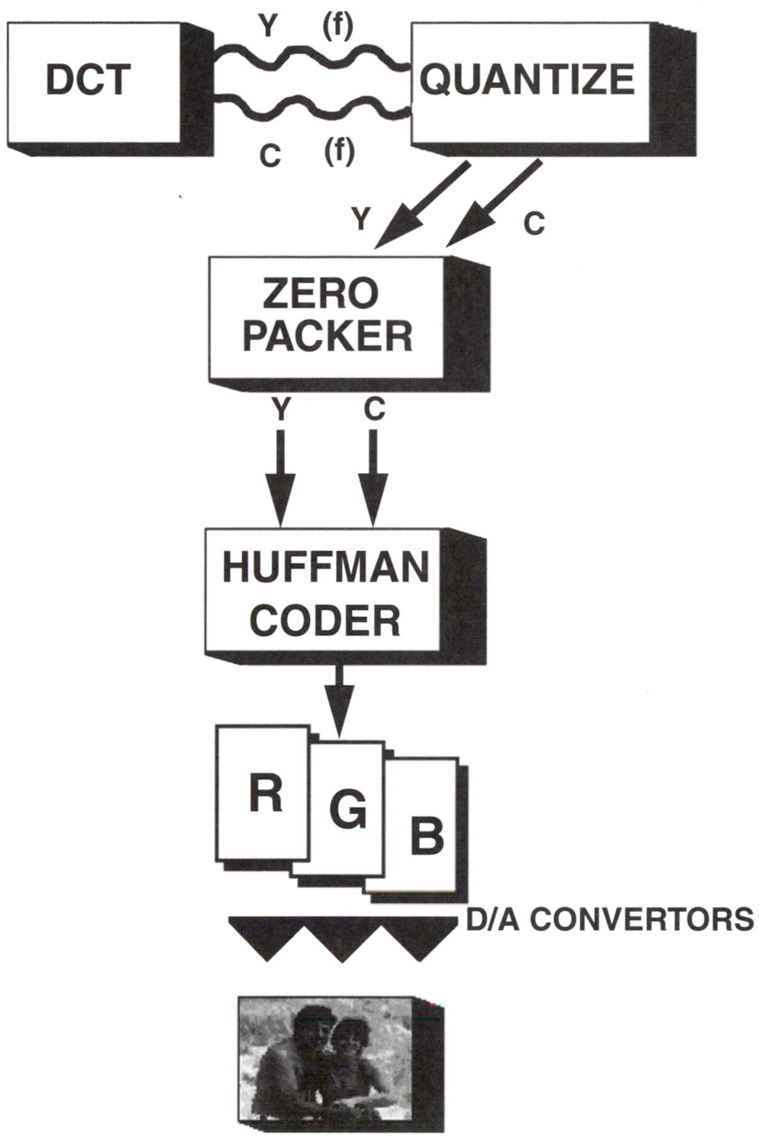

Figure 10-31 The discrete cosine transform processes YUV signals and represents them as frequencies, which then enter the quantize section. These frequencies undergo compression and are zero packed and further coded. These digitized signals undergo a D/A conversion, resulting in a viewable signal. Illustration by Jeffrey Krebs.

general, an M-JPEG compression ratio of 2:1 is relatively difficult to distinguish from the original image.

The quantization table (Q table) and the methods by which it operates are based on human visual system (HVS) studies, which seek to answer such questions as these:

Which frequencies is the human eye very good at seeing?
Which frequencies is the eye not good at seeing?
How does the eye respond to motion?
How does the eye respond to a static frame?
What luminance information can be removed?
What chrominance information can be removed?

The luminance and chrominance signals that make up a picture are not of equal importance to the human visual system. Digital video compression techniques take into account that when the eye processes a picture, the more important aspect is the picture's luminance content. Color is a much more expendable portion of a picture. Based on some estimates, up to 90% of a picture's color information can be removed without adversely affecting the recognizability of that picture. As a result, most compression schemes take into account that much of a picture's color can be sacrificed. Operating under such principles, digital video compression algorithms seek to discard information in an intelligent way.

If you think about mathematical ways of reducing a number, one basic method involves dividing that number by a higher number. Simply, the number 50 divided by 5 equals 10. If we increase the denominator to 25, we get 50 divided by 25 equals 2. A Q factor is, in essence, a denominator that reflects how marginally or drastically the frequencies will be changed during quantization. The Q factor is the bit/pixel relationship of an image.

A practical guideline is that a Q factor of 50 (Q 50) will lead to little loss of detail (and therefore retains high quality) while up to 95% of the data for that image is removed. When Q 50 is exceeded, deterioration of the image follows rapidly. Q factors of 100 and higher are typically used when image quality is secondary to storage requirements. Therefore, the relationship between the Q factor and KB/frame of images is as follows:

> As the Q factor increases, the KB/frame decreases. As a result, a higher Q factor will result in a decrease in picture quality. Conversely, as the Q factor decreases, the KB/frame increases. As a result, a lower Q factor will result in an increase in picture quality.

The goal of M-JPEG compression at this stage is to represent the 64 frequencies of each 8×8 array as smaller and shorter messages to store. For each 8×8 array, the frequencies represented by that array are arranged from DC level (0) to 63, which represents the highest frequency in the array. The quantized frequency array is the sum of the frequencies of each 8×8 array.

The quantization factor (Q factor) is then applied. Here each of the frequencies for one 8×8 array is divided by a set constant:

> Quantized frequency array = Quantized table elements (frequencies)/Q factor

The Q factor chosen has an inverse relationship to the amount of information left intact. Q factors range from 0 to 255, for a total of 256 steps. Recall that we are working in 8-bit samples, equating to 256 levels in grayscale. As the Q factor goes up, more information will be thrown away. As the Q factor goes down, more information will remain.

What is being accomplished during this stage is akin to the type of process used when long and short codes were assigned to our compacted document. The goal here is to produce a string of as many numbers as possible that are smaller than the original frequencies. By doing this, a series of numbers is created that, when taken in total, will represent transmitting less information for the original number of frequencies. By doing this, we have quantized out a large number of the original frequencies. We have compressed the array and, ultimately, the file.

The quantization process—the Q factor and the resulting quantization frequency array—represents the primary area in which the significant compression steps are taken. The "magic," if you will, with regard to what constants are chosen for the Q table, is the algorithms and formulas based on examining the perceived differences in pictures treated with different Q tables. Recall that we divide the quantized table elements (the frequencies) by a Q factor. The Q factor, in turn, utilizes a table of divisors, the Q tables. These are the tables that further influence the quality of the picture.

The "quality" of an M-JPEG compressed image is the ratio of compression (in bits/pixel), which is regulated by the Q factor and the size of the image (in pixels/second).

Our 64 frequencies have now been shortened. When we examine the quantized frequency array, we would expect to see a predominance of zeroes.

Zero Packer

The next step is to process the quantized frequency array. This is done through the use of a *zero packer.* The goal of this stage is to take the resulting zeroes and assign a code that designates how many zeroes there are, which aids in the transmission of less data as the process reaches its end. It is a lossless procedure.

Zero packing uses a process called *run-length encoding* (RLE). There is a history of using RLE processing in broadcasting equipment. Early character generators utilized run-length encoding to define the shape of characters. Run-length encoding determined when to switch a character from black (invisible) to white (visible) over the length of a horizontal line. Each character was defined by zeroes and ones, which would run for a certain length along a horizontal line.

Huffman Coder

The zero packer passes its information on to the Huffman coder. The coder runs a Huffman table. The purpose of this stage is to calculate redundancy in order to store and, therefore, to transmit less data. This is a lossless stage, and it utilizes the process of Huffman encoding.

The Huffman coding stage results in data that are stored to computer disk. When we want to view material, the data are accessed from the computer disk, undergo decompression, and are reprocessed by the three D/A convertors in the framestore. At the same time, sync is reapplied, resulting in a composite analog video signal. This signal can then be viewed and recorded to videotape.

These are the various stages of decoding, transforming, and encoding that are typically associated with the digitizing and compressing process of M-JPEG. Different manufacturers and system or software developers may vary or rearrange the order of these processes, but this provides an adequate outline.

Finally, returning to the example of the compressed document, if we were to take an M-JPEG file and run a software compacting program designed to reduce the size of that file, we would find that very little, if any, additional space can be saved. Although the compacting program will make attempts, usually the result is 0% saved, the entropy of the message having been reached long before.

Symmetrical versus Asymmetrical Compression

M-JPEG is a compression process that is symmetrical in nature. This means that it takes an equal amount of processing power to compress an image as to decompress that image. This is important because in applications designed for editing, the compression of a frame must occur in real time. Decompressing that same frame must also occur in real time. Popular examples of symmetrical methods include teleconferencing and videophones.

Asymmetric compression techniques, on the other hand, require a greater amount of processing power, almost always during the compression stage. Once the material has been compressed, it can be decompressed with fewer processing requirements. Obviously, there are limitations with regard to the editing process. Since asymmetric compression is a non-real-time process, it will require a delay while material is transferred from analog to digital, compressed, and readied for playback.

Compact disc–read only memory (CD-ROM) is an example in which asymmetric compression methods are employed. CD-ROM is an optical disc that usually stores 650 MB of data. Transferring information to and ordering it on the disc is an asymmetric process, but once the disc has been made, the data on it can be read and quickly accessed. CD-ROM is used extensively in interactive games, industry, and education, and the playback systems are quite affordable.

Fixed Frame Size versus Variable Frame Size

M-JPEG seeks to determine redundancy in a frame while preserving detail. The compression stage, where the Q factor and Q tables are employed, may or may not take into account the complexity of information for each and every frame that must be processed. M-JPEG is neither a fixed-frame-size nor a variable-frame-size compression method; that is the choice of the implementation method utilized by the DNLE system.

Fixed-frame-size implementations mean that there is a fixed amount of data that the compression algorithm will allow for each frame. It will not expand this amount of information if the frame contains more data than the algorithm is set to process.

Variable-frame-size approaches, in contrast, are set for a range of data for the frame. If some action occurs from frame to frame, the compression algorithm will, for those frames, expand accordingly and allow more data to pass in order to preserve those elements in the frames related to the temporary increase in data.

For example, let's say we aim a film camera at a boy who is sitting on a bench in a park. Behind him, in the distance, is a landscape of trees. The boy is fairly static, and the camera is not moving. A frame of this boy will yield a certain amount of data. Just for purposes of illustration, let's say that each frame will require 100 KB.

Next, we continue to film the boy, and between the bench and the trees in the distance, a woman riding a horse passes through the frame. The amount of data in our frames increases. Let's say that these frames jump from 100 KB to 125 KB because there is more going on in the frame. For the time during which the horse and rider are in frame, we will be required to store more data than if only the boy were in frame.

As a frame increases in detail content, the frame will contain more data that will have to be either processed or discarded. Because we have no way of knowing if there will be extraneous and unexpected action in our filming of the boy, how will M-JPEG compression handle the resulting frames of information?

Fixed-Frame-Size Technique

In the fixed-frame-size approach, a threshold is set for all frames with regard to the total amount of data that can be stored per frame. If the threshold is set at 125 KB, we will preserve all the information in our example with the boy, the horse, and the rider.

However, if the threshold is set lower, to 110 KB per frame, there will be a loss of information. The frames of the boy will be fine, since they only require 100 KB, but the more complex frames will usually have one of two problems. First, it may not be possible to digitize the frames. When this occurs, it is usually because the DNLE system has not been able to clear its buffers of the digitized frames before the next series of frames must enter the buffers. As a result, there is nowhere to put the incoming footage—the frames are not digitized, and the digitizing process stops.

Second, it is possible that the footage will be digitized but may have truncated (missing) data. Missing information in these cases is usually characterized by a loss of data in the coding blocks that make up the picture. When we look at the compressed file as it is being played back, entire sections (blocks) of the picture could be missing; there are no data there to be displayed. Usually what is represented in these sections are random (and incorrect) contents of memory or what can be termed *pixel confetti*. We do not have the benefit of error masking techniques associated with digital oversampling methods.

Last, we may not see any defects in the digitized files, but instead, frames may have been dropped during those instances

Figure 10-32 An example of fixed-frame-size compression with the threshold set too low. There is a resulting loss of information, often evidenced as a mosaic effect where a picture's pixels cannot be properly drawn.

where the system was not able to keep pace with the digitizing requirements. Instead of having 30 digitized frames per second, we may find that one second gives us 30 frames while another second gives us, for example, 27 frames, with 3 frames lost.

Figure 10-32 is an example of the visible defects that could occur if picture information is lost due to a fixed-frame-size approach.

Conversely, if the threshold is set too high, to 200 KB per frame, we waste valuable storage space (Figure 10-33). We continue to use 75 KB more than the 125 KB needed. But we have no choice since we cannot scale down our 200 KB algorithm. It

Figure 10-33 An example of fixed-frame-size compression with the threshold set too high. Here storage is used ineffectively with regard to the actual file size to be stored. Illustration by Jeffrey Krebs.

Figure 10-34 Variable-frame-size compression accommodates fluctuations in a picture's storage requirements by dynamically allocating the threshold as a picture requires more or less storage. As a result, the captured pictures are less likely to exhibit the artifacts associated with a fixed threshold. Illustration by Jeffrey Krebs.

is fixed, and even though the frames coming in only require 125 KB to be stored, we are quite ineffectively using extra storage.

Variable-Frame-Size Technique

In the variable-frame-size approach, no threshold is set for frames being processed with regard to the total amount of data that can be stored per frame (Figure 10-34). By dynamically changing the algorithms to facilitate the variable data size of the frames as the complexity of the image changes, several benefits are realized.

First, storage space is used intelligently. By using only the amount of storage that the individual frame requires, we are able to maximize the effective use of storage. Second, all the data necessary to display the picture properly are captured. In our example, a variable-frame-size algorithm would have accepted data based on the 100 KB frames of the boy. Then, as the horse and rider come into view and the data increase to 125 KB frames, our variable-frame-size approach expands accordingly. When the horse and rider clear frame and only the boy remains, our algorithm contracts to continue to process the less complex 100 KB frames. Last, because we have stored adequate data for the frames, we will not see defects in the captured frames or experience an inability to digitize the incoming frames.

A variable-frame-size approach involves somewhat more work to design, but the benefits derived are well worth the effort. It is therefore wise to examine the methods used in the DNLE system of choice to determine if variable-frame-size techniques are employed.

Intraframe Coding

When we watch a film or a video, each frame of information is distinct and discrete, representing an entity complete unto itself. Movement is perceived by taking into account that each

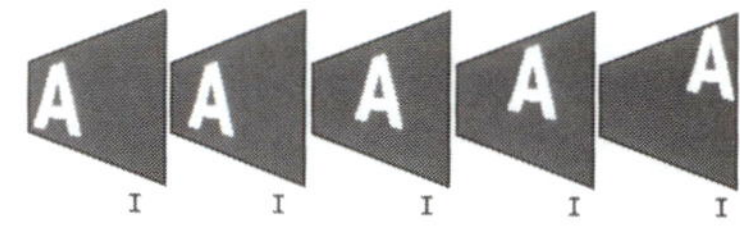

Figure 10-35 Intraframe coding allows each frame to carry its own information and to be drawn independently. Illustration by Jeffrey Krebs.

successive frame has changes that are slightly different from the previous frame. The phenomenon known as *persistence of vision* finds our eyes holding some remnant of information from a previous frame as we process the next frame. Slight, static changes within each frame are blended together to create the semblance of motion.

Intraframe coding of frames under M-JPEG compression means that each M-JPEG-compressed frame contains all the information that the frame requires for display (Figure 10-35). While the frame is dependent on the previous and successive frames to fulfill its role in the appearance of movement, an intraframe-coded frame does not need and is not dependent on the data contained in any other frame in order to be displayed.

Intraframe coding is important when we think about the editing process. When we are editing, we are always removing and adding frames, joining frames from different sources, and sometimes even removing frames from within the same shot to create jump cuts or to speed up action. This unpredictability of where previous and successive frames will be in our editing program is handled well by intraframe coding. Since each frame that we use during the editing process can be displayed without having to draw information from a previous frame, intraframe coding is currently the method of choice for editing. If we had to restrict our editing choices because we could not reliably display the correct frame at the point at which we wanted to make an edit, the creative process of editing would be hampered.

MPEG COMPRESSION

MPEG compression, proposed in 1990 by the Moving Picture Experts Group, a subset of the International Telephone and Telegraph Consultative Committee (CCITT) and the International Organization for Standardization (ISO), is a form of software compression as well as hardware-assisted compression.

Whereas M-JPEG is based on still images, MPEG is based on motion. Digital video compression based only on algorithms originally designed for still images is a logical reason why there is a need for both types of compression. There are several important distinctions between M-JPEG and MPEG.

The basic digitization and compressing processes that have already been outlined in detail are very similar to those used in MPEG. MPEG also employs 8×8 blocks during the DCT stage in which spatial redundancies are analyzed. However, larger coding blocks are employed to examine larger sections of a picture being analyzed for movement. The information regarding redundancy and that regarding movement travel together as they leave the compression engine.

The MPEG video compression algorithm has many of the same applications as other digital video compression techniques. These include DNL editing, video conferencing, video-on-demand systems, and broadcast delivery.

Different Versions of MPEG

There are actually several different versions of MPEG, including the following:

MPEG 1 Samples video at 4:2:0 for an average of 1.2 Mbits/sec, at a pixel matrix of 352×240, 30 fields/sec.
MPEG 2 Samples video at 4:2:0, supporting data rates between 1.2 to 15 Mbits/sec, at a pixel matrix of 704×496, 60 fields/sec.
MPEG 2 Professional Profile @ main level Samples video at 4:2:2 for an average of 50 to 60 Mbits/sec, at a pixel matrix of 704×496, 60 fields/sec.
MPEG 4 A proposed version that has a target data rate of between 10 kbps and 1 Mbit/sec, designed for wide area transmission.

MPEG 1 encoding has traditionally been used for providing video on media types that do not support the data rate required for full-motion signals, such as CD-ROMs.

Sending Video versus Processing Video

Note that both MPEG 1 and MPEG 2 sample video at 4:2:0, while one variant of MPEG 2—MPEG 2 Professional Profile @ main level—samples at 4:2:2. There are reasons why the 4:2:0 form of MPEG 2 may be more desirable than the 4:2:2 version. Note that for the broadcast industry, it is desirable to be able to send as many channels of video as possible through the narrowest channel. The requirement is quite simple: to transmit "good," that is, acceptable, quality over the smallest data line possible.

Once video has arrived in the consumer's home, a 4:2:2 MPEG 2 version will have no discernible benefits over viewing a 4:2:0 version. Further, most direct broadcast satellite (DBS) channels vary from between 2 to 8 Mbits/sec in the video that must be sent over this distribution channel. Broadcast television stations use as a gauge a 45 Mbit/sec channel that, ideally, would carry between two to three MPEG 2 streams.

However, if during the editing stage the program requires certain video processing stages, as is the case with chroma keying, we will find that we can achieve better results if our video has been captured and is subsequently processed with the extra chroma sampling that 4:2:2 provides. Since this 4:2:2 version requires approximately 30% more space than the 4:2:0 version, it is sensible that MPEG 2 sampled at 4:2:0 would be used primarily for distribution, while MPEG 2 sampled at 4:2:2 would be used primarily for production and postproduction.

Interframe Coding

The method by which data are stored for MPEG frames is a combination of intraframe and interframe coding. While M-JPEG uses solely an intraframe-coding scheme, MPEG uses both methods. Based on the type of interframe coding employed, a

Figure 10-36 With the interframe coding methods of MPEG compression, each frame is not drawn independently. Instead, certain frames are predicted, resulting in a decrease in the amount of storage required. Illustration by Jeffrey Krebs.

significant savings of storage over M-JPEG compression is possible. A ratio of 3:1 is the most usual estimate given for such savings. If we originally could store 30 minutes of M-JPEG-compressed material, we would realize 90 minutes of MPEG-compressed material. Such benefits seem overwhelming; why use M-JPEG at all if we can save so much space with MPEG?

As we know, in M-JPEG, each frame is compressed independently of the previous frame. However, when a series of frames undergoes MPEG compression, each frame is not compressed independently of the others. Instead, MPEG employs both intraframe and interframe coding. Because of this, certain MPEG frames when displayed require the presence of codependent frames in order to be drawn (Figure 10-36).

In interframe coding techniques, there is a series of frames that are referred to as *I, P,* and *B frames. I* is an intraframe-coded frame, in which data are independent of other frames. It is also called an *intrapicture* and a *standalone frame. P* is a predicted frame, in which data are predicted from a previous intraframe frame or from a previous predicted frame. *B* is a bidirectional frame, in which data are interpolated from the closest I and P frames.

When the MPEG compression process begins, an initial I frame is coded. This I frame is the exact type of model as used in M-JPEG. It is a standalone frame in that it is completely independent and can be drawn and displayed based solely on the data that it contains.

P frames are created based on predictive coding. For example, if we have a sequence of numbers, 2, 4, 6, 8, we can somewhat reliably predict the continuing sequence: 10, 12, 14, etc. This is *predictive coding*: A routine can be written that attempts to complete the sequence.

It is important to note that I frames and P frames do not follow one another. They are separated by B frames. A way to think about this is that an I frame is created, and then a P frame is predicted. More P frames are predicted until it is time for an I frame to be created. Between the I and P frames are B frames. In general, the I frame is created due to a change in the movement of pixels in the incoming frames to be compressed. However, in MPEG, approximately every half-second interval will have a new I frame association. This interval may vary, depending on the scheme that is chosen. This interval, or length, is known as a *group of pictures* (GOP), which begins with an I frame and extends to the last frame before the next I frame.

Motion Adaptive coding takes into account the changes that occur from frame to frame. Static frames will be encoded as a single frame. However, when movement occurs, encoding will take place on a field basis.

By coding only I and P frames, we can experience significant savings since complete data are being stored only for the I frames. P frames are predicted. What is being predicted is movement, and only the data that represent the change in movement need to be stored, not the complete data required for that individual frame.

B frames separate I and P frames. B frames are bidirectionally interpolated from the closest I and P frames. If we have an I frame with a certain amount of data associated with it, and we predict a P frame, we know that a certain amount of time has elapsed between the I and P frames. This elapsed time is represented to us visually by B frames—frames that do not truly exist in terms of their data content. They are interpolated and drawn based on the information contained in frames that do have true data: either the closest pair of I and P frames or the closest pair of P frames.

By using predictive coding (P frames) and bidirectionally interpreting frames (B frames), only storing changes in data (P frames), and only periodically storing all data (I frames), MPEG compression offers greater storage savings than M-JPEG techniques.

Storage Savings

The following numbers can vary, but in general, with MPEG compression, storing only I frames will yield only about 1.3 times better storage numbers than those of M-JPEG. Storing I and B frames, however, will yield about 2 times the storage over M-JPEG. Here, our 1 GB of storage with M-JPEG would require, for the same number of frames, only .5 GB of storage. Finally, storing I, B, and P frames would yield about 3 times the storage over M-JPEG methods.

Implications for the DNLE Process

It is important to discuss some of the aspects of MPEG as they relate to the digital editing process. Under M-JPEG, since each frame can be drawn and displayed independent of other frames, the editing process can proceed in a normal fashion. Anytime the editor wants to cut from one frame to another frame, the cut can happen instantly. However, under MPEG, frames are not independent of one another. P and B frames are dependent on the I frame. Consider the implications this could have for editing.

If we have two segments of digitized video, and we want to edit from a point in segment 1 to a point in segment 2, we will be removing some of the data that precedes the place in segment 2 where we want to make our edit. The editing process cannot proceed if we want to edit from, let's say, a P frame in segment 1 to a B frame in segment 2. The B frame can no longer receive its information from preceding frames; it is now appended to segment 1.

Logically enough, for distribution, we would want our MPEG files to have the longest GOPs (groups of pictures) uninterrupted by I frames as possible; generally, these are about 15 frames. However, for editing, a short group of pictures is desired. Yet, with I, B, P coding, if the editor suddenly wanted to cut from a B frame in one file to a P frame of another file, there would perhaps be some form of latency while the DNLE system searched its index of frames in order to display the desired frame that the editor requested.

Creating an MPEG-Based DNLE System

This was the essential problem that prevented DNLE manufacturers from creating an MPEG-based DNLE system for almost a decade, from 1988 to 1998. Many solutions were proposed: One such proposal was to restrict editing only from I frame to I frame, which is obviously unacceptable to the creative editing process, in which access to every frame is usually desired. Despite this fact, several manufacturers did create DNLE systems where only editing from I frame to I frame was possible. These systems did not succeed and were not adopted.

Cost was yet another factor contributing to the difficulty of creating an MPEG-based DNLE system. By 1992, the cost of real-time M-JPEG encoders (the chip or chip sets that power M-JPEG-based DNLE systems) were only about $200. By 1997, these encoders had dropped to about $50, while decoders cost between $20 to $30.

In contrast, in 1992, real-time MPEG 1 encoders cost in excess of $150,000. By 1997, the cost of a real-time chip set capable of encoding in all MPEG variants had dropped to $600: a 250% decline! Decoders had become quite affordable years earlier.

Finding the B and P Frames Quickly

Success in creating an MPEG-based DNLE system came in late 1997. The essential question was quite simple: how to create a DNLE system that did not restrict the editor from editing any desired frame. In order to allow the editor to choose from any frame and to cut to any frame, the DNLE system must be able to find B and P frames as quickly as I frames could be located. Otherwise, the latency in locating the frames could become so objectionable as to make the editing system unusable.

Dynamic random access memory (DRAM) chip sets are extremely fast, high-density integrated circuits. More than any other commercially available chip set, DRAM chips are perfect for incorporation into MPEG-based DNLE systems in order to perform the I, B, P frame searches that are necessary. While expensive, these chip sets will most likely decrease in cost, and, as a result, unhindered access to any frame that the editor desires to edit—in a cost-effective MPEG-based DNLE system—can be engineered.

MPEG Delivery Methods

As stated earlier, reducing the size of the video to be transmitted results in all sorts of benefits to both the sender and the receiver. There are many potential uses for MPEG-delivered video, some of which are discussed in the following sections.

Video-on-Demand

Video-on-demand (VOD) systems are those which essentially allow the consumer to make some form of request and receive a delivery. For example, if you are staying in a hotel room and want to "order" a movie in your room, this is a form of video-on-demand. However, the choices and delivery mechanism may or may not be very flexible. For example, you may have only ten movies to choose from, and may only see the movie starting at specific times, say every 15 minutes.

Other VOD systems can be more complicated to engineer, but more flexible for the user. For example, you may be able to pick among many more movies and receive the movie instantly, without having to wait for the quarter-hour to arrive before the movie begins. Further, you may even actually have control over how the movie proceeds: You could be in command of playing, pausing, rewinding, and replaying sections of the movie, if the right controls were made available.

Media and Video Browsing

There are a great number of applications for media browsing. Let's say that you are writing a quarterly report for the department in which you work, and you want to include some video of a new factory in Rome in the report. The company has a video archive where you can query a database and see small versions (often called *thumbnails*) of the video in this archive. You are thus able to preview different video clips, decide which clip is the one you want, and download that into the document.

Broadcast stations are natural consumers for media browsing. Journalists often want to see the actual pictures for which they are writing copy. Media browsing stations, from which journalists can review and choose the images that will make up the story being written for the 6 P.M. news, are natural and fundamental uses of digital video in the broadcast facility.

Digital TV Program Timeshifting

Imagine that you are on a business trip, and during the week that you were out of your home country, there was a series of news segments on an issue in which you are very interested. Since you were not able to tape these segments on your home VCR, you have missed the information. However, now consider if you were a subscriber to a digital TV timeshifting service. This service would take your specific requirements, digitally encode the segments, and store them in a data server. Upon returning from your trip, you would dial in to the server, and video would stream from the server into your home computer.

MPEG Offers Standardization

A significant factor in the widespread adoption of MPEG-based encoding is the ability to achieve standardization. With M-JPEG schemes, although the technology has been adopted as a standard, the implementation has not been standardized. This means, for example, that each manufacturer of a DNLE system that uses M-JPEG compression can implement different and proprietary algorithms, which therefore destroys any compatibility among DNLE systems. It is usually not possible for the digitized and compressed M-JPEG media from one DNLE system to be played on another M-JPEG-based DNLE system. Among the reasons is that there is no standard implementation of M-JPEG compression.

However, with MPEG, especially MPEG 2 Professional Profile @ main level, we know that we will be sampling at 4:2:2 and at a specific data rate of 50 Mbits/sec. With each manufacturer sampling under the same standard, the long-desired capability to take media files from one system and play them on another manufacturer's system will be possible.

OTHER COMPRESSION METHODS

There are a number of different compression schemes that are of interest. However, it is important to note that this particular section is not necessarily concerned with compression technologies solely as they relate to incorporation into a DNLE system. Indeed, certain compression methods may be more applicable to streaming video over the Internet rather than being used in a DNLE system.

Digital Video Interactive Compression

DVI, which began at Sarnoff Labs, was eventually continued in its development by Intel Corporation. DVI supports both still images and motion video and can be both asymmetric and symmetric in nature; it is possible to decode and encode in DVI as well as in M-JPEG. DVI-based DNLE systems had a relatively short four-year life cycle, from 1990 to 1994, and DVI eventually bowed to the widely adopted M-JPEG.

Fractals

A general overview of how fractal technology has been developing follows. Instead of breaking a picture down into frequencies, as DVI, MPEG, and M-JPEG methods do, fractals utilize fractal patterns to represent every possible pattern that can exist. By dividing a picture into small pieces, in effect, into a fraction of its whole, these smaller sections can be searched and analyzed fairly quickly. On a smaller level, instead of trying to find the pattern for the entire picture, the search is for smaller patterns of pixels.

In Figures 10-37A–D, the original pattern (A) is broken down into smaller sections (this varies in terms of matrix: one typical pattern consists of 16×16 blocks) and magnified. To find where image D exists in the expanse of image A, each subsequent magnified section (images B and C) is then analyzed and examined to find something in the fractal set that resembles the original sampled image. Once a match has been found,

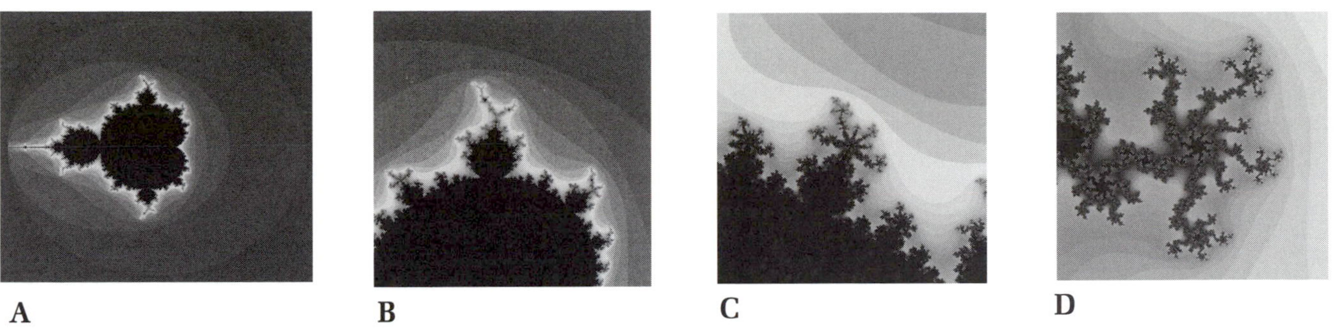

Figure 10-37 A variation of a Mandlebrot fractal set, the original pattern is magnified to reveal sections that resemble the original pattern.

only the *x, y,* and *z* coordinates of where the sampled image (image D) can be found in the fractal set space (Image A) are noted.

In this way, pixels do not have to be transmitted for each section of the original picture. Instead, the process continues until the entire picture has been broken down into subsections and analyzed. The result of this is a string of coordinates. To play back an image, these coordinates from the data stream are processed, and then, returning to the fractal set (image A), data are copied based on the coordinate locations needed. The data represented by each of these *x, y,* and *z* coordinates are then copied and merged. The result is a recreation of the original picture.

Fractals offer extremely high compression ratios. However, fractal technology is a very asymmetrical process and is extremely compute-intensive. The encoding process is very slow, whereas the decoding process is very fast. In 1993, it was widely thought that a real-time fractal compression system was on the near horizon. Five years later, there was still no real-time fractal encoding system.

Fractal compression works very well with natural shapes, such as buildings, but fares worse with created objects, such as computer animation and computer-generated imagery. Many suppliers of content for the Internet use fractal compression, where the fast decoding process is a key benefit.

Wavelets

Wavelets represent a recursive technique that is quite analogous to LZW compression. Wavelets take a picture that is to be compressed and introduce aliases.

Wavelet compression is divided into two processes: a *scaling* function and a *convolving* function. First, the scaling function is used to take the original picture and squeeze it down to reduce it on the *x* and *y* axes (Figure 10-38). Once the image has been scaled, the convolving process is run. (*Convolve*

Figure 10-38 The first step in wavelet compression is the scaling function. The original picture is reduced on the *x* and *y* axes. Courtesy of Aware, Inc.

means to roll or wind together.) This process is a set of wavelet functions (transforms) that seek to encode error. For example, the information in the original picture is compared to the differences in the scaled version. The differences represent error. The convolving process can be run approximately five times.

Once the picture has been scaled and analyzed in this manner, the result of this transformation is to achieve information based in *wavelet space*. Wavelet space is error. The goal is just to store one of four portions of the picture and then to quantize the other three portions of the picture (Figure 10-39).

Different wavelet scaling functions can be used to form the set of bases that allow a picture to be analyzed. The analog to this is the method by which M-JPEG compression uses frequencies to analyze a picture.

Wavelet compression offers an advantage over M-JPEG compression in its treatment of edges to objects in a frame. M-JPEG analyzes pictures in 8×8 coding blocks, and these boxes have edges. An edge represents an infinite number of frequencies, many of which are thrown away when an M-JPEG-compressed image is quantized. Wavelets, on the other hand, are not block-oriented. Because the entire picture is being analyzed, edges are better preserved.

One current characteristic of wavelet compression is that it has difficulty preserving textures. For example, whereas M-JPEG does a very good job at preserving the detail and textures

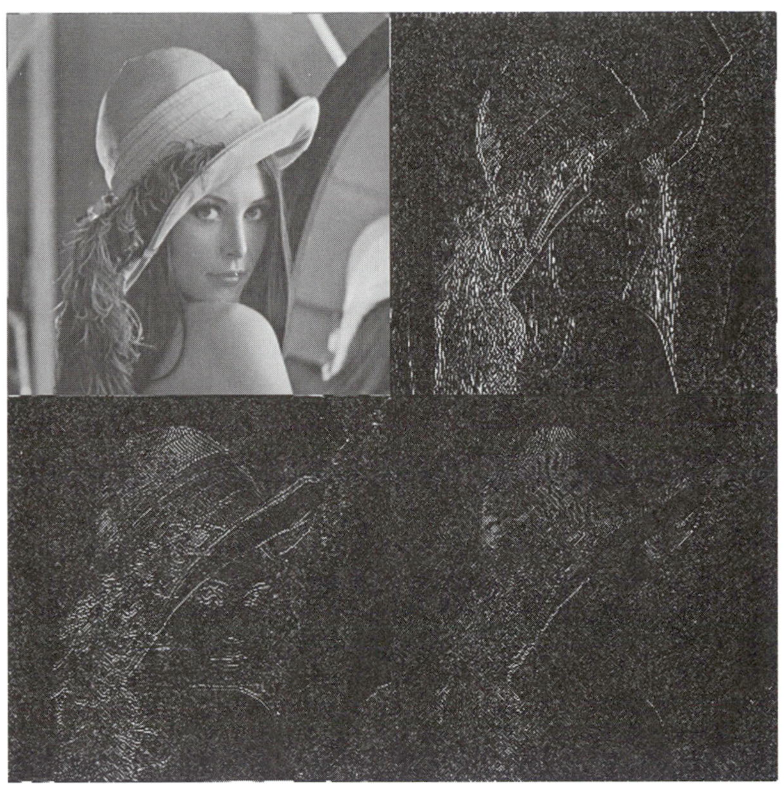

Figure 10-39 This is the result of the first level of a wavelet transform. The three portions of the picture shown in outline are represented as quantized information. This procedure continues for each cycle of transformation. Courtesy of Aware, Inc.

of a brick wall, wavelets have difficulty coding all the edges of the bricks; one side effect is that the overall texture of the brick wall is softened and compromised.

Wavelet compression was used in only one DNLE system, from 1994 to 1996, and was eventually discontinued, only to be replaced by M-JPEG compression. There were several reasons for this. The first is that wavelet compression chip sets were made available by only a few manufacturers; wavelets never achieved the industry standardization and eventual widespread manufacturer adoption that usually accompanies standardization. The second reason is that, given equally high data rates for both M-JPEG- and wavelet-based systems, the video "smoothing" artifacts of wavelets were found objectionable by the majority of DNLE users.

EVOLUTION OF DIGITAL VIDEO COMPRESSION TECHNIQUES

A possible extended chronology for the use of digital video compression techniques is as follows:

Early 1980s	Digital video interactive (DVI) for CD-ROM
1989, 1990	Software compression for DNLE systems
1990, 1991	M-JPEG for DNLE systems
1992	MPEG 1 introduced for CD-ROM

1993	High-data-rate M-JPEG for DNLE systems
1997	Losslessly compressed M-JPEG for DNLE systems
	MPEG 2 at 4:2:0 for distribution
	Fractals for distribution; Internet content
1998	MPEG 2 at 4:2:2 for DNLE systems

Looking to the Year 2000 and Beyond

It is appropriate to make some predictions concerning how digital video compression techniques are likely to mature and evolve. In general, then, basic improvements to the current methods will bring much more clarity to the actual transform. In effect, the transform process will improve, getting better and better at judging and understanding what the human eye can and cannot perceive. This factor cannot be overstated, and as more sophisticated transforms are enabled, better compression will result: We will be able to throw away more and more information in the frame without noticing that the data are gone.

MPEG-based compression, in different forms, will appear alongside traditional M-JPEG compression in order to facilitate the distribution of multiple channels of video. And, of course, there is a need for MPEG-based compression for interactive games, DVD, DVD-ROM, and so forth.

Real-time fractal transformations are also likely to finally appear on the scene.

CHARACTERIZING THE RESULTS OF DIGITAL VIDEO COMPRESSION

In the early years of DNLE systems (1988-1993), the resolution of DNLE video was very obvious; relatively high compression ratios resulted in very noticeable picture defects. Five years later, by 1998, the picture quality of DNLE systems was largely unnoticeable. Low compression ratios of 2:1, lossless compression, or completely uncompressed picture quality removed any objections concerning whether the pictures from DNLE systems were, indeed, worthy of being broadcast.

A GRAPHIC CHRONICLE OF DIGITAL VIDEO COMPRESSION

The examples shown in Figures 10-40 to 10-51 represent the evolution of digital video compression in both software-only and hardware-assisted compression techniques from 1989 to 1992. All images shown were shot with a charged-coupled device (CCD) video camera and recorded to Betacam videotape. The images were then digitized and compressed. Finally, the images were captured in a graphics program for display here.

Software-Only Compression, 1989–1991

Figure 10-40 In late 1988 through the end of 1990, software-only compression techniques yielded results similar to Figures 10-40 and 10-41. The data size for this example is 6.1 KB per frame at 4 bits per pixel. Note the significant pixillation and coding block artifacts within the image. Depending on the images being compressed, editorial decisions based on what can be seen in the frame may be difficult to make.

Figure 10-41 The data size for this example is 12.4 KB per frame at 8 bits per pixel. With more than double the data compared with Figure 10-40, this example shows an increase in detail preservation and a decrease in the coding block artifacts.

Hardware-Assisted M-JPEG Compression, 1991–1992

Figure 10-42 Hardware-assisted M-JPEG compression began to surface toward the end of 1990. DNLE systems began to offer either JPEG- or DVI-compressed images by the first quarter of 1991. Shown under this category are four examples (Figures 10-42 to 10-45). The data size for this example is 4.2 KB per frame at 15 bits per pixel. Although, as a still, the image blurred, this artifact is not as apparent when the image is in motion.

Figure 10-43 This example, at 6.4 KB per frame and 15 bits per pixel, clearly shows the advantage of M-JPEG compression over the software-only methods. If we compare Figures 10-40 through 10-43, there is a dramatic difference. Although Figure 10-40 is at 6.1 KB, and Figure 10-43 is at 6.4 KB, there is virtually no difference in storage per frame. The difference in the two images, however, is significant. Notice the decrease in coding block artifacts and the preservation of detail, especially in edge areas, such as the computer monitor and the eyeglasses.

Figure 10-44 This example, at 8.2 KB per frame and 15 bits per pixel, shows increased detail being preserved in the image. This is especially noticeable in the rims of the eyeglasses, where there is an increase in definition. There are also noticeable high-frequency artifacts shown in these areas.

Figure 10-45 This example, at 18.1 KB per frame and 15 bits per pixel, represented the state of the art of M-JPEG digital video compression by the end of 1991. At this data size, much of the pixillation has been removed from the image, while a high level of image detail remains. For many applications, this image resolution is acceptable for direct output from the DNLE system.

Second-Generation Hardware-Assisted M-JPEG Compression, 1992

Figure 10-46 At the start of 1992, improvements were realized in M-JPEG compression chips. As a result, larger frame sizes became possible as increased data rates were supported. The data size for this example is 7.9 KB per frame, 24 bits per pixel. By increasing the number of bits per pixel from 15 to 24, an improvement in both image resolution and storage capacity was realized. In addition to the increased number of bits per pixel, the sampling matrix was changed from 320×240 to 640×480. Compare this figure with Figure 10-43.

Figure 10-47 The data size for this example is 9.6 KB per frame, 24 bits per pixel. At this size, an excellent comparison can be made between Figures 10-47 and 10-44. With a slightly larger size, at just over 1.4 KB, there is noticeably less ringing in the high-frequency areas, such as the eyeglasses.

Figure 10-48 The data size for this example is 17.509 KB per frame, 24 bits per pixel. This image, at less KB per frame than Figure 10-45, shows improvements, especially in the areas of the eyeglasses.

Figure 10-49 The data size for this example is 23.0 KB per frame, 24 bits per pixel. This image, while very similar to Figure 10-48, improves dramatically when the two examples are expanded to fill the screen. With more than 6 KB per frame more than Figure 10-48, this example shows fewer artifacts and less degradation at full screen size.

Figure 10-50 The data size for this example is 37.9 KB per frame, 24 bits per pixel, slightly less than a 25:1 compression scheme. The improvement over Figure 10-49 is particularly evident in the lower- and upper-left sections of the eyeglasses. In Figure 10-49, there remains a great deal of high-frequency ringing. However, in this example, this distortion is not present.

Figure 10-51 This is the uncompressed image at its original resolution of 900 KB per frame, 24 bits per pixel. Compare this uncompressed image with the other compression levels to help determine which KB per frame may be suitable for your needs.

Third-Generation Hardware-Assisted M-JPEG Compression, 1997

Dual Field Support

By 1997, new improvements in M-JPEG chip sets supported even larger frame sizes. Very quickly, it became very difficult to distinguish between the original signal and its compressed version due to the relatively small ratio of compression that is possible in this third-generation implementation. In prior years, M-JPEG compression was based on preserving only one field of video information. The second field was discarded, and then a larger or small compression ratio was applied to the remaining one field.

With third-generation support, however, both video fields are preserved (Figure 10-52). As a result, motion artifacts are not introduced. Although it is impossible to show the benefits of video digitization and compression based on preserving both video fields in the scope of this static book, what the user notices when a single field is preserved is that there may be motion jitter, especially when a slow camera pan occurs. This, of course, is due to the fact that one field of information no longer exists. However, when we preserve both fields, this artifact no longer exists.

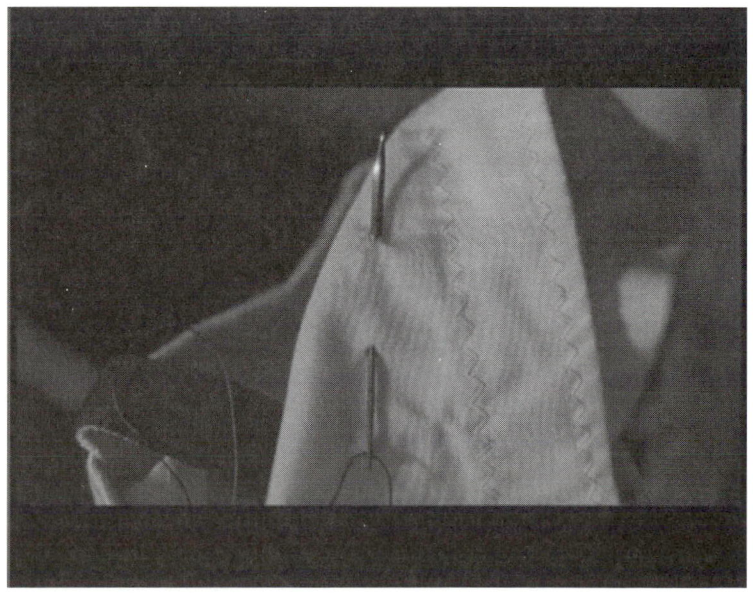

Figure 10-52 The data size for this image is 100 KB per frame, 24 bits per pixel. Due to the still print medium, it is difficult to accurately judge the image resolution because the second video field is not reproducible here.

THE IMPORTANCE OF PROPER INPUT SIGNALS

Prior to the digitization and compression stages, several steps can be taken to ensure that the detail content in a picture to be compressed is not extraneous detail. Video noise, caused by many troublesome sources such as generation loss, can have significant and detrimental effects on all digital video compression methods. Reducing video noise through the use of first-generation footage and digital noise reducers helps ensure that digital compression schemes will not attempt to process this unwanted noise as elements of detail that should be preserved.

Similarly, the type of input can be very important. If we have a Digital Betacam videocassette, we can choose to input the video into our DNLE system in a variety of ways. We could digitize based on composite video, but this would be a poor choice because both the luminance and color elements exist composited together down a single wire. We could choose to digitize based on component analog video, on the other hand, where luminance and color-difference elements are separated. Or we could digitize based on the serial digital video stream that is also available. We could also digitize based on S-Video.

Almost always, we would want to digitize based on receiving the signals in their most clear, separated form. In this case, we would digitize either component or serial digital video. With proper attention to input, we will always receive better digitized and compressed results as a consequence.

11

Digital Storage Devices

STORING TO RAM OR TO EXTERNAL DISKS

After the compression process, digitized material must be transferred to one of two places, either to the internal memory, RAM (random access memory), or to external storage disks. One reason to store material directly to RAM is that it can be manipulated much more quickly than material stored on external disks. Because RAM is resident directly within the CPU, a process can be implemented in shorter amounts of time than if the process must communicate via computer bus to treat material on an external disk.

But, of course, there is a practical limit to the amount of material that can be stored in RAM. Most CPUs used in DNLE systems have approximately 80 to 200 MB of RAM, the majority of which is apportioned for the DNLE software application. Instead, immediately after material is digitized and then compressed, it must be transferred to disk so that the entire digitization process can continue uninterrupted.

As we know, there are bandwidth issues that the CPU must address. If a series of frames is being processed, and there is more information associated with the frames than the CPU can process in a given amount of time, there will be difficulties. Either the process will not continue (in effect, the CPU stops the digitizing process), frames will be skipped, or all frames will be digitized but degraded in some unanticipated manner.

The same bandwidth issues are integrally linked to a DNLE's storage mechanism. The quality of picture (its digital density and image resolution), audio resolution and number of audio channels, and the ability to ensure real-time playback capability are dependent on the capabilities of the storage system. Disk capacities are also important if we are to store all the information that is required: We must either choose a more rigorous compression scheme or store less material on disk.

DISK CHARACTERISTICS

Disks have three characteristics that are important for digital nonlinear editing: capacity, data transfer rate, and access time.

Capacity

Capacity is measured in kilobytes (KB), megabytes (MB), gigabytes (GB), and terabytes (TB). The amount of footage that can be stored on a DNLE system is affected by the capacity of each disk drive and the number of drives that can be linked together and are simultaneously available.

Data Transfer Rate

Data transfer rate can also be termed *read/write speed* or *transfer speed.* Data transfer rate is measured in KB/sec and MB/sec.

The amount of data that a computer disk can write and read in a certain amount of time is the disk's data transfer rate. DNLE systems and the picture resolution that they are capable of providing are affected by the disk storage subsystem and the amount of data that can be written and read from the disk.

We may decide that we can work in a lower-quality, single-field picture quality because we need many hours of footage, or we may decide that we require two-field, high-quality pictures in order to finish directly from disk. Regardless of the objective, if the disk subsystem is not capable of reliably accepting the required data and returning it to us, we must reduce the picture and audio resolution and the number of audio channels. If the disk cannot keep up with accepting the data being sent to it, we must send less data. The disk's data transfer rate represents the bandwidth limitation of the disk drive.

Access Time

Once frames have been transferred to disk, and we request that the frames be played back, there is a time delay between the moment that we ask for the frames and when the data are available to the computer. This time delay represents the access time of the disk drive. Access time is measured in milliseconds (ms). A millisecond is 1/1000 of a second. Whereas the disk's data transfer rate is the amount of data that the disk can reliably read/write in the span of one second, once the material is on the disk, the issue is how quickly the disk can locate the material, process it via the CPU, and pass it on to the monitor for display. There are many delays between disk and computer screen; disk seek time is only one component.

All three characteristics—capacity, data transfer rate, and access time—must be considered not only to understand fully the present methods of digital video compression, but also to judge how improvements in disk technology affect the picture quality and the amount of information that can be stored. Although we tend to think of the capacity of the disk as the most important concern, it is not. The disk's data transfer rate is the enabling or disabling characteristic that is the most important for our purposes.

DATA RATE

To determine which disk type will be needed, we need to understand first the roles that the disk will be asked to play. The only way to do this is to ask these questions: How much material do I need? What image quality is required? And, to a lesser degree, how fast do I need the material to be accessible from the disk? With answers to these questions, the appropriate choice of disk type becomes quite apparent.

KB/Frame

We use the term KB (kilobytes; 1024 bytes) to refer to the number of kilobytes of information. This is the amount of digital data used to represent each frame. For example, if we have an uncompressed D1 frame, we have approximately 700 KB of data:

> 720 × 486 = 349,920 × 2 bytes = 699,840 bytes (~700 KB)/frame × 30 fps = ~21 MB/sec

However, after deciding on a particular picture quality, we wind up with an average of 21 KB/frame, for a compression ratio of approximately 33:1. We now identify these files as being an average 21 KB/frame.

To determine the amount of disk bandwidth that we need, we calculate the amount of data that will be digitized and compressed. Let's say that we judge that a 5:1 compression scheme gives us picture quality that is suitable for our purposes. We also require four channels of 48 KHz audio. For each second of material, how much data must the disk be capable of processing?

Formula for Determining Data Rate and Storage Capacity

The following formula is used to determine the required data rates as well as the disk's capacity to store information:

> *t* = disk capacity KB ÷ {60 ÷ [(KB/frame × fps) + (audio K × audio chans)]}

where *t* = length of material in minutes; disk capacity KB = the disk's capacity in kilobytes; 60 = the number of seconds in one minute; KB/frame = kilobytes per frame for the compressed image; fps = the digitized frame rate (30, 25, or 24); audio K =

audio kilobytes per second; and audio chans = the number of audio channels.

To determine the data rates required for each second of our 21 KB/frame and our four channels of 48 KHz sound, we calculate as follows:

(KB/frame × fps) + (audio K x audio chans)

21 KB/frame × 30 fps = 630 KB/sec + 48 KB/sec × 2 bytes (16-bit sampling) = 96 KB/sec × 4 (number of audio channels) = 384 KB/sec; Total = 1014 KB/sec. If we divide 1014 KB/sec by 1000, we have 1,014,000 bits; if we divide this by 1,000,000, we receive 1.014 MB/sec.

The material that we want to store to disk thus requires the consistent transfer of 1.014 MB each second. The disk type we choose must be capable of that data transfer rate; this is precisely the reason why image quality is dependent on the data transfer rate of the disk subsystem.

Next, when we want to determine how much of this material will fit on a 1 GB disk drive, we complete the following formula:

t = disk capacity KB ÷ {60 × [(KB/frame × fps) + (audio K × audio chans)]}

t = 1,000,000 KB ÷ (60 × 630 KB/sec + 384 KB)

t = 1,000,000 KB ÷ (60 × 1014 KB/sec)

t = 1,000,000 ÷ 60,840 KB/min

$t \cong$ 16.4 minutes

At these settings for image and sound resolution, approximately 16 minutes can be stored on a 1 GB disk. However, recall that with a variable image compression scheme, the 21 KB/frame for our picture may increase or decrease according to the image requirements of each individual frame. As a result, we may find that we can store much more material on the disk.

These formulas are not affected by variation in frame sizes when the frame size is fixed. For example, if we are using a DNLE system that provides uncompressed D1 digitizing, the frame size is fixed, and we will always see 1.26 GB of disk storage required for one minute of picture (720 × 486 = 349,920 × 2 Bytes = 699,840 Bytes (~700 KBytes) / frame × 30 fps = ~21 MB/sec × 60 = 1.26 GB/minute).

DISK TYPES

Computer disks can be magnetic or optical in terms of the actual recording medium. The process by which data are written and read to the disk can be magnetic, optical, or both. Each disk type has a unique set of characteristics with regard to data transfer rate, capacity, and access time. Which type of disk to choose will be a decision that is made when one weighs the amount of footage required (capacity), the quality of that footage (data transfer rates), and the speed with which the footage must be available (access time).

MAGNETIC DISKS

The Basic Magnetic Disk: Floppy Disks

The most commonly found magnetic disk for storing material is a floppy disk. These small 3.5" disks have a data transfer rate of 80 KB/sec, a capacity of 1 to 2 MB, and an access time of 180 ms. Floppy disks consist of a thin, flexible magnetic medium that is encased in a protective plastic shell. They are erasable and can be used many times. They come in several sizes: Older floppies still in use are in 8" and 5.25" form factors. Floppy disks are used primarily to store and transport data for text files and documents.

The 8" floppies originally had about 100 KB capacity; 5.25" disks averaged 360 KB, and 3.5" floppies average 2 MB.

Higher-Capacity Floppy Disks: 100 MB and Higher

Improvements in bit packing density have allowed for the creation of increased capacity and higher data transfer rates. Previously, if we had a spreadsheet document that required 6 MB of information to be stored, we required six high-density 1.2 MB floppy disks. However, with higher-capacity floppy disks, each floppy can hold a minimum of 100 MB of uncompressed data and 200 MB of compressed data, and we can easily store more than 15 such spreadsheets on one disk. These disks have a data transfer rate of 1.4 MB/sec and an access time of 29 ms. Zip disks, introduced by the Iomega Corporation, have a capacity of at least 100 MB and cost less than $15.

Jaz disks, also introduced by Iomega, have a capacity of 1 GB at a cost of less than $100. In addition, these disk units support reasonably high data rates of 6.6 MB/sec sustained and 10 MB/sec in bursts. These large capacities, in such a small and portable form factor, are ideal for transporting and exchanging files from one DNLE system to another.

With the higher transfer rates, a highly portable media and disk unit can be used for actual playback of full-motion video. This is especially important for desktop viewing applications (Chapter 7).

Magnetic Hard Disks

Magnetic hard disks have a long history of development and use. They are the most reliable disk technology from that point of view. They are erasable and are usually rated in terms of hours of use, on the order of about 50,000 hours mean time between failure (MTBF). Today, most personal computers have internal hard disks, ranging in capacity from 500 MB to as much as 2 GB.

DNLE systems usually do not utilize the computer's internal hard disk for storing the data-intensive picture and sound files. Normally, the DNLE software program is stored on the internal hard disk while picture and sound files are digitized to the external disks.

Inside the hard disk is usually a number of disk platters (the number varies but is usually no more than ten) that are able to store data on both sides. The reading and writing mechanisms of the disk drive consist of multiple heads on parallel stacks that align with the disk platters. These heads read and write information from tracks that are in the form of concentric circles.

Access Times of Magnetic Hard Disks

Hard disks offer extremely fast access times. These range from 6 to 16 milliseconds (ms). Fast access time means lower latency rates (the time spent waiting for the material to be shown). Fast access time also means that when we are editing, we can have a series of short edits one after another. When the cutting density is high (many cuts in a short amount of time), it is possible to experience trafficking problems in which the magnetic disks cannot keep up with the editing pace.

There are many factors that can affect trafficking issues when we are using DNLE systems. High compression ratios equate to lower data rates and make it more likely that high cutting densities will not stress the various subsystems that make up the DNLE system. Conversely, low compression ratios equate to higher data rates and make it more likely that high cutting densities will stress the DNLE's subsystems.

When there are a large number of cuts that must be played back, the tracking heads that hover over the disk platters seek and locate the required sections of data. We can easily imagine the difficulties that may occur if our cutting ratio is so high that there are too many seek requests for the disks to keep up with. When this occurs, often playback will halt. The user must then command the DNLE system to continue playing.

Revolutions per Minute (RPM)

Another characteristic of disks is the rotational speed of the disk platters. The amount of information that the disk can deliver is affected by the rapidity with which the platters revolve. SCSI 1 (small computer systems interface) disks were introduced with a speed of 3600 RPMs. Over the years, as disk technology progressed and disk packing methods improved, rotational speeds have become increasingly faster. These SCSI 1 disks delivered 1.5 MB/sec as their maximum data rate.

It is also important to note that magnetic disks cannot deliver the same data rate across the span of the platters. If we think of a vinyl record, the concentric circles that make up the vinyl recording have smaller circles toward the center of the record. Less information is available to us in the center than on the outer circles.

7200 RPM drives are able to deliver significantly more information. These disks are capable of providing approximately 9 MB/sec from the outer tracks and about two-thirds of that, approximately 6 MB/sec, from the inner tracks.

10,000 RPM drives further improve on the disk's capability to deliver data. These drives provide approximately 17 MB/sec from outer tracks and, again, roughly two-thirds that data, 11.5 MB/sec, from the inner tracks.

The result of these faster rotating drive mechanisms is that the disk can provide increased data throughput. As a result, we are able to store higher picture quality and additional audio tracks onto the disk.

Disk Form Factors

Magnetic hard disks come in three form factors: 5.25" (full height), 5.25" (half height), 3.5" (half height), 3.5" (low profile), and 2.5" (varying heights). Of the three, 5.25" disks have been in development the longest (Figure 11-1), but disk drive evolution and the ability to pack more bits into smaller sizes have resulted in the same capacity drives available in 3.5" form factors. Smaller-capacity disks, such as the 2.5" disks, are particularly important in being able to create portable hard disk-based cameras. Note that 1.8" disk form factors have not been very widely adopted.

Typical of disk drive development, changes to disk drives are usually first realized in the 5.25" form factor drives and then trickle down to the smaller size drives.

Fixed versus Removable Disks

Magnetic disks exist in a self-contained, sealed enclosure. A fixed magnetic disk has its own power supply. There are also removable magnetic drives, which are basically the same as fixed drives except that they do not have their own power supplies. Instead, a removable drive fits into a chassis that contains the power supply and disk address. Removable disks are particularly useful when footage from one system must be shared among multiple, unconnected DNLE systems.

Figure 11-1 The 5.25" half-height magnetic disk in a removable cartridge form. Courtesy Avid Technology.

Specialized Firmware

Magnetic disks have many characteristics that must be addressed before they can be successfully used as storage mechanisms for DNLE systems. Normally, any magnetic computer disk can be used to store any digital file, such as a word processing document or a spreadsheet. All of these various file types can be stored without making any specialized changes to the disk other than normal disk formatting.

However, disks used with DNLE systems are often treated with software that prepares them for DNLE use. Computer devices, such as disks, or a computer stylus or mouse, require software that allow them to be used in conjunction with the computer. These software programs are known as *drivers*. Normally, when a magnetic disk is prepared for use with a DNLE system, software drivers are loaded onto the firmware resident in the disk. *Firmware* is onboard memory within the disk that allows it to be reprogrammed.

For example, many disks perform a normal routine known as thermal recalibration (TCAL). At specific times, the disk will perform a recalibration of its heads. During this time, other processes (for example, a request for a file to be read) are delayed until the TCAL process is completed. This, of course, could severely affect the performance of a DNLE system. If we are digitizing video and audio when the TCAL process begins, we may experience a halt in digitizing, or we may find that not all the frames that were supposed to be captured were, in fact, captured.

Mode pages are yet another aspect of a disk drive that must be addressed. There are different modes under which a disk drive writes and reads its information. Normally, a disk drive is not set up to write very long file sizes, such as would be common when we are digitizing many minutes of picture and audio. If we attempt to digitize picture and sound with very low compression ratios, we may find that the disk drive, even if its technical specifications support the resolution, may not be able to keep up with the data rates required. In this case, it is a matter of programming the onboard firmware correctly before digitizing can successfully proceed.

In most cases, DNLE software, once launched, will poll the connected disks and assess what firmware is loaded within the drive. Depending on the results, the DNLE software will load the appropriate drivers into the storage firmware to facilitate successful operation.

SCSI: SMALL COMPUTER SYSTEMS INTERFACE

SCSI, pronounced "scuzzy," is short for small computer systems interface and represents a standardized connection between computers and storage devices. The Apple Macintosh computer was the first CPU to integrate SCSI 1 directly on the computer's motherboard. This onboard support is known as Asynchronous SCSI 1 Narrow and has a limit of 1.5 MB/sec.

SCSI technology is characterized by two important attributes: speed and width. Speed is defined as being either Fast or Ultra. Width is defined as being either Narrow (passing 8 bits of data) or Wide (passing 16 bits of data).

Speed	*Width*
Fast	Narrow (8 bits of data)
Ultra	Wide (16 bits of data)

These are the various available SCSI devices:

SCSI 1
Fast, Narrow SCSI
Fast/Wide SCSI (sometimes referred to as SCSI 2)
Ultra Wide SCSI

Controller Cards

Controller cards are additional hardware board(s) that are placed within the CPU and to which the external storage disks are connected. Controller cards are used to increase the bandwidth that is possible between the computer's bus and the connected SCSI disks. This is a result of the cards being DMA-capable. DMA is an abbreviation for *direct memory access*, which essentially means that other coprocessor boards can communicate with the SCSI controller card, and data does not flow through the computer's bus.

For example, SCSI 1 controller cards appeared in DNLE systems in 1993 and, with SCSI 1 Narrow disks, offered a transfer rate of up to 5 MB/sec. Without the controller card, these SCSI 1 Narrow disks offered only a 1.5 MB/sec data rate.

As SCSI disks improve, controller cards are developed to support the different types of SCSI disks. Significant advances in the data transfer rates are possible. For example, shown below are the data transfer rates supported by various types of disks and controller cards:

Fast, Narrow SCSI controllers support bus transfers of up to 10 MB/sec.
Fast/Wide SCSI controllers support bus transfers of up to 20 MB/sec.
Ultra Wide SCSI controllers support bus transfers of up to 40 MB/sec.

Consider the situation where we want to support a compression ratio of 2:1 for ITU-R 601. The effective data rate that we must pass each second is 21 MB divided by 2, or 10.5 MB/sec. Fast, Narrow drives come close but, with the addition of audio, are not able to support this data rate. Fast/Wide SCSI drives, however, do provide enough data throughput to support this resolution.

Distance Limitations

It is important to note that there are specific distance requirements when using SCSI. For example, Fast/Wide SCSI supports a maximum of 3 meters in total. Ultra Wide SCSI supports a maximum of 1.5 meters in total and is also limited to only four devices in total.

How Single-Ended Controllers and Differential Controllers Affect Distance

There are two types of controller mechanisms, each of which can affect the distance requirements of the various SCSI

Table 11-1 SCSI Throughput

	Clock Speed	*Width*	*Throughput*
SCSI 1	5 MHz	1 byte	5 MB/sec
Fast, Narrow SCSI	10 MHz	1 byte	10 MB/sec
Fast/Wide SCSI	10 MHz	2 bytes	20 MB/sec
Ultra Wide SCSI	20 MHz	2 bytes	40 MB/sec

devices. Single-ended controllers are the most popular; a conservative estimate is that 90% of the drives that are manufactured on a yearly basis are single-ended drives. Single-ended controllers allow the total SCSI bus length to be six meters. This means that regardless of the number of drives that we have, the total distance of the cabling that forms the connections between each disk and CPU must not exceed six meters. This is often seen as a limitation since many DNLE users prefer to have the disks further away from the operating environment in order to reduce the sound generated by the fans in the disk mechanisms.

Differential controllers allow SCSI bus length to be lengthened to 72 meters with one exception—Ultra Wide SCSI is limited to 1.5 meters.

Calculating Disk Throughput

The theoretical throughput as a result of using SCSI controllers is calculated by multiplying clock speed (in megahertz) and width (in bytes). Thus, we have the values given in Table 11-1.

INCREASING THE DATA TRANSFER RATES

Serial Storage Architecture

Serial storage architecture (SSA) was developed by IBM (International Business Machines) and, like SCSI, acts as an interface between the CPU and storage devices. SSA is available at 20 MB/sec and 40 MB/sec, similar to the data rates of SCSI. However, unlike SCSI, SSA is capable of offering much higher data rates as well. Further iterations of SSA can provide between

100 to 160 MB/sec. As a result, several streams of uncompressed ITU-R 601 can be supported and played in real time.

There are some significant pros and cons with regard to SSA. While the increased data transfer rate is a significant positive, serial storage architecture has not been adopted by the majority of manufacturers who would be called on to create the disk drives, host adapters, and so forth. Economically, one must take into account the price and availability of any component that is offered by only one company.

Fibre Channel

Fibre channel is another high-data-rate technology that utilizes fiber optic cabling rather than copper wire. Fibre channel specifications for data transport are 2 Gbits (gigabits)/sec, or 250 MB/sec Fibre Channel Arbitrated Loop (FC-AL) is an arbitrated implementation of fibre channel (software is used to apportion the total data throughput) that provides connection between the host CPU and storage disks at 1 Gbit/sec, or 125 MB/sec.

FC-AL is also significant in an economic sense in that many manufacturers have adopted and supported FC-AL. As a result, several different sources of disk drives, host adapters, and software are available. The result of this competition is the normal market-driven price structure that one expects to find.

As DNLE systems decrease picture compression ratios and offer more channels of high-quality audio, the amount of data that must be stored increases significantly. At the same time, the number of picture and audio streams that DNLE users want to manipulate in real time is also increasing. A high-data-rate-architecture such as FC-AL, combined with its open market availability, will most likely be the choice for widespread adoption and support.

IMPROVING DATA RATES AND DATA PROTECTION WITH RAID

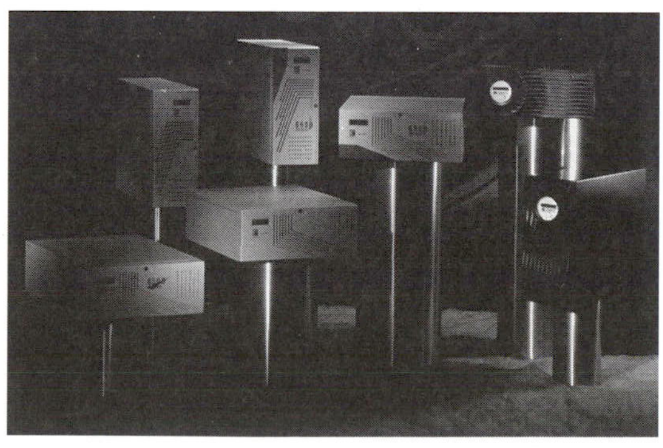

Figure 11-2 Various forms of RAID arrays from Ciprico. Courtesy Ciprico.

RAID is short for redundant array of independent disks. By combining disks, it is possible to achieve the following goals: to increase data throughput capability, to increase overall storage capacity, and to provide protection against data loss. There are several levels of RAID implementation, as described in the following sections. Figure 11-2 shows RAID systems from Ciprico.

RAID Level 0: Disk Striping

Let's say that we want to work with 2:1 compressed digital video and four channels of 44.1 KHz audio. We require approximately 10.8 MB/sec for picture. Now, let's assume that we are using an SCSI controller with Fast, Narrow SCSI drives. This provides us with a data throughput of about 10 MB/sec. We must, therefore, increase the data throughput of the storage subsystem in order to digitize the required material. But instead of purchasing Fast/Wide SCSI disks, which have a throughput of 20 MB/sec and can easily store our material, we can choose to use employ RAID Level 0.

RAID Level 0 is also called *striping*. The process of striping disks involves using software to pair like drives together. For example, if we have two 9 GB Fast, Narrow SCSI disks, we can stripe the disks together in order to increase the aggregate throughput of the drives. In this case, striping these two drives together would provide the necessary throughput to digitize the material we require. When we do digitize the material, data are spread throughout the two disks. As a result, if we remove one disk, we lose access to all the material because each disk requires the other in order to display the information to us.

There are some important caveats when disk striping is employed. It is necessary to use the same volume sizes when striping drives. Two 9 GB drives striped together are preferable to striping a 9 GB drive with three 3 GB drives. It is also important to note that Raid Level 0 does not provide any data redundancy to protect against data loss. If one drive in a striped set is lost, all data are lost.

RAID Level 1: Mirroring

RAID Level 1 involves writing identical material twice to the disk mechanisms. This is known as *mirroring*. Because material is being written twice, a small amount of additional time is necessary to accomplish this, and writing times are therefore slower. With RAID Level 1, data are fully redundant—there is an exact copy of data on a second drive set. Of course, this requires double the investment in disk storage.

RAID Level 2: Parity Recording

RAID Level 2 involves writing information to a specific disk and then using this information to recreate information should it become lost or corrupt on the other disks. When we store data onto a series of drives, we can also catalog exactly what data were stored to each drive. Should one of the main drives fail, we can retrieve the data by knowing what information was written to each drive. This is the information that is held by the *parity drive*. With RAID Level 2, data are written onto eight of the disks (one byte of data is divided into eight bits, and one bit is written to each disk), while a parity bit is recorded onto the ninth disk. The ninth disk is never used, except when data become unavailable for some reason on the other eight disks.

Figure 11-3 Stampede, from MountainGate, is a high-capacity, removable mass storage system, configurable as a RAID array. Courtesy MountainGate.

RAID Levels 3, 4, and 5: Variations on Parity Recording

RAID Level 3 is similar to Level 2 except in the amount of data that is written to each disk. Instead of one bit recorded over the span of eight drives with a parity bit written to the parity drive, there is no specific number of drives required, and the amount of data that is written is much larger (approximately 500 times greater).

RAID Level 4 is similar to Level 3 except for certain performance overhead issues that make it a bit inefficient over Level 3. Specifically, the writing performance is slower than Level 3. RAID Level 5 is similar to Level 4 except for a greater efficiency in the manner in which data are written and read to the parity drive.

In general, RAID Level 3 and Level 5 drives are the most commonly chosen forms of RAID protection against data loss.

Figure 11-3 shows a disk array that can be configured as JBOD (an acronym for "just a bunch of disks") or as a RAID array.

DECREASING PRICES AND INCREASING CAPACITIES

One of the most important trends in disk technology is that, in general, disk prices decrease on the order of every 18 months while capacity doubles. Prior to 1989, hard disks in excess of 400 MB were uncommon. In early 1989, 600 MB disks began to appear. The table below shows the evolution of magnetic disk capacities and prices for a 5.25" form factor. Note the last column, which lists the cost per megabyte.

Year	*Size*	*Price*	*Cost per MB*
1989	600 MB	$6000	$10/MB
1992	2 GB	$4000	$2/MB
1994	3 GB	$3500	$1.67/MB
1997	9 GB	$1800	$ .20/MB

Will Magnetic Storage Ever Be as Affordable as Videotape?

DNLE systems and their widespread use are dependent on having an abundant and affordable amount of storage. The continuing technological improvements in disk development are a significant enabling factor, and there is every indication that the decreasing cost-per-megabyte trend will continue. Examining the previous table, which shows the amazing drop in magnetic disk storage prices from 1989 to 1997, we can clearly see the economic trend of digital storage mechanisms supporting the advance of DNLE systems. However, digital hard disks have a long way to go before their cost per minute equals that of videotape. This is not true for magnetic streaming tape, which will certainly be on par with that of videotape.

Magnetic Tape Systems

In addition, tape backup systems can be used. These systems use cartridges that house magnetic tape in much the same way as audio tape cassettes. The cost per megabyte of tape backup is extremely low: A 2 GB cartridge averages just one cent per MB! As with all disk mechanisms, from magnetic disks to tape cartridges, the relationships are always the same: the faster the disk mechanisms, the higher the data rate and the more expensive the mechanism; the slower the disk mechanism, the lower the data rate and the less expensive the mechanism.

INCREASING THE NUMBER OF DISKS

Depending on the program being edited and the compression ratio employed, we may find that we require additional disks in order to have more footage available. But it must be noted that we cannot just indiscriminately add disk drives and expect that the host CPU can communicate with all of the drives. Different computers have different computer busses, and each type can communicate with a varying number of disks. For example, on the Apple Macintosh PCI (peripheral computer interconnect) bus, seven disks can be attached.

By adding an SCSI hardware controller card, an additional 7 drives can be attached to the CPU. This provides 14 disk drives that are available for digitizing and playback, in effect doubling the amount of footage that can be accessed at a given time. Furthermore, a dual controller card can be used; in this case, 14 and not 7 drives can be connected to the controller card. These 14 drives, coupled with the 7 drives on the internal PCI bus, result in a total of 21 drives. With 9 GB drives, this provides us with 189 GB of storage. With 23 GB drives, this provides 483 GB of storage, or hundreds of hours of footage at more than acceptable picture quality.

Disk Addresses

Each disk has a unique address, and there is a fixed number of addresses that can be addressed by the computer bus. For example, if we have seven disks, each with its own address, they can all exist on the hardware controller card. However, there are also disk "towers," which treat several disks as if they had only one address. In this case, seven drives would have only one address, and we could therefore have seven distinct towers (7 drives in one tower × 7 towers = 49 drives on one bus). Depending upon what size disk we use, we could have a staggering amount of footage online.

OPTICAL DISCS

As we know, digital storage is available in many different formats. There are floppy disks, magnetic disks, magnetic tape, and optical discs. Any of these formats can be used to store the digital files that are used by DNLE systems. However, while these different formats can store these files, they may not provide the data rates required to sustain real-time picture and audio playback. When we choose the storage mechanism that we will use in conjunction with the DNLE system, we ask these basic questions:

What is the total data rate that is required?

Do we need to back up our data?

If we want to edit with ITU-R 601 picture quality and four channels of 48 KHz audio and have four simultaneous picture streams available to us, we require a disk subsystem that can sustain just under 90 MB/sec. Clearly, magnetic disks and some form of disk striping must be used to accomplish this task. Other disk types cannot be used to provide a solution. However, there are definitely scenarios that allow us to use other disk mechanisms. Magnetic tape, since it provides a relatively low data rate, cannot be used for real-time playback of 2:1 compressed pictures. At the same time, however, magnetic tape makes an excellent choice for backing up our data.

When we ask our first question—the total data rate that is required—we will instantly be able to make our calculations and determine the disk subsystem. And, as picture quality has improved and the number of audio channels has increased, only magnetic disks have been able to sustain the required data rates.

Optical Discs Have Lower Data Rates than Magnetic Disks

When DNLE systems were first introduced, the required data rates could be sustained by optical discs. Because only high compression ratios were used, the amount of throughput required was very low. For example, consider the data rate required by the highest picture and sound quality available on DNLE systems in 1989:

4.5 KB/frame $\times$ 30 fps = 135 KB (picture) + 22.05 KHz (8 bit)/sec. $\cong$ 157 KB/sec

This data rate (which, incidentally, supported a picture compression rate of 150:1) could easily be supported by magneto-optical (MO) and phase-change optical (PCO) discs. Although both MO and PCO discs differ from manufacturer to manufacturer, in general, the maximum write speed is approximately 1 to 1.5 MB/sec.

As DNLE systems have grown in their picture and audio quality, optical discs have not increased in their capability to the extent necessary to support the required data rates. This is not to say that optical discs have not improved in their capacities or data rates, for they certainly have. However, there is certainly quite a difference between magnetic and optical discs; even the fastest optical disc has an access time that is still two to three times slower than a magnetic disk. Further, capacities of optical discs are also smaller than that of magnetic disks.

There has yet to be an optical disc that can provide the data throughput required for both the low compression ratios as well as the uncompressed picture resolutions that are available on DNLE systems. For these reasons, it is rare to find MO and PCO discs being used with DNLE systems.

Some Digital Audio Workstations Use Optical Discs

Optical discs are used for some digital nonlinear applications. Certain digital audio workstations (DAWs) use optical discs as their main storage medium. The primarily reason for this is cost. Given the evolution of disk pricing, magneto-optical discs, in volume numbers, can be purchased at approximately one-fifteenth of the cost of magnetic disks! Thus, for the same capacity in optical disc storage as a magnetic disk that costs $3000, the cost is only $200. But this ratio is not likely to continue; eventually, the cost per megabyte of magnetic disks will be comparable to that of optical discs. Gradually, the use of optical discs for DAWs will disappear and be completely replaced by magnetic disk use because of the latter's superior characteristics.

Magnetic Disks Replaced Optical Disc Usage in DNLE Systems

In 1988, optical discs were used with early DNLE systems. Since the data rate required was relatively low due to the high compression ratios used in early DNLE systems, optical discs were fast enough to provide the necessary data throughput. But data transfer rates, capacity, and access times for both magneto-optical discs and phase-change discs are far less than those of hard disks.

As we know, as years passed and resolutions improved, data rates grew. These improvements, along with the decreasing cost of magnetic storage, left optical discs with no role in the actual digitization and editing within DNLE systems. However, optical discs may make sense for a different purpose—backing up and archiving our work.

Types of Optical Discs

Erasable and Nonerasable

Optical discs come in two varieties. *WORM* (write once, read many) discs can only be written to once and then are used as playback mechanisms. *WMRM* (write many, read many) discs are erasable.

CD-ROMs are compact disc–read only memory discs and are actually different from WORM discs in that CD-ROM discs are manufactured with their data on them and are never written. CD-ROM is used for many purposes, including training, education, and computer games.

Magneto-Optical and Phase-Change

Optical discs fall into two categories: magneto-optical and phase-change. The specifications of each type of disc are somewhat different, depending on the manufacturer. However, overall, their capacities and data transfer rates are similar. The media for both types of disc are reliable, the discs are estimated to be good for 1 million uses, and they have an archival life estimated to be ten years.

Magneto-Optical Discs

Magneto-optical (MO) discs combine two technologies: magnetic and optical recording methods. While the basis for this marriage is decades old, lasers that could perform the optical function are a much more recent development. The first MO discs began to appear in the mid-1980s. MO discs are usually two-sided, although one-sided discs can be obtained. MO disc drives, however, only afford the ability to read data from one disc side at a time. The disc must be turned over to access files stored on the second side.

Magneto and *optical* refer to the method by which data are erased, written, and read. An MO disc consists of a protective polycarbon (or glass) layer. Beneath is the recording medium, which is metal based. This layer cannot be easily magnetized and therefore is not susceptible to accidental erasure. The recording layer has two possible states: positive or negative. In digital terms, this would equate to zeroes or ones. The recording surface of a new MO disc consists of spots that have the same orientation.

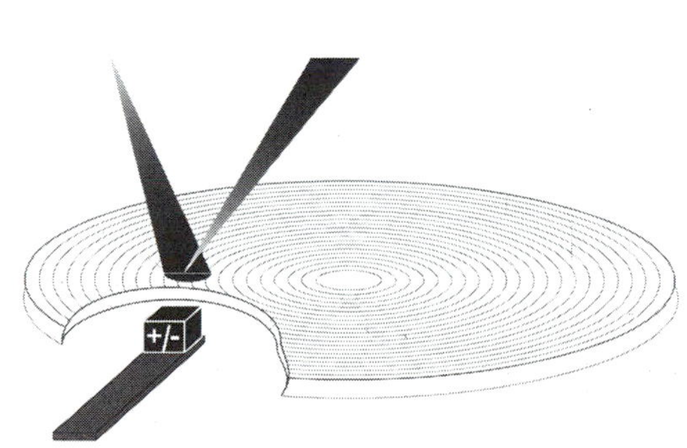

Figure 11-4 The read and write process for a magneto-optical disc. A laser (right) erases spots on the disc by heating these sections while the disc is held in a strong magnetic field. The magnet is then used to change the orientation of the spot. The same laser (shown in the illustration as another beam, left), operating at a different power level, determines the orientation of the disc spots to read information. Illustration by Jeffrey Krebs.

Before we are able to write information to the disc, whether for the first time or the 100th time, we must first erase the sections of the disc where we want to record new information. Erasing the disc is accomplished by heating the sections with a laser while the disc is in a strong magnetic field. The spot is heated such that the magnetic material loses its orientation. This is known as its *curie point.* Curie point refers to temperature. One laser, running at two different power levels, is used to heat spots and to read the orientation of these spots. While a spot is being heated, the magnet is used to change the orientation of the spot. The recording medium rapidly cools, and the spot has a new magnetic orientation. This is how material is recorded to a magneto-optical disc.

To read information from the disc (Figure 11-4), a laser beam is used to read the orientation of the spots on the disc. If the light from the laser beam is reflected off the surface in a clockwise direction, the spot has a certain orientation; if it is reflected counterclockwise, the spot has the opposite orientation. This is known as Kerr rotation.

Slower Write Rates than Magnetic Disks

Before data can be written to MO discs, space must be made for the new material. MO technology does not permit for the direct overwriting of old material by new material. The process of erasing and writing information to an MO disc can be done in either two or three passes (revolutions) of the disc. These passes add time to the process. As is the case with magnetic disks, data transfer rates are not equal over the surface of the disc. When a new disc is used, it begins to fill from the outer portion to the inner portion. The outer ring of optical discs is considered the "fast" portion, and the inner ring is considered the "slow" portion.

For overall price, performance, and capacity, magneto-optical discs offer greater benefits over phase-change optical discs.

Phase-Change Optical Discs

Phase-change optical (PCO) discs appeared in 1990. They represent a technology based on the ability of a material to exhibit two properties: amorphous (without shape; not crystalline) and crystalline (a solid having a characteristic internal structure).

PCO discs consist of a protective layer made of polycarbon or glass. Beneath are several layers of the recording medium, which is composed of nonmetallic substances that have an electrical resistance that can vary with the application of light. PCOs, like MO discs, are quite durable, and the data stored on a PCO cannot be easily erased by stray magnetic fields. They can also be dual-sided.

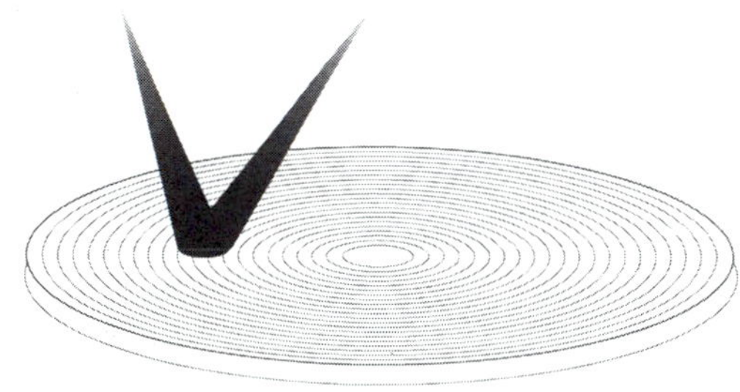

Figure 11-5 Changing a spot on a phase-change optical disc from its original state to either an amorphous or a crystalline state results in a read/write cycle that is more efficient than magneto-optical disc technology. One laser, which is shown twice in the illustration to indicate two separate power levels, serves as the read/write mechanism. Illustration by Jeffrey Krebs.

Writing data to a PCO disc involves changing the state of the recording medium from amorphous to crystalline. All recording spots on a new disc have the same property: They are amorphous. To record data to the disc, a laser beam is used to change the spot on the disc from amorphous to crystalline (Figure 11-5). The reflective properties of a crystalline spot are different from those of an amorphous state. This difference will eventually be interpreted by a read laser.

When we want to change a spot from a crystalline state to an amorphous state, we must heat the spot in the same fashion as we heated the magneto-optical disc, in effect reaching the melting point of the recording medium. The same laser, running at a more powerful rate, is used to heat the spot, which turns from its crystalline state to an amorphous state.

The important aspect of the medium that makes up a PCO disc is that it can be changed from an amorphous state to a crystalline state and back to an amorphous state simply by varying the amount of light applied. Because of this nature, writing data to a PCO disc can proceed more efficiently than writing data to a magneto-optical disc. Whereas MOs require that the spot first be erased and then magnetized, PCOs change states depending on whether the data to be stored will be represented by an amorphous or a crystalline state. This capability is referred to as a one-step read/write process, and it represents a significant time savings over the write process of MO discs. This can effectively double or triple the writing speed. Reading speed is not affected.

Information is read from the PCO disc by measuring the intensity of light reflected from a spot in an amorphous state versus light reflected from a spot in a crystalline state. A read laser is used for this purpose. Depending on the level of reflected light, data is interpreted as either a 0 or a 1. By being able to determine whether data should be interpreted as either a 0 or a 1 through an examination of the different reflected values, the PCO holds distinct advantages over the MO disc. Recall that the MO must determine the Kerr rotation to read the orientation of the recording spots. Because the laser pickup head on the PCO has a less critical task to determine what a spot's orientation is, the device can be designed to be smaller and lighter. It therefore takes less time for the head to move along the surface of the disc.

Early versions of PCO discs offered advantages over magneto-optical discs, especially with regard to access times; however, over the years, more manufacturer development was afforded to magneto-opticals, which now offer superior performance over PCO discs.

BACKUP AND ARCHIVING

As we know, computer disk storage comes in many forms. When we use a word processor to write a letter, and we want to store the letter to an external storage mechanism, we most likely will use an inexpensive floppy disk. For the cost of a few cents, we can store 2 MB of data—enough for about 1000 typewritten pages! As our data requirements grow, as would be the case if we now want to store still images that have been captured with digital cameras, each picture could require approximately 1 MB. There are many different scenarios that require storage in order for us to keep our files available.

As we edit on a DNLE system, we digitize original material to the DNLE's disk drives, edit the program, and, eventually, need to purge the disk drives so that we may load material for a different project. But what do we do if we find ourselves in a position in which it may be necessary to bring the original program back for additional editing?

Limitations of Redigitizing from Original Source Tapes

When we find ourselves in a situation in which we have purged the disk drives and have to bring back the project, we may be able to batch redigitize the material that we need. The DNLE system software directs us to reload the source videotapes and then automatically redigitizes the required footage. However, while this method works very well, we may have used sources that do not have timecode and therefore cannot be redigitized: Files such as computer graphics, audio from compact discs, and so forth cannot be automatically brought back. Therefore, it is desirable to also digitally back up this data.

Digitally Backing Up the Files

By using a digital storage medium to back up our digital files, we simply reinstall our digital files when it is necessary to re-edit the program, and we then have access to the entire program; all of the files that we require are digitally restored. There are a variety of methods that we can choose when we want to back up our files. To better understand the various backup mechanisms, some definitions are useful.

Offline: The files that we require to edit our program are not currently loaded on the DNLE storage drives.

Backup: Making a copy of the files for a program onto a different storage mechanism. After the files have been backed up, the original files are still kept on the original DNLE system's storage disks. The reason to back up? To protect the original files against a catastrophic disk failure.

Archival: The program's files do not exist on the DNLE storage disks. Instead, they have been copied to an archival storage module and erased from the DNLE storage modules.

Near-line: The program's files exist in a semi-automated retrieval mechanism, in much the same way that a multiple compact-disc audio changer can quickly access one of many CDs.

Using Magnetic Disks for Backup or Archiving Is Costly

Magnetic disks are like any other computer disk with regard to storing digital data. They can be used to store a one-page, single-lined sheet with a storage value of 2 KB, or one 35mm film frame with a storage value of 40 MB—20,000 times larger! Certainly, magnetic disks are the most sensible choice for use in DNLE systems. However, long-term storage on hard disk for archival purposes is costly. Instead, we must first determine what level of backup and archival is necessary, and then we can determine the appropriate storage medium.

The following items are important to back up:

1. The digital files that make up the program: video, audio, graphics, and so forth.
2. The sequence that was created via the DNLE software; this is a digital file that points to the picture and sound files and puts them together in their meaningful fashion.

Calculating the Transfer Time

When we are backing up data from magnetic disk to another media type, the transfer time may occur faster or slower than real time. This means that if we have one minute of material to transfer, it may take us less than a minute to back it up, or it may take us more than a minute to transfer it. To calculate the transfer time, we use the following formula:

(Amount of material ÷ Read time) + (Amount of material ÷ Write time) = Total time for backup

For example, let's say that we have 500 MB of material to back up. The magnetic disk that holds the material is capable of a read time of 5 MB/sec, and the digital tape mechanism that we are backing up to has a write time of 2.5 MB/sec. We calculate:

(500 MB ÷ 5 MB/sec = 100 sec) + (500 MB ÷ 2.5 MB/sec = 200 sec) = 300 seconds, or 5 minutes

BACKUP OPTIONS

Magneto-Optical or Phase-Change Optical

We can choose among many different storage media for backing up our data. We may decide to use either magneto-optical or phase-change optical discs. If we have 1.8 GB of digital files to back up, and each optical disc holds 500 MB per side for a two-sided disc, we require two discs to store the data.

Magnetic Tape

Magnetic tape—the same tape that is used to record video and audio as well as digital audio—can be used to store the digital files from DNLE systems. There are several different forms we can employ:

4mm tape
8mm tape
DAT (digital audio tape)
DLT (digital linear tape)

Each of the different media types is housed in its own drive mechanism, which is then connected to the DNLE system's CPU, and the 4mm, 8mm, DAT, or DLT cartridge (Figure 11-6) is placed inside its drive housing. DNLE files are backed up or archived to each of these different types of tape by using software that orchestrates the transfer of files from the source disks to the target tape (Figure 11-7).

Figure 11-6 A digital linear tape (DLT) drive, which houses a DLT cartridge for backing up work.

Additional Data Compression?
When digital files are transferred from the DNLE system's disk drives to tape, the tape drive mechanism will usually have

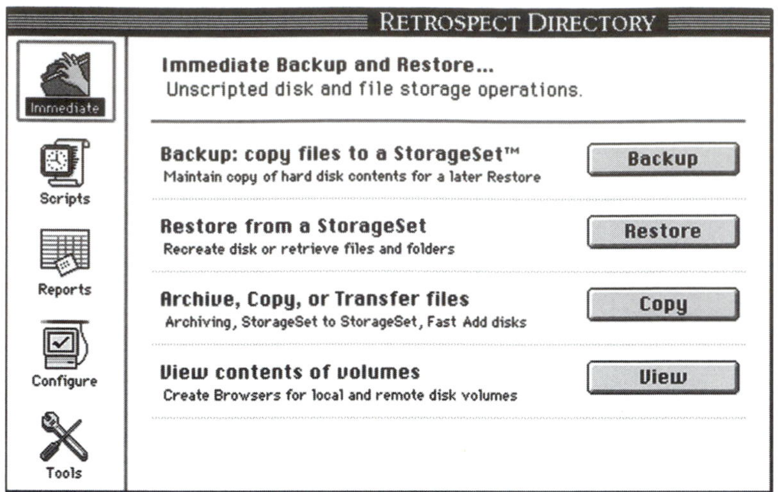

Figure 11-7 A representative interface from Retrospect, a software utility used for backup and archival purposes. Courtesy Dantz Development Corporation.

onboard data compression capabilities. Onboard compression can be used to store more material onto the tape cartridge. However, employing data compression may or may not be recommended with certain DNLE system files due to the form in which the files exist. It is best to check with the DNLE system manufacturer prior to using additional data compression.

Cost

Using magnetic tape for backup and archival purposes is extremely economical on a cost-per-MB basis. The actual disk drive mechanism will usually cost between $3000 to $5000. Media cost will vary slightly, and will always be more affordable when purchased in quantity, but the capacity-to-cost ratio is very compelling, as shown in the following chart:

Format	*Cost*	*Capacity*
Exabyte (8mm)	$25–40	25 GB
DAT	$15–20	25 GB
DLT	$99	20–35 GB

Data Transfer Rates

One of the compromises that is made when using magnetic tape for backup and archiving is that although the price of the medium is very low, the data transfer rates that the tape mechanism supports are slower than magnetic disks. The following chart shows the data transfer rate of tape devices and their chronological improvement:

First generation	8mm	2 GB	1.50 MB/sec write
Second generation	8mm	4 GB	1.50 MB/sec write
Third generation	8mm	15 GB	1.50 MB/sec write
Fourth generation	8mm	20 GB	3.00 MB/sec write
Fifth generation	8mm	30 GB	5.00 MB/sec write
First generation	DLT	10 GB	1.25 MB/sec write
Second generation	DLT	15 GB	1.25 MB/sec write

Third generation	DLT	20 GB	1.50 MB/sec write
Fourth generation	DLT	35 GB	5.00 MB/sec write
First generation	DAT	1 GB	250 KB/sec write
Second generation	DAT	4 GB	500 KB/sec write
Third generation	DAT	12 GB	1.25 MB/sec write

Although tape-based backup and archiving systems are slower than magnetic hard disks, data writing speeds are clearly improving. This fact, combined with tape's low price, makes tape an ideal choice for long-term storage.

CD-R: Compact Disc–Recordable

The same technology that is used to create audio compact discs can be used to back up and archive media. In the past, using CD-R discs for backup and archival purposes was not a common practice. This was largely due to the price of the recording mechanism, which was quite expensive: During the early 1990s, units cost well over $10,000. However, during the late 1990s, a significant decrease occurred in the cost of this technology.

CD-R employs a disk drive unit that is used to record, or burn, the information onto the surface of the recordable disc. Drive units are rated in terms of the time that it takes to burn the CD. 2× units, which are capable of burning discs at the rate of two times real time (one minute of material takes two minutes to burn) are priced at under $400, and 4× units are priced under $900. The software that is used to coordinate the transfer is usually included free of charge with the recording unit.

The blank CD-R discs can be purchased in bulk quantities, starting at under $7, and have a capacity of 650 MB. It's important to remember that CD-R discs are write-once discs and cannot be re-recorded. Normally used for compact-disc audio, they hold 74 minutes of 44.1 KHz audio.

In addition to being used for backup and archiving, CD-R and the small capital investment it requires have brought the capability of creating one's own audio compact disc on the desktop. As a result, more beginning musical groups are able to create and distribute their own audio compact discs.

Real-Time Backup and Archiving: Using Videotape to Store Digital Data

All of the backup and archiving mechanisms that have thus far been discussed all involve non-real-time backup, and most are centered on the backup of images that are compressed or equal to ITU-R 601 resolution. It may be necessary to store data that are uncompressed at ITU-R 601 quality, and to do so in real time. This is especially desirable in the commercial editorial marketplace, where rapid job changeover is necessary. As soon as one job is finished on an uncompressed DNLE system, it is often necessary to begin the next job as soon as possible. In this case, a method of digitally backing up data as fast as possible is required.

In the same way that 8mm magnetic tape is used for backing up data, it is also possible to use videotape, which can write data faster than 8mm, DLT, or DAT technology. Using D1 videotape recorders and D1 videotape, a fast enough write-time capability is achieved. Approximately 270 Mbits/sec must be written in order to store ITU-R signals, and employing a D1 recorder can provide the required data throughput.

Although data can be stored in real time, which is of tremendous benefit, this particular implementation is somewhat costly. An interface unit, which is used to transfer data from the DNLE's disk drives to the D1 recorder, along with error-correction software that ensures the integrity of the data, costs about $40,000. Additionally, a D1 recorder and tape are required, though this is less of an issue as it is reasoned that a postproduction facility will most likely already have access to a D1 recorder.

POSSIBLE FUTURE STORAGE TECHNOLOGIES

Storage mechanisms will certainly be characterized by a continued evolution and improvement of existing technologies. Magnetic disks will grow in capacity and data rate and, as important, will decrease in their cost per megabyte. For optical discs, improvements in laser technology will allow for an increase in bit writing density and will therefore allow for higher-capacity discs. There are also interesting new technologies that are being explored. One such technology is holographic storage.

Holographic Storage

Holographic storage involves using lasers to store data in an array stored in a crystal. The data are stored as optical information that requires a read laser to intersect with the crystal at precisely the right angle (Figure 11-8). When this happens, the optical information and the read laser interact to recreate a pattern of light and dark pixels that make up the data set that has been stored. One goal of investigators of this storage technology is to be able to offer tremendously dense storage in an extremely small area. One proposed scenario would be the ability to pack almost 10 GB of data for each cubic centimeter, with a data rate of 1 Gbit/sec!

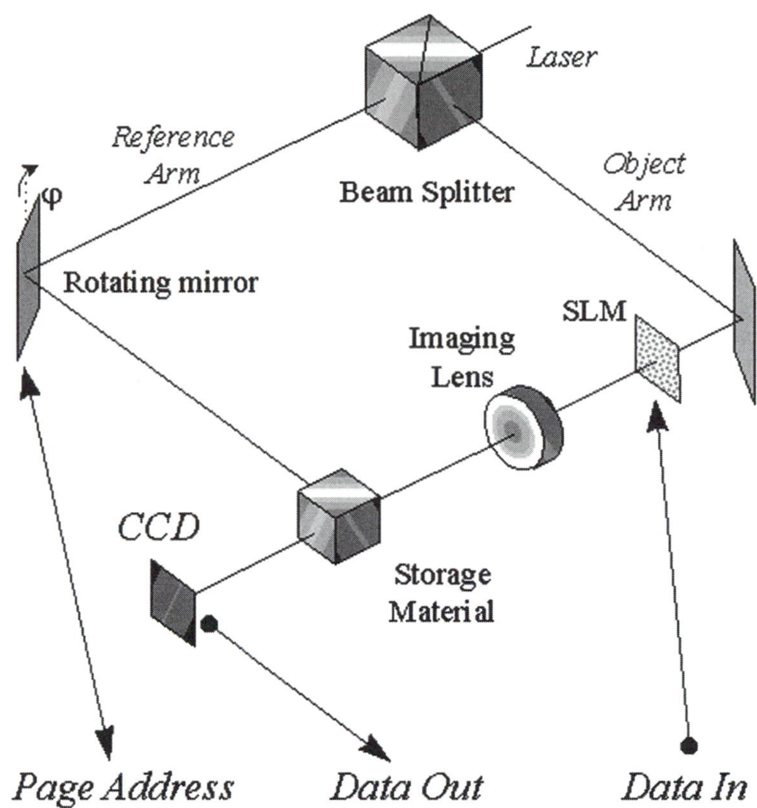

Figure 11-8 The principles of a holographic storage system. Data to be stored are formatted by the spatial light modulator (SLM) into a page of pixels. For each page, the rotating mirror changes the angle of the reference beam. These two beams interfere in the storage crystal to record the hologram. During the read process, the reference beam is directed by the rotating mirror to this same angle, which reads the data out to a CCD camera. Description and graphic Courtesy Optitek Corporation.

12

Networks, Shared Workgroups, and Transmitting Video Data

It is only natural that the creation and manipulation of digital media would bring with it the desire not only to share the work products from different workstations, but also to send data back and forth from workstation to workstation. Imagine that you are editing in New York and that special visual effects are being done in Los Angeles. If you could send digital files to Los Angeles, where they would be used to create the special effects, and these could then be sent back to you, a greater enjoyment of the parallel work process can be realized. With the correct digital network in place, these transfers can take place on a remote and automated basis—no more waiting for packages to arrive via overnight courier!

TYPES OF NETWORKS

LANs

LANs, local area networks, are defined as those that are confined to computers interconnected within short distances, from 10 to 100+ meters, as is generally the case within the same office or building.

WANs

WANs, wide area networks, are defined as those in which the computers are separated over geographic distances typically greater than one kilometer.

COMPONENTS OF NETWORKS

In order to send and share data among workstations, we require certain components. Depending on how we want to send and receive information, we will make certain choices relating to how we design the network. Figure 12-1 shows the basic components that allow a computer to network with another computer. There will be either a native network method or an add-on networking card, cabling, and software.

Network Topologies

When a network design has been chosen, it is referred to as a *topology*—the manner in which data are shared and communicated. There are four basic network topologies: point-to-point, broadcast bus, token ring, and switched.

Point-to-Point

Figure 12-2 shows a point-to-point topology using either copper or fiber cable. Point-to-point connections are perhaps the most simple in terms of the usage model: two computers transmitting data to one another. They can function in either LAN or WAN configurations and over copper or fiber wire. Transmission rates of gigabits/sec can be achieved.

Broadcast Bus

Figure 12-3 illustrates a broadcast bus topology. Here, all workstations on the network are connected by a single wire. Each computer on this type of network must share in the overall capacity that the network provides. As a result, if the bandwidth is at or near usage capacity, and another workstation requires the network, it must wait until bandwidth becomes available. Software assists in the detection of when it is possible to transmit and receive data. Bus topologies function over

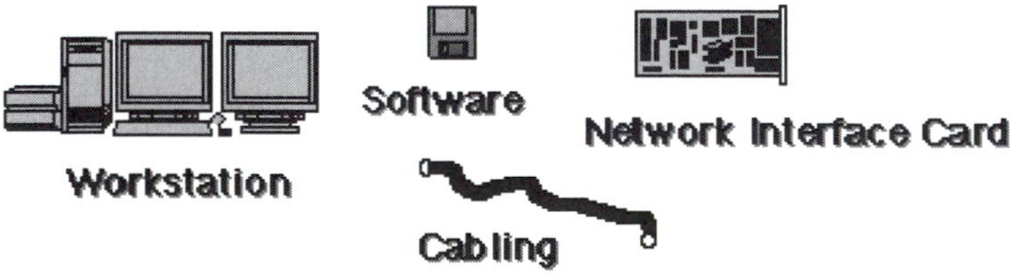

Figure 12-1 The basic components of any network. Two computers are connected via a network add-on card, cabling, and software.

Figure 12-2 A point-to-point topology. Two workstations are connected over either copper or fiber wire.

copper wire in LAN configurations, with transmission speeds in the tens of Mbits/sec.

Token Ring

Figure 12-4 represents a token ring topology, in which all workstations are connected by a single wire. However, unlike a broadcast bus topology, in which each computer must share in the overall bandwidth of the network, a token ring topology requires that only one workstation sends data at a time. A "token," in actuality read and write permission, travels among the workstations and determines which one can utilize the network at a specific time. Ring topologies function in LAN configurations over fiber digital data interconnect (FDDI) at a rate of 100 Mbits/sec.

Switched

Figure 12-5 shows a switched topology. When we make a telephone call, we are, in essence, using a switched network. There is a network in place, and when we want to make a phone call, a switch is triggered that gives us the full bandwidth of the network. We do not have to share the network with other users—we can talk without pausing for enabling bandwidth. The same applies for a switched computer network. Each computer is connected to the network via a switch. When data must be communicated, the switch is opened, and the workstation gets the full bandwidth of the network. Therefore, with a switched topology, bandwidth scales with the

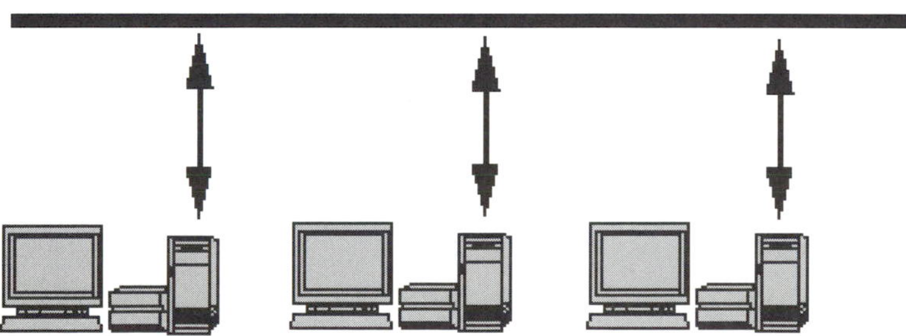

Figure 12-3 A broadcast bus topology. All workstations are connected by a single wire, and each shares in the overall capacity of the network.

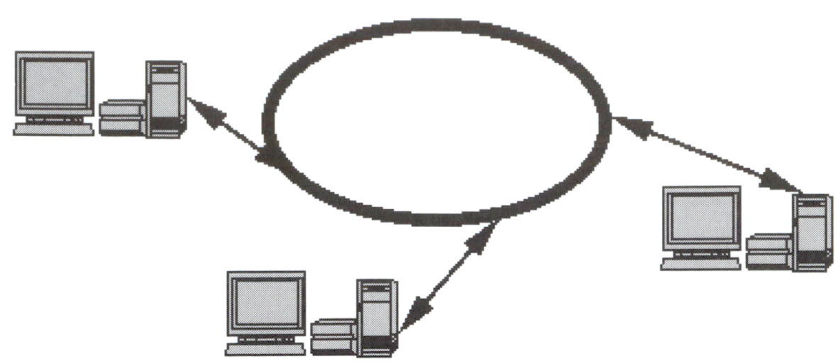

Figure 12-4 A token ring topology. All workstations are connected by a single wire and one computer must have a "token" that enables the computer to use the capacity of the network.

number of ports, and speeds of 10 Mbits/sec to 1 Gbit/sec can be realized.

Interface Cards and Software

Let's take the example of a computer and a modem. Some workstations have onboard communications capabilities. For example, some computers have a built-in modem for sending and receiving data and faxes. Add-on interface cards are used to form the connections among computers. Software operates with these network interface cards. TCP/IP, or Transmission Control Protocol/Internet Protocol, is software that is used to transmit data and to retransmit data that did not arrive at the destination. Computers equipped with TCP/IP, regardless of the actual network, can transmit and receive data among themselves.

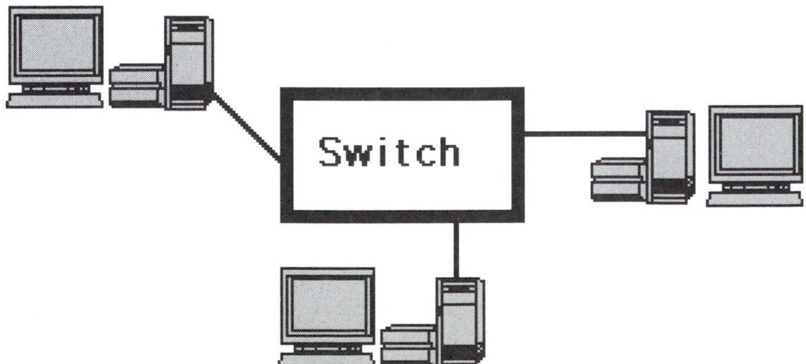

Figure 12-5 A switched topology. All workstations are connected to the network via a switch. When a computer requires the network, the switch is opened, and the workstation receives the full bandwidth of the network.

SENDING AND RECEIVING DATA

Sending digital files, whether they are word processing documents or digital video and audio files, is dependent on having the right combination of hardware and software and understanding that a certain amount of data, traveling at a certain rate, will require a specific amount of time to get to the required destination. There are many different transport mechanisms for transmitting data, such as those shown in Table 12-1.

Table 12-1 Data Transmittal Mechanisms

Transport Method	*Transfer Rate*
Modem 2400 baud	2.4 kbits/sec
Normal phone link	15 kbits/sec
Leased-line phone service	56 kbits/sec
ISDN	64 kbits/sec per channel
Computer Network	
AppleTalk (Macintosh)	230 kbits/sec
Ethernet	10 Mbits/sec
	100 Mbits/sec
	Gigabit (Gbit)/sec
T1	1.5 Mbits/sec
T3	45 Mbits/sec
FDDI	100 Mbits/sec
	200 Mbits/sec
ATM	155 Mbits/sec
	622 Mbits/sec
Fibre Channel	133 Mbits/sec
	1 Gbit/sec
	4 Gbits/sec
FireWire	400 Mbits/sec
	1 Gbit/sec
HiPPI	800 Mbits/sec
	1600 Mbits/sec

Modem

A modem (modulator/demodulator) is used to transmit and to receive digital data. The channel that the data must travel through is small, at 1.2 kb/sec. The bandwidth capability of an ordinary phone line is approximately 1 kb/sec, leaving some room for overhead and control codes that must be sent with the message.

Modems are used to turn analog information into digital information. The analog signals are in turn represented as sounds, which can travel over a phone line. The receiving modem turns these analog signals back into their original digital form. Modems operate at different baud rates, which is a measurement of the transmitting and receiving capability of the modem. Baud rate does not mean how many bits can be sent per second, but this is often thought to be the case. Most modems will operate at 14.4, 28.8, or 33.6 kbps.

Integrated Services Digital Network

Integrated services digital network (ISDN) is a transmission method that is designed to combine various sorts of information, from telephone transmissions to fax to images and sounds, into one digital network. ISDN is used for many purposes. A typical example would be a large corporation that has to communicate with its branches on a regular basis, for example, an insurance company that must regularly receive and send large database files.

ISDN requires that a communications link be placed at the transmitting and receiving sites. These installations are offered by telephone companies, who apply a use fee to such installations. At 64 kbits/sec, the bandwidth is not that much greater than dial-up service. However, up to 24 channels of ISDN can be combined, depending on how many are needed. If 24 channels are used, the data transmission rate totals 1.5 Mbits/sec, a respectable data rate. For companies that regularly must transmit many forms of digital information but do not require very large bandwidths, ISDN is a very acceptable solution.

Computer Networks

A great number of computers in business and education are networked, or linked. In an office setting or an educational institution, computer terminals on many different desks that can access a central computer have become quite commonplace. The central computers may contain databases or information that many office workers or students can tap into, query, and obtain materials from. Electronic mail (e-mail) is a very common form of networked communication. These central stores of information are often referred to as *servers* because they serve the demands placed on them by those requiring data stored on the server. Networking offers many possibilities, including transferring data files from one computer to another and actually controlling a computer on one floor of an office with a computer on a different floor.

Most of the material that users have heretofore moved back and forth has been in the form of documents, spreadsheets, graphic presentations, and files that were not particularly data-intensive. However, transferring digital motion video and audio files from computer to computer requires a great deal of network capability and places a great burden on the network.

ATM

ATM, or asynchronous transfer mode, is most commonly used in combination with fiber optic cable, although it can also be supported by twisted pair copper wire. ATM can be used to provide data transfer rates over very long distances (cross-country distances can easily be supported). ATM utilizes fixed data packet sizes that do not fluctuate. Using ATM as the physical layer for the network in conjunction with a SONET transmission method can provide for very high data throughput. SONET (synchronous optical network) and its European counterpart, SDH (synchronous digital hierarchy) are rated in terms of their OC, or optical carrier, capability:

OC 1 = 51.8 Mbits/sec
OC 2 = 155 Mbits/sec
OC 3 = 622 Mbits/sec
OC 48 = 2.4 Gbits/sec

Ethernet

Ethernet is a form of local area network (LAN), using twisted pair copper wire, that can extend to approximately 1.25 miles and can offer up to 1000 nodes (computers and peripheral devices). Ethernet operates on a principle known as *carrier sense multiple access* (CSMA). While all LANs require computers to wait their turn before sending information, CSMA allows a computer to send information, and when the cable is not in use, another computer can begin sending its information.

The two most popular forms of Ethernet are rated at 10 Mbits and 100 Mbits. The 10 Mbit version is referred to as 10-base-T, while the 100 Mbit version is referred to as 100-base-T. 10-base-T Ethernet input/output (I/O) ports come standard on most personal computers, while some personal computers offer 100-base-T I/O ports. However, because multiple computers can be waiting to transmit, the more practical throughput (the amount of data that can regularly be processed) is about 0.8 Mbit/sec (about 800 KB/sec) to any given computer. Networking computers via Ethernet affords an adequate throughput size for transmission and is a popular choice for linking systems that must transfer data-intensive files.

Ethernet capacities are not limited to 10- and 100-base-T. Gigabit (Gbit/sec) Ethernet protocols will be commonplace in the very near term.

Fibre Channel

Fibre channel, as is to be expected from its name, runs over fiber optic cable. Fibre channel is rated at 133 Mbits/sec and 1 Gbit/sec and is expected to grow to support transfer rates in excess of 4 Gbits/sec. Fibre channel supports point-to-point, loop (fibre channel arbitrated loop, or FC-AL), and switched networks.

Fiber Digital Data Interconnect

Fiber digital data interconnect (FDDI) is a transmission method that uses fiber optics to transmit and receive signals (it is also possible to use twisted pair copper wire). These fibers are transparent and are usually constructed of either glass or plastic. Fiber optics transmit energy by directing light instead of electrical signals. Electrical signals are encoded into light waves, transmitted, and received and decoded back into electrical signals.

In the past, the cost of fiber optic technology was much higher than copper. However, significant price reductions for fiber and the increased capacity that it provides combine to form a superior solution for data transfer. FDDI is offered in a 100 Mbits/sec configuration, but due to overhead, delivers from between 2 to 6 MB/sec. Compared with some of the other alternatives, FDDI is no longer very widely adopted.

FireWire (IEEE 1394)

In the late 1990s, IEEE 1394, commonly known as FireWire, was developed at Apple Computer. FireWire is a digital serial transport mechanism designed to support native DV (digital video). FireWire supports up to 63 devices on a single computer bus and a distance of 4.5 meters between nodes. Unlike SCSI, which requires that all the devices be connected together, have unique addresses, and be terminated properly, FireWire addressing is done dynamically after the device is connected. A throughput of 400 Mbits/sec (maximum) is supported under IEEE 1394, but it is not limited to that data rate—a 1 Gbit/sec mode is a future development.

FireWire is promising in several aspects. A single cable, FireWire is used to connect professional and consumer camcorders and devices directly into the DV-compatible bus of the CPU. A camcorder can be connected directly into the computer's FireWire port and digital video, and audio can be transferred very quickly into the computer's disk storage. This transfer rate can be faster than real time. Devices are also "hot swappable," which means that they may be connected without first powering down the CPU. These factors lead to the conclusion that FireWire will become a standard for connecting consumer electronics, and FireWire's capabilities may very well be adopted by segments of the professional marketplace.

With FireWire, digitization before using a DNLE system is a thing of the past. Because the video and audio files are already in digital format, they need only be transferred over FireWire before one begins editing.

HiPPI

HiPPI, or high performance parallel interface, is a very fast transport mechanism that uses fiber (although it can also support coaxial cable). The supported data rates are 800 Mbits/sec and 1600 Mbits/sec. A 6400 Mbits/sec rate is a goal for future support. In addition, HiPPI can support very long distances; coaxial cable can support 25 meters, while different fiber types will support between 1 to 25 km. One of the methods by which HiPPI achieves its very high data rates is through the use of nonblocking switches that ensure that when a connection between two machines is made, the connection receives the full possible bandwidth.

T1 and T3

T1 and T3 are best referred to as common carriers of signal that require dedicated systems installed at two sites that will be in communication with each other. Often misinterpreted as terrestrial, T1 and T3 links are not solely terrestrial in nature; they can involve communication using satellites as well as over land. T1 and T3 service, available from phone companies, is arranged in advance of use and involves hardware that, in the case of T3, offers greater bandwidth capabilities than, say, ISDN. Coaxial cables are used.

T1 links have a bandwidth of approximately 1.5 Mbits/sec (about 150 KB/sec), equal to 24 channels of ISDN. T3 links, on the other hand, have a very significant bandwidth of 45 Mbits/sec (about 4.5 MB/sec). Although T3 service is expensive to install and use, transferring data over these links is an extremely efficient method when large files are routinely sent and received.

SHARING WORK AMONG DIGITAL WORKSTATIONS

In a parallel and shared work environment, it is important to be able to connect several workstations together. Figure 12-6 shows a shared workgroup environment. Here several workstations are connected to a central storage, which all workstations share. Each workstation can play, in real time, digital video and audio files directly from central storage. Imagine that we are working on a program for which the postproduction schedule is very limited. It is determined that to finish the program by the required time, the work must be shared among several people. In a shared workgroup, each person has equal access to all the files on the central storage disks. Depending on the network that is in place, real-time play of multiple streams of video and audio is supported.

Shown in Figure 12-7 is MountainGate's CentraVision FC solution, which allows multiple workstations to share the same pool of source material.

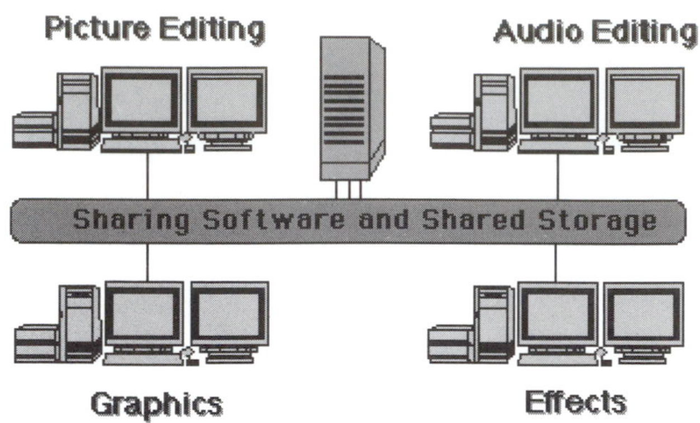

Figure 12-6 The shared workgroup environment consists of a number of users connected to a central storage system, with all users having simultaneous access to data contained on the storage modules.

Video Servers and Data (Media) Servers

There is often some confusion regarding the differences between video and media servers. A video server serves video in real time, and possibly based on the demands of the requester. For example, with video-on-demand systems, a user is able to make a selection from among several different choices. Some video-on-demand systems are very simple: A person wishes to see a particular film, makes the request, and a person literally walks to a shelf and puts the requested film into a videotape player! While functional, this implementation does not allow the user to control the viewing—the film cannot be paused, or a scene cannot be viewed over. It is certainly the goal of sophisticated video-on-demand services to allow for more flexibility and to put the user in charge of when and how material is viewed. To arrive at that goal, however, a media server is required.

Media servers provide data that allow users to retrieve, view, and, of course, edit full-motion digital video and audio

Figure 12-7 MountainGate's CentraVision FC solution allows multiple workstations to share the same pool of storage, allowing for simultaneous use of media and projects. Courtesy MountainGate.

files. There are many factors that bear on realizing a media server solution. The number of users who must have simultaneous access to the digital media, the aggregate bandwidth requirements that the media server must support, and the distance among workstations are all significant issues.

Parallel Workgroups on a Global Basis

A natural outgrowth of shared workgroups is the development of a virtual and global production and postproduction facility. If work can be shared among users, it is only natural that work will need to be shared on a more widespread basis. Let's say that we are editing in New York and want to send some shots to Los Angeles for painting while also sending some files to Rome for special effects. We can accomplish this by putting into place the required networks. Such flexibility speeds up the process of viewing and interpreting the sequence, directing changes to be made, waiting for the changes to be made, receiving the changes, and completing the program.

Transmitting the Data

Only two factors contribute to how long it takes for data to be transmitted from one location to another: how much data must be sent and the capacity of the sending/receiving network. For example, let's say that we have a 30-second commercial that we want to send from New York to Los Angeles. If we want to send the commercial in a completely uncompressed ITU-R 601 format, and we want to send it in real time, we require enough bandwidth to handle the approximately 22 MB/sec necessary to handle this resolution.

Of course, there are many scenarios that do not require real-time transfer but instead require only that data arrive within an acceptable time period. To calculate how much time it takes to transmit data, we use the following formula:

> Size per frame × Frames per second + Size of audio files × Number of audio files = Amount of data to be sent

If we are working with ITU-R 601 video at a compression ratio of 2:1, 350 KBytes per frame are required. Combined with two channels of 48 KHz audio, our calculations show:

> 10.5 MB (350 KB/frame × 30 frames = 10.5 MB/sec) + 192 KB (2 × 48 KHz (2 bytes) = ~ 10.6 MB/sec

We must transmit 10.6 MB and must choose which type of transmission method to use. We would logically seek the most rapid form of transmission, but we may not have access to the needed equipment. If we have access to an ATM network, running OC 1, with a data throughput of 51.8 Mbits/sec, our transmission time is less than two seconds in order to send one second of material, or two times real time.

Clearly, depending on the nature of the files that will routinely be sent from one location to another and the amount of money that can be invested in the network, it is possible to experience considerable differences in transfer times. Generally speaking, the faster the network, the more expensive it is. However, network technology prices are decreasing quite rapidly while capacities are increasing.

Figure 12-8A shows a software transmission calculator that can be used to determine how long it will take to send a file based on a chosen transmission method. Note that we have entered 50 feet of 35mm film (33 seconds) at a specific picture resolution, letterboxed in the 1:1.85 aspect ratio, with two channels of 44.1 KHz audio. Transmitting this data over a 28.8 kbps modem will take 6 hours and 47 minutes. However, by using a T1 line at 1.5 Mbps, our transmission time is reduced to a mere 7 minutes (Figure 12-8b).

Transmitting Video Data Around the World

Consider this possible scenario: War breaks out in a country. Military law is declared, and a ban is placed on all communication out of the country. Journalists from around the world have footage that has been shot showing the first hours of the war, but there is no way to transmit the motion video. However, there is a way to make phone calls and to send documents via modem. Some reporters use the phone to call in their reports. Others use modems in their computers to send stories. Others send still video images.

The race is on. Which network will be the first to transmit motion video from the ravaged country? A small digitizing and editing station is set up in a hotel room. The video footage of the war is digitized and stored, and the footage is edited. Next,

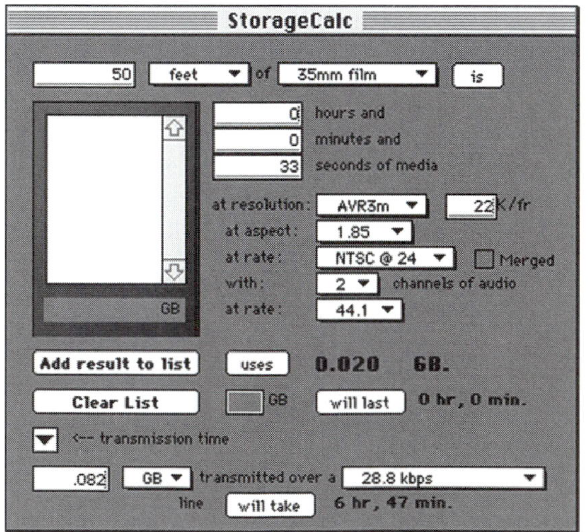

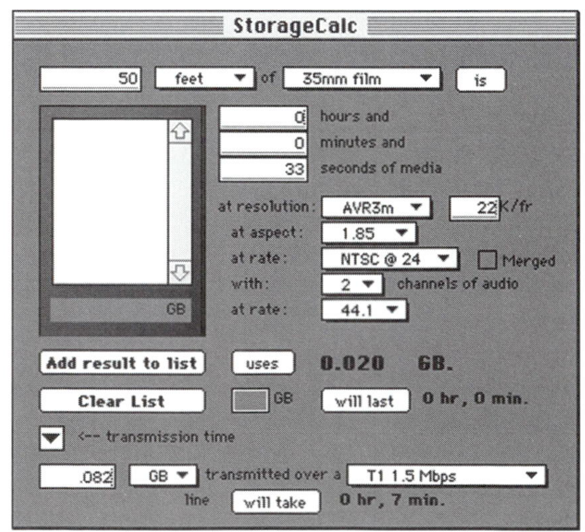

Figure 12-8 **(A)** A software transmission calculator that shows how much time is required to send a file. Based on a 28.8 kbps modem, the chosen file would take 6 hours and 47 minutes. **(B)** Using a T1 line at 1.5 Mbps reduces the transmission time of the same file to 7 minutes.

we connect to a phone line and transmit the digital files to the broadcast center, where they are then played directly to air. Even if we have a relatively low-capacity data line, and the files take several hours to get to their destination, it is really of little consequence—all that matters is that a message was gotten out of the war-torn country.

Digital Connections among Sites

Much of the technology discussed in this chapter is necessary for creating digital connections among sites. Sending video and audio signals, as well as digital data, is an integral aspect of realizing the global networked facility. Sending real-time video and audio signals must take into account the data requirements necessary for the resolution of video and the number and resolution of audio channels.

There are a number of manufacturers who are involved in the real-time transport of video and audio signals, at ITU-R 601 resolution, at 270 Mbits/sec. However, scaleable sending is also important when the user does not require that the signals be at their original uncompressed resolution. In this case, users can choose among different compressed versions of the original ITU-R 601 signal. For example, it may be acceptable to view the signals at MPEG 2 rates of 45 Mbits/sec or to seek a higher compression ratio and view the signals at 6 Mbits/sec. As the cost of the equipment required in creating these digital connections decreases, either fuller-resolution video and audio will be transferred, or the number of channels of compressed video and audio will increase.

The benefit to the user is very compelling. Let's say that we are shooting as well as editing a film in New York. However, the film is being telecined in Los Angeles. Based on the types of digital connections we choose, we can receive our digital dailies in real time and be totally free of the digitizing process. Or we can actually watch the telecine session, remotely, while it occurs and still have captured the files for later editing.

Services from Pacific Bell such as ABVS (Advanced Broadcast Video Service) provide video at 147 Mbits/sec and at 45 Mbits/sec. There are many manufacturers involved in either or both hardware and software support for video, audio, and data transport. Among them are Sprint Drums, Vyvx, EDnet, and Creative Partner.

Figure 12-9 is a representative interface of Creative Partner from Emotion Corporation. Using a friendly, object-oriented interface, it is easy to send and receive material over a network and to make comments and notations directly on the media in order to facilitate collaboration.

The Internet's Role in Delivering Content

The Internet can also be a vital, and economic, way of sending and receiving digital data. Although the Internet cannot yet provide for

Figure 12-9 Creative Partner, used for reviewing, commenting, and notating information sent over a network to further collaboration and global production. Courtesy Emotion Corporation.

real-time transfer of video at ITU-R 601 resolution, capabilities are increasing all the time. The Internet is extremely useful for sending digital data when the time factor does not require real-time transfer. For example, let's take our previous example of editing our film in New York. We want to receive some of the special effects that are being done in Los Angeles. These can certainly be sent in an overnight package, but they can also easily be posted in our e-mail system and transferred using the Internet. If it requires 30 minutes to download five examples that we can use as temporary place-holders in our sequence, and the only cost of getting the material was maintaining an extremely inexpensive monthly Internet connection, the value is very clear for maintaining a collaborative, worldwide, parallel workgroup.

ADSL

For the transmission of data into the home, supplying the conduit required for services such as video-on-demand, one possible technology is Asymmetric Digital Subscriber Line (ADSL). ADSL, capable of delivering approximately 6 Mbits/sec, can be used to transmit over the existing twisted pair copper lines that currently make up the majority of telephone services. While this data rate is not enough to deliver uncompressed video, it is sufficient for delivering MPEG-based video along with synchronized audio.

TALKING WITH EDITORS

What is your outlook for transmitting data, networking, and shared workgroups?

Joe Beirne

There are essentially two layers of data involved in digital media workgrouping: (1) the media itself, and (2) the media content and location pointers. We make extensive use of transmission, sharing and networking of the second data type: It has been neither necessary nor efficient for us to apply these methods to the media itself, except in limited cases.

We look forward to using fast and reliable networks to achieve media transmission, but our need for this ability is far outweighed by our need for comprehensive "pointer data" workgrouping, databasing, and archiving.

Peter Cohen

I have had little success with networking and shared workgroups to date, but it will evolve. In this way, we remain specialists as opposed to being forced into becoming generalists.

Alan Miller

Ultimately, networking data and shared workgroups will be the way. Right now there are still many speed issues to deal with. Also, not all projects require sharing on an ongoing basis. Now, it's easier to transfer audio and graphic files on a Zip drive.

Scott Ogden

At this point I use networking only in terms of bringing graphic files onto my Media Composer. But I definitely see this changing in the future. What a company like mine could use is a fast and dependable media-sharing capability. We have nine Media Composers and are often working on the same project. We are constantly consolidating projects and media onto different removable magnetic drives. The ability to access any project at any time would be very helpful.

As far as the more distant future, I think many editors fantasize about being able to break the bond between them and a facility. Many would like to be able to live anywhere they like and at the same time be able to work on challenging projects that only the big media centers can provide. In order for this to happen, the cheap, free flow of digitized media over WANs will have to happen. Not only will we need to send a 30-second cut or a 2 and 1/2 minute trailer quickly to a client, but eventually we would need to be able to access a three-hour film rough cut and bring it into an edit bay.

Basil Pappas

AvidNet Transfer Tool has revolutionized workgroup editing, and I see this as an area of major future growth. As networks and telephony increase in speed, it will expand the distance we can be from one another while increasing the bandwidth with which we can communicate. At *48 Hours*, we commonly assign many editors to multipart shows that may share common media. The ease with which we can eliminate duplication in the workflow has allowed us all to start thinking of new ways to apply the technology. We can truly go "on the road" and experience the same ease of use we used to have in our traditional editing environment.

Tom Poederbach

The benefit is clearly that you can get the best person for a specific part of the job without leaving your chair. Most program makers would love to have a really inexpensive desktop editing system to be able to play around with their footage. A director would do a rough cut of a scene and send the pointers back to his editor, who can then work on the scene and send it back to the director for approval.

13

The Sixth Wave: Digital Media Management and Delivery

The personnel associated with the many crafts involved in making a finished film or videotape have certain areas of expertise. These areas of specialization include audio sweetening, digital video effects, electronic painting systems, film color correction, and so on. Editing is further broken down into specialties: some people specialize in commercials, others in film documentaries, and so on.

What both film and video editing processes have in common is a very procedural way of working. Normally, one specialist, say the picture editor, makes a contribution, while the sound editor makes another contribution. And while there will always be reasons for specialists, the tool sets of fifth-wave systems, with their complete horizontal, vertical, and intraframe editing capabilities, allow users to wear several hats, performing all of the functions required to completely finish a program.

But film and television programs are only two categories from among the enormous number of programs that are of the "not for broadcast" variety: corporate industrials, training videos, and institutional uses of video. Each year in the United States, an average of 425 films are made; thousands of corporate videos are made.

The personnel responsible for creating these presentations are most likely not classically trained film and videotape editors. Very often, they have to combine many elements in creating the program: Some form of digital video, computer graphics, character generation, music, sound effects, and still photographs may all have to be combined to create the program. Managing all the different forms of media to create the finished program can be a difficult undertaking for anyone, and especially when the corporate audio-visual department is limited in terms of resources and personnel.

METADATA VERSUS MEDIA

When we use a DNLE system to create a video program, we take all of the source materials—video, audio, graphics, and so forth—and edit them together into a cohesive unit. The actual files that reside on the computer's disks can be thought of and generally labeled as *media*.

However, the identification of each of the sources that went into the making of the program must carry additional information. For example, if we are editing a film for theatrical release on a DNLE system, we must eventually return to the actual film negative in order to conform the original negative to our DNLE edit. Therefore, we must retain information about the original source material. This database—in effect, the retention of information that identifies the origin of each source and how they were combined to form the finished program—is generally referred to as the *metadata*.

Figure 13-1 illustrates the relationship between metadata and media. Metadata, in the form of a *composition*, uses references to the data contained in the *sources*. Finally, the digitized media files are in the form of *media data objects*. The metadata is the database that contains information concerning the identity and characteristics of the edited sequence that we have put together.

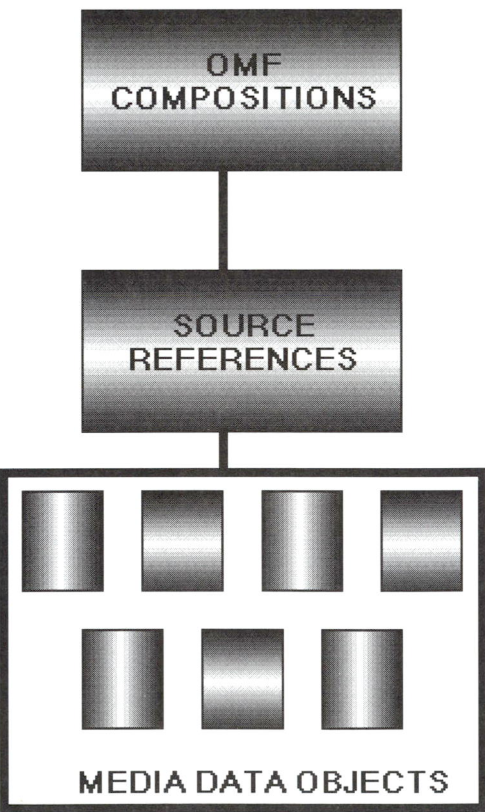

Figure 13-1 The relationship between metadata and media. Compositions utilize source references that point to the digitized media data objects.

Faced with the dizzying array of digital files, originating from many different systems and with many different file types, it will be necessary to ensure that these assets are successfully tracked, made compatible, and delivered securely from location to location. The sixth wave of digital nonlinear editing is significant because it brings widespread digital manipulation and digital asset management to the DNLE system.

THE SIXTH WAVE: DIGITAL MEDIA MANAGEMENT

The sixth wave of digital nonlinear editing involves the utilization of a number of different technologies which, when combined, create an integrated system for digital media management (DMM). The major components of DMM are

Asset management
File compatibility
Media compatibility
Metadata interchange
Open systems on open platforms

When combined with and tightly integrated into the DNLE system, the DMM becomes complete, for it is the DMM system that creates, manipulates, and orchestrates data. These data files, whether they are associated with film, video, audio, or computer-generated images, are all manipulated as data file types. The DMM system, as an integrated concept, will therefore evolve into a manager of digital signals rather than remain as a simple digital nonlinear editing system.

Asset Management

Asset management refers to software that assists the user in creating a database of original sources, or *assets*. Assets can be thought of as any of the original elements that we require to create our program, such as the script, the original footage, audio elements, and so forth. The asset management component of the DMM system allows us to catalog these sources. Figure 13-2 is an example of an asset management system that allows the user to enter user-defined fields of information and query the asset manager. The user is then presented with any clips that match the criteria of the search query.

Once our assets have been loaded into the DNLE system, additional information becomes identified with each asset. The asset's *attributes* are these additional pieces of data, such as the asset's file type, when the file was originally created, its history of revisions, and so forth.

File Compatibility

File compatibility can be defined, in general terms, as the ability to take a specific file that was created on Manufacturer A's

Figure 13-2 An asset management system is one of the most important components of the digital media management system. Shown is the interface of Cinebase, an asset manager that allows the user to set search queries and then be presented with the clips that match the search conditions. Courtesy Cinebase.

equipment and be able to read that file on a piece of equipment from Manufacturer B. With film, file compatibility is not an issue: Film in its various gauges enjoys compatibility with other similar film gauges. Television, in contrast, is extremely incompatible from country to country. Video must be brought to the most common denominator before it can be compatible. For example, if we are creating our master videotape on D1 and want to incorporate some digital video from a consumer camera, we cannot easily do so in a digital sense; therefore, the most common interchange format becomes base-band video. However, any MPEG 2 Professional Profile @ main level file can be played by any system that complies with this standard of encoding and decoding.

Computer Formats Suffer Greatly from Incompatibility

The computer industry also has not enjoyed a history of file compatibility. A word-processed document created in one word processor may not be readable by a different word processor. However, through computer format interchanges, translation programs can be written. For example, if we save our word-processed document in Rich Text Format (.rtf), a standardized method of interchanging text files, any other word processing program that has implemented .rtf support will be able to open our file.

However, if we have a graphic file that is in the PICT format and wish to use it in a system that only uses files in the RGB format, we have a situation in which we must translate the PICT file into RGB before we can incorporate it into our program.

Fear of Compatibility?

Manufacturers have traditionally been suspicious of file compatibility, which they have viewed as a potential threat. Few companies have been forthcoming in promoting a common interchange format. If there is any doubt at all about this, simply consider the situation of videotape edit decision lists (EDLs). There are a variety of formats, such as Ampex, CMX, Grass Valley, Paltex, and Sony. None of these lists can be recognized by another editing system. However, as the fourth-wave DNLE systems began to appear in the late 1990s, more manufacturers had finally understood the inevitable reality: Be compatible or perish.

The widespread adoption of DNLE systems as well as desktop-based software applications for audio, compositing, graphics, and painting demands that files be compatible. As with our word processing example, without a common standard, sharing files between different electronic painting systems or between the DNLE system and the digital audio workstation becomes impossible or results in an extremely inefficient use of time.

Metadata and Media Compatibility

File compatibility refers to the ability for one program to read the file types of another program. Media compatibility refers to a similar concept: one software application being able to read the media type from another application. Both file and media compatibility are extremely important in reducing the amount of work that is required when we find ourselves using several different applications.

Interchange

However, having file and media compatibility is only the beginning of realizing true interchange among different workstations. The concept of interchange is that of enabling different software applications to read and write both file and media types from other systems. In addition, true interchange means that the metadata created by differing systems is also interchangeable.

OMF: Open Media Framework

The Open Media Framework was introduced by Avid Technology in 1994 and is an initiative to standardize how metadata are described and, therefore, successfully interchanged among workstations on different computer platforms. One way of thinking about OMF is to consider it as one would consider a "super EDL"—an edit decision list that could describe all the edits and effects we accomplished in a form that we could take from system to system. For example, let's say that we have started putting together our program on a DNLE system and want to finish the program by mixing the audio on a digital audio workstation (DAW).

The first hurdle that we face is whether the audio and video media from the DNLE system are compatible with the DAW. If so, the DAW will be able to directly read the audio and video files. However, just being able to read the files does not instruct the DAW as to how to put the files together, that is, in what order each individual audio file should be placed in order to precisely match the sequence as it exited the DNLE system. This is the second hurdle: achieving metadata compatibility.

OMF often uses a cooking analogy that suggests that the media files are ingredients while the metadata represents the recipe that determines how the sources should be combined (Figure 13-1). The OMF components are as follows:

Composition: The composition (the recipe) is the set of instructions that chronicles how the media are played in time and the synchronization among different elements.

Source references: Specify the original sources of all elements.

Media data objects: These are the multiple types of media contained within one file structure and include: animation, audio, graphics, video, and so forth.

If we have metadata compatibility between the DNLE system and the DAW (Figure 13-3), the sequence that we have edited on the DNLE system will be precisely preserved when we open the sequence on the DAW. As a result, all the decisions that were made regarding each and every audio cut and effect are seamlessly brought into the DAW. When we contrast this to what would be required had we not had media

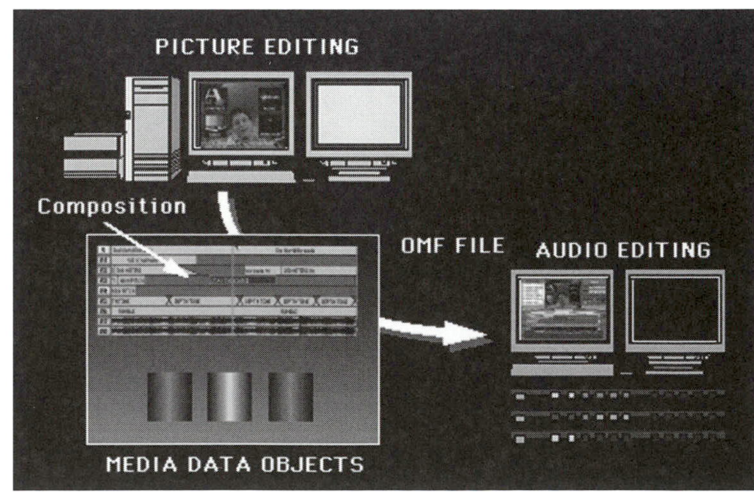

Figure 13-3 A practical example of how metadata and media type interchange is employed between the digital nonlinear picture editor and the digital audio workstation. A scene is cut on the DNL picture editor and a composition, representing the metadata, is passed to the DAW as an OMF file. The DAW reads the OMF file and uses the metadata to recreate the cut scene. The media data objects are read directly as a result of media file compatibility.

and metadata compatibility, the savings in time become quite obvious.

Open versus Closed Systems

A closed workstation is one that consists of proprietary hardware and software that perform very specific tasks. It is unlikely that the system can be used to do anything other than the tasks for which it was designed. An open system, however, is one in which hardware and software are developed for generic computer platforms. As a result, the user has the possibility of running other software programs on the same hardware. The advantages of this capability cannot be overstated. Imagine that we have a hardware system that is at one moment serving as a DNL editor. We then quit the DNLE application and start a software program that turns the hardware system into a digital painting system. This generic, nonproprietary computer that takes on its identity by virtue of what software is currently running is truly the epitome of the Turing Machine concept outlined in Chapter 1.

Java and Open Systems

Java, a computer programming language developed by Sun Microsystems in 1994, can be used to extend the capabilities of previously closed systems. When originally introduced, the goal of Java programming was to serve as a cross-platform programming language for Internet applications. As such, it served as a way for an application to run on different computer platforms.

A manufacturer of a technically "closed" system could further extend the capabilities of the system's hardware by creating a Java API. Third-party developers, writing in Java, could therefore use the hardware of the host CPU and related subsystems. Java *applets* are Java applications that can run on any computer as long as the CPU is capable of running the Java plug-in.

PARALLEL WORK AND COLLABORATION ON A GLOBAL BASIS

Integrated digital media management enables significant possibilities that further the goal of parallel work and collaboration on a worldwide basis. Imagine that we are working in Boston and need some dramatic stock footage of billowing clouds. Using a high-speed data link, we can dial into a stock footage provider in Los Angeles (Figure 13-4) and query the asset management system for different types of cloud footage. We are then able to view the various clips that the system displays.

Depending on the degree of compatibility that the stock footage provider has implemented, it may be possible to download the cloud clips that we have found in the exact file type

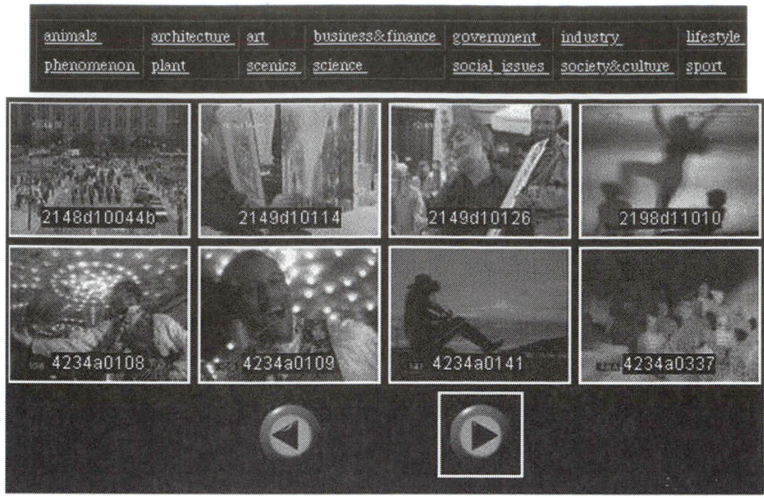

Figure 13-4 A stock footage provider whose library can be accessed over the Internet. Courtesy Energy Productions.

(file, media, metadata) that our DNLE system requires. Perhaps most conveniently, we have accomplished all of this without leaving our editing room or our home! And we have received information that can be incorporated seamlessly into our DNLE system to create our program.

The digital media manager affects how individuals work with information and how disparate forms of media are combined into meaningful wholes. This wave will be compatible with information regardless of its origin. Files will transfer back and forth and among systems that will originate the pictures and sounds, catalog the signals, edit the signals, and transmit the signals. Progressive manufacturers will create *digital media managers* in the future, not *editing systems*.

Being in Two Places at Once: Videoconferencing

Digital video compression, combined with metadata and media interchange, can assist us in solving the age-old problem of trying to be in two places at one time. Through the use of various types of data links—some capable of transmitting large amounts of data, others capable of transmitting smaller amounts of data—we are able to communicate with individuals. There are many different software programs that allow us to connect a small camera atop the CPU and capture and transmit video and audio. Depending on the data link, we may achieve real-time transmission. An example of this technology is VDO Phone created by the VDO Corporation (Figure 13-5).

Figure 13-5 VDO Phone software allows two or more users to share simultaneous communications for sending live video and audio over the Internet. Courtesy VDO Corporation.

DIGITAL MEDIA DELIVERY ON A MASS-MARKET SCALE

As thousands of programs are created within a digital media production environment, it is critical to have a strategy for the delivery of digital programming to the desktop and living room on a global scale. Certainly, some of these delivery mechanisms will be directly to the user's computer as well as directly to the television.

In addition, advances in digital media disc recording and playback will influence the educational and entertainment programming (referred to as *edutainment*). This "portable" edutainment will be contained on new forms of mass-market-produced digital discs.

Compact Discs

The term *compact disc* (CD) is a very generic term that does not refer solely to the popular audio compact discs that have enjoyed great success in the consumer marketplace. In reality, compact discs come in several forms.

CD-DA: Compact Disc–Digital Audio (Red Book)

The term *Red Book* refers to a classification of the various compact disc types. CD-DA discs store 73 minutes of stereo 44.1 KHz audio at 16 bits per sample onto 650 MB.

Enhanced CD

An enhanced CD is one that conforms to the Red Book classification, but in addition to the normally found audio, an enhanced CD contains graphics, video, text, and other forms of still media. A computer is used to view the extra material.

CD-ROM: Compact Disc–Read Only Memory (Yellow Book)

CD-ROM was developed as a storage mechanism for computer data. There are actually two types of CD-ROM. Mode 1 is used for the storage of non-media-related data, such as large numerical and textual databases. Mode 2 discs are used for media-intensive video, audio, and animation files, as is the case for CD-ROM-based interactive games.

CD-i: Compact Disc Interactive (Green Book)

A CD-i disc is one that contains both the system's operating system and programming on disc and that uses special hardware. Alone, the hardware system cannot function; with the CD-i disc, the entire system can be reconfigured. For historical purposes, however, it should be noted that CD-i technology was never widely adopted.

Video CD (White Book)

Video CDs are used to play 30 fps MPEG 1 video for a total of approximately 74 minutes. Video CDs, although originally thought to be a possible successor to recordable VHS machines, have not been widely adopted, and a general reason is that they are not capable of storing an entire two-hour film.

CD-R: CD-Recordable (Orange Book)

Both magneto-optical (MO) and phase-change optical (PCO) discs (see Chapter 11) are examples of CD-R discs. Although these discs were originally used as storage modules for video and audio playback from DNLE systems, only MO discs were widely adopted for use in digital audio workstations. In general, though, CD-R discs are now used for storage of other, non-video- or audio-related media.

CD-RW (CD-rewritable) discs are a variant of CD-R discs, but are not compatible with CD-R discs.

DVD: Digital Video Disc or Digital Versatile Disc?

DVD is sometimes referred to as either digital video disc or digital versatile disc. With Video-CD, an entire movie could not be stored on one disc. As a result, DVDs were initially proposed to develop a consumer-oriented disc for full-length feature film playback. Originally, a series of disagreements by major hardware manufacturers delayed the standardization of DVDs; an eventual agreement was reached in 1995, resulting in an initial standardization that provided for 133 minutes of video (at approximately 4.6 Mbits/sec) on each DVD—an amount of time sufficient to fit the average feature film.

The characteristics of DVDs are listed below.

Aspect ratio:	4:3 (1.33:1), 4:3 (1.33:1) Pan & Scan, 16:9 (1.77:1) Widescreen
Audio:	AC-3 Stereo or 5.1 Surround
Language:	3–5 languages
Subtitles:	32 languages
Video:	MPEG-2 (4:2:2)

Disk Density

There are various disc types and densities provided for within the DVD standard:

Single-sided, single layer (SS,SL): 4.7 GB
Single-sided, double layer: (SS,DL): 8.5 GB
Double-sided, single layer: (DS,SL): 9.4 GB
Double-sided, double layer: (DS,DL): 17.0 GB

It should be noted that disk density will be affected by the accuracy of the write/read capabilities of the DVD's laser writing/reading mechanism. 40 GB capacities in a DS,DL disc are possible.

Audio for DVD: Dolby AC-3

The audio contained on a DVD is AC-3, a development from Dolby Laboratories. AC-3 (AC is an acronym for audio coding) is a compression scheme designed to remove redundancy as well as to analyze which extraneous audio frequencies may be removed without detriment to the aural experience. AC-3 delivery is in both stereo as well as in 5.1 surround format. The 5.1 separate channels consist of left, center, right, rear left, and rear center. The remaining fractional channel (.1) is dedicated to low frequencies with high bass content. AC-3 also serves as the primary audio format for high-definition television (HDTV) as well as for direct broadcast satellite (DBS).

As a result of AC-3 compression, a great deal of disc space is saved, while simultaneously high-quality, multichannel digital audio is delivered. As a result, it is possible to combine the overall aspects of DVD to offer intriguing programming. For example, we could have a single 5.1 surround audio track for our film, while having several different language versions, along with different subtitled tracks—any combination of which can be chosen by the viewer!

DVD-R (DVD-Recordable) and DVD-RAM (DVD–Random Access Memory)

DVD-R discs are recordable, whereas DVD-RAM discs are rewritable. We may judge both DVD-ROM and DVD-RAM as the evolution of CD-R and CD-RW discs. Although the capacities of DVD-R discs will undergo continual change and improvement, even the first generation of discs offers between 3.9 GB and 7.8 GB of storage capacity. When compared to the 650 MB of CD-ROM technology, it is clear that substantial leaps can be made in bringing full-motion, full-resolution MPEG-2, AC-3 encoded programming to a variety of markets previously served only by CD-ROM.

THE INTERNET AND THE WORLD WIDE WEB: COLLABORATING AND DELIVERING ON A GLOBAL BASIS

The Internet and the global network of interconnected computers known as the World Wide Web (WWW) that forms a part of the Internet are perhaps the most exciting developments to occur in the mid-1990s. The Internet is a network that had its origins in strategic military defense and institutional usage.

Each computer that is connected to the Internet is known as an *Internet host* and is completely independent of all other computers. An Internet service provider (ISP) is any carrier who provides access to this network of computers via a dial-in service. For example, if we are editing a program, and we find that we want to audition some sound effects of crashing surf sounds, we may find that we can simply locate an Internet host that, as a service, has provided a site for downloading these sound effects. We then download the sounds and edit them into our program.

World Wide Web sites offer information via the use of Web pages, which are created using a variety of programming. The interactive nature of these pages is achieved via hypertext markup language (HTML) which, for example, allows the user to click on a specific word, which then references other files related to the word. For example, in Figure 13-6, clicking on the underlined *Terran Interactive* will then link the user to a different page or to an entirely different Web site.

Internet Searching

It is possible to search for desired information on the Internet using computer-based language, but most users find these commands difficult to master; certainly, the massive increase in Internet use in the late 1990s was due to a solution to this vexing problem. By using Internet browser software applications, it suddenly became very easy to find exactly what the user was looking for. Figure 13-7 is an example of Netscape Navigator, which can be used for making inquiries on the WWW.

Watching and Delivering over the Internet

An Internet connection and how it is made have significant implications for how quickly we can receive data from an Internet host.

Internet connections for the vast majority of consumers were originally limited to 14.4 kbps modems. Gradually, of

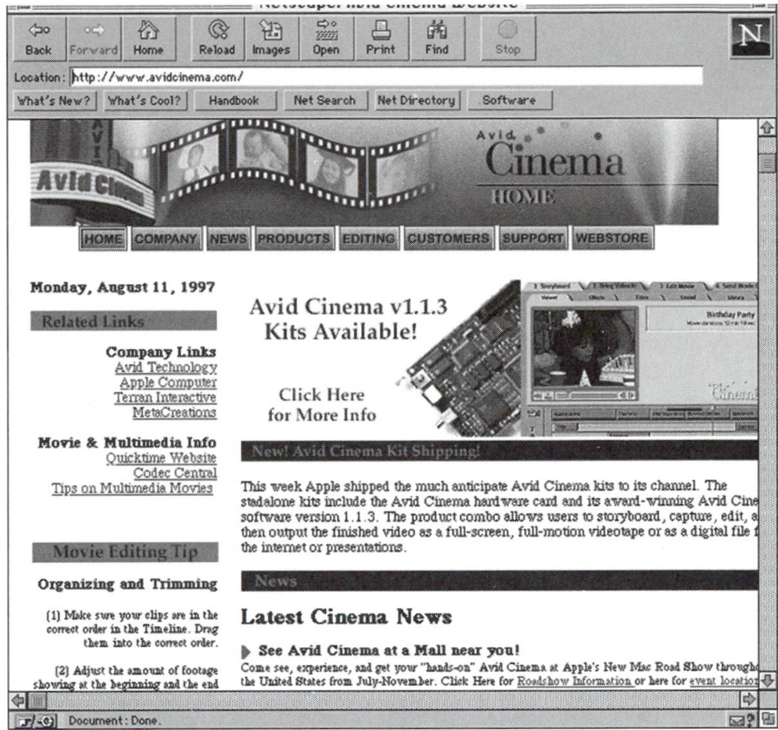

Figure 13-6 A World Wide Web page that employs hypertext markup language (HTML) and provides interaction among related pages.

course, that connection grew—to 28.8 kbps, then to 56.6 kbps. Connections of this type, however, cannot deliver real-time full-screen video—the data rates simply cannot be supported. Figure 13-8 shows a typical size and resolution of an MPEG image delivered over the Internet with a 28.8 kbps modem.

Preparing Web-Ready Material

When we want to prepare material for posting on a Web site, we must make decisions regarding the size, resolution, color

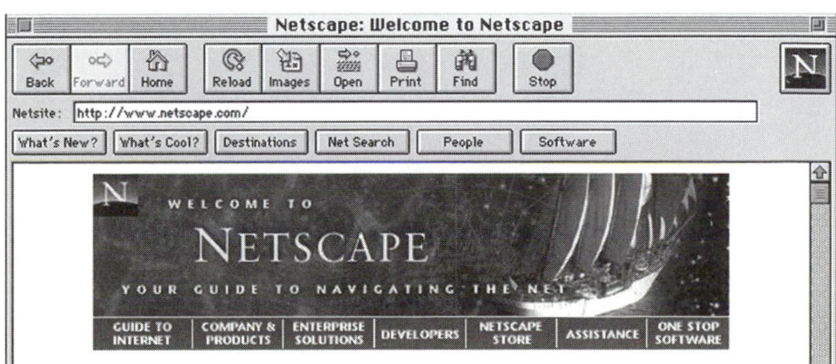

Figure 13-7 Netscape Navigator, an application that can be used as an Internet browser. Courtesy Netscape Communications.

Figure 13-8 An image of motion video playing over the Internet. The size, frame rate, and color depth of motion images can increase only with larger Internet connections. (Footage from Discovery Channel. ECO-Challenge provided by Discovery Channel Images.)

depth, and frame rate of the images that we post. Figure 13-9 shows an example of Movie Cleaner Pro, an application that is used to optimize files and make them Web-ready. Various image dimensions are shown in Figure 13-10.

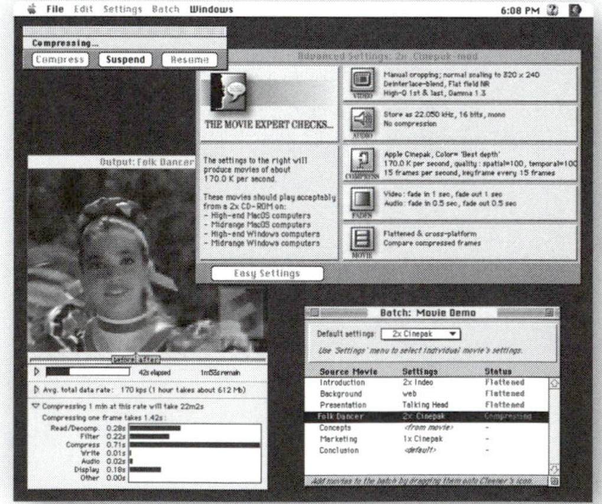

Figure 13-9 Movie Cleaner Pro, a powerful application that can be used to prepare material for distribution on the World Wide Web. Courtesy Terran Interactive.

Faster Connections: Cable Modems

There are a variety of ways in which Internet data can travel more quickly into the consumer's home. Cable modems are convertors that utilize the larger bandwidth provided by coaxial cable that runs into the home and is used for delivering cable television programming. Imagine that you are at home watching a feature film on cable and that you are able to navigate through a series of graphic and text pages that provide more information about the film you are watching—how certain scenes were filmed, the actor's filmography, and so forth.

Or imagine that you are watching a television sitcom where the subject of that night's show is about football, and all the characters are arguing because no one wants to order a pizza. An interactive, on-screen pizza could be displayed on the television screen in your home, and you would then be able to click on the pizza, place an order to the local pizza delivery service, and receive your pizza in a matter of a few

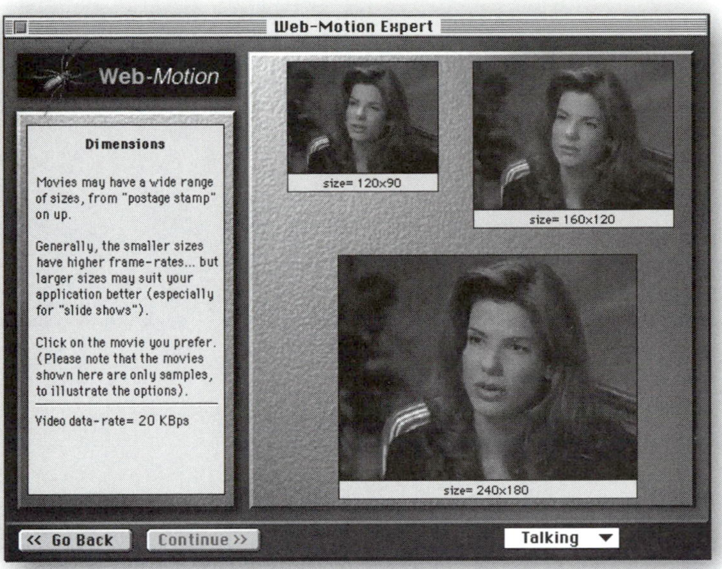

Figure 13-10 Various image dimensions that make up common choices for Web posting. Courtesy Terran Interactive.

minutes. All of this becomes very possible with interactive programming and larger Internet connections.

Streaming versus Downloading

When a file is posted on an Internet host's server, we must first *download* the file to our own, local computer and then open the file. In the case of video and audio media, we must wait for the download to complete before we can begin watching the clip.

However, a technique called *streaming* does not require that we wait until the entire file arrives before we can begin hearing or viewing it. Instead, with streaming techniques, we can establish a link to a Web site and open the desired file. With the correct audio and video plug-in support loaded into our Internet browser, the video and audio portions of the file will begin streaming to our computer via the Internet connection.

There are a variety of companies that provide streaming software and architecture. Progressive Networks, creator of RealVideo and RealAudio, uses Web-specific codecs (coders-decoders) to compress video and audio signals and prepare them for Internet users (Figure 13-11). With plug-ins from manufacturers who support such streaming techniques, it becomes possible to open a file at a Web site and begin receiving video and audio material instead of waiting for a full download to take place. Another role played by the software streaming applications is to be able to stream the required amount of data from the Internet host to the recipient in such a way that the user does not receive interruptions. For example, if we were

Figure 13-11 RealAudio Player, a codec used for streaming audio and video over the Internet. Courtesy Progressive Networks.

sent too little data, we may find ourselves looking at a blank or frozen screen until the new pictures arrive at our computer.

Real-time streaming protocol (RTSP) is a method for delivering media via streaming techniques. When streaming software is written such that it adheres to the requirements of RTSP, the software is operable across multiple platforms. Additionally, this provides a way for the creator of streaming content to ensure that the streaming is completely scaleable. The consumer could be streaming the content at 28.8 kbps, could be an intranet user at 56.6 kps, or could require marginally compressed video at higher transmission rates (typically a LAN, local area network).

Intranets

An *intranet* is one or more Web sites that are reserved for a corporation. Unlike the Internet, an intranet's Web site is usually accessible only by the members of the corporation or those with proper password authorization. An intranet is similar to any Web site that we would find on the Internet, although there are usually two specific differences. First, the throughput of the network is often greater than normal Internet connections. Minimally, a 56 kbps path is found, although a T1 intranet connection path is also fundamental to some organizations. Second, there will be protection in place to prevent outsiders from moving past the intranet's *firewall*. A firewall is the software layer between the corporation's internal Web site and the area reserved for external visitors to the company's official Web site.

Intranets are important with respect to digital media management because they represent a method by which many potential users could be accessing and moving multiple media types and incorporating them into presentations of all sorts. Using video and audio compression, full-screen and full-frame-rate material can be easily accessible to all members of the organization.

VRML

VRML, virtual reality modeling language, is another implementation that will further affect the content provided over Internet and intranet services. VRML is the method by which content can be delivered fully animated and in 3D. Imagine that you are at home and want to play an interactive game in 3D with a friend in another state—VRML programming can enable this form of interactivity, and streaming techniques can be used to provide little, if any, time delay.

Figure 13-12 is an example of Catalyst, an authoring tool used to create commercial-quality 3D games for the WWW. Figure 13-13 is an example of Torch, an Internet entertainment player for real-time playback of content created with Catalyst.

Figure 13-12 Catalyst, an authoring tool used to create 3D games for the World Wide Web. Courtesy Newfire, Inc.

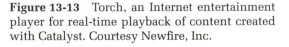

Figure 13-13 Torch, an Internet entertainment player for real-time playback of content created with Catalyst. Courtesy Newfire, Inc.

Figure 13-14 "Floops," VRML star of the world's first episodic Web cartoon. Courtesy Protozoa.

Characters can be created using VRML for use on Web pages, Web cartoons, and programs. Figure 13-14 is an example of a VRML character.

THE COMPUTER VERSUS THE TELEVISION

In the late 1990s, the issue of whether the computer or the television would serve as a worldwide communications medium began to develop. Essentially, data, regardless of their form, can be presented on both computers and traditional television. The notion that only moving video and audio signals—what traditionally used to be thought of as "television"—are suitable for presentation on television is clearly a notion that is being challenged.

Indeed, streaming techniques that can provide real-time audio and video from Internet hosts to the home fall into one category of the computer-versus-television debate. There are also several other technologies that may play a role as these services develop:

Broadband: Broadband refers to the ability to send multiple channels via a single wire. For example, cable television into the home consists of a single cable that, originally, was designed solely to deliver video programming. However, this cable can also carry a variety of other signals, including those related to computer data. We could find ourselves watching a program on television but being able to navigate through a variety of text and interactive programming. It certainly brings forth an interesting question: Is this still "television"?

WebTV: WebTV is a general term that refers to the ability to access the World Wide Web via a conventional television. WebTV can function via either telephone or the more capable broadband connection.

DirecPC: DirecPC, developed by the Hughes Network, consists of a small satellite dish and computer card that can deliver Internet requests at approximately 400 Kbps—more than 15 times faster than a standard 28.8 Kbps modem.

SECURITY

In the new era of digital media collaboration and delivery, a significant effort must be made to ensure the security of digital assets. Whenever we find ourselves in a position of sending our digital assets from location to location over any type of network, we must consider if the assets must be protected. If we do not, the files may easily be intercepted as they travel along.

Watermarking is a security measure that embeds information into a file. It should be impossible to distinguish where in the file the information has been embedded, while it should also be impossible to remove the embedded information. Consider that you have taken a photograph and want to send it to someone; during transmission, the file is intercepted, and someone begins selling your photograph. Having embedded watermarking information that identifies you as the owner, you can prove that you are the rightful owner of the photo. Figure 13-15 shows an example of a watermarking program. At the top is the encoding section, allowing the user to set the level of

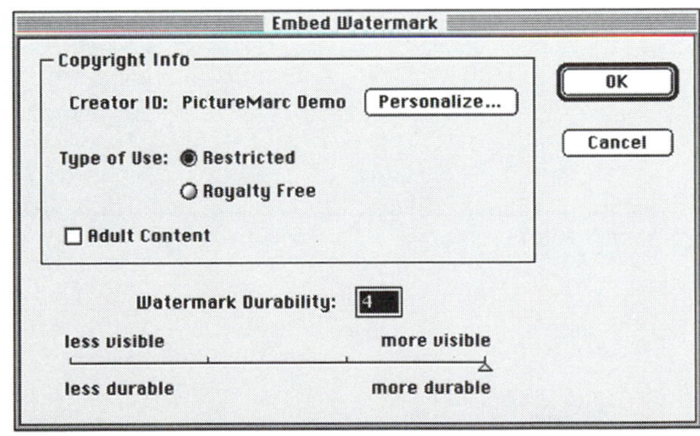

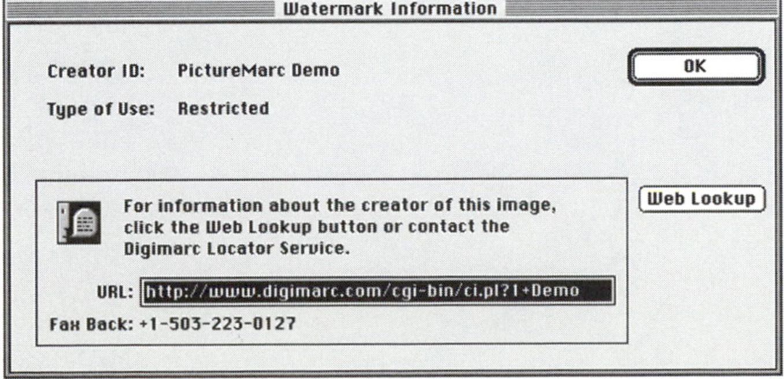

Figure 13-15 PictureMarc, a watermarking software program shown here as a plug-in to Adobe Photoshop. The encoding section (top) allows the user to set the level of watermarking. The information window (bottom) is visible only upon decoding. Courtesy DigiMarc Corporation.

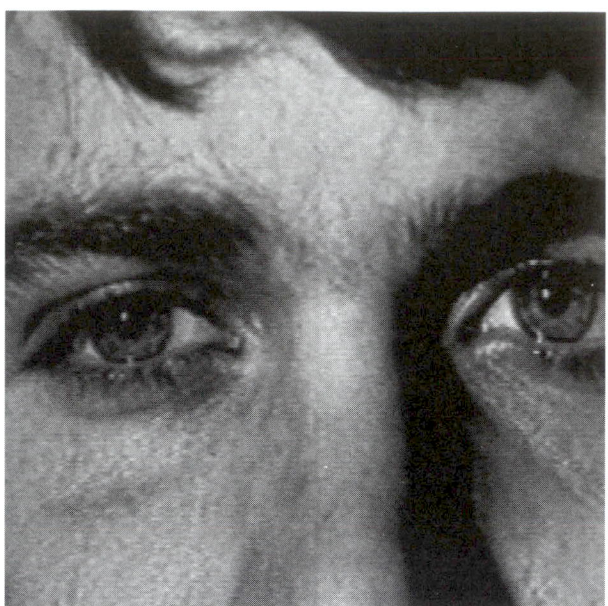

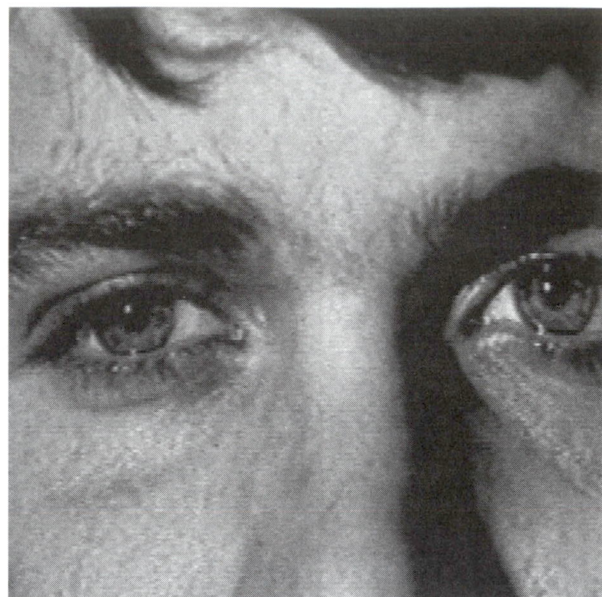

A B

Figure 13-16 **(A)** An original file sampled at 300 dots per inch. **(B)** The file after watermarking information has been embedded into the file. Can you discern any difference between this and part (A)? Courtesy Digimarc Corporation.

watermarking. Below is the information window that has been embedded in the file; it is only visible upon decoding.

Figure 13-16A is an original file sampled at 300 dpi (dots per inch); Figure 13-16B shows the file after watermarking. It is extremely difficult to discern the watermarking when comparing these two images.

TALKING WITH EDITORS

What are your views on open versus closed systems and the Internet?

Joe Beirne

> Favoring open systems is like favoring goodness: Everyone agrees, but they are not agreeing on the same thing. The theory is that one can write software freely for an open system product and that will yield cooler, more flexible applications. That doesn't help much if the "open system" is adopted by only one manufacturer. Also, it is less than helpful for a developer or manufacturer to advertise compliance with an open standard (like OMF) and not deliver. But generally we believe that adoption of professional standards (where they are actually a standard) and compliance with publicly available systems (where they are actually useful) are a healthy, productive trend.

We have been working with Webcasting and find that the concept is promising but that the configuration specs for the user are so complex at this point that it is not realistic for wide audiences: It's a geek thing today. We use the Internet widely for nonstreaming media and will follow the infrastructure for streaming media as that becomes more interesting. It doesn't matter that we have a T1 line today because our audience have, say, 14.4 kpbs modems, and the pain level for video or complex animation is too high for all but the most dedicated enthusiast. This is changing, and we look forward to revisiting Webcasting in the not-so-distant future.

Alan Miller

Open systems always let you interface to new ways of doing things. Closed systems work but are still closed. Closed systems can't survive; editors and clients want it all and won't settle for part. Using the Internet for program delivery is still pretty far off. Eventually, it will be great, but the other available transmission modes, whether satellite, cable, or over the air, are far superior.

Scott Ogden

Open systems are wonderful. I am currently typing this using Microsoft Word on my Media Composer system. The ability to bring many different tools onto the same system can only help my ability to be more things to more people. As for using the Internet for program delivery, I can't wait to do it. But let's talk about bandwidth . . . !

Basil Pappas

Desktop video never would have exploded without open environment systems. The downside to this is the increased upgrade costs that traditional editing technologies had managed to escape or put off for longer periods between major upgrades. The Internet does not offer me anything in the way of program delivery, yet. It only offers a way to promote the kind of programming I make at the current time.

Tom Poederbach

I believe in open systems and feel that it will be normal to purchase and download software from the Web to accomplish whatever you have to do.

14

Editing Film on the Desktop

Feature films, television shows, and even commercials have world markets. Programming that originates in one country can be remarkably successful in other countries; the United States film industry has a proven record that attests to the international popularity of its films.

Consider the path that a network television show in the United States could take. The show is a one-hour episodic that is shot on film. The footage is transferred to videotape, and a DNLE system is used to edit the program. Either the direct video output from the DNLE system is used as the final program, or an edit decision list (EDL) is conformed during online editing. Dupes are then made of this master and delivered to the network for broadcasting. At a later date, the international syndication rights to the show are sold, and it is necessary to provide a videotape master of each show in the series in PAL format. What is the recourse for the show's owner? If only an NTSC videotape master for each show had been created originally, how does the seller of the show provide the PAL masters?

One method is to take each videotape master and perform a standards conversion from NTSC to PAL. Depending on the scan conversion process used, there may be noticeable visual artifacts whenever videotape images in one transmission scheme are translated into another scheme. The most common detriments are degrees of temporal aliasing and an overall softness to the images. Postproduction facilities offer different methods of scan conversion. Real-time scan conversion, converting a one-hour show in one hour's time, offers varying results. Excellent results can be achieved with techniques that take more time to process the individual frames. These non-real-time scan conversion methods are usually more expensive than real-time methods, however. As technology has improved, real-time frame analysis that yields excellent results has become available in real-time machines, although they tend to be quite expensive.

Being able to move easily between film and videotape formats and to interject computer technology into these formats requires that there be methods whereby projects started in a particular format can be "matched back" to the original form regardless of the processing done to the images during the postproduction process.

CREATING VIDEOTAPE MASTERS FROM AN ASSEMBLED FILM NEGATIVE

In the example of the television episodic, the problem is that a PAL videotape master must be realized from an NTSC videotape master. There is no common ground for the formats, and the recourse is to scan convert from NTSC to PAL. The solution to this dilemma would have been to create the PAL videotape master from the correctly assembled film negative.

This is precisely the benefit of using a DNLE system to create a film cutlist. The selected film negative is transferred to videotape and edited on the DNLE system. The resulting film cutlist is used to indicate to the negative cutter which pieces of negative should be assembled and in what order. The final negative assembly can be thought of as a neutral element that can then be transferred to the required format and is thus used to create both NTSC and PAL masters. The benefit is that no scan conversion method has to be used to translate from NTSC to PAL or from PAL to NTSC. The film is simply projected at an appropriate rate to create either a PAL or an NTSC videotape master.

Another emerging requirement for the coexistence of film, videotape, and computers involves the area of digital imaging. Film images that are manipulated digitally by computers must originate on film, be transferred to digital data, be manipulated digitally, and then be transferred back to film.

As an example, consider a motion picture that is aimed at a family audience. One scene involves two children who are first filmed in a dark room. The boy waves his hands and talks to a character who is not visible. Later, a three-dimensional computer-generated dragonfly is designed and rendered into final form. This element is then composited with the background plate of the boy. The compositing process involves taking the original film and the dragonfly animation and creating a new piece of film, which is then used in the finished motion picture.

Special visual effects done strictly in either the film, videotape, or digital domain, are being replaced by methods that include a combination of all three. In the same scene, it is quite commonplace that some effects will have been achieved by a combination of all three techniques. Data must be manipulated, and these data are visual information that can be affected in any way but that most often must wind up in the same form in which it originated.

EDITING FILM ON A DNLE SYSTEM

When our final program will take the form of a finished film that will be projected in a theater, a DNLE system can be used to edit the material and to generate a film cutlist, which is then used to conform the original film negative. This digital film-making process requires several steps.

Film to Tape: The Telecine Process

Film to tape (FT) is a transfer process. Footage is shot on film and transferred to videotape. The machine that accomplishes this is called a *telecine*. The videotape is then edited, and either the direct output of the DNLE system becomes the final master, or an EDL from the DNLE system is conformed to create the final videotape master.

Using a DNLE system to edit film for a theatrical release involves using a telecine to transfer the film to videotape or directly to the disk drives of the DNLE system.

Film and Videotape Speeds

The normal play speeds for film and videotape are different, and the normal play speeds for videotape itself are different, depending on its format.

Format	*Normal Speed* (fps)
16mm film	24
35mm film	24
NTSC videotape	30 (actually 29.97)
PAL videotape	25

Correlation of Film to Videotape

There simply can be no 1:1 relationship between film and videotape, for 24 fps will never equal 25 or 30 fps. For example, when transferring film originated at 24 fps to PAL (25 fps), one extra video frame must be generated from every 24 frames of film. For NTSC videotape, six extra film frames must be created to compensate for the difference between 24 and 30 fps.

One way to avoid the necessity of creating video frames to achieve a 1:1 correlation is to alter the shooting speed. If the eventual goal is to achieve a PAL videotape master, the film is shot at 25 fps. Twenty-five frames of film transferred to 25 video frames creates a 1:1 relationship and ensures that for each frame of film there is a corresponding video frame. This is similarly achieved in NTSC if film is shot at 30 fps. Thirty film frames transferred to 30 video frames again results in a 1:1 relationship.

Sometimes these alternatives are taken. Often, a film shot in Europe will be shot at 25 fps because the film will first be seen on television, and then it may be released theatrically. But rarely will film be shot at 30 fps for NTSC because those six extra frames each second can, given the total amount of film shot, add significantly to the overall budget. After all, why shoot more film per second unless a specific effect or benefit is realized?

Direct Correlation of Film Frames to Video Frames

There are situations in which a direct correlation of film frame to video frame is beneficial. When the FTF (film-tape-film) situation involves using electronic techniques to perform some type of digital imaging, a 1:1 correlation is necessary.

For example, if a segment of film must be manipulated electronically, such as with computer painting, each frame is transferred to the digital device, painted, and returned, frame for frame, back to film. For visual effects that must be created in the world of videotape, a 1:1 correlation often lessens the frequency of aliasing and motion artifacts. (Recall that interpolating fewer frames into a medium that requires more frames than the original requires interpretation; in essence, this is yet another form of sampling except that instead of information being discarded, information must be generated: Redundancy must be introduced from fewer samples.) Being able to capture one film frame, process it, and return it back to one film frame without interpreting whether the film frame consists of two or more fields is very advantageous.

HOW TELECINES OPERATE

The telecine process involves the use of a sophisticated film projection machine that ensures that a certain number of film frames are projected each second. The machine does not waver and delivers an exact number of frames. The speeds at which the telecine machine can run vary. Some can only run the film at 24 and 30 fps, while others can run the film at slower and faster rates.

To put it simply, in the telecine process, film is threaded between a feed reel and a take-up reel and run through a projection system. The film is pulled down from the feed reel and held for a time, during which the image is actually transferred from its optical state to an electrical state. These electrical signals are then recorded to the videotape. Telecine systems work in conjunction with color-correction systems that affect the images being transferred to videotape. The color of the film frames can be altered, or special effects such as enhancing or reducing film grain artifacts can be introduced.

The sync sound for the program is played from a 1/4" audio tape or DAT, and both the picture and the sound are transferred to videotape, which is then digitized into the DNLE system. Note that the transfer to videotape can be completely bypassed by transferring directly to computer disk.

Edge Numbers

It is easy to locate videotape frames because a timecode number is associated with each frame. Locating a specific frame of film within a roll is also easily accomplished because the film edge numbers provide a method of locating specific footage. These edge numbers are placed on the edge of the film by the manufacturer. These latent edge numbers are struck directly into the film negative. Whenever the film is transferred, a unique identifying number for each frame of film becomes part of the transfer. This data will be used to successfully match back to the original film negative when the editing stage is completed. Edge numbers are also called *key numbers*.

Edge numbers appear at specific intervals on a strip of film. In 35mm 4-perf film, an edge number appears every 16 frames, or once every foot. In 16 mm film, there are 40 frames for each foot of film; edge numbers appear every 20 frames, or every half foot. Every 1000-foot 35mm film roll translates to approximately 11 minutes.

In Figure 14-1, a strip of 35mm film is shown. The edge number is an alphanumeric identifier. In this case, KeyKode™, from Eastman Kodak, is used to identify the individual film

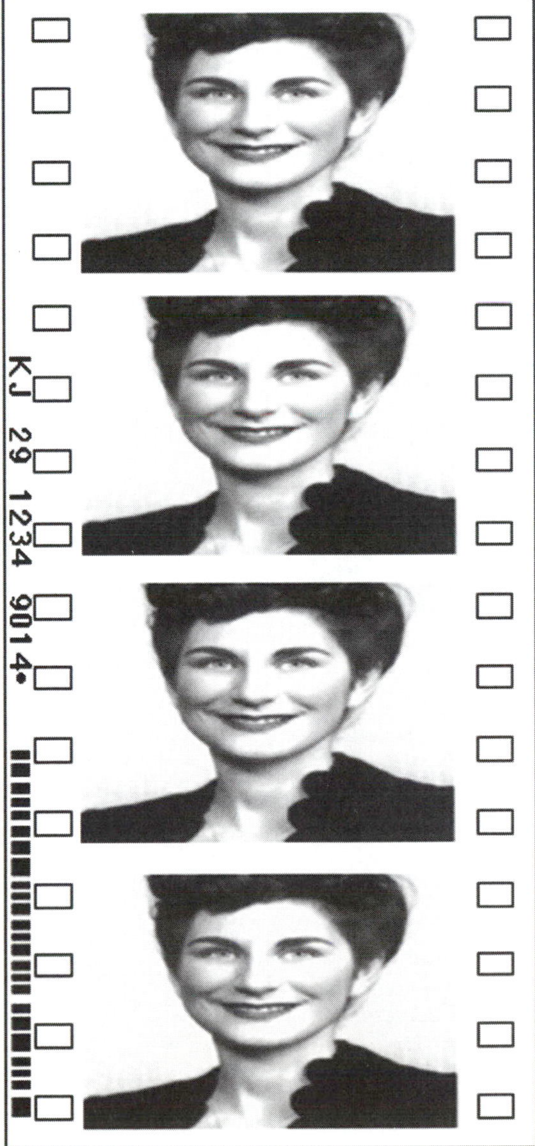

Figure 14-1 This piece of 35mm 4-perf film shows the KeyKode edge number and the accompanying machine-readable bar code that is used to identify each film frame on the camera roll. Illustration by Jeffrey Krebs.

frames. The edge number, KJ 29 1234 9014, has two parts. KJ 29 1234 is the reel identifier; this code reflects the film manufacturer, film type, and reel number. 9014 is the footage counter; this code reflects the location of the frame in terms of feet of film.

A zero frame indicates where the edge number begins. Since the edge number requires the span of several film frames to be displayed, there is an indication of where the 16-frame counting process should begin. A filled-in circle indicates whether the zero frame is at the beginning or at the end of the edge number.

If we want to label a frame within the 16 frames per edge number, we identify that frame by using an offset to the previous edge number. This offset would appear as "+00." The frame offset number is important because there is one edge number for every 16 frames of film. In this example, there is no frame offset because shown is a zero frame reference edge number. But if the chosen frame showed, for example, KJ 29 1234 9014 +12, the offset would indicate that the selected frame is plus twelve frames from the edge number. Edge numbers, like timecode numbers, ensure that we can find a particular film frame. By using frame offsets, we can find frames within the boundaries of two edge numbers.

Pulldown

As shown in Figure 14-2, when transferring film to videotape, a method must be used to create more video frames than there are film frames. *Pulldown* refers to the method by which additional video frames are created from their film counterparts. Since we start out with 24 film frames for each second of action, we must arrive at 30 video frames for that one second. How do 24 frames become 30 frames? The answer lies in the act of "pulling down" the film and holding it for a specific amount of time while it is projected and transferred to videotape.

A 24-to-30 conversion provides us with a ratio of 4:5; for every four frames of film, there will be five frames of video. Six sets of four film frames and six sets of five video frames represent each second of material. For PAL transfers of material shot at 24 fps, the transfer proceeds at 24 fps while one additional film frame is created, for a total of 25 frames of video from 24 film frames.

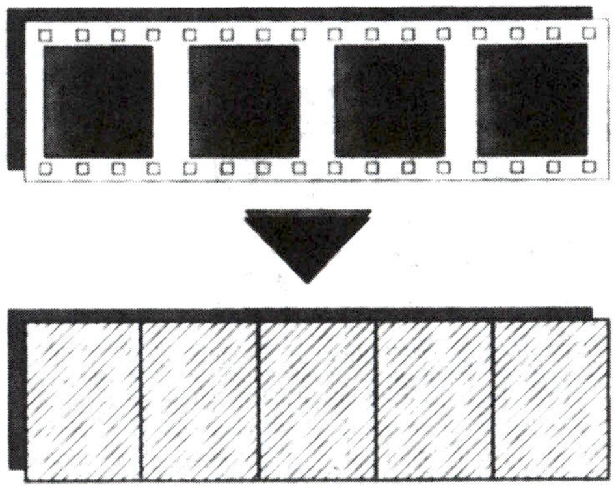

Figure 14-2 This is the pulldown sequence when transferring 35mm film to NTSC videotape. Six extra frames must be "created" when 24 fps film is transferred to 30 fps videotape. This results in a ratio of four film frames to five video frames. Illustration by Jeffrey Krebs.

2:3 and 3:2 Pulldown

Creating five video frames from four film frames does not involve duplicating frames. Instead, the process of pulldown creates duplicate fields. At specific times, a frame of film is recorded as either two video fields or as three video fields.

Since each video frame consists of two fields of information, the extra six frames of video are created by duplicating fields. The telecine machine ensures that a frame of film is pulled down into the projection gate and held for a specific

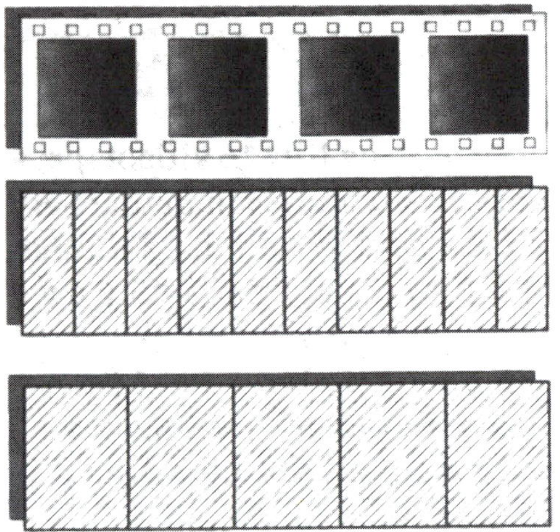

Figure 14-3 In a 2:3 pulldown conversion, four film frames are represented by ten video fields, which in turn create five video frames. Illustration by Jeffrey Krebs.

amount of time while a specific number of fields are recorded onto videotape. It is for these reasons that a telecine must be used. Another type of transfer device is a film chain, which is similar to the projection methods described but which cannot ensure specific pulldown. Film chains cannot be used when a negative cutlist is required because the pulldown cannot be guaranteed to take place in the same specific 2:3 or 3:2 sequence.

In a 2:3 pulldown, the first film frame is transferred for two fields to the videotape. The next film frame is transferred for three fields to the videotape. The process continues, and the result is that for every four film frames, ten video fields, or five video frames, will be artificially created. This ratio of four film frames to five video frames provides us with the 24-to-30 frame conversion that is required (Figure 14-3).

Although duplicate video fields are created, the action represented in the film frame is not altered. All that is happening is that one frame of film is transferred to videotape as either two fields or three fields.

There may be confusion regarding whether to use 2:3 or 3:2 pulldown. It is often thought that one method is better than another. In actuality, the only difference between the two methods is where the duplication of fields begins. When we use the term *pulldown sequence,* we are merely describing the location where the duplication begins. Whether a transfer is in 2:3 or 3:2 pulldown sequence is of little consequence; the result of both is that the additional video fields are created. However, there is usually a preference for the 2:3 sequence because in a 2:3 transfer, the first film frame is associated with two video fields; therefore, there is a direct correlation of one frame of film equaling one frame of video. 2:3 pulldown is also referred to as the *SMPTE-A* transfer method. 3:2 pulldown is referred to as the *SMPTE-B* transfer method.

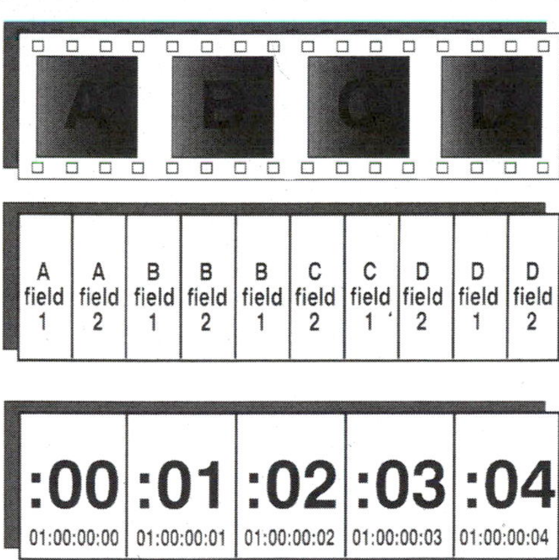

Figure 14-4 Pulldown mode refers to the location of a particular video frame within the pulldown sequence. This diagram shows a 2:3 pulldown sequence and the pulldown mode. Illustration by Jeffrey Krebs.

Pulldown Mode

In Figure 14-4, there are four film frames labeled A, B, C, and D. The A frame is transferred, and two video fields are created. The B frame creates three video fields. The C frame creates two video fields, and so on. The transfer of four film frames yields the following video fields:

Video Frame	*Film Frame*	*Video Fields*
1	A	A + A
2	B	B + B
3	C	B + C
4	D	C + D
5	None	D + D

When we edit with film footage that has been transferred to videotape, it may be possible to edit on frames that do not have a direct correlation to a piece of film. For example, video frame 3 (:02) consists of a B frame and a C frame. The B frame is a remnant of the 2:3 pulldown sequence from video frame 2 (:01). Some DNLE systems compensate for this by displaying only video frames that have a direct correlation to the film. In this case, the B frame would not be displayed. Instead, the C frame would be displayed. In this way, the editor would be able to see the direct relation of the video frame being chosen to the film frame that exists on the negative.

Pulldown Mode Identification

The pulldown sequence refers to how duplicate video fields were created: Either the first duplicate consists of two fields in a 2:3 sequence or three fields in a 3:2 sequence. The pulldown mode allows us to determine what position a frame will take in the pulldown sequence. If we are given a videocassette that was transferred from film in a 2:3 sequence, and we are asked to determine what the pulldown mode of a particular frame is, we can find the answer by looking at specific information on the videocassette.

In Figure 14-2, we see that five video frames are created from the four film frames. If the zero frame consists of two fields, it must be either an A frame or a C frame because only A and C frames take part in creating two video fields. When we jog the videotape through the two fields, if the timecode does not change, the zero frame is an A frame. If the timecode does change between fields, the zero frame is a C frame.

If the zero frame consists of three fields, it must be either a B frame or a D frame because only B and D frames take part in creating three video fields. Now, we jog through the videocassette and find the zero frame. If the timecode changes between fields 2 and 3, it is a B frame. If the timecode changes between fields 1 and 2, it is a D frame.

SYNC POINT RELATIONSHIPS

When the film is being transferred to videotape, a database needs to be created. The film transfer will most likely be a one-lite process in which only cursory attempts are made at color correction. The goal of the one-lite is to provide an overall exposure to the film to make editorial judgments. When it is finally determined which pieces of film will be used in the finished film, final color correcting will take place. The database created during the one-lite consists of sync points, or common relationships among the various media that are associated with every strip of film being transferred.

Sync points include the following:

- Edge numbers, which relate to the sync point of film footage.
- Timecode, which relates to the film's position on the videotape.
- Pulldown mode, which relates to the position of the video frame in the pulldown sequence.

These three sync relationships are the minimum needed to provide a negative cutlist. There may be additional sync relationships. If a sound cutlist is required, the sync points will expand to include these as well:

Audio timecode, which relates the sync point of the original sound recording to the film frame.
Ink number, which relates the sync point of the sound transfer to the sync point of the film frame.

For each sync point, the scene and take number can be noted.

Punching the Printed Film

One method of quickly identifying the sync point is to make a physical punch to the printed film. By looking at the resulting videotape, the punch hole will indicate that a sync relationship has been established. The database for the sync point illustrated in Figure 14-5 shows the following:

Video reference frame (04:09:28:00.1). This shows the timecode that is being recorded to the source videotape. The ".1" designates field 1.
Film edge number (111590+00A). This indicator shows the edge numbers in feet and frames. The "A" indicates the pulldown mode.
Audio timecode number (01:04:27:01). This indicates the timecode for the audio recording. This format is usually center track 1/4" reel-to-reel audio tape or DAT with timecode.

Once these relationships have been established, we can determine the correct profile for each ensuing frame since the rules of counting have been established. When a new sync

Figure 14-5 Making a physical hole directly on the film permits the easy identification of the sync point, which becomes known as the *punch frame*. Also shown is the *smart slate,* which includes a visual reference for the audio tape timecode.

relationship has been made, that is, when any of the sync points is changed, as is the case when a new punch frame is made, a new database entry must be created. We cannot simply continue to count through a different set of sync points because at least one of those sync points has now changed.

The largest criticism of manual methods of database entry is that mistakes can occur. If a video timecode number is given for a particular key number, and the timecode is incorrect, when we create the negative cutlist, the incorrect frames of film will be used from the negative. All it takes is one manual entry error for the wrong piece of film to be used.

Automatic Key Number Readers

Removing the possibility of human error in creating the database of sync relationships is the goal of machine-readable key numbers. The essential method of these systems is similar to the bar code information contained on various products. By placing machine-readable edge numbers or timecodes directly on the film, edge readers can be placed on the telecine machine to capture sync points automatically. One example is Eastman Kodak's KeyKode, which consists of the usual edge number information but also includes a bar code alternative. This bar code is deciphered by a reader that is housed on the telecine (Figure 14-6).

Telecine machines pass on information about the items being synchronized. The controlling device can be a laptop computer that runs software capable of orchestrating the various machines involved in the telecine process. If the film footage has machine-readable edge numbers, and the telecine

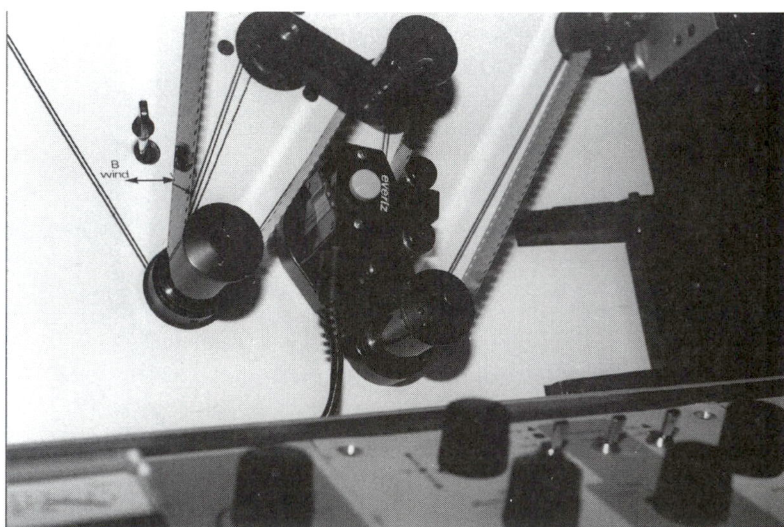

Figure 14-6 The KeyKode reader processes the bar code information contained along the edge of the film. Courtesy Evertz Microsystems, Inc.

machine is outfitted with a bar code reader, the relationship of items in the transfer can be automatically captured. Software and hardware to control the telecine include a means of remotely operating videotape and audio machines. The purpose of machine-controllable telecine transfer and bar code information on the film is to provide a complete database for all film transferred to videotape, thus avoiding any manual entry of information to the film database.

When the film footage is transferred to videotape or directly to disk, a database will be created automatically and should include the following:

Film edge number. The film edge number is captured via the bar code reader.

Video reference frame. The videotape timecode for that sync point is captured by the timecode reader connected to the telecine and the videotape recorder.

Pulldown mode: A frame. The pulldown mode for that sync point is established. Depending on the system being used, a sync point may consistently be the same type of frame, usually an A frame. If not, the pulldown for the sync point will be calculated by referencing the position of the frame within the pulldown sequence.

Pulldown sequence. The method of transfer is established as either a 2:3 or a 3:2 sequence.

Audio timecode. The audio timecode for that sync point is captured by the timecode reader connected to the audio tape player.

Additional. The scene, take, and description entries for the sync point are entered manually. Since these entries are not critical to the creation of an accurate negative cutlist, errors here can be tolerated.

The automatic creation of such a database is a great step forward in reducing errors in cataloging how film frames relate to video frames. Once the methods of automatic capture are in place, the steps are as follows: The film is placed on the telecine, and the audio tape to be synched to the picture is loaded onto an audio tape player; this will be either 1/4" or DAT playback. A videotape is placed in the videotape recorder. All machines are then under the control of the telecine transfer system. The telecine operator cues the film to the first sync point. If the film has been punched, the film is stopped on the punch. This sync point may include clapsticks.

Next, the proper piece of audio for the sync point is located. If the commercial footage we have shot includes sync sound, such as two people talking, we may elect to sync the sound to the picture during the telecine process. Locating the right sound for the sync point may be a very easy process if the shooting stage included the use of clapsticks that displayed the timecode of the audio recorder. These clapsticks are called *smart slates* or *digi slates.*

When the operator parks on the sync point of the film frame, a visual timecode is displayed on the smart slate. This timecode number is then typed into the telecine controller, which remotely operates the audio tape player. The result is that the correct sound for this visual sync point is found. When the film is run forward, the sound is in sync with picture. Both picture and sound are then recorded to the videotape.

When all the film has been synched with the corresponding audio and transferred to tape or to disk, the work products of the telecine session will include one or both of the following:

> *Computer printout of sync relationships.* A hard-copy printout of all the sync relationships involved is generated. The relationships are correlations: This edge number equals this videotape timecode equals this pulldown mode equals this audio timecode, and so on.
>
> *Software file of sync relationships.* In addition to the hard copy, database information is usually provided on a floppy disk.

A comprehensive telecine system provides both work products. Figure 14-7 shows an example of a computer-generated database using Aaton software. The minimum one should accept is a computer-generated hard copy of the sync points. A handwritten copy must be carefully scrutinized, as vagaries in handwriting could severely affect the integrity of the data. More than one negative cutlist has been affected by a handwritten telecine log that confused a B frame with a D frame.

The capability of providing a floppy disk that contains all the information regarding the telecine transfer is extremely important. In the case of a printout only, the data must be

Figure 14-7 The computer-generated database showing sync relationships. Created by Aaton software.

```
*GLOBAL
TRANSFER_FACILITY  AATON LAB-GRENOBLE-FRANCE
AATON_KEYLINK  Eq*069 Version 5.17
FILM_TITLE  PEPIN MERHI  HOLOGRAM MAN
TELECINE_SPEED  23.98
VIDEO_REEL  HOUR0010 (30 ndf NTSC)
FILM_GAUGE  35mm 4perf 24fps
AUDIO_FPS  24
AUX_TC_FPS

*EVENTS
      video tc     audio tc     aux tc        keycode           date/tag  cam/lr
     -----------  -----------  -----------  ------------------  --------  ------
001  10:00:00:24  14:04:17:05               KL162518 4956+03    94 10 10  A
     10:00:47:19  14:05:04:00               KL162518 5026+07    51469     551597
     Scen 86E     Take 1       CmR A48      SnR 14

002  10:00:47:23  14:05:27:05               KL162518 5026+10    94 10 10  A
     10:02:02:18  14:06:42:00               KL162518 5138+14    51472     551597
     Scen 86F     Take 1       CmR A48      SnR 14

003  10:02:02:23  14:06:53:13               KL162518 5139+01    94 10 10  A
     10:02:26:28  14:07:17:18               KL162518 5175+05    51475     551597
     Scen 86G     Take 1       CmR A48      SnR 14

004  10:02:27:02  14:07:17:23               KL162518 5175+09    94 10 10  A
     10:02:54:07  14:07:44:28               KL162518 5216+05    51481     551597
     Scen 138     Take 1       CmR A48      SnR MOS

005  10:02:54:16  14:07:45:06               KL162518 5216+12    94 10 10  A
     10:03:17:21  14:08:08:11               KL162518 5251+08    51484     551597
     Scen 138     Take 2       CmR A48      SnR MOS
```

entered manually into the editing system being used to correlate the material to be edited to the negative to be cut. If a computer disk is available that has all the sync points as a database file, this digital data can be entered automatically into the DNLE system as long as the file structures are compatible. This avoids the manual entry of data when we enter the stage of moving information from telecine to DNLE system.

EDITING AND DELIVERY ON VIDEOTAPE AND FILM

The next stage in creating the film is digitizing the footage into the DNLE system. Of course, if we have transferred our film footage directly from telecine to disk, this stage is unnecessary. The footage is then edited into the appropriate form to create the finished film.

Film Cutlists

Once the film has been edited, the DNLE system utilizes its database of film edge numbers to create a film cutlist for the cutting and assembly of the original film negative. The basic set of film lists includes the dailies report, pull list, assemble list, dupe list, and optical list. Additional film lists include the scene pull list and the change list.

Dailies Report

The dailies report is the list of sync points that is created during telecine. A dailies report is usually more sophisticated than the telecine report in that it contains ending edge numbers and the duration of film and video segments.

Pull List

The pull list shows the film segments that must be cut from each camera roll. The various pieces of film that will be used in the conforming process exist on different camera rolls. The pull list provides the negative cutter with the information required to pull all the scenes required from each original camera roll. If a section of film has been used twice or is involved in an optical effect, the pull list usually indicates that the one piece of original negative must be duplicated.

Assemble List

The assemble list indicates how the individual film segments should be ordered. The assemble list is, in essence, the final EDL. It is used in conjunction with the dupe list and the optical list to conform the negative.

Dupe List

The dupe list indicates all film segments that must be duplicated because the film frames have been used more than once. The dupe list is only used for those frames that are related to straight cuts.

Optical List

The optical list shows the specific film edge numbers used to create fades and dissolves optically. The optical list shows the scene start and end and the effect start, center, and end points. It is referenced by the assemble list.

Scene Pull List

The scene pull list is a scene-by-scene list that is pulled from the negative. The scene pull list differs from the pull list in that it lists the scenes that must be pulled but not the exact cuts within each scene. While the pull list indicates all segments that must be pulled from the individual camera roll, the scene pull list indicates all scenes that must be pulled from all camera rolls. The scene pull list is usually ordered by edge number.

Change Lists

Prior to negative cutting, when a film work print is used and screened, changes may be requested. The change list compares the original assemble list with the new assemble list and shows only the changes made to the original. In this way, the person conforming the work print can go only to the sections requiring changes rather than interpreting an entire assemble list.

Conforming the Negative

Using the various film lists, the negative cutter pulls the different film segments from each camera roll. If film needs to be duplicated because it was used more than once in the program, the dupe list will indicate this, and dupes will be ordered from the lab. Using the optical list, fades and dissolves also will be ordered from the lab.

When all the required elements are available, the negative cutter assembles each segment in the order determined by the assemble list. The completed negative is then duped and color-graded, and additional film prints are struck. These are the prints that will be used for theatrical distribution.

Sound

The original recordings are referenced by either the timecode numbers or the slate IDs. An audio-only assemble list can be created because the telecine process included entries for sound timecode sync points. By using the timecode information relating to the audio, entire audio tracks are reassembled to create a first-generation sound track.

Alternatively, if the original sound recordings were digitized into the DNLE system, they can be used directly from the DNLE system and will become components for the mixing of the film's final sound track.

Again, it should be noted that the automatic key number reading systems may not be available on every telecine system because telecines must first be outfitted with the required bar code readers. It remains necessary to be aware of all the potential pitfalls that exist in the conforming of film negative to the DNLE system's negative cutlist. There should always be a visual inspection made of the original film negative to ensure that the integrity of the database is, in fact, correct. Figure 14-8 shows a negative cutlist, generated from the DNLE system.

Editing at 24 fps

Although DNLE systems first appeared in 1989, it was not until 1992 that DNLE systems that played back at 24 fps were introduced. There are several benefits to be gained from editing at 24 fps. The first and most significant benefit is that the material shown on the DNLE system's screens is running at its native speed. The movement originally seen in the film camera is preserved. Without this capability, we would be forced to view original material playing back at 30 fps; as a result, we would see the pulldown frames, and consequently, movement would not be natural.

The second benefit of editing at 24 fps is a savings of overall storage time. If 24 frames instead of 30 are stored for each second of material, 20% more material can be stored for each second of footage. Over the course of ten hours of footage, the savings are indeed considerable.

An additional benefit can be gained from *letterboxing* the film as it is transferred to the DNLE system. Letterboxing, which preserves the aspect ratio in which the film was originally shot, consists of two black bands across the top and bot-

Figure 14-8 A negative cutlist generated from the DNLE system, which is used to cut the original film negative in the exact fashion that editing proceeded on the DNLE system.

```
Project: The Clueless and the Dead
Assemble List for edl file Serpentine:

  Seq  First Edge Number     Last Edge Number     Length  Total   Camera Conform
  ---  -----------------     ----------------     ------  -----   ------ -------
/-001     OPTICAL Number 1              FADE IN       24     24             0.0
       Record: 00:00:00:00  00:00:00:00

| 002   end of optical 1 to   start of optical 2   258    282       P8  -1.0 -1
       Record: 00:00:00:00  00:00:11:23
       Scene:   10/1

\-003     OPTICAL Number 2             DISSOLVE       24    306            -1.0
       Record: 00:00:00:00  00:00:00:00

  004  FN 20 2852-5257+15•3  FN 20 2852-5265+11•2    168    474       P7  -1.0
       Record: 00:00:12:23  00:00:19:23
       Scene:   11/1

  005  FN 20 2852-5318+21•3  FN 20 2852-5325+15•1    145    619       P7  -0.5
       Record: 00:00:19:23  00:00:25:24
       Scene:   13/1

  006  FN 20 2599-5498+09•3  FN 20 2599-5509+08•2    235    854       P8   1.0
       Record: 00:00:25:24  00:00:35:17
       Scene:   14/4

  007  FN 20 2852-5338+07•2  FN 20 2852-5339+17•3     32    886       P7  -1.0 -1
       Record: 00:00:35:17  00:00:36:28
       Scene:   13/1

  008  FN 20 2599-5510+20•3  FN 20 2599-5531+18•3    447   1333       P8   0.5
       Record: 00:00:36:28  00:00:55:16
       Scene:   14/4

  009  FN 20 2852-5360+21•3  FN 20 2852-5366+14•3    122   1455       P7  -0.5
       Record: 00:00:55:16  00:01:00:19
```

tom of the screen (Figure 14-9). This is necessary because film footage shot at a 1.85:1 ratio (or higher) must now temporarily exist in the 1.33:1 ratio of video. These two black bands consist of zero information to a JPEG-based digital video compression scheme. Therefore, the KB per frame that would normally have been concerned with the areas of picture above and below the frame can now be applied to the material within the letterbox. Higher-quality pictures at the same KB per frame are the result.

A DNLE system running at 24 fps is ideal for editing film-originated material when the goal is to generate a negative cut-list. Although it is also possible to edit 24 fps material at 30 fps and then generate a "matched back" list, one disadvantage of this is that 24 fps material is shown on the screen at 30 fps. However, at true 24 fps playback, there is no doubt as to what will be seen once the original film negative is conformed. The benefit of digital nonlinear editing in the world of film is quite significant, and, along with the database and footage search functions of the DNLE system, editing films is made easier as a result.

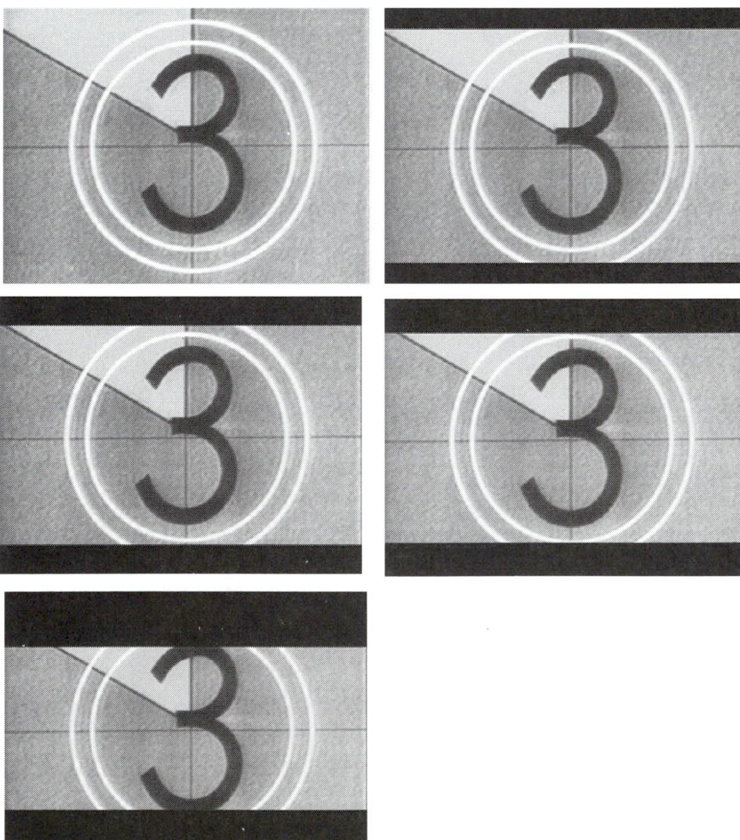

Figure 14-9 Letterboxing preserves the original shooting aspect ratio. Shown is the 1.85:1 aspect ratio of 35mm Academy film.

TALKING WITH EDITORS

How do your clients view you these days as opposed to in 1992, when JPEG-based DNLE systems were just arriving?

Joe Beirne

In 1992, we were outsiders looking in. We no longer need to prove our ability to perform, or to justify the underlying context or paradigm involved in using this technology. In 1992, producers were primarily looking for significant cost savings associated with nonlinear editorial and desktop media in general. This is no longer the primary focus: DNLE is simply the standard. The rates for machine time have dropped, and the value added by our services has increased enormously in this time. The producers realize that DNLE systems can increase the quality of a cut and can save time if used thoughtfully.

Producers also better understand the DNLE process today, and this has made the process faster, better looking, better sounding, more dynamic, and (sometimes) cheaper.

We are also now often doing everything for a post project under our own roof: A television client who may have done, in 1992, a rough cut at our facility now does offline, graphics, animation, sound design, compositing, and "online," all on desktop or workstation systems, and at a very high quality level. That was never our plan, but it has made sense for us and for our clients as well.

Peter Cohen

Before moving over to DNL editing, I spent nearly a decade as a high-end video effects and online editor. This was a great education in the art of compositing. I became involved with DNL editing in the late 1980s. This was a great education in content. I am now watching these worlds collide on the desktop. I work mostly on episodic television, and the time restraints make it impossible for me to do it all myself, so I have moved into a supervisory position.

Alan Miller

Today we are no longer a curiosity. In fact, there are so many systems out there that people no longer use my services just because I have a DNLE system. Believe it or not, now they look for talent and creativity. The DNLE explosion obscured this for a while, but people are seeking quality again. For a time, it seemed clients thought if you just owned a DNLE system, you must be able to edit. Boy, were they proved wrong! Some things aren't as easy as they seem.

Scott Ogden

They see me as a creative editor who has to do more in a shorter amount of time.

Basil Pappas

Fortunately, they view me as the same creative editor that I always was. Picture quality is now a given, so the distinction between offline and online has disappeared. My background as a film editor is now worth more than ever, as producers get finished products in less time, with an uncomplicated post schedule using fewer people.

Tom Poederbach

I actually cannot answer this question, but I suppose that customers expect you to have a DNLE system. If not, you are "old fashioned"!

15

Digital Nonlinear Editing Systems

FOR MORE INFORMATION

Due to the rapid rate at which DNLE systems progress and new systems are offered by manufacturers, included below are World Wide Web addresses for various manufacturers of DNLE systems. In this way, the latest information may be made available to the reader by browsing the specific Web site.

Adcom, Inc.	www.adcom.com
Adobe Systems	www.adobe.com
Avid Technology, Inc.	www.avid.com
Discreet Logic	www.discreet.com
D-Vision Systems	www.dvision.com
Fast	www.2fast4u.com
Jaleo	www.jaleo.com
JVC	www.jvcinfo.com
Lightworks	www.tek.com
Macromedia	www.macromedia.com
Matrox Video Products Group	www.matrox.com
Media 100	www.media100.com
Montage	www.mgl.com
Panasonic	www.panasonic.com
Play, Inc.	www.play.com
Quantel	www.quantel.com
Scitex Digital Video	www.scitex.com
SoftImage	www.softimage.com
Sony	www.sony.com
Videomedia	www.videomedia.com

Glossary

A/B roll An editing system composed of three videotape machines: two source machines and one record machine. The A/B roll system allows the editor to make transitions, such as dissolves and wipes, and involves the use of a video switcher.

Access time The amount of time from when an inquiry for information is made until the information becomes available.

ActiveMovie An API (application programming interface) that can be used to create synchronized full-screen video and audio.

AES/EBU American Engineering Society/European Broadcasting Union.

AIFF Audio interchange filter format.

Analog Electrical signals that vary constantly. In analog recordings, the changes to the recording medium are continuous and analogous to the changes in the waveform of the originating sound or are analogous to the reflectance of the original sound.

Answer print The first version of the entire film with optical effects and complete mixed optical sound track.

ASCII American Standard Code for Information Interchange. Represents the manner in which binary definitions are assigned to numbers and letters. It provides a standard for exchanging different types of files.

Asymmetric compression Asymmetric compression techniques require a greater amount of processing power to compress a signal than is required to decompress the signal.

ATM Asynchronous transfer mode (ATM) is not in and of itself a network, but rather a packaging scheme for data.

ATV Advanced television.

Audio layback When the final audio mix is completed, the process of recording it back onto the original video master. The completed tracks are laid back onto the videotape.

Audio layup The process of transferring audio from the master tape in progress to a multitrack audio editing system to add additional sounds and complete a sound mix.

Audio-assembly The process of using an edit controller to implement the edit decision list to create a videotape master. A cuts-only auto-assembly process involves one source machine and one record machine.

AVI Audio/video interleaved. Similar to QuickTime, AVI is the corresponding extension to Intel-based CPUs.

Bandwidth The number of bits per second of material. The computer is tasked with processing a number of bits per second when digitizing; that number becomes a limiting factor. The computer can process only a certain number of frames and a certain amount of information for each frame every second.

Betacam A recording videotape process that utilizes a variation of component techniques.

Betacam SP The "superior performance" version of Betacam videotape. It uses magnetic particle videotape.

Bins In film editing, a canvas container used to hang film strips. In nonlinear editing systems, the location where footage is stored is also called the *bin*.

Bit The smallest piece of information in the digital world. The term is short for "binary digit."

Blow-up The ability to enlarge a section of a picture.

Blue screening Technique by which selective colors (usually blue or green) are removed in order to composite layers of film.

CAV laserdisc Constant angular velocity. A laserdisc that is capable of slow motion, step frame, and freeze frame. Used for laserdisc-based nonlinear systems. CAV discs offer 30 minutes per side (54,000 frames).

CCD Charged-coupled device.

CD-I Compact disc interactive

CD-ROM Compact disc–read only memory.

Chroma subsampling A technique used to reduce the file size of an image by reducing the amount of color information it contains.

Circled takes In film, the takes that will be printed from the exposed camera negative.

CLV laserdisc Constant linear velocity. A laserdisc that is not usually capable of slow motion, step frame, and freeze frame. Used for playback purposes, CLV discs offer 60 minutes per side (108,000 frames).

Coding The way in which information is represented in file size reduction programs.

Component analog (Y, R-Y, B-Y) A component analog signal is one in which the original red, green, and blue signals (RGB) are separated into their luminance and chrominance components. Specifically, luminance is known as Y, while chrominance is separated into R-Y (red) and B-Y (blue).

Composite A composite video signal is one in which the luminance and chrominance signals are combined. Composite video is an analog signal, coded in either NTSC, PAL, or SECAM. The biggest criticism of composite video connections is that the signal is created by adding chroma signals to the luminance channel. As a result, there may be difficulties in separating the two, and chroma interfering (bleeding) into the luminance channel may result.

Compression To reduce in volume and to force into less space.

CTDM Color time division multiplexing. A basic technique used in the record and playback processes of Betacam videotape.

D1 An SMPTE standard for recording digital videotape recordings. D1 is a component recording process.

D2 A standard for recording digital videotape recordings. D2 is a composite recording process.

D3 A recording process for digital composite 1/2" videotape.

D5 This component digital tape format (1/2") employs 10-bits-per-pixel sampling. As a result, D5 provides superior performance to D1, especially with regard to keying operations for multilayering.

Dailies The circled takes that have been printed. Dailies are reviewed every day that a film is in production. Also called *rushes.*

DAT Digital audio tape.

Data transfer rate The amount of information that a computer storage drive can write and read in a certain amount of time. Also called *read/write speed* and *transfer speed.*

DAW Digital audio workstation. DAWs use optical discs or magnetic disks to offer random-access nonlinear editing of audio.

Decimation The removal of a great portion of elements that make up a whole. This form of subsampling occurs at the pixel level.

Destructive An operational process that causes original audio or video files to be altered. Nondestructive processes do not alter the original files.

Dial up Dial-up phone service is exactly that: an ordinary telephone in a home or office. A modem is used to transmit and to receive digital data. The channel that the data can travel through is small, at 56 Kbits/sec (Kilobits; Kbps).

Digital The conversion of an analog signal into a binary form. In digital recordings, digits are used to represent quantities, and digits in a rapid sequence represent varying quantities.

Digital backlot Footage that is many years old that is reconstituted through digital technology and digitally composited.

Digital Betacam This component digital tape format uses the ITU-R 601 standard and then employs discrete cosine transform (DCT) compression at a very low ratio (1.77:1).

Digitize To convert continuous analog information to digital form for computer processing. Also known as digitizing and digitization.

DFW Digital film workstation.

Disk default The average amount of information that can be stored based on the digitizing parameters chosen and the capacity of the computer disk.

DNLE Digital nonlinear editing.

Double system The film recording method in which picture and sound are recorded as two separate elements.

Down convert To convert video files from normal play rates to less than normal rates. This type of conversion is primarily used to increase storage capacity.

DS-0 DS-0 is the basic unit used to measure fiber optical capacity. At 64 kbps, one DS-0 channel is required to send a single voice call.

DS-1 DS-1, also known as digital service-one, has a capacity of 1.5 Mbps.

DS-2 DS-2 (digital service-two) has a capacity of approximately 6 Mbps.

DS-3 DS-3 (digital service-three) has a capacity of approximately 45 Mbps. At 45 Mbps/sec, a DS-3 line can be used to transmit compressed video.

Dual-finish cognizant The desire to leave the editing process with lists that can be used to create a finished videotape master and a cut film negative for both videotape and film releases.

Dubbing In film, when the entire film becomes available for final audio mixing. As a reel is projected, all the various sound elements for that reel are mixed together. In video, the process of making copies of the master tape for distribution.

DV Digital video.

DVA code Discovision Associate code. These five-digit codes are encoded onto the glass laserdisc master by the laser. They represent the manner by which the disc can be searched. DVA code is related to the timecode of the premaster tape.

DVC Digital video cassette.

DVCAM A digital video variant introduced by Sony Corporation.

DVCPRO A digital video variant introduced by Panasonic Corporation.

DVD Digital video disc or digital versatile disc.

DVE Digital video effects device used to alter and manipulate images.

DVI Digital video interactive. A compression method consisting of a programmable chip set and software. DVI supports both still images and motion video and can be both asymmetric and symmetric in nature. A current implementation can decode and encode in DVI as well as JPEG.

DRAM Dynamic random access memory.

Edge numbers Identifying numbers for 35mm and 16mm film. Film negative has edge numbers that identify the film frames. In 35mm four-perforation film, an edge number appears every 16 frames, or once every foot. In 16mm film, there are 40 frames for each foot of film; edge numbers appear every 20 frames, or every half foot.

EDL Edit decision list. In videotape editing, a list that indicates how a program was put together. The EDL is based on SMPTE timecode, and it forms the basis for the interchange of information between the offline and online editing stages. A minimal form of EDL shows the timecode numbers of the source tapes used and the transitions between images.

Ethernet A form of local area network. It consists of a coaxial cable that can extend approximately 1.25 miles and can offer up to 1,000 nodes (computers and peripheral devices). Ethernet is rated at a bandwidth capacity of 10 Mbits/sec, but practical throughput is about 1 Mbit/sec.

4 FSC 4× subcarrier frequency. The sampling frequency that is most often used for digitizing composite video signals (14.3 MHz NTSC and 17.7 MHz PAL).

FDDI Fiber digital data interconnect. A transmission method that uses fiber optics to transmit and receive signals. FDDI is often offered in two configurations: bandwidths of 100 Mbits/sec and 200 Mbits/sec. A 100 Mbits/sec FDDI network will most likely deliver about 2 MB/sec.

Fibre channel A high-data-rate technology that utilizes fiber optic cabling rather than copper wire.

Film cutlist The film counterpart of an edit decision list. Instead of providing numbers that relate to the timecodes of the videotapes, the film cutlist indicates which film edge numbers should be cut from the original film negative.

Final cut The point at which the picture portion of the editing is complete, or "the picture is locked."

FireWire IEEE 1394, also called FireWire, is a standardized method for high-speed connections.

Fixed frame size In compression methods, as implementation in which there is a fixed amount of data that the compression algorithm will allow for each frame. It will not expand this amount of information if the frame contains more data than the algorithm is set to process.

Flash convertor A device used to convert analog signals to digital signals. With the flash convertor, it is possible to convert frames of video into data that can then be interpreted by computers.

Floppy disks A thin, flexible magnetic medium encased in a protective plastic shell. Floppy disks are erasable and can be used many times. They come in three sizes: 8", 5.25", and 3.5".

Flops Done to reverse the line of action so that left and right are switched.

fps Frames per second. The normal playback of 35mm and 16mm film is 24 fps.

Fractals A compression technology that uses fractal patterns to represent every possible pattern tat can exist. By dividing a picture into small pieces, these smaller sections can be searched and analyzed fairly quickly. On a smaller level, instead of trying to find the pattern for the entire picture, the search is for smaller patterns of pixels.

Framestore A digital device that stores from one to several frames of video.

Freeze frame An optical effect that is created by repeating a single film frame while the new negative is exposed for as many frames as are necessary to arrive at the required duration for the freeze.

FTFT Film to tape to film to tape refers to the ability to generate a color-corrected edit decision list (EDL) from a one-lite EDL.

GUI Graphical user interface. The operating environment defined by computer software programs.

HDTV High-definition television.

HiPPI High-performance parallel interface. A very fast transport mechanism that uses fiber (although it can also support coaxial cable).

Hybrids A nonlinear system that combines a variety of storage methods, including videotape, optical disc, and magnetic disk.

IEEE Institute of Electrical and Electronics Engineers.

Image tracking The ability to place, or attach, an object to another object in the frame.

Image stabilization Designating certain areas of an image that should be mapped to each other regardless of the motion that occurs from one or more frames to the next.

Ink numbers The process of coding numbers on the mag track and film print. Also known as *inking.*

Interframe coding A method for compression in which certain film or video frames are dependent on previous or successive frames. Interframe coding offers a major benefit of MPEG compression: a significant savings of storage compared with JPEG methods.

Interlaced scanning Television signals are created by interlacing odd and even scan lines to form the viewable, interlaced image.

Internet A global network of computers. The World Wide Web (WWW) is part of this network of interconnected computers.

Intraframe coding A method for compression in which each film or video frame is independent of previous or successive frames. In intraframe coding, each JPEG-compressed frame contains all the information that it needs to be displayed.

Intranet A term for one or more Web sites that are reserved for a corporation's internal use.

ips Inches per second. The term is used to describe audio tape consumption. The normal recording and playback speed of 1/4" reel-to-reel audio tape is 15 ips.

ISDN ISDN (Integrated Services Digital Network) is a transmission method that is designed to combine various sorts of information, from telephone transmissions to fax to images and sounds, into one digital network. ISDN requires that a communications link be placed at the transmitting and receiving areas. At 64 kbits/sec, the bandwidth is not that much greater than dial-up service. However, multiple channels of ISDN can be combined, up to 24 channels, depending on how many are needed.

Java A computer programming language developed by Sun Microsystems.

JPEG Joint Photographic Experts Group. A form of hardware-assisted compression. JPEG is based on still images and employs discrete cosine transforms, which are lossy algorithms. When a file is compressed using a JPEG-based processor, information about the original signal is discarded and lost.

Keycode Refers to all edge number formats that can be read by a bar code reader.

KeyKode™ A numbering system introduced by the Kodak Corporation that consists of the usual film edge number information but also includes a bar code alternative. This bar code, which is deciphered by the KeyKode reader, is physically housed on the telecine.

LAN Local area networks are those which are confined to computers interconnected within short distances, from 10 to 100+ meters.

L cut A transition in which audio and video are not cut together as in a straight cut. In an L cut, either audio or video precedes the straight cut. Also called *overlap* or *split edit.*

Letterboxing Film transfers that preserve the aspect ratio of the film as originally shot.

Linear editing A type of editing in which the program is assembled from beginning to end. If changes are required, everything downstream of the change must be re-recorded. The physical nature of the medium dictates the method by which the material placed on that medium must be ordered.

Lossless compression The process of compressing information without irretrievably losing any of the data that represent that information. To be lossless, a great deal of analyzing must be done.

Lossy compression The process of compressing information that results in a loss of some portion of the data in the original message.

Macros Used by computer applications to "record" a certain repeated function.

Magnetic disks A computer storage method. Magnetic disks are erasable and highly reliable. They typically have a fast access time and offer a data transfer rate that is faster than that of any other computer disk technology.

Mag track Magnetic track. Sprocketed magnetic audio tape used in the double-system method of film editing. The picture elements are contained on the film, and the sound for those pictures are contained on the mag track.

Magneto-optical discs A computer storage method that combines two technologies: magnetic and optical recording methods.

MetaData Information that identifies the origin of each of the original sources and how they were combined to form the finished product.

MIDI Musical instrument digital interface. The interface responsible for the translation of musical information into digital terms.

Mix-to-pix The process of mixing audio to the final video master. Mixing to the picture is accomplished as sections of the program are played on the video monitor.

MOS Refers to film that has been shot without sound being recorded.

MPEG Moving Picture Experts Group. A form of hardware-assisted compression. Whereas JPEG is based on still images, MPEG is based on motion. It is a lossy compression method.

Multiple versions The nonlinear editing system's ability to provide multiple versions of a sequence without requiring additional copies of footage or degrading the signal by losing generations.

Multithreading The ability for several different processes from either the same or different software packages to simultaneously process a file.

Nagra Professional-grade reel-to-reel audio tape recorder that is most commonly used for field recording.

Negative cutter Person who is responsible for recreating the cuts on the original camera negative, yielding an exact duplicate of what the editor created on the work print.

Nonlinear editing A type of editing in which the program need not be assembled from beginning to end. The physical nature of the medium and the technical process of manipulating that medium do not enforce or dictate a model by which the material must be physically ordered. Changes can be made regardless of whether they are at the beginning, middle, or end of the sequence being edited.

NTSC National Television Standards Committee, which standardized the color television transmission system in the United States. Motion video is normally played back at 30 frames per second. (Actually, it is 30 fps for non-drop frame and 29.97 fps for dropframe.) The scan rate is 525 lines at 60 Hz.

Nyquist limit One-half of the highest frequency at which the input material can be sampled. Also called *Nyquist rate.*

Offline An editing process that does not result in a finished product. The resulting program is in a form of preview.

OMF Open Media Framework is a format for file compatibility to fully describe all relationships between source material and effects.

Online An editing process that results in a finished product that is ready for final viewing and distribution.

Opticals Transitions in film, other than cuts, that require two or more pieces of film to be printed together. Optical effects, such as dissolves and wipes, are created with an optical printer.

PAL Phase alternate line. A color television standard in which motion video is normally played back at 25 fps. The scan rate is 625 lines at 50 Hz.

Phase-change optical discs A computer storage method based on the ability of a material to exhibit two properties: amorphous and crystalline.

Pixel A single point of an image's makeup.

Pixel matrix The number of pixels that are contained vertically and horizontally over the span of the viewing screen.

Playlist A list of items to be played back in a certain order. The playlist is the principle behind virtual recording.

Plug-ins Software tools created by third-party manufacturers that can be used directly by other digital systems.

Predictive coding A method of creating routines that attempt to complete a model by analyzing the existing sequence.

Previsualization Techniques used to create and judge concepts in a form that is not for final viewer consumption as part of the film proper.

Progressive scanning Each line is drawn progressively, or sequentially, resulting in the final viewable image.

Quantization The loss that results from the process of sampling.

QuickTime A set of operating extensions to the Macintosh computer platform that allows Macintosh computers to display time-dependent media such as video, audio, and animation and to combine these media with time-independent media such as text and graphics.

QuickTime VR (QTVR) QuickTime virtual reality.

RAID Redundant array of independent disks.

RAM Random-access memory.

Random access The ability of an editing system to find a section of material without having to proceed sequentially through other material to reach that location.

Raster A pattern of scanning lines covering the area on which an image is displayed.

Release print The final version of a film project from which additional film copies are made to distribute to theaters.

Rendering When an effect is desired that cannot be accomplished in real time, the entire effect, or a portion of it, must be recorded to disk or RAM in order to see the effect play in real time.

Repositions Moving a picture north, south, east, and west on predefined fields.

Resolution dependent The highest resolution that a system can provide is fixed.

Resolution independent The highest resolution that a system can provide is variable.

RISC Reduced instruction set computing.

Rough cut This first cut is the first complete viewing of the entire film.

Run-length encoding A process used to determine messages by defining the message as a string of zeroes and ones that would run for a certain length of time before changing characteristics.

S-Video S-Video signal is one in which the luminance channel is separated from the chrominance signals, but, unlike component analog, the chrominance signals are not separate.

Sampling Measuring an analog signal at regular intervals. A sample is a smaller part of a whole that represents the nature or quality of that whole.

Sampling theorem A theorem that states that a signal must be sampled at least twice as fast as it can change in order to process that signal adequately. Sampling the signal less frequently can lead to aliasing artifacts.

Scaling The process of reducing the size of the matrix for an image by removing pixels.

Scrubbing Representing the analog waveform of audio to the human ear with an accompanying change of pitch as the audio playback is decreased or increased. Also called *audio scrub with pitch change.*

SCSI Small computer systems interface. A chain consisting of a 50-pin cable and a protocol and format for sending and receiving commands. It is used to connect computers and peripheral devices. Pronounced "scuzzy."

SECAM *Séquential couleur à Mémoire.* A television standard that, like PAL, has a normal playback of 25 fps with a similar scan rate. It is primarily used in Eastern Europe and France.

Serial digital A serial digital interface (SDI) provides connections for both ITU-R 601 and composite digital video and four channels of digital audio. SDI has a transfer rate of 270 Mbits/sec.

Single system The videotape recording method in which picture and sound are simultaneously recorded onto the single element of the videotape.

Skip frames Used when motion needs to be accelerated by skipping frames during the printing. This will create a sped-up effect when the new element is played back at sound speed.

SMPTE Society of Motion Picture and Television Engineers.

Sound sweetening The process of taking sounds and changing them in some way.

Spatial aliasing The distortion of the perception of where items are positioned in two- and three-dimensional space.

SDTV Standard-definition television.

Serial storage architecture (SSA) A digital storage method developed by IBM Corporation.

Steenbeck A film editing machine.

Storyboard A visual arrangement of shots that can be easily rearranged to experiment with the flow of a sequence.

Straight cut A transition in which audio and video are cut together. Also called *both cut.*

Subsampling Subsampling refers to a technique in which the overall amount of data that will represent the digitized signal has been reduced. When more samples are thrown away than meets the sampling theorem, subsampling is being done. When the sampling theorem is violated, many types of aliasing can be noted.

Symmetrical compression A compression technique that requires an equal amount of processing power to compress and decompress an image. In applications designed for editing, the compression of a frame must occur in real time. Decompressing that same frame must also occur in real time.

Synchronous optical network (SONET) SONET is an optical fiber delivery method that operates at higher rates than DS3 or T3 technology. STS signals can be combined to provide greater bandwidth. The optical channels (OCs) come in the following versions: OC-1, a 51 Mbits/sec channel; OC-3, a 155 Mbps channel; OC-12, a 622 Mbits/sec channel; and OC-48, multiple 45 Mbps optical channels for a total of 2.4 gigabits.

T1 and T3 Common carriers of signal that require dedicated systems installed at either end of two sites that will be in communication with each other. T1 links have a bandwidth of approximately 1.5 Mbits/sec; T3 links have a bandwidth of 45 Mbits/sec.

TBC Timebase corrector. An electronic device used to correct and stabilize the playback of a video signal.

Telecine A device that is used to transfer film images from a film roll to either videotape or to digital disk.

Temporal aliasing The distortion of the perception of movement over time.

Timecode A signal that is recorded onto videotape and that identifies each video frame. Timecode takes the form of hours, minutes, seconds, and frames. Longitudinal timecode is recorded onto an audio track. Vertical interval timecode (VITC) is recorded onto a section of the video track. Address track timecode is recorded simultaneously with picture recording.

Trafficking problems The conflicts that can arise when there are many items to be cued and played back and too few playback devices.

Trim Material not used for a take. Everything before the start frame being used is the *head trim.* Everything after the end frame being used is the *tail trim.*

Turing Machine A general-purpose machine that is capable of any operation if given the appropriate software instructions.

Variable frame size In compression methods, an implementation in which there is no fixed amount of data for each frame. If action occurs from frame to frame, thereby increasing the complexity of those frames, the compression algorithm expands accordingly and allows more data to pass.

Video tap The output of a film camera that is converted to a video signal and that allows the image to be recorded and reviewed on videotape.

Virtual recording A "recording" process for nonlinear editing systems that is actually a record-keeping process that lists the edits that will eventually be made instead of actually transferring video and audio signals from several source tapes to a record tape.

VITC Vertical interval timecode.

VRML Virtual reality modeling language.

WAN Wide area networks are defined as those in which the computers are separated over geographic distances typically greater than one kilometer.

Wavelets A compression technology in which a picture is scaled, and a set of wavelet functions (transforms) are run that seek to encode error. The information in the original picture is compared to the differences in the scaled version. The goal is to store just one of four portions of the picture and to quantize the other three portions.

Widow dub Timecode information placed as an overlay window over copies of source footage as a step in the offline process. Also called *burn-in dub.*

WMRM Write many, read many. In laserdisc, optical disc, and magnetic disk technology, an erasable medium.

Work print The developed and printed film used for editing purposes.

WORM Write once, read many. A medium that can only be written once but can be read many times. It is nonerasable.

Bibliography

1. Advanced Television Standards Committee. *ATSC Digital Television Standard.* September, 1995.

2. Ohanian, Thomas A., and Michael E. Phillips. *Digital Filmmaking: The Changing Art and Craft of Making Motion Pictures.* Boston: Focal Press, 1996.

3. Ohanian, Thomas A. *Digital Nonlinear Editing: New Approaches to Editing Film and Video.* Boston: Focal Press, 1992.

4. Zettler, William, John Huffman, and David C. P. Linden. *Application of Compactly Supported Wavelets to Image Compression.* Cambridge, Mass.: Aware, 1991.

Index